ACC
SYDNEY

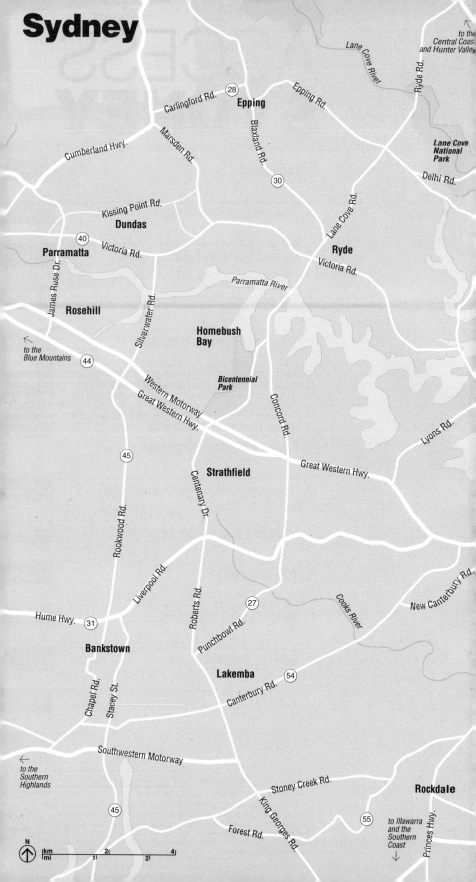

Sydney

to the
Central Coast
and Hunter Valley

Lane Cove River

Ryde Rd.

Carlingford Rd.

(28)

Epping

Epping Rd.

Marsden Rd.

Blaxland Rd.

Cumberland Hwy.

Lane Cove
National
Park

Delhi Rd.

(30)

Kissing Point Rd.

Dundas

Lane Cove Rd.

(40)

Victoria Rd.

Parramatta

Ryde

Victoria Rd.

James Ruse Dr.

Rosehill

Parramatta River

Silverwater Rd.

**Homebush
Bay**

to the
Blue Mountains

(44)

*Bicentennial
Park*

Western Motorway

Great Western Hwy.

Concord Rd.

Lyons Rd.

(45)

Strathfield

Great Western Hwy.

Rookwood Rd.

Centenary Dr.

Liverpool Rd.

Roberts Rd.

(27)

Cooks River

New Canterbury Rd.

Hume Hwy.

(31)

Punchbowl Rd.

Bankstown

Lakemba

(54)

Canterbury Rd.

Chapel Rd.

Stacey St.

Southwestern Motorway

to the
Southern
Highlands

Stoney Creek Rd.

Rockdale

(45)

King Georges Rd.

(55)

to Illawarra
and the
Southern
Coast

Forest Rd.

Princes Hwy.

N

km
mi

1   2   4

2

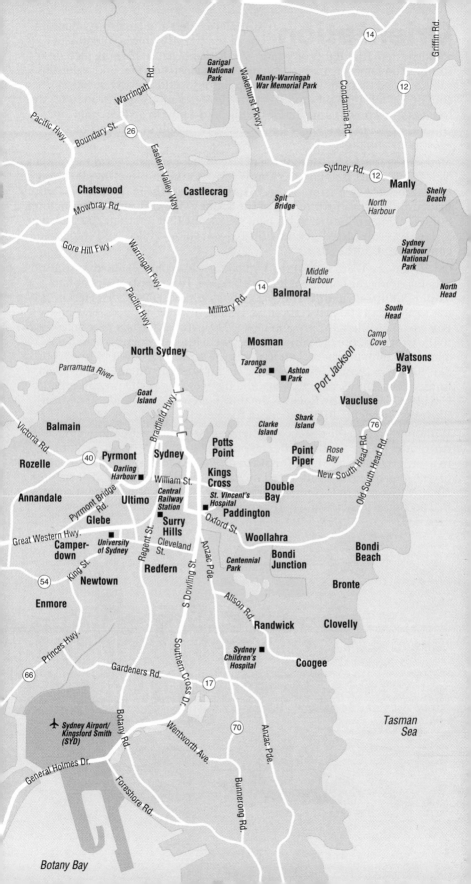

Orientation

Australia's oldest and largest city is also one of the country's most vibrant and sophisticated. Highlights of Sydney's remarkable natural beauty include a stunning aquamarine harbor, 34 golden and clean beaches, and waterside suburbs filled with eucalyptus trees and birdlife. Add a relatively balmy climate for at least eight months of the year, gregarious Sydneysiders (as the residents are known), innovative dining, and a host of architectural and cultural wonders, and you've got a surefire prescription for a spectacular vacation destination.

A good way to start a visit to this gateway to "Down Under" and the capital of New South Wales is to take the **Manly** ferry northeast from **Circular Quay** (pronounced "key") across **Sydney Harbour**—past the massive steel **Harbour Bridge** and the pearl-white sails of the **Sydney Opera House** on **Bennelong Point**. Taking in these sites, it's hard to imagine that less than 200 years ago Sydney was considered a brutal British penal colony, filled with colonists, convicts, and cutthroats.

On 26 January 1788, several years after James Cook had claimed Australia for Britain (giving the continent its British name, **Terra Australis**), Captain Arthur Phillip sailed into Sydney Harbour with his famous First Fleet of 300 free settlers and 700 petty criminals. He and his crew decided that **Botany Bay** was an unsuitable port, and proceeded eight kilometers (five miles) north to the western shore of **Sydney Cove**, where his motley crew cleared the land and set up tents and bark shelters along the sandstone outcrops to establish a new British outpost. At that time the land was a lush, untamed gray-green forest of eucalyptus, native palms, and fig trees. Today this area around Circular Quay and **The Rocks** is the threshold to the city and the **Central Business District (CBD)**, and one of the world's busiest ports.

Without regard to the distance and danger associated with journeying to the **Antipodes** (as the South Pacific was often referred to by its early colonizers), free settlers soon came from Britain in droves to start new lives. Convicts who had been pardoned or had served their time also looked for land or sites for family businesses in the new colony. Within 30 years of settlement, Sydney had become a busy trading port long before the rest of the country was explored.

Sydney Skyline

Sydney became more cosmopolitan as the city's wealth of resources—deep natural harbor, neighboring farmland, and subtropical climate—drew people from all over. In addition to immigrants from the British Isles, who came in shiploads up until World War II (when the number became a trickle), Greeks, Italians, Eastern Europeans, Lebanese, and Chinese, among others, made Australia their new home. These new arrivals dramatically changed the face of Sydney by introducing new foods and styles, and renovating the Victorian terraces in today's fashionable suburbs of **Paddington, Woollahra,** and **Glebe.** More recently, Vietnamese, Thais, Koreans, and Pacific Islanders have added to Sydney's melting pot (with an ensuing increase in racial tension), bringing more new customs and cuisines to the area, and establishing ethnic enclaves in the suburbs. Today this diverse population of over 4 million covers a 3,700-square-kilometer (1,430-square-mile) bustling sprawl known as **Greater Sydney.**

Despite its size, Greater Sydney is a manageable destination for visitors. Most of the city's attractions and public events are in and around the beautiful harbor of sparkling waters and such city beaches as **Bondi, Bronte,** and **Coogee**—all located within a 10-kilometer (6-mile) radius of the city center. Naturally, the harbor view is prized here, although Sydney has been fairly cautious in the last 20 years about its harborfront developments. There are very few skyscrapers casting afternoon shadows over the ocean waters in the bustling CBD, and most of the buildings on the foreshore are low-rise residential. **The Royal Botanic Gardens** and **The Domain**, park belts adjacent to the CBD, also preserve the area's tranquillity. Several relatively new redevelopments are tucked away down from the harbor, including the ultramodern **Darling Harbour** complex of stores, hotels, casino, and exhibition spaces just west of **Chinatown** at the end of the CBD. And farther west up the **Parramatta River** is **The Inner West,** where old buildings have been conscientiously revitalized. **Homebush Bay** farther up the river was once mangrove swampland that has been reclaimed and is now the site of the **Olympic Village** for the **Sydney 2000 Olympic Games.**

The **Eastern Suburbs** also provide visual diversions, such as the harborfront mansions and blocks of apartments of **Potts Point, Elizabeth Bay,** and the grander homes of **Point Piper, Rose Bay,** and **Vaucluse.**

Across the Harbour Bridge is the **North Shore.** Much less developed than the southern side, the North Shore has its own set of treasures, including a leafier and greener foreshore. It is also home to **North Sydney**—a second high-rise business center of Sydney, the tranquil suburb of **Mosman, Taronga Zoo** (well hidden behind a dense natural green camouflage), tranquil **Balmoral Beach,** and the lively tourist beach town of **Manly.**

While wealthier residents occupy the harborfront and beachside properties, such former working-class suburbs as **Surry Hills** (south of the city center), Glebe (to the southwest), and **Balmain** (due west) are now popular because of their proximity to the CBD and their splendid Victorian architecture. Thanks to the local obsession to restore anything built before 1950, many of these suburbs have been transformed into refined neighborhoods, full of beautifully painted Victorian terraces, chic cafes, and stylish boutiques.

Similarly, the neighborhoods of **Kings Cross, Darlinghurst,** and **East Sydney** were once far less trendy—they were known more as the city's red light district than for the elegant restaurants and happening nightclubs that dominate the area today.

Some of Australia's most interesting landscape can be found within a two-hour drive of the city. **Parramatta** to the west is most notable for its historic buildings. In the **Blue Mountains** farther west, towns and small villages are built alongside sheer cliffs that drop into deep green valleys of eucalyptus forest. Southwest of the city and also a part of this mountain range are the **Southern Highlands,** once the playground for Sydneysiders in search of a milder, more English climate. About 120 kilometers (74 miles) northwest of the city is New South Wales's wine country, **Hunter Valley,** abounding with vineyards, restaurants, hotels, and historic country towns. South along the coastal road—the **Princes Highway**—are the pristine beaches areas of **Kiama, Seven Mile Beach National Park,** and **Jervis Bay,** while north along the **Sydney-Newcastle Freeway** leads to more populated—but equally impressive—beach towns, including **Avoca** and **Terrigal.**

Sydney has a rich history, but in many ways it is a city of the future: It is ethnically diverse, environmentally aware, democratic, and cosmopolitan, yet it carefully holds on to its individuality. Beware of comparing Sydney to any other urban area; after a couple of days here, it will become apparent that this metropolis is in a class of its own, as Sydneysiders are eager to remind visitors. It's no wonder that the city was chosen to host the **Sydney 2000 Olympic Games.**

How To Read This Guide

ACCESS® SYDNEY is arranged by neighborhood so you can see at a glance where you are and what is around you. The numbers next to the entries in the following chapters correspond to the numbers on the maps. The text is color-coded according to the kind of place described:

Restaurants/Clubs: Red **Hotels:** Blue
Shops/ Outdoors: Green **Sights/Culture:** Black

Rating the Restaurants and Hotels

The restaurant star ratings take into account the quality, service, atmosphere, and uniqueness of the restaurant. An expensive restaurant doesn't necessarily ensure an enjoyable evening; however, a small, relatively unknown spot could have good food, professional service, and a lovely atmosphere. Therefore, on a purely subjective basis, stars are used to judge the overall dining value (see the star ratings at right). Keep in mind that chefs and owners often change, which sometimes drastically affects the quality of a restaurant. The ratings in this guidebook are based on the information that was available at press time.

The price ratings, as characterized at right, apply to restaurants and hotels. These figures describe general price-range relationships between other restaurants and hotels in the area. The restaurant price ratings are based on the average cost of an entrée for one person, excluding tax and tip. Hotel price ratings reflect the base price of a standard room for two people for one night during the peak season.

Restaurants

★	Good
★★	Very Good
★★★	Excellent
★★★★	An Extraordinary Experience
$	The Price Is Right (less than $10)
$$	Reasonable ($10-$20)
$$$	Expensive ($20-$30)
$$$$	Big Bucks ($30 and up)

Hotels

$	The Price Is Right (less than $125)
$$	Reasonable ($125-$200)
$$$	Expensive ($200-$275)
$$$$	Big Bucks ($275 and up)

The prices above and throughout this look are in US dollars. At press time, the exchange rate was about $1US to $1.60 Australian.

Map Key

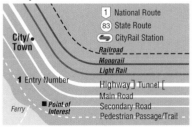

To call Sydney from the US, dial 011-61-2, followed by the local number. When calling from within Australia, dial 02 and the local number.

Getting to Sydney

Airports

Sydney Airport/Kingsford Smith (SYD)

Sydney Airport (also known as "Kingsford Smith Airport") is located 12 kilometers (7 miles) south of the city on the shores of Botany Bay.

The airport's international terminal is the gateway to Australia and is divided into four sections (**A, B, C, D**). The smaller eastern terminal services all domestic flights. A shuttle bus carries passengers between the two for a fee.

Airport Services

Airport Emergencies/Security	9667.9111
Currency Exchange	9317.2100
Customs	9317.7000
Immigration	9219.7777
Information	9667.9111
Interpreters	9221.1111
Lost and Found	9667.9583
Parking	
international	9669.3693
domestic	9669.6303
Police	000

Airlines

Air New Zealand	13.2476, 800/262.1234
American	9299.3600, 800/433.7300
Ansett Australia	13.1300, 888/442.9626
Canadian	9299.7843, 800/426.7000
Hazelton Air Services	9235.1411
Qantas Airways	13.1313, 800/227.4500
United	13.1777, 800/241.7522

Getting to and from Sydney Airport/Kingsford Smith

By Bus

The **State Transit Authority**'s green-and-gold *Airport Express* buses (13.1500) are a common sight around Sydney. They travel on two routes between the city and the airport, departing daily from 5AM to 11PM. *Route 300* leaves every 10 minutes and includes such stops in the city center as The Rocks, **Town Hall,** and Circular Quay. *Route 350* departs every 20 minutes and goes north to **Kings Cross,** Potts Point, and Elizabeth Bay. Both buses stop at the **Central Railway Station.** Tickets may be purchased from the bus driver or at **State Transit Authority** ticket kiosks in the city and outside the airport terminals.

At the airport, *Airport Express* shuttle buses carry passengers between the domestic and international terminals for a nominal fee.

Kingsford Smith Bus Service (9667.3221) is an alternative private service that operates every day between selected hotels in the city, Kings Cross, and Glebe every 10-15 minutes from 6AM to the last flight.

By Car

The airport is about a 20- to 25-minute drive from the city. During the afternoon rush (5-7PM), it's a good idea to allow an extra 10-15 minutes, particularly for the trip to the airport. From the city center, head south on **Cahill Expressway** along the **Palmer Street and Bourke Street Bypass** to **South Dowling Street.** This street turns into **Southern Cross Drive,** which goes to the airport. From the **North Shore,** take the **Harbour Tunnel** rather than the Harbour Bridge to save a few minutes. Take **King Street** through **Newtown** from The Inner West, and follow the signs. From the south, **Princes Highway** goes directly to the airport. Reverse the directions when coming from the airport.

Short-term parking is available at the domestic (9669.6303) and at the international (9669.3693) terminals; a long-term (9669.6163) lot is located in the southeast section of the airport.

Rental Cars

The following car-rental companies have counters at **Sydney Airport.** They are open daily from 6AM to midnight, and all have quick dropoff:

Avis	9353.9000, 800/831.2847
Budget	13.2727, 800/527.0700
Hertz	13.3039, 800/654.3131
Thrifty	008/652.008, 800/367.2277

By Limousine

Limos are not a popular mode of transportation in Sydney, but there are several limousine services offering airport transfers around the clock, seven days a week. Two of the better services, charging around $50 each way, depending on waiting time, are **Astra National Limousines** (13.2121) and **Legion Limousines** (9699.9722).

By Taxi

Cab stands are located outside each of the terminals. Taxis are usually plentiful, except from 5 to 7PM. Be forewarned: The lines (or queues) are sometimes slow at the domestic terminal's taxi stand.

Australia is currently a commonwealth of the United Kingdom. Its official head of state is Queen Elizabeth II of England, who is represented in Australia by the Governor General. The monarchy has had little to do with directly governing the nation since the dismissal of Prime Minister Gough Whitlam in 1974 for allegedly engaging in shady business deals. The queen (through her representative) still retains the power to veto any major decision made by Australia's parliament.

By Train

Stick with other modes of transport—it's too complicated and time-consuming to take the train to and from the airport.

Bus Station (Long-Distance)

Long-distance bus services (depending on the company) usually leave from two main terminals in Sydney—**Oxford Square** (Riley and Oxford Sts) and **Central Railway Station** (Eddy Ave and Pitt St). Call 9281.9366 for information on destinations and appropriate terminals. Some of the carriers include **Greyhound Pioneer** (13.2030), **Kirklands Coach Service** (9281.2233), and **McCafferty's** (9361.5125). There are taxi stands at both bus terminals.

Train Station (Long-Distance)

All regional and interstate trains arrive at **Central Railway Station** (see above, 9219.8888). Most city center **CityRail** train stations are only one or two stops from this station. For reservations and information, call **Countrylink** (13.2232). Ask about the "New South Wales Discover Pass," which allows rail travelers to make several stops within a certain time period for no extra charge.

Getting Around Sydney

Sydney's public transportation system, operated by the **State Transit Authority** (13.1500), is the best way to get around town, especially as city streets become ever more congested with cars. Buses, trains, and ferries operate on a regular schedule and on time, and buses have designated lanes on some major roads, making rush hour more bearable.

The three-day "SydneyPass" allows unlimited travel on any public bus, including the *Airport Express,* the *Sydney Explorer* bus, the *Bondi & Bay Explorer* bus (see "Buses," below, for a discussion of both *Explorer* coaches); **CityRail** train; ferry; and three harbor cruises. It is available at all **CityRail** stations, the airport, the ferry ticket office and the bus terminals at Circular Quay (both at Alfred St and Circular Quay E), and Wynyard Park (York and Margaret Sts), the **Queen Victoria Building** (455 George St, between Druitt and Market Sts), and **State Transit Authority** ticket kiosks at the **Central Railway Station** and Circular Quay. The pass costs $60 ($20 for children under 16).

Bicycles

Cycling on city and suburban streets is permitted, but it is not that desirable a means of transport because the thoroughfares are usually hilly. **Bicycle New South Wales**'s (209 Castlereagh St, at Bathurst St, 9283.5200) handbook, *Cycling Around Sydney,* contains maps of designated and easy bike routes around the city. It is also sold at bookstores throughout the city.

Centennial Park in Paddington, with its grassy hills, gardens, and ponds, has one of Sydney's best cycling paths and picnic spots. Both **Centennial Park Cycles** (50 Clovelly Rd, at Avoca St, 9398.5207) and **Wooly's Cycles** (82 Oxford St, between Hopewell St and Kidman La, 9331.2671) are close to the park and have a range of bicycles and tandems (as well as in-line skates) for rent. Reserve ahead on weekends and public holidays.

Buses

Sydney's blue-and-white public buses connect with most train and ferry services and have huge windows that allow for great sight-seeing. Bus stops are easy to spot, with their quirky shelters and yellow-and-black posts, which usually have timetables displayed. The main city bus terminals are at Circular Quay (see above, 9219.4316) for the beaches and southern Sydney, and Wynyard Park (see above, 9299.8521) for northern destinations across Harbour Bridge. Tickets can be purchased on board, at **State Transit Authority** kiosks (see above), and at the **Tourism New South Wales Visitors' Centre** in The Rocks (55 Harrington St, between Essex and Argyle Sts, 9931.1111; fax 9931.1424).

Route 777 through the city center, and *Route 666* from **Wynyard Rail Station** to the **Art Gallery of New South Wales** are two free bus routes.

The red *Sydney Explorer* is a 35-kilometer—22-mile—circuit of the city's top attractions (see map on page 206). The blue *Bondi & Bay Explorer* (or *Route 222*) travels to the eastern harbor and beach areas—including Kings Cross; Paddington; **Double Bay**; and Bondi, Bronte, and Coogee Beaches (see map on page 206). Both *Explorer* buses offer passengers unlimited travel along the specific routes. Riders can get on and off at any of the stops along the way. Drivers offer some commentary and information, and are usually happy to answer questions.

Driving

Two important rules to remember: stay on the left-hand side of the road, and always wear a seat belt. For those undaunted by heavy traffic and long searches for a parking spot, driving in Sydney isn't too onerous. A good street map (*Gregory's* and *UBD* are two of the most popular) and a patient navigator will make getting around easier as street signs are sometimes hard to find. Driver-safety and traffic laws are taken seriously in Sydney and New South Wales and hefty fines are administered when they are violated. Be forewarned: It's common to see police "booze buses" (blood-alcohol–level test units) pull over motorists at random. Ask the rental car company for an outline of the statutes or contact the **National Roads and Motorists Association (NRMA**; 151 Clarence St, between King and Erskine Sts, 13.2132), which also has free maps.

An international driver's license is not required in Australia.

Ferries and Water Taxis

Ferries and other speedier modes of water transport—catamarans, hydrofoils, and water taxis—are an integral part of Sydney's lifestyle and allure. Not only do commuters use them, tourists and natives alike also take advantage of their accessibility to explore the miles of Sydney's harbor inlets and coves. Ferry, hydrofoil, and catamaran services are operated by the state-run **Sydney Ferries** (Alfred St and Circular Quay E, 13.1500) to over 30 places in the harbor, as well as west to Homebush Bay and Parramatta (see map on page 205). The main services run to Manly, **Taronga Zoo, Neutral Bay, Milsons Point,** and Mosman on the North Shore; and to Balmain, Double Bay, Rose Bay, and **Watsons Bay** on the south side. Destinations are clearly marked above each wharf. Ferry services run daily from 6AM to midnight at half- to one-hour intervals (depending on the route). Buy tickets from the ticket booth or an automated ticket machine at the pier. Hydrofoils and catamarans ply the waters daily from 6AM to midnight at one-hour intervals.

The **Ferry Information Centre** (Sydney Ferries, Wharf No. 4, 9247.5151), a must-stop tourist spot, also has information on the "Zoo Pass" to **Taronga Zoo;** "Aquarium Pass" to Darling Harbour; and the Morning River, Afternoon Harbour, and Evening Harbour Lights cruises.

Water taxis are a good way to zip around to any place on the harbor that's near a wharf, but keep in mind that cruising at high speeds doesn't necessarily allow for the best viewing. The average cost of a trip is $35 for the first person and $5 for each additional passenger. Although water taxis often wait for fares near the wharves at Circular Quay, it's best to book one at least an hour in advance through the following private companies: **Taxis Afloat** (9922.4252), **Aboat Taxis** (9555.1155), **Harbour Taxis** (9555.1299), and **Water Taxis** (9955.3222).

Light Rail
Sydney Light Rail (**SLR**; 9660.5288) began operation in July 1997 to link the **Central Railway Station** to the city's key tourist and entertainment venues in an effort to reduce pollution levels from the staggering increases in automobile traffic. Jointly run by the New South Wales Department of Transport and a private company, the **SLR** stops include Chinatown, the **Exhibition Centre,** Darling Harbour, the **National Maritime Museum, Sydney Casino,** and the **Sydney Fish Markets.** Future plans include extending the line farther north to Circular Quay, west to the suburb of Lilyfield, and south to **Sydney Airport.** Tickets may be purchased at electronic kiosks at each stop. The **SLR** runs Monday through Saturday from 6AM to midnight, Sunday from 7AM to 11PM, every 5 minutes during peak times and every 11 minutes off-peak.

Monorail
The **TNT Harbourlink Monorail** (9552.2288) runs through the retail-heavy southern end of the CBD to Darling Harbour and is one of the quickest and easiest ways to get around the area. Considered by many to be an eyesore, this controversial mode of transport has been a part of the Sydney cityscape since the mid-1980s. Although some of the finer old buildings aren't visible from it, the monorail is a good way to avoid pedestrian and car traffic, and explore the city center, Chinatown, and Darling Harbour. It runs every five minutes Monday through Saturday from 7AM to midnight; Sunday from 8AM to 9PM. The stops on the monorail loop are **City Centre,**

Darling Park, Harbourside, Convention Square, Haymarket, World Square, and **Park Plaza.** It connects with **Town Hall** station. Tickets and the "Monorail Day Pass," which allows unlimited one-day travel, are on sale at all stops.

Parking
Street parking in the CBD is next to impossible on weekdays. Be forewarned: parking police are vigilant—cars will be towed in clearways (high traffic areas) from 3:30 to 6:30PM in most places. Call the 24-hour **Sydney Traffic Control Center** (9211.3000) if your car is towed and impounded. It's best to use hotel, shopping mall, and office block parking lots that are marked by blue-and-white "P" signs. Metered parking is common in the suburbs. Street parking is usually free Saturday afternoon, Sunday, and public holidays.

Taxis
A cab ride in Sydney often makes visitors feel as if they are in a small town. Drivers are known for their chattiness and homespun philosophies, and in keeping with this spirit, it's common to see passengers riding up front with the driver. Taxis may be found cruising the streets, at stands marked by red-and-white signs, and at major hotels. Alternatively, call one of the following cab companies (a $1 surcharge is added to the fare): **Legion Cabs** (9289.9000), **Premier Cabs** (9897.4000), **RSL Taxis** (9581.1111), and **Taxis Combined** (9332.8888). Tipping is appreciated, but not essential.

Tours
Regardless of the kind of excursion you're looking for—a historic district walking tour, a motorcycle trip, a guided city sight-seeing expedition, a harbor cruise, or a day's jaunt—a good place to start your search is at Circular Quay, where numerous tour operators have offices. Alternatively, try one of the following companies:

AAT King's (Wharf 6, Alfred St, between Circular Quay E and George St, Shop W1, 9252.2788, 800/33.4009) has a Half-Day Southern Surf Beaches tour leaving from Circular Quay or major city hotels. This afternoon bus trip, complete with running commentary, provides a quick overview of the city, taking in visits to the **Opera House, The Royal Botanic Gardens,** Darling Harbour, Chinatown, Vaucluse, and Bondi Beach. Another well-run outfit, **Australian Pacific Tours** (Circular Quay W, north of Argyle St, Shop 4, 13.1304), has a morning tour to Northern Beaches, including Milsons Point, Manly, and then back to the city for highlights of the historic Rocks region. Both operators also offer day trips to outlying areas of Sydney, including the Blue Mountains, Hunter Valley, Canberra, and excursions to Sydney's wildlife parks. For smaller group tours around the city, try **Dal Myles Special Tours** (Museum of Contemporary Art, 140 George St, between Alfred and Argyle Sts, 9977.5567). This company can also customize trips for parties of four or more.

Although many of the bus tour companies have packages that include harbor cruises, they are often only one part of the tour and usually don't allow you to make the most of the splendid harbor. For a half- or full-day circuit around the harbor, the government-run **Sydney Ferries** (Alfred St and Circular Quay E, 13.1500) is highly recommended as the company uses its fleet of passenger ferries, catamarans, and hydrofoils. **Captain Cook Cruises** (Wharf 6, Alfred St, between Circular Quay E and George St, 9206.1111) is the largest private operator, offering tours of harbor inlets and coves and several packages including decent seafood lunches and big dinners. If you prefer sailing, try **Matilda Cruises** (Sydney Harbour Cruise Centre, Wheat Rd, west of the Western Distributor, 9264.7377), which features the 18th-century–inspired tall ship, the *Solway Lass.*

One of the best operators for walking tours trips is **The Rocks Walking Tours** (106 George St, between Argyle St and Hickson Rd, 9247.6678). This 75-minute tour gives visitors a wonderful insight into the birthplace of British settlement and a taste of some of Australia's oldest architectural treasures. Guides are always well informed and enthusiastic.

Eastcoast Motorcycle Tours (Wharf 6, Alfred St, between Circular Quay E and George St, 9555.2700) offers a number of different trips around The Rocks, CBD, and beaches. The operator also has day trips to various locations and customized tours.

Nothing seems to beat the exhilaration of flying over one of the world's most beautiful harbors. A company with years of experience is **Sydney Harbour Seaplanes** (Rose Bay Jetty, Lyne Park, New South Head Rd, between Vickery Ave and Wunulla Rd, 9388.1978). For the right price, the operator will also customize flights. **Sydney Helicopter Service** (Sydney Airport, Ross Smith Ave, east of Sir Reginald Ansett Dr, 9637.4455) offers chopper tours of the city and harbor.

Bridge Climb (5 Cumberland St, between Gloucester and Lower Fort Sts, 9252.0077) is for the ultra-adventurous. Anyone can drive over it, walk over it, or simply marvel at its size from the harbor's edge, but some people prefer to scale it. This tour operator provides specially designed bridge-climbing clothing and shoes, harnesses, and headsets to communicate with the guide for its excursions to the peak of the arch. Those who have tried it aren't sure which is more breathtaking, the experience or the views. A maximum of 10 people leave at 20-minute intervals for the half-day climb.

Trains
Sydney's state-run rail system, **CityRail** (13.1500), runs five easy-to-follow train lines from downtown to the northern suburbs, east to **Bondi Junction,** west to the Blue Mountains, southwest to the Southern Highlands, and south to **Cronulla** (see map on page 205). All lines run through **Central Railway** (Eddy Ave and Pitt St) and **Town Hall Stations** (George St, between Bathurst and Druit Sts). The trains operate daily from 4:30AM to midnight, and are perfect for day trips within and outside the city.

Tickets may be purchased from machines or ticket windows at the stations. Ask about various passes for the train, bus, and ferry system, including the

"TravelPass" (weekly, monthly, or quarterly travel); "CityHopper" (for trips within the city area—bounded by Kings Cross, North Sydney, and Redfern); "DayRover" (unlimited travel anywhere in the city); and the "Rail Weekly" (for train trips between two designated stations—and those in between—for seven consecutive days). To get onto the platform, insert tickets into the automatic turnstiles. Be sure to keep them until journey's end—inspectors are known to check them en route, and they are also needed to exit at the destination station.

Walking
Exploring Sydney on foot is one of the best ways to see the CBD, city beaches, and the parkland. Remember to cross at the lights or at the zebra crossings marked by black-and-yellow signs.

Some of the best walks are around The Rocks and Circular Quay in the city, Bondi Beach to **Clovelly Beach,** Manly Beach to **Shelly Beach,** Vaucluse, Watsons Bay, and **The Gap.** Ferries and buses connect to all of these destinations and have walking tour suggestions.

FYI

Accessibility for People with Disabilities
Most modern public buildings and major hotels are fitted for wheelchair access, while many older buildings have installed ramps (some of which are not visible from the street) to meet current laws.

Airport buses, some ferries, the **Sydney Light Rail,** and taxis are wheelchair accessible (call 9339.0200 for cabs with raised roofs and hoists). For those traveling by train, call **CityRail** (13.1500) to get the phone number of the departing station to ask for assistance. **Avis Australia** (9353.9000, 800/831.2847) and **Hertz** (9360.6621, 800/654.3131) both have vehicles with hand controls available. There's plenty of designated street parking for disabled drivers around the city (stickers must be displayed).

Hearing- and visually impaired travelers can also be assisted during their stay in Sydney. The **Deaf Society of New South Wales** (9633.9718) may be contacted for social events, travel services around the city, and TTY telephones. It also has a 24-hour TTY Relay Service for communication with non-TTY telephone users. The **Royal Blind Society** (9334.3390) has numerous services—support groups, guide dogs, escorts, travel, etc.—available to the traveler.

Australian Council for Rehabilitation of the Disabled (**ACROD;** 55 Charles St, between Morrison Rd and Kenneth St, Ryde, 9809.4488) publishes *Accessing Sydney,* which lists accessibility details for all the city's major venues and facilities. It's available at most major bookstores. *Getting Around the City of Sydney,* a free map designed to help people with disabilities navigate around the city and its buildings, is available through the **Council of the City of Sydney** (9265.9027).

The **National Parks and Wildlife Service** (9585.6333) publishes *Outdoor Access for*

Everybody. This book provides information on access to the state's various national parks and is available at most major bookstores. For information on sporting facilities, including city beaches, contact the **New South Wales Sports Council for the Disabled** (9763.0155).

Accommodations

Although new hotels have been popping up all over Sydney in recent years, a shortage of accommodations still exists. It is essential, therefore, to make reservations ahead, particularly from December through March when the festivals are on and Sydney is at its warmest. Expect that a harbor view will add 30 percent to the room rate at most hotels.

In addition to the hotels listed in each chapter, there are a variety of bed-and-breakfast establishments in the city. Contact **Bed and Breakfast Sydneyside** (9449.4430) for more information. The homestay is also becoming a popular alternative to the guest house and bed-and-breakfast, but be sure to check how far from the city the accommodations are. Call the **Homestay Network** (9498.4400) to inquire about this alternative form of housing.

Many pubs in Sydney are also called hotels, stemming from the time when the liquor laws dictated that pubs/bars also had to provide lodging for patrons in order to receive a license. A few pubs still have some rooms upstairs, but they are usually not the best accommodations available in the city. (The Rocks area is an exception to this rule.)

Climate

Sydney has a subtropical, almost Mediterranean, climate—the summers are often steamy and the winters mild. The seasons are the reverse of those in the Northern Hemisphere, so the best months to be in Sydney are October through March when the average temperature is around 75 degrees F. Sydney averages 342 days of sunshine a year, making the odds of having great weather for a ferry ride or stroll along a city beach high. The metric system is in force Down Under, so all weather is usually listed in Celsius (double the Celsius reading and add 30 for a quick conversion to Fahrenheit).

Months	Average Temperature ($°C$)	($°F$)
December-February	19-26	69-82
March-May	15-25	60-80
June-August	10-18	51-67
September-November	14-22	59-75

Drinking

The legal drinking age throughout Australia is 18. Most bars and pubs are open Monday through Thursday from 10AM to 10PM, Friday through Saturday from 10AM to midnight. In the busy tourist areas, however, many establishments have 24-hour licenses or live entertainment that allow them to stay open until 3 or 4AM. On Friday night office workers spill into the street outside pubs to party hearty.

Electricity

The current is 240 volts, with three-square-pin outlets. North American appliances will need a converter.

Embassies and Consulates

Note: All embassies are in Canberra, Australia's capital.

British Consulate (The Gateway, 1 Macquarie Pl, at Reiby Pl, Level 16, 9247.7521)

Canadian Consulate (111 Harrington St, between Essex and Argyle Sts, Level 5, 9364.3000)

US Consulate (MLC Centre, 19-29 Martin Pl, between Castlereagh and Pitt Sts, 9373.9200)

Health and Medical Care

Sydney's medical standard is one of the world's best, with state-of-the-art technology and well-trained professionals. Australia's national health policy, "Medicare," applies only to Australians and visitors from the United Kingdom. It's advisable, therefore, for nationals from other countries to have travelers' medical insurance. For medical emergencies, call 000 for an ambulance or walk in to the emergency room at any public hospital. Otherwise, look in the Yellow Pages under "Medical Centres." Pharmacies (generally referred to as "Chemists") are scattered throughout the city, although most have limited hours. For vaccinations and travelers' medical information, contact **The Travellers' Clinic** in Kings Cross (13 Springfield Ave, at Earl Pl, 9358.3066) or **Travellers Medical and Vaccination Centre** (428 George St, between Market St and Strand Arcade, Seventh floor, 9221.7133).

Hours

Sydney seems to have found a happy medium in its work hours between North America (where the 9-to-5 work day prevails) and Europe (where leisure time is paramount). Museums and cultural institutions are generally open daily from 10AM to 5PM. Store hours are usually open Monday through Wednesday and Friday from 9AM to 5:30PM, Thursday from 9AM to 9PM, and Saturday from 9AM to 4PM. Some major department stores and boutiques are also open on Sunday. Restaurants are generally open for lunch from noon to 2:30PM; for dinner from 6 to 11PM, with last orders at 10:30PM. Many cafes only serve breakfast and lunch, and pub hours are more irregular. Places with an entertainment license stay open until the wee hours.

Opening and closing times for shops, attractions, coffeehouses, and tearooms, etc. are listed by day(s) only if normal hours apply (opening between 8 and 11AM and closing between 4 and 7PM). In all other cases, specific hours will be given (e.g., 6AM-2PM, daily 24 hours, noon-5PM).

Money

The Australian dollar ($AUS) is the country's colorful currency. The largest bill (or "note") is $100, the smallest $5. There are $1- and $2-coins, as well as 5-, 10-, 20-, and 50-cent pieces.

Banking and cash machine facilities are located throughout the CBD and the suburbs. The **Commonwealth Bank, National Australia Bank, Westpac, ANZ,** and **St. George** are Sydney's main banks. All offer ATMs and the best rates on currency exchange. Banks are generally open Monday through Thursday from 9:30AM to 4PM; Friday from 9:30AM to 5PM. In addition, most major foreign banks have offices here, as Sydney is Australia's financial capital. The hours are the same as Australian banks and provide similar services for the visitor. **American Express** (92 Pitt St, between Martin and Penfold Pls, 9239.0666) and **Thomas Cook** (44 Market St, at York St, 9234.4000) also provide foreign money transaction services.

Exchange rates are displayed in the window or at the entrance of most banks and independent *bureaux de change.* The latter are good sources for changing money in such outlying neighborhoods as Kings Cross, Potts Point, Bondi Beach, Darling Harbour, and Manly. After hours try **Thomas Cook** (call 9264.1133 for the nearest location), **Travelex** (call 9241.5722 for the closest office), and **Interforex** (Wharf 6, Alfred St, between Circular Quay E and George St, 9247.2082).

Personal Safety

Sydneysiders' laid-back demeanor and the city's lack of obvious urban poverty give visitors the impression that Sydney is relatively crime-free. But as with most major cities, Sydney has its share of drug-related crimes, muggings, and vehicle thefts. It's a good idea to exercise the same caution here as in any other metropolitan environment. Be particularly careful after dark on deserted city streets—call a cab to play it safe. In addition, stick to the main streets of Kings Cross, Potts Point, Darlinghurst, Bondi Beach, Newtown, and Glebe, as the side streets are not as friendly at night. Most city streets are well patrolled by pairs of police officers, while mobile police units are set up in tourist-heavy areas, and public transport has "Nightsafe" areas.

Beach safety is another big issue in surf-loving Sydney. Surf life savers (lifeguards) are on duty at all city beaches in the daytime and swimmers are monitored with a hawklike vigilance. If nobody is patrolling the beach, take that as a good indication that it's not a good day for a swim.

Approximately 25 percent of the Sydney work force takes either the bus, ferry, or train to work.

Australia's government is based on the Westminster system: An elected prime minister and his or her selected cabinet are responsible for all matters of national importance. States vote for a premier to lead their governments. Each local community within a state elects a leader (usually a mayor) to direct local public works and projects and to lobby for attention from the state government.

Public Holidays

New Year's Day	1 January
Australia Day	26 January
Good Friday	21 April 2000
	13 April 2001
Easter Sunday	23 April 2000
	15 April 2001
Easter Monday	24 April 2000
	16 April 2001
25 April	Anzac Day (Veterans Day)
12 June	Queen's Birthday
Bank Holiday	7 August 2000
	3 August 2001
Labour Day	2 October 2000
	1 October 2001
25 December	Christmas Day
26 December	Boxing Day

Publications

The Sydney Morning Herald ("The Herald") is Sydney's premier daily newspaper. Its front-page "Column 8" amuses readers with local trivia, jokes, and anecdotes. The "Metro" section on Friday lists most of the city's best arts and entertainment for the following week. *The Australian* (national newspaper) and *The Daily Telegraph Mirror* (local) are other popular dailies. *The Bulletin* is a weekly news magazine and *The Financial Review* is a business journal that's published Monday through Friday. The *Sydney Star Observer* is the major free gay and lesbian weekly newspaper. All are available at newsstands ("newsagents") around town.

Finding a newsagency that stocks interstate and major international newspapers can be difficult (although they are available at the city's better hotels). Two major outlets are **Sydney Library** (Town Hall, 456 Kent St, between Bathurst and Druitt Sts, Level 3, 9265.9694) and **World News Centre** (Harbourside Festival Marketplace, Darling Dr, between Pier and Murray Sts, 9281.3707).

Restaurants

Imaginative chefs and savvy restaurateurs have created a buzzing foodies' paradise in Sydney, so reservations are highly recommended at major dining spots—especially on weekends. With a few exceptions, restaurant and cafe cuisine is generally a well-presented, eclectic mix of Mediterranean and Australian English-style food. Much of it reflects Australia's multicultural influences and superb local products. A recent phenomenon is the emergence of "Modern Australian" cooking (for more information, see "So What Exactly is Modern Australian Cooking?" on page 149), a cuisine well worth sampling. Many pubs (also known as "hotels") are serving both old (steak and chips) and new (marinated kangaroo kebabs with couscous) Aussie fare in a bistrolike setting.

Like its lifestyle, the dining dress code in Sydney is relaxed, but not too casual. (Jackets and ties are sometimes required at private clubs.) This is also true of the service: Waiters generally don't fawn over their customers and tipping is not usual except in the more expensive restaurants. A 10-percent surcharge is often added to the check (the "bill") on Sunday and public holidays.

BYO ("Bring Your Own") on a menu means that the establishment has no liquor license. Most restaurants don't object to patrons bringing their own wine, they merely add on a corkage charge.

Shopping
Sydney has a number of excellent shopping areas. The CBD and The Rocks are notable for major department stores and international labels. Double Bay, Paddington, and Woollahra are renowned for smaller boutiques, antiques, art, craft, and homeware stores. For the hip, funkier crowd, the streets of lower **Oxford Street** in Paddington and **Crown Street** in Surry Hills are filled with young designer, music, and homeware shops. Newtown, Glebe, and Balmain are also popular shopping domains for Sydney's more alternative student set.

Smoking
Smoking is permitted in designated areas of restaurants and is usually acceptable in all areas of cafes and pubs. It's prohibited in most commercial buildings, department stores, and on all public transport and taxis.

Street Plan
The CBD is on a loose grid plan from **Haymarket** to **Alfred Street.** Beyond this area, the city seems to have been planned so that as many buildings and residences as possible have a harbor view. This makes for some rather confusing and complicated trips by car, especially with lots of one-way streets, dead-end roads, and numerous zebra crossings to help the traffic flow around the city. Street names are very colonial: the main thoroughfares are **George, Pitt, Castlereagh, Elizabeth,** and **Macquarie Streets.** Street signs are often difficult to find, although most indicate which numbers are on that particular block. If you lose your way, look for the harbor—this is usually north—or ask a friendly pedestrian.

Taxes
Sydney has no sales tax on purchases or services. Payment of a departure tax can be made at the airport or prearranged through airlines and travel agents.

Telephone
Australia's telephone system is generally reliable and efficient. The two main telephone companies are **Telstra** and **Optus.** Most numbers have eight digits, while some major companies and government organizations have only six.

A local call made from a public telephone cost 40 cents at press time. Phone cards can be purchased from stores displaying the blue-and-gold **Telstra** sign. Dial 013 for directory assistance.

Tickets
Ticketek (over 50 outlets throughout the city; main location at 195 Elizabeth St, between Park and Market Sts, general information 9266.4800) and **Firstcall** (66 Hunter St, between Chifley Sq and Bligh St, 9320.9000) are the two major booking agencies for opera, ballet, theater, and other performing arts and major sporting events. Both are open Monday through Friday; Saturday from noon to 4PM. For day-of bargains, visit **Halftix** (Martin Pl and Elizabeth St, 0055.26655 toll-free in Australia), Monday through Friday noon to 5:30PM; Saturday noon to 5PM.

An Australian Icon: The Flying Kangaroo

Qantas, Australia's national airline with its hub in Sydney, and its mascot—the mythical flying kangaroo—are perhaps Australia's most famous commercial symbols. Australians are very proud of their airline (and in true Aussie style, they won't be afraid to tell you), and with good reason. This government-run carrier not only holds the world's best airline safety record, but is also the oldest in the English-speaking world (and second on the planet).

Founded in Queensland in 1920 by pioneer aviators Paul McGinness and Wilmot Hudson Fysh and grazier Fergus McMaster, **Qantas** takes its name from the original registered title—Queensland and Northern Territory Aerial Services. The airline was one of the first (in 1931) to start long-haul services from Australia to the United Kingdom. It also played a vital role in the war effort from 1939 to 1945, when the airline flew regular supply drops at treetop level in New Guinea. **Qantas** was also the pioneer in flying from Australia to San Francisco and Vancouver in 1953.

In 1992, **Qantas** took over **Australian Airlines** (formerly TAA), and today is the world's 11th-largest carrier, with 99 aircraft and 565 flights per day.

Time Zone
Sydney is approximately 15 hours ahead of New York City. Daylight savings (an hour is added) usually starts on the last Sunday in October and ends the last Sunday in March.

Tipping
As wages are considered decent in the Australian hospitality industry, tipping is appreciated rather than expected. In fancy restaurants, leave 10-15 percent if the service has been outstanding; if not, round up the check. Some establishments will add a gratuity to parties of six or more. The standard tip for porters and housekeeping staff is a dollar or two. Round up a taxi fare to the nearest dollar.

Visitors' Information Centers
The **Tourism New South Wales Travel Centres** at The Rocks (55 Harrington St, between Essex and Argyle Sts, 9931.1111; fax 9931.1424) is open daily. The **Sydney Airport** location (International Arrivals Hall, 9667.6050) is open daily from 6AM to midnight. The **Darling Harbour Visitor Centre** (Palm Grove Carousel, just south of the Panasonic IMAX Theatre, 9286.0111) and **The Rocks Visitors' Centre** (106 George St, between Argyle St and Hickson Rd, 9255.1788) are both open daily. All offer maps, information about attractions, some hotel and restaurant listings, and booking services.

Web Sites
Some handy web sites for desk- and laptop exploration of Sydney and beyond are:

The Australian Financial Review:
www.afr.com.au

The Sydney Morning Herald:
www.smh.com.au
Current news from two of the country's leading papers.

Australian Tourist Commission:
www.australia.com.au
General information on Australia and its six states and one territory.

Blue Mountains:
www.bluemts.com.au
Details on these mountains, just 1.5 hours from Sydney.

Hunter Valley Tourism:
www.winecountry.com.au
Facts on the vineyards and towns of Hunter Valley.

National Library of Australia:
www.nla.gov.au
Australian literature and library's archives.

Sydney Convention and Visitors' Bureau:
www.scvb.com.au
•Sydney data, including lists of current hotel rates and tour operators.

Telestra's White/Yellow Pages:
www.whitepages.com.au; www.yellowpages.com.au

Maps and phone numbers of destinations throughout Australia.

Tourism New South Wales:
www.tourism.nsw.gov.au
Sydney information, and tours of the city and New South Wales.

Phone Book

Emergencies
Ambulance/Fire/Police 000
Dental Emergencies 9211.1011
Hospitals:
    Children's..9382.1111
    St. Vincent's..9339.1111
    Sydney Hospital 9228.2111
NRMA Emergency Road Service 13.1111
Pharmacy (24 hours) 9235.0333
Police 000
Victims of Crime....................................9217.1000

Visitors' Information
AIDS Hotline..9332.4000
CityRail...13.1500
Customs..9317.7000
Disabled Visitors' Information (ACROD)
....9809.4488
Monorail...9552.2288
Road Conditions (Sydney Traffic Control Centre)
....9211.3000
Postal Service 13.1317
State Transit Authority 13.1500
Sydney Ferries 13.1500
Time..1194
Travellers' Clinic.....................................9358.3066
Weather 0055.14450

Koalas, heavily sedated by their diet of eucalyptus leaves, have been known to go into such a deep sleep that they lose their grip on tree branches and fall to the forest floor below. Thus, one of their nicknames is "Drop Bear."

Sydney is one of the most flammable cities on earth because of its large number of eucalyptus trees. In the summer of 1995, bush fires raged throughout the city, destroying many homes on the North Shore and much parkland.

Celebrating in Sydney

January

Australia's largest and most eclectic arts festival, **Sydney Festival,** runs all month and features international and Australian performing and visual artists, multicultural celebrations, free outdoor events, and plenty of sporting events. For information, call 9266.4111

The annual cricket tournament, **The Test,** is played at **Sydney Cricket Ground (SCG)** throughout the month. Check newspapers for the schedule of international matches when Aussie supporters are loud and ferocious. Tickets may be bought at the fields on the day of the game, but advance purchase through **Ticketek** (9266.4800) is essential for the weekend matches.

The **Opera Australia** performs **Opera in the Park** in **The Domain.** It is usually held on the first Saturday of the year. For information, call 9319.1088.

The **Australia Day Eve Concert** on 25 January in The Domain features Australian artists performing a range of music, from chamber to country. For more information, call 9265.0444.

Australia Day (26 January) commemorates the 1788 landing of the British First Fleet in **Botany Bay.** Expect fantastic fireworks and plenty of harborside partying. A **Tall Ships Race** celebrating the First Fleet docking is held in the morning. **Ferrython,** an annual ferry race on **Sydney Harbour** that raises money for various organizations, also takes place on this day. Passengers fill several ferries as thousands of picnickers cheer from the shores. For more information, call 0055.20455.

The **Sydney Writers' Festival** takes place the last week of the month. International and Australian authors come together for talks, panel discussions, readings, performances, lunches, afternoon teas, and dinners. Most events are free and held during the last week of the Sydney Festival at venues around the city. For information, call the **Sydney Writers' Festival Hotline** (9230.1515).

February

Bondi Beach Coke Classic is held on the first Sunday of the month. Swimmers from 13 to 70 years of age compete in this well-organized 4-kilometer (2.5-mile) swim at Australia's most famous city beach. For more information, call 9259.6666.

The **Bondi to Bronte Coast Walk** is the venue for the **Sea Theatre Festival,** a performing arts carnival, also on the first Sunday of the month. From noon to sunset, artists dance, sing, contort their bodies, tell stories, and even do the old fire-eating routine at ten stations along the walk. The finale is held at **Bronte Park** at 7:30PM. For more information, call 9361.3391.

The pre-events and -parties for Sydney's famous **Gay and Lesbian Mardi Gras** can be as exciting as the outrageous parade itself, especially on the Saturday before Lent. What started out as a gay rights protest in 1978 has turned into one of Sydney's best local and tourist attractions. Now Mardi Gras mania features a full festival starting as early as late January with visual and performing arts shows, sporting events, and parties all around the city center. For more information, call 9361.5344.

Sydney celebrates **Chinese New Year** in **Chinatown** with glowing red lanterns, New Year dragons, and fireworks. For more information, call 9281.1377.

What started as a quirky Australian short film festival has grown into the **Tropicana Film Festival,** a daylong event that has reached cultlike status. Relatively unknown film makers have their shorts judged one Sunday in the month by a panel of film industry peers and a trendy crowd of jeering viewers. For more information, call 9360.9809.

March

The **St. Patrick's Day Parade** on 17 March goes from **Hyde Park** to **Prince Alfred Park.** Many pubs serve ghastly green beer, while some cafes and take-out places dye their food a peculiar version of the verdant hue. For more information, call 9440.0695.

The **Royal Easter Show** hits **Sydney Showground** (at **Homebush Bay**) 12 days before Easter. This extravaganza has been the ultimate country-meets-city experience for decades. Features include the best of Australia's livestock, sheep dog trials, enormous quirky displays of fruit and vegetables, and sample bags from major food and beverage companies. The carnival atmosphere is great for children of all ages. For more information, call 9704.1111.

April

ANZAC Day, 25 April, honors Australia's war veterans. A dawn memorial service starts the day's events, followed by a parade down **George Street.**

Australia's most prestigious fine art prize entries are exhibited to the public throughout the month at the **Art Gallery of New South Wales.** The categories for the Archibald, Wynne, and Sulman prizes are drawing/portraiture, landscape and sculpture, and genre works or murals. For more information, call 9221.7200 or 9225.1800.

May

Sample a bit of Australian domestic heritage at the **Australian Antique Dealers Fair** at the **Sydney Showground** (at Homebush Bay) the first weekend of

KEELY EDWARDS

15

the month. European and American antiques are also on display. For more information, call 9327.2286.

The Sydney Morning Herald hosts a 20-kilometer (12-mile) **Half Marathon** the last Sunday of the month. The race starts from **Pier One** at **Dawes Point.** For more information, call 9282.2822.

June

Come see the next *Priscilla Queen of the Desert* or *Strictly Ballroom* at the **Sydney Film Festival.** Held at several cinemas around the city for two to three weeks of the month, the festival introduces the latest innovative Australian productions and usually includes a major retrospective as well. For more information, call 9660.3844.

July

With opposite seasons to the Northern Hemisphere, many Sydneysiders like to make the most of the "chilly" winter months with **Yulefest** in the **Blue Mountains** (a 1.5-hour drive from the city). This quasi-Christmas experience runs all month at most hotels and guest houses in the region. For more information, call 4739.6266.

The one-week **Australian Book Fair** opens mid-month at **Darling Harbour**'s **Convention and Exhibition Centre.** Australian publishers tussle with one another during the week and on the weekend the public can attend author readings, panel discussions, and children's events. For more information, call 9977.0888.

August

Avoid driving around the city on the second Sunday of this month when the **City-to-Surf Fun Run** takes over the town. This 15-kilometer (9-mile) mini-marathon seems to be a misnomer, as thousands of runners sprint (and wearily plod) down **William Street,** struggle up hilly **New South Head Road,** and reach the finish line on the coast at **Bondi Beach.** For more information, call 9282.6616.

As winter ends, seafarers gear up for the **Around Australia Yacht Race** the last week of the month. This race is one of the world's biggest and most grueling sailing events.

September

In even-numbered years, the **Biennale of Sydney** opens for two months at the **Art Gallery of New South Wales** and other museum and public venues. This often controversial exhibition features some of the best Australian and international contemporary visual artists. For more information, call 9368.1411.

The **Festival of the Winds,** a multicultural, kite-flying extravaganza, takes place on Bondi Beach the second Sunday of the month. Beachside entertainment includes performance artists and musicians, and the whole event provides a great spectator activity for children. For more information, call 9130.3325.

The **Rugby League Grand Final** is played at **Sydney Football Stadium** late in the month to a crowd of 40,000-plus spectators and millions of armchair viewers. Most teams are from the Greater Sydney area, so the rivalry is in the air as supporters don

team colors and some homes are decorated. For more information, call 9232.7566.

The Royal Botanic Gardens Spring Festival takes place toward the end of the month with displays of spring blooms, sculpture, dance, and food at these magnificent public gardens. For more information, call 9231.8182.

October

Aurora Blessing of the Fleet on the Sunday of Labour Day weekend is held at Darling Harbour. In this Greek and Italian traditional event, brightly decorated fishing boats are blessed by Christian Orthodox and Catholic priests. For more information, call 9286.0111.

Also on Labour Day weekend is the **Manly Jazz Festival,** when both Australian and international jazz musicians play at different venues in this beach town. For more information, call 9977.1088.

November

At 3:20PM on the first Tuesday of the month, Australians stop whatever they are doing for a few minutes to watch or listen to the **Melbourne Cup,** the nation's most famous horse race. Sydney's pubs, cafes, and restaurants usually offer special meals on this day and the city's legal betting houses are mobbed with punters. For more information, call 03/9371.7123.

Sydney to the Gong Bicycle Ride, the first Sunday of the month, attracts over 10,000 cyclists. The 100-kilometer (62-mile) ride goes from **Moore Park** to the city of Wollongong in the south. For more information, call 9287.2929.

December

On the Saturday before Christmas each year is the **Carols in The Domain.** This magical evening of carols by candlelight is shared with families and groups who often settle into a spot on the huge lawn hours before the event starts. For more information, call 9319.7874.

At **Christmas Day on Bondi Beach,** this unofficial party attracts hordes of travelers and locals in search of sun, sand, surf, and a great place to spend the day. Beware of the drunken masses later in the afternoon.

On **Boxing Day,** 26 December, the harbor and its shores are buzzing with the **Sydney to Hobart Yacht Race.** The harbor is crammed with thousands of small sailboats following the racing yachts on their way to Tasmania. Some of the best views are from **The Royal Botanic Gardens, Rushcutters Bay, Darling Point,** and at **The Gap** near **Watsons Bay.**

Traditionally, **New Year's Eve** is celebrated in The Rocks area with street parties and overflowing pubs. At midnight, fireworks begin over the harbor and light up the **Harbour Bridge, Opera House,** and city. The Rocks, **Circular Quay,** and the **Opera House** are the best viewing places to be if the crowds aren't a problem. Otherwise, try the harborfront in the **Eastern Suburbs** or the **North Shore** near **Kirribilli** and **Milsons Point.**

Bests

Tanya Plibersek
Member of Parliament for Sydney

The best way to spend the day in Sydney is to walk around and soak it up.

Here's my ideal Saturday:

Wake up in **Darlinghurst** or **Woolloomooloo.** Have breakfast at **bills** on Liverpool Street in Darlinghurst. The ricotta hotcakes are must-haves. I tend to linger over the weekend crossword, but there are loads of glossy magazines to flick through while eating. Wander over to **Oxford Street** (perhaps walk up to the markets) or walk to the **Art Gallery of New South Wales.**

Have a wander in **The Royal Botanic Gardens**— smell the **Rose Garden** (it's amazing how different each variety smells) and check for tadpoles in the water lily ponds. Do not miss the walk around **Farm Cove** to **Mrs. Macquarie's Chair.** This is the best view of the **Harbour Bridge** and the **Opera House,** although you might have to squeeze between tour buses to see it.

Start the evening with a cocktail at the **Bayswater Brasserie,** then try one of our fantastic restaurants. If you want a truly memorable meal try **Paramount, Morans** (goat-cheese soufflé is a must-have), **Wockpool,** or **Mezzaluna.**

Cheap and cheerful: **Stanley Street, East Sydney** for Italian; **Burgerman** hamburgers; **Box** for Thai. Finish with dessert at **Morgan's.**

Some final words: catch a ferry, swim in the ocean, stay close to the water, and walk everywhere!

Cathy Sidoti
Lawyer, Michell Sillar Australian & International Attorneys

Yum cha (dim sum) at **Marigold** in **Chinatown**— Popular (especially on Saturday morning) Cantonese brunching/snacking/gossiping activity.

Watsons Bay Hotel Beer Garden—Spend a whole afternoon sitting in the sun, with gun-barrel views down the harbor for the price of a couple of beers (or as many as you like!).

Ride an inner harbor ferry—To see Sydney as a working seaport, beautiful early-20th-century maritime architecture with a city skyline backdrop.

Go to the horse racing at **Royal Randwick Racecourse**—wear a hat.

In summer, spend a day at the **Sydney Cricket Ground**—See a test match if you're a true fan or a "one-day international" if you're uninitiated.

Walter Norris
Retired (Australian Broadcasting Corporation)

Most people will want to see the "sails" of the **Sydney Opera House,** the colonial **Rocks** area, the **Sydney 2000 Olympic Games** site.

The **Museum of Sydney** recognizes the site of the first public building in Sydney. It doesn't take a half-day to visit, has a fine bookshop and cafe, and provides a background to the early settlement that became Sydney.

While still in the city, go to the **Strand Arcade** off the **Pitt Street Mall,** a restored 19th-century collection of individual shops—or for a wider selection, the **Queen Victoria Building.** Also take a bus along Oxford Street to **Paddington** for the younger "cool" shopping.

The recreational prize of Sydney must be the beaches, accessible from many suburbs. If you are not able to spend time at a beach, you can always view them. At **Rose Bay** there are two seaplane services that can fly you to **Palm Beach,** or farther, taking in wonderful views of the harbor and the beach-lined coast on the way.

More visible from the air are the many small islands in the harbor. If you want a break from the crowds and to see more of the harbor, it is possible to visit some of these islands. To do this, visit the water transport centers at **Circular Quay.**

Many visitors to Australia are intrigued by the unique vegetation and wildlife. Much can be seen without traveling far. **The Royal Botanic Gardens** and **Taronga Zoo** are situated on the harbor shores and easily accessed.

Adrian Read
Public Relations Consultant, Read McCarthy Group

The 280° panorama of Sydney, old and new, from **Observatory Hill,** above **The Rocks;** the observatory itself; the **Agar Steps** from Observatory Hill down to Kent Street; and the tunnel under the **Harbour Bridge** from Observatory Hill to Cumberland Street are the first places I would take a visitor to Sydney, night or day, in a vehicle or (best) on foot.

Eastern side of **Macquarie Street** from **Hyde Park** to the **Opera House**—the past and the present in context. Take the pedestrian-only **Tarpeian Way** past **Government House** and walk down the stairs to the **Opera House** forecourt. Rub the shiny nose of the big bronze pig outside **Sydney Hospital.**

The Inner West suburb of **Leichhardt** and its rough-and-ready Italianness—especially **Bar Italia**—there are many smarter places but this one is *simpatico.*

Being early for a concert on a fine, clear evening (any season) and taking in the view of the city, **Circular Quay,** and the **Sydney Harbour Bridge** from outside the front foyer of the **Opera House Concert Hall.**

The **Fleet Steps** off Mrs. Macquaries Road and the city view across **Farm Cove.**

Looking up into the Harbour Bridge while crossing it in a convertible—preferably as a passenger!— especially at night when flocks of gulls catch the light as they wheel around and above the structure.

Circular Quay/The Rocks

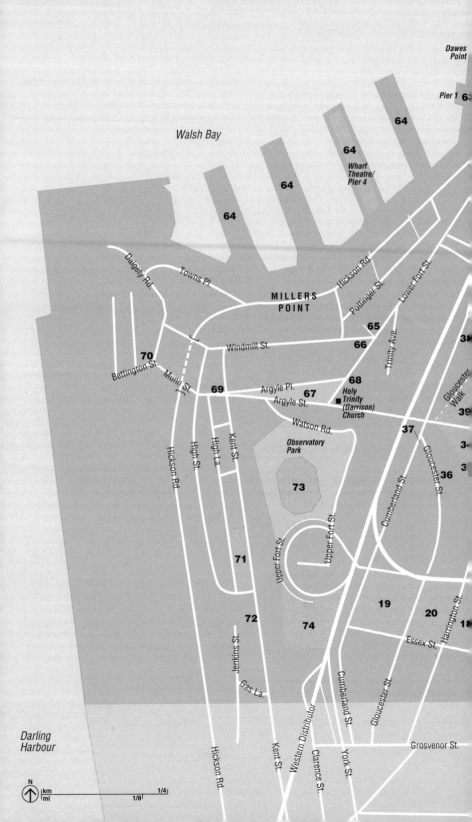

Dawes Point

Pier 1 63

64

Walsh Bay

64

Wharf
Theatre/
Pier 4

64

64

Dalgety Rd.

Towns Pl.

MILLERS
POINT

Hickson Rd.

Pottinger St.

Lower Fort St.

65

66

Windmill St.

Trinity Ave.

3

70

Bettington St.

Munn St.

69

Argyle Pl.

67

Argyle St.

68

Holy
Trinity
(Garrison)
Church

Gloucester Walk

39

Watson Rd.

37

3

Observatory
Park

Cumberland St.

Gloucester St.

36

73

High St.

High La.

Kent St.

Hickson Rd.

Upper Fort St.

Upper Fort St.

71

19

20

Harrington St.

72

74

Essex St.

1

Jenkins St.

Gas La.

Kent St.

Western Distributor

Cumberland St.

York St.

Gloucester St.

Grosvenor St.

Darling
Harbour

Hickson Rd.

Clarence St.

N

km
mi

1/8

1/4

Circular Quay/The Rocks

As the gateway and birthplace of Sydney, this area is appropriately flanked by two of Australia's greatest architectural icons—the **Sydney Opera House** and the **Sydney Harbour Bridge.** The opera house sits majestically on **Bennelong Point** at the eastern end of **Sydney Cove,** and the single-span arch bridge—the world's largest—connects the city center with the more residential North Shore.

At the southern part of Sydney Cove is Circular Quay (pronounced "key"), once more accurately known as **Semi-Circular Quay.** Built on reclaimed land at the mouth of the colony's first freshwater supply, it is now Sydney's harbor gateway and one of the city's major public transport hubs. Just south of the quay is where Captain Arthur Phillip of the First Fleet raised the Union Jack in 1788 and declared the land a British colony. A flagpole at the beginning of Loftus Street designates the spot where this event occurred. It also marks the beginning of Sydney's **Central Business District (CBD)**, the site of several historic public buildings, including the **Customs House** and the **Water Police Court** (now the **Justice and Police Museum**).

On the western side of Sydney Cove is The Rocks, an area that starts where **George** and **Alfred Streets** meet and finishes just under the shadows of the Sydney Harbour Bridge at **Millers Point.** The First Fleet sailed into the cove in January 1788, after determining that Botany Bay, a few miles south, was an inadequate site for a new colony. Soon after—with considerable disregard for the local Aborigines—camps were set up in the rocky sandstone outcrops along the cove's western shore (hence "The Rocks"), and the tiny British penal colony gradually grew into a huge, bustling port.

The Rocks was Australia's oldest and most heavily populated urban community in the 19th century. It owes much of its development to the heavy use of convict labor that built many of the dwellings, storehouses, and the **Argyle Cut**, which joined the port to **Darling Harbour.** By the end of the 19th century, The Rocks had become a disorderly port, rife with squalor, plague, gang wars, and prostitution. By the 1920s the area was so dilapidated and neglected that the public barely resisted the idea of demolishing entire streets and rows of old Victorian terrace homes in order to clear the way for the construction of the Sydney Harbour Bridge.

It wasn't until the 1950s, when Sydney was beginning to take interest in its history, that The Rocks was salvaged. Since then the area has changed dramatically. Many of the Georgian and Victorian buildings, such as **Cadman's Cottage, The Sailors' Home,** and **The Argyle Centre,** have been carefully restored and refurbished, thus transforming the neighborhood into the harborfront village it once was and making it one of the city's safest districts. Sydneysiders are proud of this area and its heritage, and often congregate here to honor their city, celebrate major events, grab a beer after work, visit the **Museum of Contemporary Art (MCA)**, and picnic at the harbor parks at **Observatory Hill** and **Dawes Point.** Today The Rocks is a maze of cobblestone lanes, courtyards, and wide streets.

For those who seek harbor views and access to the harbor and city, The Rocks is the place to stay. The major international hotel chains have long staked their claims here, while several smaller boutique hotels and pubs offer simple, clean rooms. And some of Sydney's top restaurants, including **Bel Mondo, Kable's, Rockpool,** and **Sailor's Thai,** can be found in this area.

The usual souvenir stores selling stuffed koalas and factory-produced boomerangs are plentiful here, but they are balanced with a more refined retail opportunity at the **Argyle Department Store**, which is full of quality

Australian-brand homewares, jewelry, and clothing. **The Rocks Market** features vendors selling handmade crafts and food, and street performers doing the latest renditions of their art.

The **East Promenade** heading toward Circular Quay is one of Sydney's most famous walkways. During the day it is filled with locals and tourists gazing at the harbor or clicking their cameras. For the sake of the view, some stop for a beer at the **Sydney Cove Oyster Bar,** or eat lunch at one of the cafes. Others may be spotted gazing at the ground, reading the plaques along the **Writers' Walk.**

The Circular Quay and The Rocks remain one of the best parts of Sydney to explore on foot. Use the hulking steel Sydney Harbour Bridge and the famous **Sydney Opera House** as directional guides and enjoy the stroll through history.

1 Sydney Opera House Jutting out from Bennelong Point on the eastern end of Sydney Cove, this opera house (pictured below) is Australia's most famous landmark. No other building in the country has attracted as much public awe, passion, delight, and controversy as this internationally renowned architectural wonder. With its intriguing roof line (commonly considered to resemble waves or sails), walls made of huge sheer glass panels, and high roof vaults, the entire building is a tribute to daring design and engineering.

Public demand for a performance complex in Sydney mounted through the 1950s. The then-premier of New South Wales, Joseph Cahill, set up an appeal fund and "Opera House Lotteries" to raise money for its construction. He also launched an international competition for designers, and Danish architect **Jorn Utzon** was announced as the winner in January 1957. **Utzon**'s original design was so boldly conceived that it proved structurally impossible to build. After four years of research, **Utzon** altered his schematics by giving the roof vaults a defined spherical geometry that would enable them to be built in a pre-cast fashion. This greatly reduced both the time and cost of the project. But from the first day of construction in 1959, the opera house was dogged by controversy. There were budget problems and political interference with the design, including the reversal of the positioning of the **Concert Hall** and opera theater. **Utzon** resigned in dismay in 1966, and the building was completed by a team of Australian architects. Queen Elizabeth II officially opened the complex in 1973.

Despite its early problems, the opera house has since proved a triumph. Everything about the building is extraordinary (see floor plan on page 22), especially the logistics of its design. There are 11 acres of floor space, 67,000 square feet of glass walls, and nearly 1,000

Sydney Opera House

rooms, including the **Concert Hall** (2,690 seats), the **Opera Theatre** (1,547 seats), the **Drama Theatre** (544 seats), and **Playhouse** (398 seats). The highest roof vault, above the **Concert Hall,** is 221 feet above sea level. The roofs are constructed of 2,194 pre-cast concrete sections weighing up to 15 tons each, and are all held together by 217 miles of tensioned steel cable. They are covered with more than one million ceramic tiles arranged in an intricate pattern that allows the shell to expand and contract. **Concert Hall,** the largest of the theaters, is an acoustic and visual wonder. Its ceiling soars 82 feet above the stage, and 18 adjustable acoustic rings or "clouds" located overhead enhance the music by reflecting the sound back down to the platform. The Grand Organ, with 10,500 pipes, is the largest mechanical tracker organ in the world. The building's shape is another marvel. While his design was commonly perceived to be modeled on waves or spinnakers of a yacht, no one really knows what inspired **Utzon.**

Beyond its amazing design, the opera house has been a major catalyst in the development and elevation of the arts in Australia, and a symbol of performance excellence and endeavor. The **Reception Hall** and large foyers of the **Concert Hall** and the **Opera Theatre** all offer spectacular views overlooking Sydney Harbour. Take a stroll to the harbor's edge during intermission to admire the nighttime vistas. Four restaurants and bars are located in the foyers. ♦ One-hour tours of the theaters and foyers: Daily 9AM-4PM. Ninety-minute backstage tours, including the stages and rehearsal areas: Su 9AM-4PM. Farm Cove Crescent (north of Circular Quay E). 9250.7111

At the Sydney Opera House:

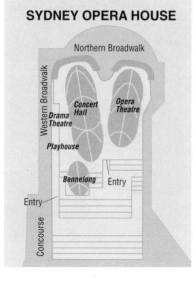

SYDNEY OPERA HOUSE

Northern Broadwalk

Western Broadwalk

Concert Hall

Opera Theatre

Drama Theatre

Playhouse

Bennelong   Entry

Entry

Concourse

Bennelong ★★★$$$$ Minimalism is a way of life at this temple of gastronomy: No flowers or table settings (they arrive with the meal) detract from the business at hand—fine dining and a spectacular view. A recent change in management saw the introduction of a crustacean counter where the chef sports a headset to communicate with the kitchen. The day's catch—lobster, crabs, oysters, and marrons—is arrayed behind him in stainless-steel tubes filled with ice. This is simply the restaurant with the best address in Sydney. A more informal level for traditional drinks and pretheater snacks perches above the main dining room.
♦ Modern Australian ♦ M-Sa dinner and supper. Reservations required. 9250.7548

The Concourse ★★$$ The food at this dining spot runs a distant second to its outstanding views of Circular Quay, the Harbour Bridge, and North Shore's **Luna Park.** Typical of Sydney's eateries, this cafe/ restaurant features outdoor dining on aluminum chairs and tables set under market umbrellas, and a large indoor space with lime-colored wooden chairs and stainless steel and granite finishes. Morning and afternoon teas (try the cookies) and a light supper after the opera or theater are the best bets here, although a harborside lunch is also hard to beat if the hordes of tourists don't overwhelm. Try the smoked Tasmanian salmon or a dozen Sydney rock oysters, and wash it down with a bottle of Australian sparkling wine. ♦ Modern Australian ♦ M-Sa 10AM-11PM; Su. Lower concourse. 9250.7300

2 **Man O'War Steps** Construction of these steps and the jetty began in the late 1830s and was completed in the 1850s. The Australian Station of the Royal Navy used the jetty until the late 19th century; later the Royal Australian Navy held military ceremonies here. Today water taxis and smaller private craft dock at the jetty. ♦ Farm Cove Crescent (north of Circular Quay E)

3 **Circular Quay** Once known (more accurately) as **Semi-Circular Quay,** this is one of the most historically significant stretches of harborfront in Australia. It is set on Sydney Cove, which originally ended in a small tidal estuary where the Tank Stream, the city's first freshwater supply, emptied into the harbor. In 1837 Governor Macquarie ordered an extension of the shoreline at Bennelong Point to allow ships to sit along the length of the cove. This worked until the city grew and required more docks. In 1853 colonial engineer George Barney constructed the **Semi-Circular Quay** seawall, and reclaimed most of the mudflats by filling the area with material excavated from The Argyle Cut in The Rocks. Some 20 years later, the first ferry wharves, as well as larger commercial docks,

were built. The opening of the overhead railway and **Circular Quay Station** of the **City Circle Railway** in 1956 provided a direct ferry-train link for Sydney. ◆ Between Farm Cove Crescent and Hickson Rd

Along Circular Quay:

Writers' Walk Set in the walkway is a series of bronze plaques that depict the impressions of famous writers—both Australian literati and visiting people of letters—of Sydney. The observations of some, including Peter Carey and Mark Twain, are not that rosy.

3 Portobello Caffe ★★$ This one-time gelato bar on the promenade between the ferry terminal and the **Opera House** has become one of the better cafes in the Circular Quay area. Pick up an ice cream to go or sit at one of the tables and watch the ferries chug by while munching on an Italian sandwich or pastry. Top it off with a well-made espresso. ◆ Cafe/ Takeout ◆ Daily. Circular Quay E (between Alfred St and Farm Cove Crescent). 9247.8548

4 Sydney Cove Oyster Bar ★★$$ Before the opera, stop at this quayside bar for a half-dozen Sydney rock oysters and a glass of Champagne. Seating is available for those who want to relax and take in the view. ◆ Seafood/Bar ◆ Daily 11AM-11PM. 1 Circular Quay E (at Macquarie St). 9247.2937

5 Circular Quay Ferry Terminal Four of the five main wharves at this terminal service the government-run **Sydney Ferries.** The destination and time of the next ferry is clearly displayed above the entrance of each dock. The **Sydney Ferries Information Office** is opposite **Wharf No. 4.** In addition, several major tour companies operate out of these wharves, offering cruise, coach, and car tours of Sydney harbor, the city, and its outskirts. ◆ Alfred St and Circular Quay E. 13.500

5 Circular Quay Railway Station The aqua tiles and beautiful marine-inspired details make this station look more like an aquarium entrance than a two-platform commuter railway station. A **CityRail Information** kiosk is positioned at the entrance along with a number of restaurants and cafes. ◆ Alfred St and Circular Quay E. 13.2232

Within Circular Quay Railway Station:

City Extra ★$$ This fast, brash, and loud cafe/restaurant hasn't changed much since it was built in the early 1980s. The food and service match its newsroom theme—the place is abrasive, and open around the clock, every day of the year. The fare is largely along the lines of an American diner (hamburgers, big calorific desserts), with such touches for the tourists as the "Aussie burger." And everything is cooked or baked on the premises. ◆ American/Australian ◆ Daily 24 hours. Shop E4. 9241.1422

6 Merrony's ★★$$$ A few laps of the Circular Quay promenade are definitely in order after eating the superb (but heavy), French-inspired food at this open dining room with lots of glass. Try the blue-eyed cod with vinaigrette or the delicious, diet-defying duck confit. Desserts are also hefty but tasty, especially the vanilla bean crème brûlée. The place is popular at lunchtime with the business crowd and later in the day with the post-opera and -theater set. ◆ French/Modern Australian ◆ M-F lunch and dinner; Sa dinner. Reservations recommended. Quay Apartments, 2 Albert St (at Phillip St). 9247.9323

7 Justice and Police Museum Sydney has always had—and continues to have—an active underworld, teeming with colorful crime figures, a fair share of notorious crimes, and memorable police operations. A history of this intriguing, though decidedly unglamorous, side of the city's past is found at this museum, where visitors are invited to "enter the world of crims and coppers." Relics from Sydney's wild colonial days are displayed, including the death mask and pistols of infamous bushrangers Captain Moonlite and Ben Hall. Check out the collection of weird and wonderful memorabilia from notorious and legendary crimes, such as the Battle of Broken Hill, the Pyjama Girl Case, and the Thorne Kidnapping, along with many other items from sensational episodes of crime and punishment. The building originally housed the **Water Police Court** (1856), the **Water Police Station** (1858), and the **Police Court** (1885), and has been restored to its early character. Heavy blocks of sandstone, spiked gates, winding steps, and a corridor of cells reinforce the museum's themes of crime and punishment, law and order. In the **Magistrate's Court,** groups that reserve in advance can participate in mock trials. There's also a re-created police charge room and remand cell where visitors may experience the lives of both police and prisoners; a gallery of mug shots of Sydney's early criminals; an array of spine-chilling weapons; and a slide show tracing 200 years of change through the eyes of the law. ◆ Admission. Th-Su Jan; Su Feb-Dec. 4-8 Phillip St (between Bridge and Albert Sts). 9252.1144

Restaurants/Clubs: Red	**Hotels:** Blue
Shops/ ◆ Outdoors: Green	**Sights/Culture:** Black

8 AMP Tower and Plaza This 43-floor office tower (pictured at bottom right) was built in 1972 and is joined to the original AMP building at Circular Quay. Until the early 1960s the old AMP structure was the tallest building in Sydney and stood out on the harborfront. Looking at the old edifice brings home how much Sydney has developed since then. **AMP Plaza**—two floors of retail shops and restaurants—is housed in the newer building. ♦ M-F. 50 Bridge St (between Phillip and Young Sts)

ANTHONY HARVEY

9 Customs House By the mid-1800s Sydney was a major trading port for Australia and the Pacific and needed government offices near the Circular Quay to control imports. Designed by **Mortimer Lewis,** the original 1844 **Customs House** was a Georgian-style sandstone building located next to the Tank Stream's outlet. Some 40 years later, architect **James Barnet** designed a two-floor addition to the structure. Polished granite columns, carved stone balusters, and an elaborate clock with a dolphin and trident motif are among its many characteristics. Today the building has been renovated into a cultural center. ♦ Free. Customs House Sq (between Young and Loftus Sts)

Within the Customs House:

Djamu Gallery of Aboriginal and Pacific Islander Art A branch of the Australian Museum, this recently opened gallery houses most of the museum's collection of Aboriginal art that was previously largely inaccessible to the public. *Djamu* means "I am here" in the Eora language. ♦ Admission ♦ Daily. 9320.6429

10 Gallipoli Memorial Club This 1870s complex, originally **F.L. Barker's Wool and Produce Stores,** was conveniently located near Circular Quay for easy access to shipping. In 1946, the Gallipoli Legion of ANZAC (Australia-New Zealand Army Corps) took over two of the four stores. The legion removed some of the interior walls to enlarge the floor space, renovated the facade, and renamed it **Gallipoli Memorial Club** in honor of World War I veterans. The other two demolished stores are now office blocks. Two restaurants occupy the club's ground floor. ♦ 12-14 Loftus St (between Bridge St and Customs House Sq)

Within the Gallipoli Memorial Club:

Rock Fish Cafe ★★★$$ Wonderful sandstone walls and wooden floors are just two reasons why this informal seafood restaurant is popular for a business lunch or a seafood dinner after a long walk around Circular Quay. The justifiably famous salt-and-pepper calamari is a meal in itself. Or try the grilled catch of the day, accompanied by a wide, tasty selection of dipping sauces. A glass of chilled Australian white wine completes the meal. ♦ Seafood ♦ M-F lunch and dinner. Reservations recommended. Level 1. 9252.3114

11 Macquarie Place This paved triangular area is of historical and geographical importance to Sydney, as well as being a famous meeting place. A sandstone obelisque, designed in 1818 by colonial architect **Francis Greenway,** features markings that show the distances to various places in the colony. Look for an anchor and cannon from the *HMS Sirius,* the ship that escorted the First Fleet from England. ♦ Just west of Loftus St

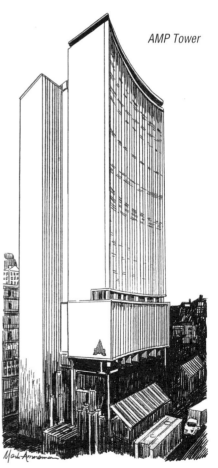

AMP Tower

12 Paradiso Cafe ★★$ When the weather is fine, so is this cafe that offers coffee, alcoholic beverages, and simple fare. All tables are outside, most under the shade of Macquarie Place's fig trees. Good bets are the Turkish-bread sandwiches and salads. Start the day with coffee and scrambled eggs while watching the business crowd scurry to their offices. ♦ Cafe/Takeout ♦ M-F 7AM-6PM; Sa 10AM-4PM. 7 Macquarie Pl (southwest of Reiby Pl). 9241.2141

13 Customs House Bar This old business district pub is a Friday evening institution in Sydney, with the city's bankers and corporate types bellying up to the bar. People flock here by the hundreds, spilling into Macquarie Place as they guzzle gallons of beer. ♦ Daily 10AM-10PM. Macquarie Pl (southwest of Reiby Pl). 9259.7000

14 The Basement *The* place for jazz and blues in Sydney, this popular nightclub has all the makings of a remarkably cool music spot—it's tucked away in a small lane way behind Circular Quay, and hosts some of Australia's (and the world's) best folk and jazz talent. ♦ M-F noon to end of last show; Sa-Su 7:30PM to end of last show. 29 Reiby Pl (between Macquarie Pl and Pitt St). 9251.2797

RENAISSANCE.
SYDNEY HOTEL

15 Renaissance Sydney Hotel $$$$ Harbor views and location are the lures at this 579-room hostelry with both indoor and outdoor pools. It's ideal for business travelers—the Central Business District is literally at the hotel's doorstep; it specializes in meetings for up to 200 people; and the **Renaissance Club** offers complimentary breakfast, tea, and cocktails for guests staying on the top four floors. The **Bulletin Bar** in the lobby has become a haunt for cigar aficionados; the **Customs House Bar** (see above) is a watering hole. There also are two restaurants and a gym. ♦ 30 Pitt St (between Bridge St and Bulletin Pl). 9259.7000, 800/468.3571; fax 9252.2352

16 Neptune Palace ★★$$$ As the name suggests, seafood is prominently featured at this dining spot. The bounty from the sea is prepared Chinese style—steamed red emperor fish and snapper with chili peppers are two of the delicacies offered. Such well-presented Malaysian standards as beef *rendang* (cooked in coconut milk, chili peppers, and other spices) and curry puffs are also on the menu. True to the name, the décor is palatial. Come for the great food, not the view, and opt for the banquet menu if the many choices overwhelm. ♦ Chinese/Malaysian ♦ M-Sa lunch and dinner. Reservations recommended. Gateway Bldg, Alfred St (between Loftus and Pitt Sts), Level 1. 9241.3338

17 Jackson's On George Popular with both the business crowd and the backpacker set, this big and bold pub has four bars, a restaurant, and a disco. It claims to offer the largest range of beers in Australia, with over 100 beers from 26 countries. Nightly entertainment starts around 7PM, just as the crowd is getting revved up. ♦ M-Sa 10AM-midnight; Su noon-midnight. 176 George St (at Crane Pl). 9247.2727

A FOUR SEASONS HOTEL

18 Regent Sydney $$$$ When this 596-room, high-rise property opened in the early 1980s (complete with brass, glass, and tons of granite and marble), it was hailed as Australia's best hotel. Now part of the Four Seasons hotel group, much of that reputation remains intact—the service and room facilities are superior and the location ideal. The hostelry is very popular with business travelers, particularly because of its meeting rooms, secretarial services, health club, salon, and 24-hour butler service. The pillar-free grand ballroom has been the venue for some of Sydney's most lavish balls and gala events, and the two restaurants, cafe, and bars are popular with local businesspeople. High tea at the **Mezzanine Lounge** has become an institution. Room rates vary according to the view. ♦ 199 George St (at Essex St). 9238.0000, 800/332.3442; fax 9251.4745

Within the Regent Sydney:

Kable's ★★★$$$$ Hotel restaurants are often uninteresting and overpriced, but this eatery is an exception. Graceful space, immaculate service, and a passionate chef with impeccable technique all contribute to making this one of Sydney's finest dining institutions. Executive chef Serge Dansereau is a stickler for the finest products and spends much of his time seeking out and encouraging Australia's best growers and producers. His menu reads like a regional map, with Hunter Valley quail and Hervey Bay king prawns, and the wine list features an excellent range of Australian wines. ♦ Modern Australian ♦ M lunch; Tu-F lunch and dinner; Sa dinner. Reservations required. Mezzanine. 9255.0226

ANA HOTEL SYDNEY

19 **ANA Hotel Sydney** $$$$ The glass and marble that stand out at this luxury hotel on the southern edge of The Rocks are softened by some well-chosen contemporary Aboriginal and other modern art work. The building was designed to reflect the curves of the adjacent freeway, and nearly all of its 573 large guest rooms have magnificent views of the harbor. An executive floor caters to those who want to sleep as close as possible to the wide range of business facilities. Two of the four restaurants feature Japanese fare and the top-floor **Horizons Bar** has floor-to-ceiling windows that offer a panoramic vista of the harbor. ◆ 176 Cumberland St (at Essex St). 9250.6000, 800/228.3000; fax 9250.6116

Within the ANA Hotel Sydney:

Unkai Restaurant ★★★$$$ Chef Hiroshi Miura's exquisitely prepared and presented cuisine competes with the restaurant's fantastic 36th-floor harbor views and serene Japanese atmosphere. Be forewarned: The menu can be overwhelming, especially in the seafood department. If confusion sets in, opt for the set menus of three to nine courses, or ask the staff for suggestions. Enjoying the three-tiered, red-lacquered lunch boxes is a memorable experience, especially as the server ceremoniously reveals each delicate layer. ◆ Japanese ◆ M-F, Su breakfast, lunch, and dinner; Sa dinner. Reservations recommended. 36th floor. 9250.6123

Unkai Sushi Bar ★★★$$ This intimate sushi bar featuring the finest seafood is considered one of Australia's best. Two *itamae* (sushi chefs) prepare such treats as spicy salmon handrolls and prawn sticks for the only 15 diners, max, that the space holds. The view of the Blue Mountains on a clear day makes dining here an even more pleasant experience. ◆ Japanese ◆ Daily lunch and dinner. Reservations required. 36th floor. 9250.6123

20 **Quay West Sydney** $$$$ Just on the fringe of The Rocks, this apartment building has 132 one- and two-bedroom suites—complete with sofa beds and kitchen facilities—available for overnight and long-term guests. The service here is as good as, or better than, that of any luxury hotel. The health club should win a prize for its view over the harbor to the Harbour Bridge and North Sydney. Other perks include conference facilities. ◆ 98 Gloucester St (just north of Essex St). 9240.6000; fax 9240.6060

QUAY WEST
SYDNEY

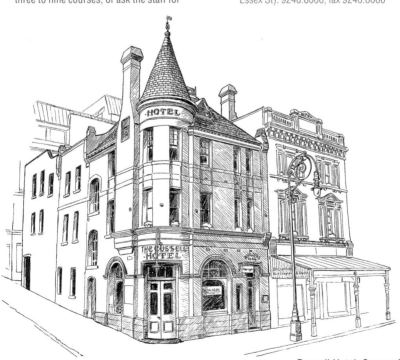

Russell Hotel, George Street

*Australian Craftworks/
Old George Street North Police Station*

21 Bicentennial Plaque Set here in 1988, this elaborate marker commemorates the British First Fleet's landing. It depicts Sydney Cove and the Circular Quay area in its pre-European state. Several walking tours of the **Opera House** and The Rocks leave from this point. ♦ Alfred St (just east of George St)

22 First Fleet Park Generally considered to be the site of the 26 January 1788 landing of the British First Fleet, this spot is not the most tranquil park in the city. But a good view of Circular Quay and lots of available people watching are good reasons to stop here. ♦ George St (between Alfred and Argyle Sts)

23 Russell Hotel $$$ This 29-room boutique hotel (see illustration on page 26) has been carefully decorated to maintain the charm of the century-old building that houses it. Just across from **First Fleet Park,** Circular Quay, and the **MCA** (see below), the location can't be beat. It's a little pricey, though the complimentary breakfast compensates somewhat. ♦ 143A George St (at Globe St). 9241.3543; fax 9252.1652

Within the Russell Hotel:

Boulders At The Rocks ★★$$ Standard Modern Australian cuisine generally relies on local products prepared with Mediterranean

and Asian influences. This dining spot has jumped on the bandwagon and offers a slightly gimmicky menu. The fare however, is always top-notch, but be prepared for slow service. While away the time with a glass or two of Australian wine and relax in the tranquil, warm yellow dining room. ♦ Modern Australian ♦ M-F lunch and dinner; Sa-Su dinner. Reservations recommended. 9241.1447

24 Australian Craftworks/Old George Street North Police Station Telltale signs of the former residents of this 1882 building designed by **James Barnet** (pictured above) include a stately British stone lion with a baton clenched between his teeth at the entrance and a front door that's reinforced with iron studs. The police beat here was once considered one of the toughest in the country. Today it has a more genteel air as a local arts and crafts gallery. Don't be put off by the huge selection of souvenirs—mixed among the cute things are some beautiful Australian-made leather goods, pottery, glassware, and woodwork. Some displays are in the old jail chambers, complete with cell doors and hanging rings to support prisoner hammocks. ♦ Daily. 127-31 George St (between Globe St and Suez Canal). 9247.7156

25 Done Art and Design Sydney artist Ken Done and his wife Judy have teamed up to sell their distinctive, bright-colored prints on T-shirts, swimwear, and accessories. Their gear seems to be everywhere, although it is most popular with tourists. ♦ Daily. 123 George St (between Globe St and Suez Canal). 9251.6099

25 Flame Opals The opal is Australia's most famous gemstone, but with hundreds of types and grades, choosing one is no easy task. From the "milk" variety to the famous black opals of Lightning Ridge, this store has them all. ♦ Daily. 119 George St (between Globe St and Suez Canal). 9247.3446

26 Aboriginal and Tribal Art Center Everything from traditional dot paintings to painted souvenir boomerangs is displayed at this visual arts gallery. The staff is happy to explain what's what and who's who in Aboriginal art. ♦ Daily. 117 George St (between Globe St and Suez Canal). 9241.5998

27 Museum of Contemporary Art (MCA) This stark, Art Deco building dominates the western bank of Sydney Cove. Erected in the 1930s as offices for the Maritime Services Board—notice the sculptured relief above the entrance of the building that depicts wharf laborers—it reopened in 1991 as a spacious contemporary art museum. More than 5,000 modern and contemporary works comprise the permanent collection, most of them acquired from the bequest of John Wardell Power, Australian medical practitioner and artist, to the **University of Sydney.** The museum also offers an ever-changing international and Australian exhibition program that includes experimental, performance, and electronic art. In addition, it features an extensive collection of contemporary Aboriginal works and presents regular exhibits of all forms of indigenous art. The ground-floor store is stacked with unique books, catalogues, and gift ideas, and is well worth a browse. ♦ Admission. Daily. 140 George St (between Alfred and Argyle Sts). 9252.4033

Within the Museum of Contemporary Art:

Sydney had only two major international hotels—the Sydney Hilton and the Wentworth—until 1982 when the Regent Sydney was built. This construction was the catalyst for a hotel boom in the city.

The opera *The Eighth Wonder* was produced in 1995 by the Australian Opera Company. The libretto has an unusual theme, recounting the story of the politics, people, and a country divided over the building of Australia's most famous icon, the Sydney Opera House.

MCA Fish Cafe ★★★$$ Regardless of what's on the menu, the dining experience here is consistent—stylish, memorable, and affordable. Owned and operated by Neil Perry of **Rockpool** (just across the street) fame, this restaurant/cafe is Modern Australian cuisine at its best—carefully selected local products are prepared creatively and quickly. The blue-eyed cod with honey and chili sauce is superb, as is the grilled swordfish with eggplant salad. It also boasts a good wine list and great desserts. Sit outside under one of the canvas umbrellas and enjoy views of the **Opera House** and sometimes a performance or art installation on the museum's front lawn. ♦ Modern Australian ♦ M-F lunch; Sa-Su breakfast and lunch. Reservations recommended. 9241.4253

ROCKPOOL
★

28 Rockpool ★★★$$$$ Don't be put off by the attitude at the door or the crowd of dazzling and good-looking patrons. Neil Perry's glamorous flagship restaurant, with its cool steel and wood interior, can be a very special Sydney experience. Perry is considered to be one of the fathers of Modern Australian cuisine, and his seasonal menu remains a consistently impressive blend of local seafood with Southeast Asian, Indian, and European flavors. Try the sea urchin or local caviar for an exotic taste treat, and the herb- and spice-encrusted tuna is a favorite. The Australian cheese selection is outstanding, and the sticky date tart keeps people coming back for seconds. Selections from all of the country's wine regions are featured on the extensive list. ♦ Modern Australian ♦ M-F lunch and dinner; Sa dinner. Reservations required. 107 George St (between Globe St and Suez Canal). 9252.1888

28 Dorian Scott Colorful Australian wool knitwear is the lure here. The clothing is either handmade or manufactured in Australia. ♦ Daily. 105 George St (between Globe St and Suez Canal). 9247.4090

29 Suez Canal The original name of this laneway was "Sewers Canal"—a self-explanatory nomenclature. In the early 20th century, the lack of decent plumbing in The Rocks contributed to the spread of the bubonic plague, which killed over 100 people in the area. ♦ Between George and Harrington Sts

30 Nurses' Walk This stretch of walkway is named after and dedicated to Australia's first nurses, many of whom were transported female convicts. ♦ Between Globe St and Suez Canal

31 Argyle Cut In 1843 hundreds of convicts started cutting through the solid sandstone with hammer and chisel to create this roadway joining Sydney Cove, Millers Point, and Darling Harbour in the west. The engineering feat took 18 years and extra local government labor to complete. It also earned the dubious reputation at the time of being a hangout for cutthroats, gangs, prostitutes, and drunks. The road was widened in 1930 to accommodate the construction of the Sydney Harbour Bridge. Look for the marks in the stone at the thoroughfare's beginning (the corner of George and Argyle Streets) showing where the convicts worked. ♦ Argyle St (between George and Kent Sts)

32 Stafford Apartments $$$ A combination of seven smartly restored, two-story terrace houses built in the 1870s and 54 adjacent studio rooms make up these accommodations. All guest rooms have kitchens and many feature balconies and views of Circular Quay and the **Opera House.** Efficient business and valet services and a gym make this property ideal for professionals. ♦ 75 Harrington St (between Essex and Argyle Sts). 9251.6711; fax 9251.3458

33 Harbour Rocks Hotel $$ Built over a hundred years ago, this 55-room, landmark hotel (pictured below) is located in a converted former warehouse and a row of Victorian terrace houses that were carefully renovated and retain their original facade. Some new guest rooms have been added in the rear, but the older accommodations are more in keeping with the area's historic ambience. A friendly staff and room service are two pluses. ♦ 34-52 Harrington St (between Essex St and Suez Canal). 9251.8944; fax 9251.8900

34 Clocktower Square The modern clocktower atop a sandstone building makes this shopping center hard to miss. With Aboriginal art galleries, and sheepskin, opal, and jewelry stores, this is souvenir heaven. ♦ Daily 7AM-9PM. 35 Harrington St (at Argyle St). 9247.6134

35 Gumnut Tea Garden ★$ Since the mid-1980s, this 1830s cottage built by convict William Reynolds has been run as a quaint cafe. Most of the tables are made from the wrought-iron bases of antique sewing machines collected by the owners. The cafe's paved, shady outdoor courtyard is occasionally the venue for jazz and classical concerts in the summer. The regular menu includes homemade scones and pies. ♦ Cafe ♦ Daily. 28 Harrington St (at Argyle St). 9247.9591

36 Susannah Place Built in 1844 for Edward and Mary Riley and their niece Susannah, this museum of four terrace houses and a turn-of-the-century corner store is indicative of the life of The Rocks' working-class community. Visitors get a sense of the routines of domestic life from the mid-1840s to the late 20th century. Behind the houses are the original brick privvies and open laundries—some of the city's earliest surviving washing and sanitary facilities. The re-created general grocer's store sells goods from the 1900s, from flypaper to boiled lollies (candy), from honey dibble sweets to marbles. ♦ Admission. Daily Jan; Sa-Su Feb-Dec. 58-64 Gloucester St (southeast of Cumberland St). 9692.8366

37 The Australian Given its name, this old Aussie pub has a lot to live up to—and it succeeds. So naturally it has both the major Australian beers and some boutique brews on tap. Views of the Harbour Bridge make the outdoor seating even more prized. Try one of the gourmet pizzas while sampling the local ales. ♦ Daily 10AM-11PM. 100 Cumberland St (at Gloucester St). 9247.2229

38 Glenmore Hotel $ The four guest rooms at this small landmark hotel have been beautifully restored. The only possible negative is that the bathroom facilities are shared, but the rooftop beer garden has grand views of this historic area. ♦ 96 Cumberland St (between Gloucester and Lower Fort Sts). 9247.4794; fax 9247.4973

Harbour Rocks Hotel

Wild and Woolly

Accounts of how startled the British were when they first caught sight of some of Australia's animals fill the country's history books—giant rodentlike animals with pouches hopped through the beaches and grassy plains (kangaroos and wallabies), slow, gray, bearlike animals sat in trees and munched on eucalyptus leaves (koalas), animals with mammalian characteristics defied classification by laying eggs (platypuses), and large, colorful flocks of birds screeched in the skies and laughed in the trees (galahs and cockatoos). Many of the animals that fascinated the colonists and zoologists more than 200 years ago may still be seen around Sydney today.

The abundance of wildlife in and around Sydney has much to do with the fact that the city is encircled by a leafy harborfront, surrounded by national parks, and lined with beaches. And in the suburbs, the streets are filled with trees, and many homes cultivate large green gardens that attract native birds, possums, and bats. But the chance of seeing a kangaroo hop or a koala lumber down George Street in the city or even along Parramatta Road out west is next to none. Marsupial lovers will have to travel out of **Greater Sydney,** or visit one of the wildlife parks on the city's fringes.

A Walk on the Wild Side

The following are some native animals and birds that may be seen in and around Sydney, including some that are indigenous to the area, but today are found only in Sydney's zoos and wildlife parks.

Australian Magpie This black-and-white birds is a common sight throughout Sydney's parks and reserves. It has a distinctive call and is worth avoiding during spring when it is building its nests and may be aggressive.

Brush-tailed Possum With its long bushy tail, big eyes, and tiny claws, this nocturnal animal is commonly found in Sydney city parks and suburbs. It feeds on fruit and some insects.

Eastern Grey Kangaroo This marsupial grazes on grasslands close to woodlands throughout Eastern Australia. Its offspring are carried in a front pouch and are called joeys. Although the animal is one of Australia's national icons, many farmers kill kangaroos because they consider them pests, destroying crops and increasing soil erosion. Kangaroo meat has become a popular item on many restaurant menus, pleasing some diners and disgusting others. The marsupial can be viewed in national parkland and wildlife parks.

Echidna With its protective spikes and a long nose that allows it to burrow into ant and termite mounds for food, this egg-laying mammal (a monotreme) is

Galah

also known as a spiny anteater. When threatened, it rolls itself into a ball and lies still. It is found throughout Australia, but may be spotted in Sydney's bushland and reserves.

Fruit Bat This nocturnal mammal with its black coloring and huge wingspan can be a frightening sight as it swoops down into trees at night. It is relatively harmless, however, and may be spotted throughout Sydney (especially in the warmer months) as it scours the city in search of fig and other fruit trees on which to feast.

Galah Often seen in flocks, this red and gray large bird grows to more than 30 centimeters (12 inches) in length and is common in Sydney's national parks and some outlying suburbs. It makes an eerie screeching sound.

Goanna Resembling enormous garden lizards, this creatures grows up to 1.5 meters (5 feet). It's found throughout Australia; in Sydney, look in the outlying bush areas.

Koala

Koala This cuddly gray animal with a black nose is not a bear. It's a marsupial and a close relative of the wombat, which is mainly found in Southeastern Australia. A koala grows up to 50 centimeters (1.75 feet) in height and eats eucalyptus leaves. It is extremely rare around the outer suburbs of Sydney, so it's best to look in the zoo or wildlife parks.

Kookaburra Also known as the "Laughing Kookaburra," this noisy bird is usually deep blue, gray, and white in its coloring and is a member of the kingfisher family. At dusk and dawn in Sydney, its laugh may be heard in the trees of Sydney's parks and gardens. Some say it sounds a little like a monkey.

Kookaburra

Pink Cockatoo This large pink and white bird with

sulfur and red crests may be spotted in Sydney's outlying bushland and plains. It is related to the galah (see above).

Platypus

Platypus
Another monotreme, this egg-laying aquatic mammal has a peculiar body—it is furry and elongated with webbed claws and a duck bill. It is rarely sighted in the wild, but may be found in the fresh waterways along the East Coast. Some biologists consider it to be the missing link between mammals and reptiles.

Rainbow Lorikeet This multicolored bird with a red beak is similar to a parrot. It's usually found in pairs or flocks around Sydney and eats nectar and fruit.

Rosella Some of these fast, chirpy crimson and indigo birds are so tame they will eat from the hands of humans. They are located throughout Sydney and the forests of Eastern Australia.

Sugar Glider This tiny acrobatic mammal from the possum family can glide from tree to tree, thanks to a large body surface area when it extends its limbs. The glider is usually found in Eastern and Northern Australia, though generally not in Sydney.

Tasmanian Devil No longer found in mainland Australia, this nocturnal and carnivorous animal spends its days sleeping underground or in enclosed spaces. It comes out at night to hunt, uttering a terrifying scream and using its ferocious teeth. Tasmanian Devils can be viewed in Sydney at **Waratah Park.**

Tasmanian Devil

Wallaby Like its larger relative, the kangaroo, the wallaby is a marsupial, and carries its young in a pouch for about six months. The Wallaby, however, prefers the protection of the forest and jungle during the day when it feeds on the underbrush. Nocturnal wanderings in search of food include forays into tall grass. Housed in **Taronga Zoo,** the wallaby can also be seen bounding around a number of the region's national parks.

Wombat

Wombat Short stumpy legs, a bearlike face, and gray/brown fur distinguish this thickset marsupial that moves relatively slowly through the bush. The burrowing animals grow to around 60-80 centimeters (23-31 inches) and can be seen in the bushland surrounding Sydney. Many wombats are killed under the wheels of vehicles because they cross the roads too slowly.

Where the Wild Things Roam

Much of Sydney's bird life can be spotted around the city and suburbs, but to catch a glimpse of a kangaroo with her joey or a koala munching on a bunch of eucalyptus leaves, head out to the bushland or visit the zoo or a wildlife park. The following are some choice spots:

Koala Park Sanctuary This is one of the first private koala sanctuaries in the country, and is also known for successfully breeding koalas in captivity. Pet a koala or two and learn about their peculiar habits. And don't miss the dingos, wallabies, and wombats. ♦ Admission. Daily. 84 Castle Hill Rd (between New Line and Victoria Rds), West Pennant Hills. 9875.2777

Ku-ring-gai Chase National Park Accessible to those with a car or who want to hike, this national park has an abundance of birds and other native creatures. Sighting depends on the weather and season, but that's half the fun. Take the train to **Turramurra Station** and connect with a bus to **Bobbin Head.** ♦ Admission charge for cars. Daily 8AM-sunset. Visitors' Center: Ku-ring-gai Chase Rd (east of Sydney-Newcastle Fwy). 9457.9322

Taronga Zoo Famous for keeping all kinds of Australian and foreign animals in "fenceless" enclosures, this zoo also has a petting farm that allows direct contact with a wide variety of creatures. ♦ Admission. Daily. Bradleys Head and Beach Rds, Mosman. 9969.2777

Waratah Park Visitors can touch a range of native animals—including wombats, koalas, kangaroos, and Tasmanian devils (be careful, they bite!)—here at one of Sydney's oldest wildlife parks. ♦ Admission. Daily. Namba Rd (west of Birramal Rd), Duffys Forest. 9450.2377

Wallaby

39 The Argyle Centre This group of four large fortresslike stores around a cobblestone courtyard, built between 1826 and 1887, is the former home of the **Argyle Bonded and Free Stores.** The complex was used mainly as a warehouse until 1976 when the Sydney Cove Redevelopment Authority took over and developed it into retail and office space. ♦ 12-20 Argyle St (between Playfair St and Gloucester Walk)

Within The Argyle Centre:

Reds ★$$ Australian bush food is served here in a large, open dining room with native flower arrangements. The kitchen produces lots of barbecued meat and seafood dishes with a modern edge. Try the salted bush lamb cutlets. It's a popular spot with tour groups. ♦ Australian ♦ M-Sa lunch and dinner; Su dinner. 12 Argyle St. 9247.1011

The Argyle Department Store Built in 1828, this former warehouse retains the original sandstone, Australian timber beams, and floorboards. Some of Australia's leading names in retail have stores here. They include **Country Road** (clothing and homewares), **Brian Rochford** (swimwear), **Surf Dive 'n Ski** (surf- and beachwear), **Diesel** (clothing), **Oroton** (handbags and luggage), and **Dinosaur Designs** (jewelry and housewares). Enter through a sandstone arch on Argyle Street or from adjacent Playfair Street. ♦ M-F 10AM-8PM; Sa-Su. 16 Argyle St. 9251.4800

Within The Argyle Department Store:

bel Mondo

Bel Mondo ★★★★$$$$ This New York–loft-style space with views of the Harbour Bridge is run by one of Sydney's super chefs, Stefano Manfredi (author, food writer, and deli owner), and his ex-wife Julie. The restaurant was lovingly restored to reflect its historic ambience. For example the open kitchen was built above the original floorboards and sits on a platform. Here a busy hive of chefs captained by Stefano and assisted by his mother, Franca, are on view. The food has traditional Italian elements with a modern take (delicate potato gnocchi with sea scallops and crayfish with cannelli beans), while the wine list featuring Italian and Australian labels carefully complements the food. The **Anti-bar** features more relaxed and less expensive dining and live jazz on Friday night. ♦ Italian ♦ M-Sa lunch and dinner; Su dinner. Reservations required. Level 3. 9241.3700

40 Argyle Terrace Originally called **Tara Terrace,** this row of seven late-Victorian terrace houses were built between 1877 and 1884. Once occupied by boat builders, blacksmiths, and engineers, they now house souvenir stores and quaint cafes. ♦ Playfair St (between Argyle and Atherden Sts)

41 The Rocks Puppet Cottage This restored sandstone cottage is now a store crammed with hundreds of handmade puppets from around the globe. A huge cast of shadow puppets and marionettes gives free performances on weekends and local school holidays. ♦ Sa-Su. Kendall La (between Argyle St and Mill La). 9241.2902

42 Orient Hotel ★★$$ Now popular for bachelor parties and with office workers continuing the week's gossip over a few beers, this grand old Australian pub opened its doors in 1844. When more in the mood for Australian food and wine than Australian beers, try the **Orient Hotel Grill,** a well-run bistro inside offering inexpensive steaks and fresh fish. ♦ Bistro ♦ Daily noon-10PM. 89 George St (at Argyle St). 9251.1255

43 Weiss Art Signature black-and-white koalas, echidnas, and platypuses are printed on everything from T-shirts and shorts to umbrellas and mugs. ♦ Daily. 85 George St (between Argyle St and Mill La). 9241.3819

44 G'day Cafe ★★$ This quirky little cafe's name suggests that it is trying hard to attract the overseas tourists. The food is surprisingly decent. It's already very popular with local workers who cram in at lunchtime for kebabs, sandwiches, salads, and cakes. ♦ Cafe/Takeout ♦ Daily 5:30AM-midnight. 83 George St (between Argyle St and Mill La). 9241.3644

44 The Rocks Hatters/Bennelong 2000 Rows and layers of Australian felt, leather, sun, and cricket hats are on sale at this small store. The popular Australian oil-skin all-weather coats are also sold here. ♦ Daily. 81 George St (between Argyle St and Mill La). 9252.4169

45 Ken Duncan Gallery This photography gallery's namesake is the owner and the main artist exhibiting here. Duncan's photography of Australian landscapes and streetscapes is postcard-perfect. ♦ Daily. 73 George St (between Argyle St and Mill La). 9241.3460

46 Observer Hotel In the 19th century this pub was a public house for sailors and was called **The Waterman's Arms.** Although it exudes more history than style, the place remains a typical old-Sydney, working-class pub, attracting hordes of lunchtime and after-work beer lovers. It has been said that patrons "enter at own risk." ♦ M-W, Su 11AM-11:30PM; Th 11AM-1AM; F-Sa 11AM-2:30AM. 69 George St (at Mill La). 9251.5847

47 Bottom of the Harbour Antiques/Old City Coroner's Court Filled with maritime bric-a-brac, this curious store was once the **City Coroner's Court.** Built in 1908, it was designed by government architect **Walter Liberty Vernon,** in the Arts and Crafts style that was more typical of private homes. It's a fine example of the Federation Free Style of architecture, defined by the use of brick with sandstone, different sizes of windows, and tall chimneys. In 1972, the court moved to Glebe and the Sydney Cove Authority turned the place into a Visitors' Information Center. In 1994, the building was leased to this antiques store. ♦ Daily. 102-04 George St (between Argyle St and Hickson Rd). 9247.8107

ℱʰᵉROCKS

48 The Rocks Visitors' Centre/The Sailors' Home This three-story building erected in 1864 provided sailors with comfortable lodgings until 1980. It then became a puppet theater, and in 1994, a visitors' center. On the ground floor be sure to catch the video that describes the area in detail, and pick up some free maps. This is the best place to start a tour of The Rocks and to book accommodations, a tour of the harbor, or a day trip out of Sydney. The staff here are helpful about the available tours. The second level has a permanent exhibition of artifacts and photographs highlighting the social, archaeological, and architectural heritage of The Rocks. The top floor has changing exhibits relating to Sydney's European heritage and a permanent display of a re-created sailor's sleeping

cubicle. ♦ Daily. 106 George St (between Argyle St and Hickson Rd). 9255.1788

Within The Sailors' Home:

Sailor's Thai ★★★$$$ David Thompson's innovative Thai food and minimalist dining room at **Darley Street Thai** can also be experienced here, but for less money. The formal dining space features carefully restored sandstone walls. The same genius and finesse of Thompson's flagship restaurant is apparent here, evident in such dishes as deep-fried quail, trout with pork and sweet fish sauce, and roasted duck salad. The heavy desserts may have Asian ingredients, but they have definitely been designed for the European palate. ♦ Thai ♦ M-F lunch and dinner; Sa dinner. Reservations recommended. Basement. 9251.2466

Sailor's Thai Canteen ★★★$$ This busy street-level noodle shop, run by David Thompson of the **Sailor's Thai** (see above), is well worth a stop. It has a long communal table that seats 50 people and a few prized tables on the balcony with views of Circular Quay. The one-bowl meals are tasty, satisfying, and a good value. The green papaya salad makes a savory side dish. ♦ Thai ♦ Daily noon-8PM. 9251.2466

49 Cadman's Cottage Few of the historical buildings in the area are as closely linked to Sydney's colonial and maritime past as this tiny sandstone structure (pictured below) erected in 1816. The oldest surviving building

Cadman's Cottage

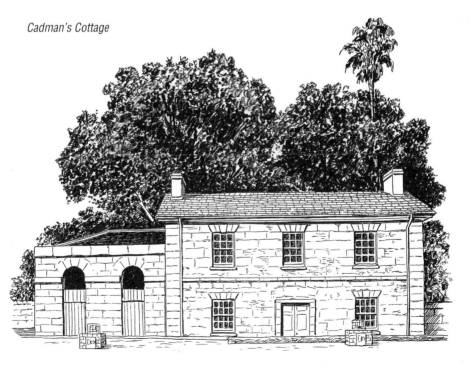

in Sydney, it was originally constructed as a coxswain's barracks (a coxswain was the master in charge of small vessels). Later the cottage served as a base for the supervision of government boats that were used to transport government officers around the harbor, move stores to Parramatta (western Sydney), and carry convicts to their work assignments. This was a time when Sydney's waterways provided the main form of transport, as roads were few and unreliable in bad weather. A small fleet of 20 vessels linked the colony's fledgling settlements and this building was the hub of that activity. The cottage is named after the last and longest-serving government coxswain and superintendent of boats, John Cadman, who retired in 1845 just as the role of government boats was diminishing. Cadman was a convict transported to Australia in 1798 and later pardoned because of his services to the government. He lived here with his wife, Elizabeth, and her two children. The cottage has also served as the headquarters for the water police and accommodations for sailors and officers of visiting merchant ships. By the 1960s the cottage had become vacant and derelict. With the development and years of reclamation of land around Sydney Cove, it was no longer on the water's edge (it now stands 300 feet inland). In 1972, the cottage was in major disrepair and was declared a historic site, and an ongoing conservation program was started to ensure the building's long-term survival. In 1996, the cottage was refurbished as the **Sydney Harbour National Park Information Centre;** staff here give out information on education programs, activities, and special events related to Sydney's harbor parks. ♦ M-F; Sa-Su 11AM-4PM. 110 George St (between Argyle St and Hickson Rd). 9247.8861

50 Overseas Passenger Terminal (OPT) It's a common sight to see a massive cruise ship like the *QEII* offloading thousands of passengers here. This massive steel and concrete structure was renovated in 1986 to allow more unobstructed views of the harbor from The Rocks. The alterations to the terminal work well and the circular tower is a nice addition to what would otherwise be a big drab dock. ♦ Circular Quay W (north of Argyle St)

Within the Overseas Passenger Terminal:

Quay ★★★$$$$ This dining spot on **OPT**'s upper level offers sweeping views of the **Opera House,** harbor, and Circular Quay. It's often said that the view eclipses the food, but thanks to Parisian-trained chef, Guillame Brahimi, the food takes its own bow. His signature dishes include grilled beef with Merlot sauce and mashed potatoes, and crème brûlée with hints of passion fruit. A serious, extensive wine list with some famous old Australian reds adds to the sense of

occasion. Service and decor are fussy, but the food and location still make this a perfect place to savor Sydney. ♦ Modern Australian ♦ M-F, Su lunch; M-Sa dinner. Reservations recommended. Upper level. 9251.5600

51 The Rocks Market On the weekend a long, sail-like canopy transforms this stretch of George Street (near the southern end of the Harbour Bridge) into one of Sydney's favorite street markets. No matter the weather, 150 vendors are here selling local crafts, housewares, antiques, flowers, books, and bits and pieces of every description. Street performers and musicians surround the market and add to the fun, while local pubs and cafes try to keep the beers and cappuccinos coming. ♦ Sa-Su. George St (between Hickson Rd and Gloucester Walk). 9255.1717

51 Old Sydney Parkroyal $$$ It's hard to imagine there's so much history outside after stepping into this modern, brassy hotel. An eight-story atrium dominates a lobby that's filled with huge native floral arrangements. The 174 guest rooms are simple, while the service is subtle. The rooftop pool has views of the harbor over the tops of landmark historic buildings. ♦ 55 George St (at Playfair St). 9252.0524; fax 9251.2093

Within the Old Sydney Parkroyal:

Playfair Terrace ★★$$ The generic hotel restaurant decor here is compensated by the view of old Playfair Street and a menu that features Australian products with Mediterranean and Asian influences. Lamb dishes are cooked to order. Morning and afternoon teas are also popular here, as is the lunchtime prix-fixe buffet. ♦ Modern Australian ♦ Daily lunch, tea, and dinner. Reservations recommended. 9252.0524

52 Westpac Museum Westpac Bank, formerly the Bank of New South Wales, is one of Australia's oldest and largest banking institutions. It is also the sponsor of this museum devoted to the history of Australian banking and business. Permanent exhibits include displays of the "holey" dollar to the current currency used in Australia. Another feature is the re-creation of a working bank branch from the 1890s. ◆ Free. M, Sa-Su 1-4PM; Tu-F 10:30AM-4PM. 6-8 Playfair St (at Atherden St). 9251.1419

53 Merchants' House Museum The Sydney Cove Authority restored this house to its original 1850s look; it was occupied at that time by James Combes and John Martyn, who used it as a storehouse for their painting and plumbing business. Today the National Trust of Australia runs it as a historic house, children's museum, and exhibition space. Take a self-guided tour of the permanent exhibition, which includes children's toys, dolls, books, and games from the 19th century to the present. Many of the comic-book characters and games will be familiar only to Australians. ◆ Admission. W-Su. 43 George St (between Playfair St and Gloucester Walk). 9241.5099

54 Swagman's Post Cafe ★★$ At the entrance to this old terrace house is a plaque in memory of its longtime resident, Nita Louise McCrae (1929-95), who campaigned against overdeveloping The Rocks. In keeping with her wishes, the current owners have maintained the wooden floors and fireplace, which give the place a cozy, rustic feel. The leafy courtyard, with its two-story-high sandstone wall, is an ideal spot to enjoy such simple fare as salads, sandwiches, ploughman's lunches, scones, and pots of Australian tea. ◆ Cafe ◆ Daily 8AM-midnight. 35 George St (between Playfair St and Gloucester Walk). 9241.5557

55 Mercantile Hotel $$ The massive steel Harbour Bridge looks as though it's about to engulf this quaint hotel (pub) built in 1914. Now considered one of Sydney's most famous Irish pubs, the 19 guest rooms are noted for their original Art Nouveau–style tiles. Most rooms have shared baths. Breakfast in the ground-floor bistro is included. ◆ 25 George St (at Gloucester Walk). 9247.3570

56 Center for Contemporary Craft In addition to being the administrative headquarters for 20,000 Craft Council members, this 1886 Victorian building houses the **Craftspace** gallery and the **Designed and Made** store. The former features contemporary Australian crafts and design, while the latter offers Australian crafts, jewelry, accessories, and housewares. Don't expect to find cuddly stuffed toy koalas and mass-produced boomerangs here—this is the place for special, well-made Australian crafts. ◆ Daily. 88 George St (between Hickson Rd and Lower Fort St). 9247.9126

Adjacent to Centre for Contemporary Craft:

Santos ★★$ Strong coffee and simple snacks are what this friendly cafe set inside a historic building offers. For those looking to socialize, a 14-seat table in the middle of the room is the place to sit, sip a coffee, read the newspaper, and chat with other customers. The view stretches all the way to the **Taronga Zoo** on the North Shore. The friendly staff will help you select one of the 12 Arabica blends of coffee. Baked goods include "spotty" and "dotty" cookies. It's the perfect spot for a quick, easy breakfast. ◆ Cafe/Takeout ◆ Daily 6:30AM-6:30PM. 9247.6061

57 Australasian Steam Navigation Company Building With its distinctive Flemish tower and gables and cat-head beams, this is one of Sydney's unique landmark buildings. Designed by **William Wardell** and built in 1883, the structure was restored (at great expense) in 1992 to its original appearance and leased to various tenants, including a gallery space for Sydney artist Ken Done. ◆ 1-5 Hickson Rd (at George St)

Australasian Steam Navigation Company Building

Ferry Folklore and Facts

Sydney's passenger ferries have been an integral part of harbor life since 1861 when five entrepreneurs started the **North Shore Ferry Company.** It was a risky venture, given that less than a thousand people lived on the northern side of the harbor at that time, but one that paid off—many people bought land on the **North Shore** as a result of this new service and the company prospered. The first boat, *Kirribilli,* carried up to 60 passengers between **Circular Quay** and **Milsons Point.** By the 1920s (after two name changes), **Sydney Ferries Limited** was transporting about 40 million passengers a year.

Later that decade the company suffered various economic ups and downs and encountered some fierce competition from other smaller companies. The reputation of ferries also changed because of a series of disasters that took place over the years— the bisection of the *Greycliffe* by the liner *Tahiti* in 1927, the capsizing of the *Rodney* in 1938, the collision of the *Baragoola* with a whale, the sinking of the *Kuttabul* by a torpedo from a Japanese midget submarine in 1942, and the beaching of the *Dee Why* with 700 passengers on Christmas night of 1946.

In 1951, after years of upsets, **Sydney Ferries** was bought by the government and regulated by the **State Transit Authority.** The *Manly* ferry became part of the system some 23 years later.

The current fleet boasts over 30 vessels, serving 32 wharves throughout **Sydney Harbour.** Boats include the *Manly* ferry, *JetCats* and *RiverCats* (hydrofoils), catamarans, and the smaller "Lady Class" ferries. The *Manly* ferry is one of the city's most famous, perhaps because of its large size and relatively slow speed that allows passengers to take in the sights as the boat cuts its way through the harbor. Other noteworthy excursions include the ferries to **Mosman** and **Watsons Bays,** and the *RiverCat* run

that goes as far as **Parramatta.** *RiverCats* will also be used to carry spectators to the site of the **Sydney 2000 Olympic Games** at **Homebush Bay.**

Special passes may be purchased through **Sydney Ferries,** and some include land transport and entry to major harborside attractions. The following are some options:

Aquarium Pass Explore the landmarks on and around Sydney Harbour, then discover what's below the surface at the **Sydney Aquarium** at **Darling Harbour.**

Ocean Pass Take a trip to **Manly,** passing the **Opera House, Fort Denison, Eastern Suburbs,** and the leafy **Lower North Shore.** Once there, explore **Oceanworld,** famous for its shark feeding and submarine walkway.

Zoo Pass The ferry to **Taronga Zoo** cruises by some major landmarks and harborside homes. Harbor and city views seen from the zoo are magnificent.

The **Ferry Information Centre** (Circular Quay Ferry Terminal, Alfred St and Circular Quay E, Wharf 4, 9247.5151), also has brochures on harbor foreshore walking tours. For more information about harborside cruises, call the **State Transit Authority** (13.1500). Contact both for details about passes, including schedules and prices.

58 Campbell's Storehouse Robert Campbell was one of the early colony's most successful merchants. He started building a private wharf and stores in 1839 for his imports of liquor, tea, sugar, spices, and textiles from India. By 1861 he had erected 12 sandstone bays, and in 1890 an additional floor in brick was added. Today the storehouses are filled with restaurants and galleries. The small harbor inlet in front of the storehouses is called Campbells Cove; here replicas of 18th-century tall ships dock and add to the sense of history. ◆ 7-27 Circular Quay W (north of Argyle St)

On 1 November 1792, just four years after British settlement of Sydney, the US ship *Philadelphia* was the first foreign trading vessel to enter Sydney Harbour.

Within Campbell's Storehouse:

The Waterfront ★$$$ There are a few big restaurants in the **Campbell's Storehouse** complex catering to the flow of tourists; this place offers some simple, well-prepared seafood. Try the mud crabs and Balmain bugs, both of which are tastier than they may sound. Be sure to ask for an outdoor table. ◆ Australian ◆ Daily lunch and dinner. Reservations recommended. 27 Circular Quay W. 9247.3666

59 Pancakes On The Rocks ★$$ Pancakes aren't the only draw at this Sydney institution that's open around the clock, every day of the year. You name it, they probably serve it, but it's best to stick to the breakfast menu if possible. ◆ American/Australian ◆ Daily 24 hours. 10 Hickson Rd (north of George St). 9247.6371

60 Park Hyatt Sydney $$$$ Constructed in the mid-1980s, this hotel was praised for its thoughtful design and development. The building snakes around the natural contour of the harborfront at Campbell's Cove and has a pre-cast concrete facade that blends into the neighboring masonry structures. In addition, because the 158-room property is only four stories high, views from **Dawes Point Park** behind it aren't blocked. City hotels don't get more luxurious and extraordinary than this: The service is impeccable and the guest rooms have 24-hour butler service and remote-control everything for those in need of overindulgence. Champagne on the balcony just before sunset is a must-have experience. Be sure to ask for a room with a view when reserving; a few lack the vista. There's also a small rooftop lap pool with a bar and a lobby bar. ♦ 7 Hickson Rd (north of George St). 9241.1234, 800/233.1234; fax 9256.1555

Within the Park Hyatt:

No. 7 At The Park ★★$$$$ Located at the southern end of the hotel with views of the **Opera House,** this glitzy restaurant doesn't have to try too hard to impress its patrons with the food. Even so, the kitchen manages to dazzle diners with a range of Australian local products (lots of red meats) prepared in a European style. ♦ Modern Australian ♦ M-F lunch and dinner; Sa dinner. Reservations recommended. 9256.1630

61 Dawes Point Park This park is the site of Sydney's oldest fortified position (1788) and was once thought to be the perfect vantage point for protecting the small colony from the possible threat of French and Russian invaders. Today the five original black cannons of Dawes Point Battery look rather powerless, sitting here pointing out toward The Heads at the east end of the harbor. It's a splendid spot for a picnic, with the Sydney Harbour Bridge as a backdrop and palm trees framing a view of the harbor. ♦ Hickson Rd (north of George St)

62 Sydney Harbour Bridge The world's largest single-span arch bridge, this hulking steel structure (pictured below) connects the city with the North Shore and is as much a Sydney landmark as the **Opera House.** It took 1,400 workers (16 of whom lost their lives) 8 years to build this 1,650-foot bridge, often referred to as the "Coathanger." The span was completed during the Depression and when it was inaugurated on 19 March 1932 it was hailed as an economic and engineering triumph. (Before this, it took hours to travel by car into the city from the North Shore or commuters had to take the ferry.) The opening-day ceremony for the bridge has earned extra space in Australian history books, thanks to a royalist named Francis de Groot who charged forward on his horse and cut the ribbon to honor "The King and Empire" before anyone had realized what happened. He was promptly arrested and stole the following day's newspaper headlines. Today the traffic congestion on the bridge is alleviated by the Harbour Tunnel, which opened in 1992, just four years after the

Sydney Harbor Bridge

government had finally paid off the cost of the bridge. With eight traffic lanes, two railway lines, a walkway, and cycling path, this bridge begs to be visited. Walking across and catching the train back from Milsons Point on the north side is a good way to see the bridge and some wonderful views of the city. Alternatively, daily tours of the Pylon Lookout on the southeastern side are a good way to learn about the "Coathanger." Take the Harbour Bridge pedestrian walkway off Cumberland Street to get to the lookout. ◆ 9247.3408

63 Harbourside Brasserie This is the place to hear loud live rock 'n' roll and smooth jazz. Performances usually start at about 9PM and feature new local talent and some regular acts. On Sunday afternoon, the atmosphere is a little more sedate with *a capello* numbers. Come for the music rather than the food. ◆ Daily 6PM-3AM. Pier 1, Hickson Rd and Lower Fort St. 9252.3000

64 Walsh Bay Finger Wharves The arrival of the bubonic plague at the turn of the century motivated the government to clean up Sydney's waterfront, especially the docks area (known as Walsh Bay) between Sydney Cove and Darling Harbour. Four finger wharves used for international shipping were then built here between 1906 and 1922. ◆ Hickson Rd (between Lower Fort St and Towns Pl)

On Walsh Bay Finger Wharves:

Wharf Theatre/Pier 4 In 1984 the **Sydney Theatre Company** helped to develop this gigantic once-derelict space into a theater, rehearsal studios, and administrative offices. It's a real treat to walk down the wharf's never-ending corridor and look at posters of past theater productions lining the walls. The **Sydney Dance Company**'s headquarters and rehearsal spaces are also here. The views of the Harbour Bridge and harbor from the northern end of the wharf are spectacular. ◆ Theater 9250.1777; Dance 9221.4811

Within the Wharf Theatre:

About half of Sydney Harbour has a depth of 9 meters (30 feet) or more at low tide. The maximum depth is 24.4 meters (80 feet) at the harbor's entrance.

Three Japanese midget submarines were spotted in Sydney Harbour on the evening of 31 May 1942. The subs were on a mission to blow up the US ship *Chicago,* but instead killed 19 sailors on a floating barracks near Garden Island. This was the only time in Sydney history that the city was directly attacked by enemy fire.

Wharf Restaurant ★★★$$ Who needs a snappy interior when you've got a floor-to-ceiling view of Sydney Harbour? Sitting high up on the edge of the wharf on a sunny day, the vista is breathtaking, while at dusk it's just magic. The decor is simple—a touch rustic—but elegant, echoing the style of food and service.

The chef favors integrating Mediterranean flavors into local lamb and seafood dishes. Costs are kept down by promoting a small and manageable menu and wine list. Be sure to leave space for the small, delicious desserts and/or the Australian cheese plate. On a warm night, ask to have coffee on the balcony. The restaurant caters mainly to the pre- and post-theater crowd. ◆ Modern Australian ◆ M-Sa lunch, dinner, and late-night supper. Reservations recommended. 9250.1761

65 Colonial House Museum Six rooms on the first two floors of this four-story terrace house built in 1884 are devoted to a museum of early Sydney. With authentic Victorian furniture and decor, photography, prints and etchings, it is a popular spot on the walking tour circuit. ◆ Admission. Daily. 53 Lower Fort St (at Ferry La). 9247.6008

66 Hero of Waterloo This wedge-shaped pub on the corner of Lower Fort and Windmill Streets is not only a bar and restaurant, but a museum as well. Sydney's folklore has it that this place, built in 1843, was where the merchant navy "press ganged" unsuspecting drunks by trapping them in the sandstone cellars and quickly dragging them down a tunnel that led to the harborside. Today the maze of cellars beneath this popular watering hole is a small museum that exhibits 19th-century domestic and maritime tools.

Louise's inside the pub is one of the oldest dining rooms in Sydney; its atmosphere may sometimes be a little more exciting than the standard pub fare offered—old-fashioned Australian cuisine featuring lamb roasts and various fish dishes, and damper (unleavened bush bread). ◆ Admission to museum. Pub and restaurant: Daily 10AM-11PM. 81 Lower Fort St (at Windmill St). 9252.4553

67 Argyle Place At the bottom of Observatory Hill where Argyle and Lower Fort Streets meet is this square filled with elegant Georgian and Victorian terrace houses. **Holy Trinity Church,** more commonly known as "Garrison Church," faces the square. It was built in 1848 using convict labor to quarry and place the sandstone. Architect **Edmund Thomas Blacket** oversaw the extensions on the church in 1878. ◆ Between Lower Fort and Munn Sts

---

Restaurants/Clubs: Red   **Hotels:** Blue
Shops/♟ **Outdoors:** Green   **Sights/Culture:** Black

How to Speak Like an Aussie

Over the years, Australia has developed its own brand of English or "Strain" (as many of the locals pronounce it), and there are plenty of theories about its origins. Not only is this language very different from North American English, no one would think it's the Queen's English either. But as long as you have the list below, you're sure to fit right in.

Note that it is common in Australia to hear people speak in "rhyming slang"—the intended use of a phrase that rhymes with the word. For instance, "to take a Captain Cook" at something is "to have a look" while "to hit the frog and toad" is "to hit the road" or "to get going." New ones appear regularly. Don't be afraid to ask for translations!

arvo	afternoon	no-hoper	an incompetent person, a social misfit
Aussie	(pronounced "Ozzie") Australian		
barbie	barbecue	nick	steal something
bewdy	from "beaut" as in beautiful, good, the best	ocker	the archetypal uncultivated Australian male
bludger	lazy person, loser	outback	the inland country far away from the cities
bloke	male		
bonnet	(car) hood	petrol	gas, fuel
boot	(car) trunk	pissed	drunk
bumper bars	(car) fenders	plonk	cheap wine
bushed	lost, also tired	Pom	a Briton
cheesed (off)	fed up, annoyed	power point	electric socket
chewy	chewing gum	prang	minor car accident
cobber	friend, buddy	queue	line up for something
dead set	a certainty; also used as an exclamation meaning "really"	ratbag	a dishonest person
		sangers	sandwiches
dinky-di	genuine	schooner	large glass of beer
drongo	stupid person, idiot	serviette	napkin
duco	car paint	shonky	poor quality, shoddy
dunny	an outdoor toilet, also general slang term for toilet	sickie	a day taken off work, but not necessarily because of illness
entree	appetizer	shout	pay for someone
esky	a portable icebox (brand name used in a generic way)	skiting	boasting
		smoke-o	coffee, tea, or cigarette break
fair dinkum	honest, genuine	snags	sausages
fair go	a chance, also an appeal for fairness	station	large ranch
flog	sell	stubby	small beer bottle
footpath	sidewalk	supper	late-night dinner
fossick	search for something	sweets	dessert
g'day	good day, hello	ta ta	good-bye, bye-bye
good one	an exclamation of approval (sometimes ironic)	ta	thanks
		taxi rank	taxi stand
good on ya	term of approval (sometimes ironic)	tea	dinner; also sometimes just tea
grog	booze, liquor	tinnie	a can of beer
homewares	housewares	tops	excellent, great
Kiwi	New Zealander	true blue	genuine
knock	criticize, find fault	wag it	play truant
lay-by	lay-away	whinge	complain, whine
lift	elevator	windscreen	windshield
lingo	language	Wogs	derogatory term for person of Mediterranean decent
lollies	candy		
loo	toilet	yakka	hard or heavy work, often "hard yakka"
mate	good friend; also used to greet someone as in "G'day mate"		
		Yank	North American
middy	small glass of beer	yobbo	a person lacking refinement

68 Garrison Gallery, Historical and Military Museum When this tiny museum next to the **Holy Trinity (Garrison) Church** opened in 1969, its focus was on early Sydney's history. It has since added a military component (complete with mannequins in uniform and photographs), thanks to the traditional association of the **Holy Trinity Church** with the Australian military. ◆ Free. Tu-Su 10:30AM-2:30PM. 60 Lower Fort St (between Argyle St and Trinity Ave). 9247.2664

69 Lord Nelson Brewery Hotel $$ Sydney's oldest continually licensed pub was constructed in 1841 with convict labor. It's now a boutique hotel, pub, and restaurant rolled into one. The 12 guest rooms are well kept and decorated with both antiques and modern fixtures, bathrooms are shared, and breakfast is included. **Nelson's Brasserie** features local fare, including kangaroo, emu, and some other more traditional dishes. The pub is packed to the rafters with locals Thursday through Saturday. ◆ 19 Kent St (at Argyle Pl). 9251.4044; fax 9251.1532

70 Palisade Hotel Dining Room ★★★$$ The menu at this comfortable, modern dining room of the **Palisade Hotel** features a modern mix of flavors with a twist—rolled pumpkin ravioli with burnt butter and parmesan, and deep-fried snapper with fresh tamarind and chili dressing are just two examples. Owners Annie Parmentier and Brian Sudek hail from Palm Beach (an hour's drive north of Sydney), and at press time it was expected that the success they had with the **Beach Road** restaurant in Palm Beach will be repeated at this delightful, as-yet largely under-recognized restaurant. Annie is the person many people claim is responsible for the invasion of sticky toffee pudding in Australia. The wine list features mostly Australian labels. ◆ Modern Australian ◆ M-F lunch and dinner; Sa dinner. Reservations recommended. 35-37 Bettington St (at Dalgety Rd). 9251.7225

The City of Sydney is Australia's wealthiest municipality.

Australia has over 17 million inhabitants and over 4 million mobile phone users.

Sydney Observatory

71 Observatory Hotel $$$$ With its sandstone and whitewash exterior, this new, 100-room hotel was built to blend in with The Rocks' historic sites and buildings. Inside, it is filled with expensive Australian antiques and paintings and state-of-the-art facilities. The indoor pool (with a side-lit, star-covered ceiling), gym, sauna, spa, float tanks, and massages, all add to the hotel's luxurious style. It's a short walk from Observatory Hill. Two restaurants and a bar make the property even more appealing. ◆ 89-113 Kent St (at High St). 9256.2222; fax 9256.2233

Within the Observatory Hotel:

Galileo ★★$$$ The hotel's classic club decor and service is carried over to its restaurant. Although this dining spot bills itself as having a Modern Australian kitchen, Italian ingredients dominate the menu. Such dishes as pancetta with Muscatel grapes, guinea fowl, and oxtail broth are complemented with fine Italian breads, a fruity olive oil, and balsamic vinegar. Wines may be ordered by the glass. ◆ Modern Australian/ Italian ◆ M-F breakfast, lunch, and dinner; Sa-Su breakfast, dinner. Reservations recommended. 9256.2215

72 Misto ★★$$ This slick metal and mirrored space more than lives up to its name (*Misto* means "mixed" in Italian). Everything from three-course, sitdown meals to take-out prepared dishes and various food items are offered here. Chef Danny Russo focuses on standard Italian fare with a modern twist, such as *risotto frutta di mare* (with seafood) that's topped with charcoal-grilled octopus. The deep-fried ricotta cheesecake with Sambuca ice cream is a deliciously calorific way to end a meal. Another plus: Portions are generous here. ♦ Italian/Cafe ♦ Daily 7AM-11PM. Highgate Complex, 127 Kent St (between Gas La and High St). 9251.9669

73 Sydney Observatory Outfitted with equipment from Great Britain, this time-ball tower/observatory (pictured on page 40) opened in 1858. In the 1880s the observatory gained international recognition when astrologer Henry Russell took some of the world's original astronomical photographs for the *Astrographic Catalogue,* the first complete atlas of the night sky, here. The Sydney section alone took 80 years and 53 volumes to complete. The observatory supplied local newspapers with the rising and setting times of the sun, moon, and planets throughout much of the 20th century. But by the mid-1970s, the increasing problems of air pollution and city lights made work at the observatory more and more difficult.

In 1982 it was converted into a museum of astronomy and related fields. A regular program of exhibitions, films, talks, and night viewings gives visitors a chance to explore some of the world's most advanced technology. An evening program includes a short talk, tour of the building, and telescope viewing of the night sky. The surrounding grounds offer fabulous views of Sydney Harbour and make for a popular picnic spot for Sydneysiders (and visitors, too!). ♦ Admission; free during the day. M-F 2PM-5PM; Sa-Su. Reservations required for night program. Upper Fort St (south of Watson Rd). 9217.0485

74 National Trust Centre The headquarters of the National Trust of New South Wales (illustrated below), which is charged with preserving any historically important commercial site or residence, was built in 1815 as a military hospital. Highlights include good harbor views, a gift shop, and a cafe. ♦ M-F; Sa-Su 2-5PM. Upper Fort St (south of Watson Rd). 9258.0123

Adjoining National Trust Centre:

S.H. Ervin Gallery A permanent collection of Australian paintings, sculptures, and woodcuts, donated by its benefactor, Samuel Henry Ervin, are housed in this remarkable gallery. Changing exhibitions emphasize Australian heritage and history. ♦ Admission. Tu-F 11AM-5PM; Sa-Su noon-5PM. 9258.0123

National Trust Centre

CIRCULAR QUAY

Grosvenor St.

70

Lang St.

York St.

69

Jamison St.

Bond St.

Margaret St.

68

67

Curtin Pl.

Hunter St.

Carrington St.

George St.

Erskine St.

64

Wynyard St.

Barrack St.

King St.

61
63 62

59
60 58

57

56

55

54

Market St.

52
53

51

50

Druitt St.

St. Andrew's
House

Sydney
Square

49

48

Bathurst St.

47

46

43

45

Wilmot St.

Central St.

44
42

41

Liverpool St.

Sussex St.

Kent St.

Clarence St.

York St.

George St.

World
Square

CHINATOWN

Goulburn St.

Bridge St.

Gresham St.

4

Spring St.

Loftus St.

Young St.

Farrer
Place
3

Bent St.

5

O'Connell St.

6

7

Bligh St.

10

Chifley
Square

Hunter St.

Pitt St.

11

Hosking
Pl.

12

Martin Pl. 13

12

14

King St.

19

Strand
Arcade

20

21

23

Imperial
Arcade

24

25

Pitt St. Mall

City
Centre

26

27

Park
Plaza

35
36

Park St.

Pitt St.

22

Castlereagh St.

30

29

28

34

32

33

Elizabeth St.

40

Castlereagh St.

37

38

Clarke St.

39

Nithsdale St.

Commonwealth St.

1

2

Farrer
Place

Phillip St.

8

9

Macquarie St.

16

17

12

15

Elizabeth St.

18

St. James Rd.

Prince Albert Rd.

Hyde Park
Barracks

Archibald
Fountain

Phillip
Park

College St.

Sandringham
Gardens

31
Hyde Park

William St.

Australian
Museum

Stanley St.

Francis St.

ANZAC
Memorial

Liverpool St.

Wentworth Ave.

Brisbane St.

Oxford St.

The Royal
Botanic
Gardens

The
Domain

N

km
mi

1/8

1/4

1/4

1/2

Central Business District (CBD)

If the heart of a city is a place where business is conducted, politics is played out, and historic landmarks are found, then Sydney's pulsing center is the Central Business District (better known as the "CBD"). The city's growth as a business hub for the Pacific Rim spurs continuous expansion but, at the moment, the CBD is bounded roughly by **Phillip Street**, Darling Harbour, **Liverpool Street** and Chinatown, and **Bridge Street** and Circular Quay.

The CBD has an intense morning rush, a brief lunchtime bustle, and an evening peak-hour crush but, like the business districts of other cities, it's virtually deserted at night—with exceptions, of course. Something is always going on at (or near) the **Museum of Sydney**, a terrifically popular spot where the unique history of this city holds center stage.

Heading south along the main thoroughfares of business—**Elizabeth, Castlereagh**, and **Pitt Streets**, renowned for some of Sydney's megastore retailing—there is an all-day buzz of shoppers, tourists, and visiting suburbanites. **Chifley Plaza** with its upmarket international and local boutiques and restaurants is a mighty rival to the **MLC Centre** off **Martin Place**, while along vehicle-free **Pitt Street Mall** you can reach the elegant 19th-century **Strand Arcade** or the glass-and-steel modernism of the **Skygarden** complex—both centers offering some of the better Australian clothing, jewelry, and home furnishings.

The green-canopied expanse of **Hyde Park** teems with office workers jogging along the paths or laying out a picnic lunch (from the famous **Food Hall** at **David Jones** department store across the street) on the manicured lawns. The streets bordering **Hyde Park** feature several high-rise chain hotels, many of which have sprung up over the last decade, catering to the desires of global travelers.

Leaving the tranquillity of **Hyde Park** behind, a stroll west along Liverpool Street leads to **George Street.** This busy thoroughfare stretches out like one of the grand avenues of New York or Chicago. **Sydney Square**, between **Bathurst** and **Druitt Streets**, is dominated by sandstone architecture and leafy trees. Some of Sydney's finest 19th-century Victorian buildings are found here, including the **Sydney Town Hall, St. Andrew's Cathedral**, and the Renaissance-style **Queen Victoria Building**—formerly the city's market-place and now a meticulously renovated retail space. Here visitors get a glimpse of the city's turn-of-the-century grandeur.

North on George Street is the monolithic **General Post Office** ("GPO") and the entrance to **Martin Place.** This open-air mall, which runs east from George Street all the way to **Macquarie Street,** is another civic focal point, with its war memorial **Cenotaph**, a huge outdoor amphitheater for lunchtime shows, several grand public and bank buildings, and some luxury boutiques.

Taken all together this area is an intriguing melange of Victorian landmark buildings, modern steel-and-glass skyscrapers, and upscale boutiques. Remote though Sydney might seem to folks from the Northern Hemisphere, visitors quickly learn that this is very much a world-class city, and nowhere is that more evident than in the CBD.

---

1 Museum of Sydney (MOS) What better place to begin an exploration of Sydney's history than at the ruins of the city's first government building? Built by order of Governor Arthur Philip in 1788, the

Government House of New South Wales served as home and office for the colony's first nine governors and remained the seat of authority for the colony until the building was demolished in 1846. In 1983, archaeologists unearthed the original foundation, a discovery that sparked a campaign to preserve the site. The find also ignited heated debate about the merits of preserving a symbol of the colonial yoke. The preservationist forces eventually prevailed, and a public plaza—**First Government Place**—was developed here. But the controversy continued as Sydneysiders argued about whether the arrival (or, some would say, the invasion) of Europeans on Australian soil was grounds for celebration. In an attempt to resolve the sensitive issue, the government announced plans for a new museum that would be dedicated to telling *all* the stories of Sydney. In 1995 this contemporary and inspiring museum opened, its entrance marked by tall totem poles, that explores the many meanings of 1788 (the year Britain claimed Australia as a colony). Within, exhibits chronicle the social history, identity, and culture of Sydney from the time of the first Government House to the present, covering stories of power, authority, rights and fights, injustices and triumphs, including the impact of European settlement on the indigenous Eora people, whose culture is re-told through images, objects, and oral histories by today's Aboriginal people. Convict Sydney, in all its color and brutality, is explored in a giant showcase of goods and chattels recovered from over 25 archaeological digs. State-of-the-art technology projects ghostly images of the past that recount their memories to visitors. The museum does an admirable job of detailing Sydney's story—and it also raises interesting questions about the city's future. Changing exhibitions of art from around the world explore themes of place, identity, culture, and communication in Australia and beyond. The **Museum Shop** offers stylish cards, books, and reproductions of artifacts, while the cafe serves up classy Modern Australian cuisine. ◆ Admission; discounts for families and children. Daily. 37 Bridge St (between Phillip and Young Sts). 9251.5988

Within the Museum of Sydney:

MOS Cafe ★★★$$$ With its solid sandstone walls, slate floors, low ceiling, and contemporary furnishings, this is not your run-of-the mill museum cafeteria. No ham and cheese sandwiches on the menu—only truly delicious, well-presented Modern Australian cuisine. Try the blinis with Tasmanian smoked salmon, or spiced blue-eyed cod with saffron glaze. Whether they're serving breakfast, lunch, afternoon tea, or dinner, the staff (usually wearing bright orange aprons) is formal yet never too fussy. Outside the cozy dining room are tables on a covered terrace overlooking the tall Aboriginal totems; request outdoor seating in advance. ◆ Modern Australian ◆ M-F 7AM-10PM; Sa-Su. Reservations recommended. 9241.3636

2 **Christensens** ★★$$$ Surrounded as it is by the skyscrapers of the CBD, this 19th-century two-story terrace house seems a bit anachronistic. But the smartly renovated town house is just the place to entertain clients for a long business lunch. The food style is traditional Australian, with Asian and Italian touches—grilled meats and fish, hearty salads, and pastas. On a fine day, ask for a table in the courtyard, which abuts the **Governor Phillip Tower**. ◆ Australian ◆ M-F lunch. Reservations recommended. 45 Phillip St (between Bent and Bridge Sts). 9247.6966

3 **Governor Phillip Tower and Governor Macquarie Tower** In 1988, five years after archaeologists unearthed the foundation of Government House, an international architectural competition was launched with the goal of developing the site's commercial possibilities while preserving its historic status. Sydney architects **Denton Corker Marshall** won the commission, with plans that encompassed a whole city block, including incorporating the **Museum of Sydney** with twin towers named for two of Australia's famous governors. These towers, completed in 1993 and 1994 respectively, adjoin the museum building. The twin skyscrapers have received all of Australia's most prestigious architectural awards. Clad in polished granite of gray and mauve with orange veins, the color of the building appears to change with the quality and intensity of the light. ◆ 1 Farrer Pl (at Young St)

4 **Lands Department Building** A stellar example of the Renaissance Revival style, this large three-story sandstone building was built in two stages: the Bridge Street frontage was constructed between 1876 and 1881, and the rest of the building went up between 1888 and 1891. It was designed by **James Barnet,** a colonial architect who was responsible for other notable buildings of the time, including the **General Post Office** on Martin Place, the **Customs House,** and the **Medical School** at **the University of Sydney.** This was **Barnet**'s largest building, and it has suffered least from alteration. Used continually for its original purpose, today it serves as the head office for the New South Wales Department of Land and Water Conservation. The building features marble flooring on the ground floor, intricate carving and paneling in the cedar joinery, elaborate moldings in the cornices, and other ceiling detailing. This is a working building and so is not open for inspection. Enjoy what you can from the exterior. ◆ 23-33 Bridge St (between Loftus and Gresham Sts)

5 Euro Caffe ★$$ Bright and airy, this Italian cafe combines good food with efficient service and style. In the morning it's coffee and pastry, at lunchtime it's salad and pasta. The risotto of the day is usually tasty and filling. ♦ Cafe ♦ M-F breakfast and lunch until 5PM. 15-19 Bent St (between Bligh and O'Connell Sts). 9221.4982

6 City Grind ★★$ They run a tight ship at this busy eatery, offering a simple breakfast and lunch menu at super speed. Salads are delicious, and the good strong coffee makes an excellent eye-opener or midday pick-me-up. Most customers opt for takeout, but there are comfortable bistro-style tables and chairs for customers with time to spare. ♦ Cafe/ Takeout ♦ M-F breakfast and lunch. 23 Bligh St (between Hunter and Bent Sts). 9223.1370

7 New South Wales Club/31 Bligh Street Boasting a sandstone facade and brick interior, this late Victorian Renaissance–style building was formerly **the New South Wales Club.** Designed by **William Wardell,** it was constructed between 1884 and 1886. After operating as an English-style men's club for nearly 100 years, the building was sold in 1972 and developed into office space. ♦ 31 Bligh St (between Hunter and Bent Sts)

8 The Wentworth $$$ This grand hotel is named after the famous Australian explorer who crossed the Blue Mountains in the west. Centrally located in the middle of the CBD, this semicircular hotel has 423 rooms, including 46 suites. Rooms are simply decorated in dark wood, with yellow and beige furnishings. The hotel caters to a business clientele and is a popular venue for mid-size conferences and meetings. Valet service is available, and rooms are equipped with irons and ironing boards. The **Garden Court** (9221.5405) offers Modern Australian cuisine and a large antipasto bar. The lobby bar, dotted with large chairs and lounges, has a piano player most evenings. ♦ 61-101 Phillip St (between Chifley Sq and Bent St). 9227.9153; fax 9227.9145

9 Chifley Tower After a great deal of speculation about its appearance and its financing, this 49-story office tower was completed in 1992. Thanks to architects **Kohn Pedersen Fox,** its postmodern design makes this high-rise a wonderful addition to Sydney's skyline. The first two floors house **Chifley Plaza,** a luxury shopping mall filled with such specialty stores as **Gucci, Cartier, Kenzo, MaxMara,** and **Tiffany & Co.** On the 41st floor, the tony **Forty One** offers fine dining—and even finer views. ♦ 92-122 Phillip St (at Chifley Sq). 9221.4500

Within Chifley Tower:

Forty One ★★★$$$$ Here's the ultimate big-night-out restaurant, with fine food and wine and supreme service—and what a view! Special occasion or not, a meal here includes one of the best vantage points in town. When the sun goes down and the lights go on, the mood becomes exclusive, glamorous, and very romantic. The decor may be a little hotel-like, but the food will satisfy any gourmet's taste. Highlights from chef Dietmar Sawyere's kitchen include prawns in potato jackets with Indian spices, and exotically herbed and spiced game meats. The wine list is impressive, although pricey. All this splendor means you have to book well in advance, especially for the private dining rooms. ♦ Modern Australian ♦ M-F lunch and dinner; Sa dinner. Reservations required. 41st floor. 9221.2500

Brasserie Cassis ★★$$$ The little sister of **Forty One** is far less formal. Situated above the retail arena of **Chifley Plaza,** it's a sleek, city bistro that caters mainly to a business crowd. The chef applies French touches while keeping the menu simple and comforting. The lemon tart is out of this world. ♦ French ♦ M-F lunch and dinner. Reservations recommended. Level 1. 9221.3500

Matsukaze ★★★$$$ It's a serene oasis amid the bustle of **Chifley Tower,** providing the setting for stylish Japanese food. Regarded as Sydney's best (and first) tempura bar, it is said that no one whisks up a batter as light or as fine as master chef Takaaki Nakoji. At lunchtime, offerings consist of tempura priced by the piece and lunch boxes with combinations of sushi and sashimi. The dinner menu is more extensive. ♦ Japanese ♦ M-F lunch and dinner. Reservations recommended. Level 1. 9229.0191

New South Wales Club/31 Bligh Street

Aborigines—The Original Australians

Anthropologists believe that the Aboriginal peoples arrived in northern Australia from Asia more than 50,000 years ago, and subsequently made their way down the coast to Sydney and throughout the rest of the continent. Their history, recorded in cave paintings and stories passed down through the generations, began in a time called the "Dreaming" or "Dreamtime," when it is said that the ancestor spirits came up from the earth and created the landscape.

Traditionally, Aborigines banded together in family-based, hunter-gatherer clan groups, rather than in large villages. Sometimes they moved from spot to spot in the bush—usually in an ancestral circle route. In the course of their long, uninterrupted settlement of the continent, the Aborigines were the world's first known people to create sophisticated, sharpened stone tools, and to represent themselves, their natural environment, and their mythology in rock and bark paintings.

Several tribes—totalling about 3,000 people—were living in the area that is now **Greater Sydney** when the first Europeans colonized Australia in 1788. The resident clans spoke three different dialects—Ku-ring-gai in the area north of **Botany Bay,** Dharawal in the south, and Dharud near the **Blue Mountains**—as well as dozens of subvariations of these languages. Tribes like the Eora lived close to the shore, particularly in the summer when fish were plentiful. Other tribes in the **Sydney Basin** included the Gandangara, Awabakal, Darkinjang, Wiradjuri, and the Wadi Wadi. Today, most native Australians in New South Wales refer to themselves as Koori.

COURTESY OF DREATIME GALLERY, SANTA FE, USA

LAMICKEY

Shores of Goreng Goreng

One year after British settlement, Australia's Aboriginal population was estimated to be 750,000, although the tribes that lived nearest the colony in **Botany Bay** were almost totally obliterated by smallpox. Subsequently, conflicts with settlers, forced removal from ancestral lands, the destructive introduction of domesticated sheep and cattle, and attempts by whites to assimilate the Aborigines all took their toll on the indigenous people. By 1840 only about 300 Aborigines survived in Sydney, living in small remnant groups. Today there are approximately 250,000 Australians of Aboriginal descent in the whole country. There are still some very small Aboriginal communities in parts of Sydney today, especially in the southern suburb of Redfern, near Botany Bay, and in the more remote western suburbs.

Over the years, Aborigines have endured a great deal of discriminatory behavior from the government and from white settlers. For example, tribes were systematically displaced and dispersed from ancestral lands, children were forcibly removed from their parents and placed in foster care, farm workers endured extremely hard living and labor conditions, and Aborigines weren't given the right to vote until the early 1960s. Attitudes started to change in the next decade, and in 1972 the government instituted a policy of self-determination in which Aboriginal communities were encouraged to take an active role in their own affairs through regional governing land councils and economic development planning authorities. And during the 1990s, such activists as Eddie Mabo finally convinced Australia's Supreme Court that Aborigines had once owned land and had a right to claim back the continuously occupied territory. Despite this seeming admission of wrongdoing, this decision, and others like it, have caused a great deal of controversy with conservative lawmakers and white landowners and farmers. The Aboriginal people still have a long way to go before they feel that they play a central role in the stewardship of their motherland.

Artistic expression has always been a central part of Aboriginal life. Crafters painted intricate white, red, brown, yellow, black, and ochre designs onto wood, rock, or flattened, dried tree bark and carved patterns onto tools and implements. To create distinctive hand outlines on rock walls, people ground shells into chalky powder, mixed it with water, and spat the pigment onto the rock's surface around the hand—a signature in the Dreaming. Today there are at least 5,500 known sites of rock decoration in the Sydney area. In what is now **Ku-ring-gai Chase National Park** lived the tribe for whom the park is named. Like the Eora, they left behind hundreds of rock paintings and engravings depicting hunting, fishing, rivers, large and small creatures in their world—both material and mythical—sharks, echidnas, wallabies, and creator-spirits. Animal designs and totems, often those of powerful or important animals such as snakes, kangaroos, eagles, and crocodiles, were often painted in what is known as "x-ray style," with the creatures' bones and internal organs represented in the images. Paintings typically have a cross-hatched or dotted pattern. Other areas with some of these images include **Sydney Harbour National Park,** the **Pittwater** district, and the **Royal National Park.**

Tribal elders traditionally presided over ceremonial life—particularly initiation, marriage, and burial rites. Often they were the only people in the community who knew the songs, dances, and poems that told of the bold and monumental deeds of the spirits back in the days of the Dreamtime. All of the cultural lore and wisdom was transmitted orally and learned by demonstration because there was no written language. *Corroborees* (celebratory dances) and cave paintings reflected the Dreaming ideal of a timeless spiritual and physical bond with the land and all the creatures living on it. Tribal members decorated their bodies almost as elaborately as they did the rock walls, with scars applied to the flesh, signifying adulthood or tribal status, along with ochre designs, necklaces of animal teeth, and feathers.

Today, Aboriginal art and performance have rebounded from obscurity and can be found in many venues in Sydney. The **Aboriginal Islander Dance Theatre** (3 Cumberland St, between Gloucester and Lower Fort Sts, The Rocks, 9252.0199), the **Aboriginal Dance Theatre** (88 Renwick St, at Turner St, Redfern, 9699.2171), the **Bangarra Dance Company** (Pier 4, Hickson Rd, between Lower Fort St and Towns Pl, Dawes Point, 9251.5333), and the **Doonooch Aboriginal Dancers at Gavala** (Harbourside Festival Marketplace, Darling Dr, between Pier and Murray Sts, Shop 377, Darling Harbour, 9212.7232) all bring to life traditional stories and dances while adding modern styles.

The *didgeridoo,* a long, wooden hornlike instrument made from a tree branch that has been hollowed out by termites, its bark stripped off, and its surface intricately decorated, is an important part of Aboriginal tradition and performance. Branches of different lengths create different pitches of an eerie, pulsing, otherworldly hum. The performer plays it using uninterrupted or "circular" breathing, vibrating the lips to create the resonance. The *didgeridoo* has been played for at least 20,000 years. Aboriginal music, like the totemic imagery, ties the artist to the Dreaming and to the land. Such contemporary Aboriginal recording artists as Yothu Yindi, Archie Roach, and Christine Anu have in recent years blended traditional themes and sounds with contemporary pop and rock performance styles.

Since the early 1970s Aboriginal painting has acquired some prominence in the art world. Among the genres are acrylic dot designs on bark, unique paintings executed outdoors on unstretched canvasses, aerial-view and abstract paintings, silk-screen prints and, most recently, murals.

A number of Sydney's museums and galleries feature both ancient and contemporary Aboriginal

Night Hunt

LAMICKEY

COURTESY OF DREATIME GALLERY, SANTA FE, USA

art. The **Museum of Sydney** has a collection of anthropological artifacts, exhibits that address the troubled history of colonization, a sculpture with the names of all of Sydney's clans, and a noted contemporary sculpture by two women—one Aborigine, one Caucasian—at the main entrance. The **Australian Museum** showcases a large natural history and anthropological exhibition. Most of its collection of Aboriginal materials has been moved to a branch of the museum, the **Djamu Gallery of Aboriginal and Pacific Islander Art,** at the **Customs House.** The **Australian National Maritime Museum** includes material and artifacts relating to Aboriginal seafaring, fishing, and boat-building. The **Museum of Contemporary Art** features works by such noted 20th-century Aboriginal artists as Albert Namatjira and Charlie Maliburr Djurrtjini, among others. And the **Art Gallery of New South Wales** contains the **Yiribana Gallery,** which displays a wide variety of types of Aboriginal painting and sculpture. Other places to see Aboriginal work include **Boomalli Aboriginal Artists' Co-op** (191 Parramatta Rd, between Young and Macquarie Sts, Annandale, 9698.2047); **Hogarth Galleries/Aboriginal Art Centre** (7 Walker La, between Brown and Liverpool Sts, Paddington, 9360.6839); and **Utopia Art Sydney** (50 Parramatta Rd, between Bridge Rd and Northumberland Ave, Stanmore, 9550.4609).

It is also possible to buy Aboriginal sculptures, bark paintings, and other crafts in the following establishments: **Aboriginal and Tribal Art Center** (117 George St, between Globe St and Suez Canal, The Rocks, 9247.9625), **The Rainbow Serpent** (Sydney Airport, 9388.7684), the **Coo-ee Aboriginal Emporium & Art Gallery** (98 Oxford St, between Hopewell St and Kidman La, Paddington, 9332.1544), and **National Aboriginal Cultural Center** (1-5 Harbour St, at Day St, 9283.7477), among many others.

10 Qantas Center Housed in a 1960s-style building are two floors filled with Qantas staff, who will help change tickets, book flights, and recommend tours for both domestic and international destinations. Stop by and browse through racks of brochures, or speak to one of the unflaggingly cheerful employees. **Qantas**'s flying red kangaroo mascot adorns every available surface—from lapels to the revolving doors. ♦ M-F; Sa morning. 70 Hunter St (at Chifley Sq). 9951.4294

11 Capita Centre Completed in 1989, this 31-story office tower is supported by an exposed steel truss that zigzags down the front of the building. The modern design was created by Australian architects **Harry Seidler and Associates.** ♦ 9 Castlereagh St (between Hosking Pl and Hunter St)

12 Commonwealth Building One of the most prominent buildings along Martin Place serves as a suitable headquarters for the Commonwealth Bank of Australia. This stately Georgian-style building with its thick, tall columns, was built in 1928 for what was then the Government Savings Bank of New South Wales. Apart from its impressive size, the building is noted for its pink granite facings on the lower floors, ceramic tiles on the upper floors, and the original wooden counters. ♦ 48 Martin Pl (at Castlereagh St)

13 Martin Place Developed in 1891 and made traffic-free in 1971, this open-air mall is always busy—populated by a mixture of preoccupied window shoppers, office workers eating lunch on park benches, and tourists watching free entertainment in the amphitheater next to the **MLC Centre** (see below). The western end is marked by the **Cenotaph** war memorial, which was designed by Bertram MacKennal and dedicated in 1929. It's the site of the annual ANZAC Day (25 April) dawn memorial service for veterans. To the east is the striking **Dobell Memorial Sculpture**. In 1979, Australian artist Lloyd Rees donated this tall sculpture composed of silver cubes by Bert Flugelman as a tribute to William Dobell, the Australian painter. ♦ Between Macquarie and George Sts

14 MLC Centre This octagonal office building and retail center's strange claim to fame is that it is supported by the tallest reinforced concrete tube in Australia. Built in 1975 and designed by **Harry Seidler and Associates,** the building (pictured at right) boasts 68 column-free floors to allow for maximum use of space. Its smaller Martin Place extension contains some exclusive boutiques, including **Adrienne Vittadini, Cartier, Moschino, Crabtree & Evelyn, Red**

Earth (a local skin-care company), and the **Dendy Cinema** (see page 49). The food court has over 300 seats with bars and a selection of take-out meals. ♦ Castlereagh St (between King St and Martin Pl). 9224.8333

Within MLC Centre:

Edna's Table ★★★$$$ Whether or not the over-the-top outback theme (think boomerang chairs, Aboriginal art, and ochre-colored walls) works is a matter of taste. What is certain, however, is that this restaurant consistently turns out some of Sydney's most innovative Modern Australian cuisine. Ingredients include such native products as fresh bush plums and paper bark (the soft bark of an indigenous tree), along with an assortment of Asian vegetables. Try the kangaroo broth or smoked emu breast as an introduction to Aussie-inspired delicacies. ♦ Modern Australian ♦ M lunch; Tu-F lunch and dinner; Sa dinner. Reservations recommended. Level 8. 9231.1400

MLC Centre

Criterion ★★★$$ Lebanese culture has been a part of the great Australian melting pot for more than 50 years. Like other immigrant cultures, the Lebanese have "married" into their new Australian family—and this restaurant offers delicious proof of that. The dining room is contemporary with a few Moorish touches, and the kitchen prepares traditional Lebanese food with a Modern Australian spin. The *mezza* plate of assorted appetizers, such as oven-baked fish with date paste, is a meal in itself. The wine list, featuring Lebanese and Australian wines, is quite extensive. ♦ Middle Eastern ♦ M-F lunch and dinner; Sa dinner. Reservations recommended. Lobby. 9233.1234

Dendy Cinema Sydneysiders come to this art-house cinema to engross themselves in the latest foreign-language films. Commonly referred to as the "Trendy Dendy," the cinema is also the place to see local independent Australian productions and serves as one of the venues of the Sydney Film Festival. ♦ Daily. 19 Martin Pl (between Castlereagh and Pitt Sts). 9233.8166. Also at: 261 King St (between Church and Mary Sts). 9550.5699

Within the Dendy Cinema:

Dendy Bar and Bistro ★★$$ The **Dendy**'s modern bar is probably more popular than the bistro, and maybe even more popular than the cinema, especially during the two-for-one Happy Hour Monday through Friday 5-7PM. Drinks deals aside, the well-prepared, uncomplicated bistro menu is worthy of some attention. The basic salads, sandwiches, and seafood dishes all have Mediterranean touches. Adventurous eaters order the kangaroo burger with chutney and potato wedges. ♦ Modern Australian ♦ Daily noon-10PM. 9221.1234

15 Banc ★★★$$$$ This former bank space was converted by **Stan Sarris** into an airy, elegant restaurant tailored to the needs of a high-powered CBD business crowd. The service is polished, without being fussy. The 25-footlong walls of the dining room are buttery yellow, blending in with the polished marble floors and enormous emerald-green marble columns that encircle the space. The food is also impressive. Chef Liam Tomlin has found the way to blend old-fashioned formal dining with Modern Australian cuisine. Traditional French brasserie-style items, including a whopping cheese trolley and a daily special—tuna niçoise on Monday—star the menu. Other choices include a number of delicately flavored salads, roasted Australian lamb on grilled peppers with mashed potatoes, and a few simple vegetarian dishes. Fine wines are sold by the glass, which makes it easy to sample a different wine with each course. Try the terrific four-dessert sampler plate if you still have room at the end of a languid lunch or dinner. ♦ Modern Australian ♦ M-F lunch and dinner; Sa dinner. Reservations recommended. 53 Martin Pl (at Phillip St). 9233.5300

16 Percy Marks Owned and run by the same family since it opened in 1899, this jewelry store specializes, now as then, in rare opals and Argyle diamonds from Western Australia. Rings, necklaces, and earrings are available in traditional and contemporary styles. ♦ M-Sa. 60-70 Elizabeth St (between King St and Martin Pl). 9233.1355. Also at: Regent Sydney, 199 George St (at Essex St). 9247.1322; Hotel Inter-Continental, 117 Macquarie St (at Bridge St). 9239.0200

17 Caffe Simpatico ★★$ This relatively small cafe offers an eat-in or take-out menu featuring hearty salads, focaccia, and Turkish-bread sandwiches with a true Mediterranean flair. Try the chicken salad with char-grilled vegetables, artichokes, and aioli, or the focaccia filled with rosemary lamb, goat cheese, grilled mushrooms, and zucchini. ♦ M-F breakfast and lunch. 140 Phillip St (between Martin Pl and Hunter St), Shop 2A. 9233.3069

18 Paspaley Pearls The warm northern waters of Australia produce some of the world's most exquisite cultured and natural pearls. As the flagship retail outlet for Australia's largest family-run pearling company, this place has a staff that knows their business. The fine pink-, white-, silver- and gold-colored pearls are mainly from the Paspaleys' farming beds off the northwest coast of Australia. Traditional and contemporary settings are available, and employees are more than willing to provide window shoppers with a history of pearling in Australia. ♦ Daily. 142 King St (between Elizabeth and Castlereagh Sts). 9232.7633

19 Pitt Street Mall Pitt Street, between Market and King Streets, is closed to vehicles, one reason that it's become the mid-city shopping hub. Many of the city's most popular shops, arcades, and department stores—including **Mid City Centre, Strand Arcade, Glasshouse, Centrepoint Tower, Skygarden, Imperial Arcade,** and **Grace Brothers**—can be reached directly from the mall. Currency exchange, souvenir, and information booths round out the options. ◆ Pitt St (between Market and King Sts)

COUNTRY ROAD

19 Country Road From casual beachwear to power suits to simple accessories, in Australia this fashion label is synonymous with the casual elegant lifestyle. The store, situated at the beginning of the **Pitt Street Mall**, is a regular haunt of stylish men and women in need of a fashion fix. ◆ 142-46 Pitt Street Mall (at King St). 9394.1818

20 Strand Arcade Designed by **John Spencer**, this shopping arcade dating from 1892 stands as an elegant reminder of Victorian days. A fire severely damaged the building in 1976, but the three-floor shopping arcade has been restored to its original splendor, complete with tile floors, cast-iron balustrades, dark wood finishes, and a magnificent glass-arched ceiling that lets in natural light. You'll find numerous small boutiques—everything from hip local fashion and jewelry retailers to old antiques stores and cafes. There is even a button shop. ◆ Daily. Between Pitt Street Mall and George St. 9232.4199

Within Strand Arcade:

Old Sydney Coffee Shop ★★$
Established in 1891 as the Harris family's coffee and tea shop, this unpretentious place has the honor of being Australia's oldest cafe. Located on the street-level main walk of the **Strand Arcade,** it serves generous pots of tea, consistently good coffee, and delicious snacks. ◆ Cafe ◆ M-F 7AM-5PM; Sa Su 11AM-3:30PM. 9231.3002

Strand Hatters Both urbanites and rural folks have been coming here since the turn of the century to purchase everything from top hats to Akubra bush hats. For the new breed of Australians who are conscious of sun damage, the store now offers a large selection of wide-brimmed straw hats to keep the rays away. ◆ Daily. Shop 8. 9231.6884

Paraphernalia for Gifts High design aesthetics seem to be the only prerequisite for what's on offer here. From leather-bound notebooks to chrome ice-cream scoops, a complete array of beautifully crafted goods adorns this small but well-stocked store. ◆ Daily. Shop 22. 9231.2474

Morrissey Edmiston–Woman and Man This supertrendy Sydney fashion house is a favorite with both real and wannabe stars and starlets. Broken into two stores opposite one another, the shop has clothing that's just what's required for lounging around in one of Sydney's hip cocktail bars. If you see something you like, buy it immediately—the clothing is too up-to-the-minute to hang around for long. ◆ Daily. Men: Shop 63. 9221.5616; Women: Shop 68. 9232.7606

DINOSAUR DESIGNS

Dinosaur Designs The molded resin jewelry and homewares here are wildly colorful objets d'art—as suitable for the contemporary urban dwellings as for Fred Flintstone's stone-age home. Check out the Adam and Eve molded salad servers and the wacky shot glasses and accessories. The stained-glass hues emanating from the back-lit display shelves can be mesmerizing. ◆ Daily. Shop 77. 9223.2953

Love and Hatred Once the place for Gothic clothing, this jewelry store remains moodily eccentric, with burning candles and incense. Proprietor Giovanni D'Ercole's style is exemplified in his trademark rings. All the jewelry is crafted with precious metals and stones, and items may be made to order. ◆ Daily. Shop 79. 9233.3441

Victoria Buckley Every piece of jewelry in this tiny store and workshop is crafted on the premises by Victoria and her able assistants, using precious metals and gem stones. The prices are very reasonable. ◆ Daily. Level 2. 9231.5571

21 Mid City Centre Another multilevel shopping center along the **Pitt Street Mall,** this complex is best known for the **HMV** music store in the basement and the busy food hall on the ground floor. There are also clothing, jewelry, and eyewear stores with decent selections. ◆ Daily. Pitt Street Mall (between Market St and Strand Arcade). 9221.2422

Within Mid City Centre:

Marcs Trendy Sydneysiders have been flocking to this hip clothing shop for years. One of the main attractions is the selection of shirts of all sorts and, seemingly, all colors—at least the season's latest hues. Another draw is the imported cutting-edge men's and women's fashions from around the globe; labels include Issey Miyake, Comme des Garcons, Dries van Noten, and Diesel. ◆ M-Sa. 9221.5575

22 Skygarden This three-level complex is one of Sydney's better retail emporiums. The boutiques include **Country Road, Saba,**

Sportsgirl, Aquila Shoes, Benetton, and **Hermès,** along with some luxurious salons. ♦ Pitt Street Mall (between Market and King Sts). Other entrance: 77 Castlereagh St (between Imperial Arcade and King St). 9231.1811

Within Skygarden:

Hardy Brothers Australia's oldest jewelry store was established in the early 19th century. Stocking very traditional jewelry designs, the proprietors feature pearls from Broome and Argyle diamonds from the Kimberleys. ♦ M-Sa. 77 Castlereagh St. 9232.2422

23 Angus & Robertson BookWorld Booksellers since 1886, this store's current claim to fame is somewhat curious— "Australia's largest book shop trading on one level." With a stock of more than 250,000 new books, the store provides a specialist for each area to assist customers. It also sells classical music CDs, and in the Classical Music Lounge customers may listen before they buy. ♦ Daily. Imperial Arcade (between Castlereagh St and Pitt St Mall). 9235.1188

24 Emporio Virtually a mini–department store on four floors, this shop is dedicated to foot fetishists of all persuasions. Each floor features a different shoe trend—from disco platforms to smart office pumps. An entire floor is devoted to wacky European creations. ♦ M-Sa. 182 Pitt St Mall (between Market St and Imperial Arcade). 9233.4520

25 Centrepoint Tower This bronze-colored tower (pictured at right), topped with a spire 31 meters (102 feet) high, dominates the Sydney skyline. Measuring 325 meters (1066 feet) above sea level, it's the tallest public building in the Southern Hemisphere. The tower, built in 1981, rises above the Centrepoint shopping complex and is anchored to it by 56 thick wire cables. Each cable weighs seven tons; if their strands were laid end to end they would stretch 1,000 kilometers (620 miles) from Sydney to Alice Springs. At the very top is the **Turret,** with four floors of restaurants and lounges, as well as an observation deck with a not-to-be-missed panoramic view of the city and harbor. Extend the views with the available high-powered binoculars or take advantage of one of the various audio (self-guided) or guided tours. A nighttime visit reveals Sydney at its most glamorous. ♦ M-F, Su 9:30AM-9:30PM; Sa 9:30AM-11:30PM. 100 Market St (between Castlereagh St and Pitt St Mall). Observation level 9229.7444, group bookings 9229.7427, restaurants 9233.3722

26 Piccadilly London-style arcades like this one may seem a little on the quirky side these days, but in the 1960s and 1970s, they were *the* places to shop. Today the collection of stores here has been eclipsed—literally and figuratively—by the enormous **Pitt Street Mall,** but it still provides some very good salons, clothing, jewelry, and take-out food stores, including **Raymond Castles** for women's shoes and **Mug Mania** for—well, mugs. ♦ M-Sa. 210 Pitt St (between Park and Market Sts). 9267.3666

27 Sydney Hilton $$$$ Built in the early 1970s, this 585-room hotel looks like other hotels in the chain the world over. Since it was built, the city has developed around it, so the spacious rooms can't boast the harbor views of some of the other major hotels. But the hotel is comfortable, well maintained, and centrally located on the monorail line that connects it to other parts of the CBD and Darling Harbour. The quality of service and staff is high, with 24-hour butler and room service. There are four restaurants, five bars, and one nightclub. Nearly everyone pays a visit to the famous **Marble Bar,** and the exclusive **America's Cup Bar** and the rowdy **Henry IX Bar** are almost as popular. ♦ 259 Pitt St (between Park and Market Sts). 9266.0610, 800/445.8667; fax 9265.6065

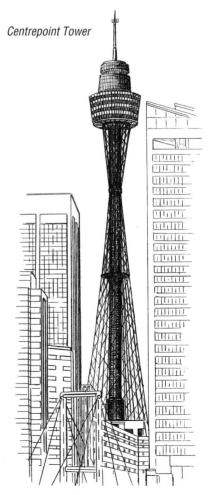

Centrepoint Tower

Within the Sydney Hilton:

Marble Bar This cozy nook was originally the bar for George Adams's **Tattersall's Hotel,** built in 1893. When **Tattersall's** was demolished in 1969, laborers refused to destroy the beloved bar, so the Hilton chain bought the marble columns and the wood and stained-glass fixtures and reconstructed the Italian Renaissance–style bar in the basement of the new hotel. Today it's still one of Sydney's most popular after-work bars; on the weekend it's a venue for live music, attracting a much younger, rowdier crowd of drinkers. ◆ M-F noon-11PM; Sa 3PM-2AM. Basement. 9266.0610

28 David Jones (Men) Just across the street from its sister store (see below) is the men's domain. The first three floors carry ties, shirts, shoes, suits, and casual gear, while the top floors get more domestic with kitchenware and home furnishings. The basement houses the huge **Food Hall,** where specialty foods, fresh fruit and vegetables, and the house brand of prepared goods may be purchased. Take a number and order everything you need to create your own picnic in nearby **Hyde Park.** Or grab a stool at the counter for a sit-down afternoon tea break or light meal. ◆ Daily. 65-77 Market St (between Castlereagh and Pitt Sts). 9266.5544

29 David Jones (Women) Referred to as "DJ's" by the locals, this department store is to Sydney what Harrod's is to London and Bloomingdale's is to New York. One of the most striking aspects of this—the original store—is the elegant marble and mirrored ground floor retail space where native floral arrangements abound and the house pianist fills the air with soothing gentle tunes to prevent shopper's burnout. Within its seven stories are books, stationery, cosmetics, women's casual- and eveningwear, plus babies' and children's clothes and toys. ◆ Daily. 86-108 Castlereagh St (between Market and King Sts). 9266.5544

30 Bar Coluzzi ★$ In Sydney, the Coluzzi name is synonymous with good, strong coffee and simple Italian fare. This is the second outpost of the successful chain. For breakfast, try raisin toast; for morning or afternoon tea, sample the dense Italian cakes. This is a casual place—cutlery is rarely required, as the menu consists mainly of sandwiches and other take-out foods. Indoor and outdoor seating is available. ◆ Cafe ◆ M-F 7AM-5:30PM. 99 Elizabeth St (between Market and King Sts). 9233.1651. Also at: 322 Victoria St (between Surrey and Craigend Sts). 9380.5420

Restaurants/Clubs: Red   Hotels: Blue

Shops/ 🌳 Outdoors: Green   Sights/Culture: Black

31 Hyde Park This grand city park, divided in half by Park Street, is surrounded by some of Sydney's most famous 19th-century buildings including the **Great Synagogue, Hyde Park Barracks,** and the **Australian Museum.** Originally, the park occupied more land and marked the outskirts of the town. It was used for farming and garrison exercises until 1810 when Governor Macquarie ordered the area fenced in and named after London's Hyde Park. From 1820 to 1821, the park contained Sydney's racecourse and from 1827 to 1856 it was used as cricket grounds. The north-south walkway, once a part of historic Macquarie Street, is lined with enormous fragrant fig trees that are illuminated at night by twinkling lights. On the fringe of today's CBD, the park serves as a weekday haven from the city bustle. **St. James** and **Museum Stations** are also located within the park. ◆ Bounded by College, Elizabeth, and Liverpool Sts, and Prince Albert and St. James Rds

Within Hyde Park:

Archibald Fountain On the north side of the park sits this impressive bronze fountain featuring the Greek god Apollo and the Roman goddess Diana. The fountain commemorates the French-Australian alliance during World War I. Completed in 1932, it was designed by sculptor Francois Sicard and donated by J.F. Archibald, founder of *The Bulletin* magazine.

Sandringham Memorial Gardens As the name implies, this garden is veddy British—and very pretty. Formerly the site of the **Band Rotunda,** the space was converted into a quaint sunken garden and opened by Queen Elizabeth II in 1954 as a memorial to Kings George V and George VI.

ANTHONY HARVEY

ANZAC Memorial Located at the southern end of the park, this Art Deco war memorial was designed by **Bruce Dellit** and dedicated in 1934 to commemorate the soldiers of ANZAC (Australian and New Zealand Army Corps) who fought and died for Australia in World War I. At 11AM each day, a brief memorial remembrance takes place in the **Tomb of the Unknown Soldier.** A permanent photography and military exhibition is located in the base of the memorial. A tree-lined "Pool of

Remembrance" stretches out at the foot of the memorial, reflecting its image. ♦ Free. Daily. 9267.7668

Hyde Park Cafe ★★$$ This rustic-looking cafe behind the **Museum Railway Station** at the southwestern edge of the park is a convenient place for a quick snack or a coffee break. At lunch, the three-course, prix-fixe menu is the way to go—the food is tasty and the portions manageable. Save room for the excellent desserts. ♦ Modern Australian ♦ M-Sa breakfast and lunch. Elizabeth and Liverpool Sts. 9264.8751

SHERATON ON THE PARK

32 Sheraton On The Park $$$$ On entering the hotel, the first-time visitor is dazzled by the opulence of the marble-and-granite lobby. Obviously, there are no cutting corners when this 599-room property was built in the early 1990s. Guest rooms are equipped with all the modern amenities, and many of them have views of **Hyde Park** or Sydney Harbour. The hotel is convenient to some of Sydney's best shopping and has a covered access to the monorail, which connects to Darling Harbour. The lobby bar is a surprisingly quiet place for a chat or meeting, while the **Riva** nightclub is for those who love to groove. ♦ 161 Elizabeth St (between Park and Market Sts). 9286.6000, 800/325.3535; fax 9286.6686

Within the Sheraton on the Park:

Gekko ★★$$$$ It's not that common to find a cozy and relatively casual restaurant in a plush hotel, but happily, this one fits the bill. Maybe it's the outback decor or the simple Modern Australian cuisine. The lunchtime crowd runs to business people, while evening patrons tend be include a lot of international tourists. Try the fine salads, ocean trout rolls, or the seared tuna steak. There's an extensive list of domestic wines, which are also available by the glass. ♦ Modern Australian ♦ M-F lunch and dinner; Sa dinner. Reservations recommended. 9286.6669

33 Great Synagogue Consecrated in 1878, this synagogue has the longest established Jewish congregation in Australia. The Byzantine–inspired synagogue was designed by architect **Thomas Rowe.** Its distinctive

features include a domed roof, round stained-glass windows, and a ceiling decorated with hundreds of painted gold stars. The wrought-iron gates are usually closed, so enter from the back of the synagogue on Castlereagh Street. ♦ Tours: Tu and Th noon-1PM. 187 Elizabeth St (between Park and Market Sts). 9267.2477; tours enter at 166 Castlereagh St (between Park and Market Sts)

34 Crave ★$ This small espresso bar and sandwich joint is buzzing at lunch hour with people ordering at the counter for "take away" and "eat here" coffees and focaccia. Sandwiches are filled with good-quality Italian meats and fresh vegetables. ♦ Cafe/Takeout ♦ M-F 7AM-5PM. 149 Castlereagh St (between Park and Market Sts). 9264.1384

35 Windsor Bistro ★$$ A few years back, the hotel on this site was in total disrepair and the ground-floor pub was infamous for its less-than-friendly patrons. These days, there's a swank pub downstairs and an equally hip, large bistro-style restaurant upstairs. Both have been renovated using blond wood and brushed steel. Seafood and salads star on the restaurant menu; look for such adventurous dishes as tuna-and-sea-urchin tartare and Vietnamese pork-stuffed squid. ♦ Modern Australian ♦ M-F lunch and dinner. New Windsor Hotel, Park and Castlereagh Sts. 9283.3362

36 Park Regis $$$ Except for a small hotel lobby on the ground floor, the bottom five floors of this building house business offices. The hotel's 120 rooms take over the sixth floor and above. The rooms are large and comfortably furnished, with such extra amenities as refrigerators and mini-bars. The outdoor rooftop swimming pool is a bonus in the hot months. Room service is provided, but there is no restaurant. ♦ 27 Park St (at Castlereagh St). 9267.6511; fax 9264.2252

37 Hyde Park Inn $$ This no-frills, 85-room hotel looks over **Hyde Park** and is on the fringe of the business district, closer to Chinatown and just a stroll across the park to Oxford Street. All rooms are well furnished and have small kitchens and bathrooms, plus surprisingly large closets. The house restaurant serves simple meals. ♦ 271 Elizabeth St (between Liverpool and Bathurst Sts). 9264.6001; fax 9261.8691

Sydney has an average of 6.7 hours of sunshine per day.

Centrepoint Tower on Market Street is the city's tallest structure. It has a 360° view of the Sydney basin.

Multicultural Sydney

The term "New Australian" was once used to describe someone not long off the ship from a Mediterranean country (unlike the original Anglo-Saxon settlers) who immigrated to this seemingly friendly, laid-back place. Today more and more people from non-European countries are making Sydney their home, and are having a great impact on the city's culture and cooking. This is evident with the emergence of a Modern Australian cuisine that infuses the flavors of Asia and the Mediterranean with Australian products, and in the proliferation of the cultural festivals of various nationalities.

KEELY EDWARDS

Sydney is one of the world's most ethnically diverse places, one reason it is such a vibrant, cosmopolitan city. In such neighborhoods as **Darlinghurst,** Italian cafes operate next to Thai restaurants and old Australian pubs sit across from Lebanese dining spots. Synagogues coexist peacefully across from cathedrals, and suburbs are filled with Anglo-Australians living next door to Greeks, Croatians, and Chinese. This isn't to say that Sydney is a multicultural utopia. As in any large metropolitan area, the city has its share of political and social debates and conflicts.

The following groups are the most conspicuous of Sydney's cultural cornucopia:

Chinese This community flourishes in Sydney, clearly apparent in a bustling **Chinatown** that's bursting with restaurants, take-out places, and supermarkets. The population continues to grow as more people arrive from Hong Kong and mainland China. Chinese New Year and the annual Dragon Boat Festival at **Darling Harbour** are major events on Sydney's cultural calendar.

Greeks Although Melbourne boasts Australia's largest Hellenic population, Sydney also has an enormous number of Greeks who migrated to Australia after World War II. A hub of cultural activity is in the **Inner West** suburb of Marrickville where the Mediterranean-style St. Nicholas Church is located.

Irish A majority of Australians claim to have some type of Gaelic heritage, understandable given England's transportation of Irish convicts from 1788 to the mid-1800s, and the steady stream of immigration from Ireland throughout the 20th century. They lived in **The Rocks,** today the location of a number of Irish-style pubs and the obvious choice for the city's St. Patrick's Day celebrations.

Italians Coffee and other culinary traditions have made this population a major part of the cultural fabric of Sydney. Italian delicatessens, restaurants, and cafes serving focaccia sandwiches, pizzas, and pastries are ubiquitous throughout the city. The Inner West neighborhood of **Leichhardt** is full of cafes and restaurants, and an annual parade is held here along **Norton Street.**

Jews The **Eastern Suburbs** have a significant number of Jews, apparent in the abundance of kosher delicatessens, cafes, and restaurants found from **Rose Bay** to **Bondi Beach.** Sydney's Jewish population originally came from Eastern Europe, the Middle East, Russia, and China, although some say there was a small Jewish community in the early colony. The **Great Synagogue** on Elizabeth Street in the **Central Business District (CBD)** and the **Sydney Jewish Museum** in Darlinghurst are two of Sydney's major Jewish landmarks.

Lebanese Many of Sydney's Lebanese live near the southwestern suburb of Lakemba, where they have built a huge mosque. Sydney's early Lebanese community was Christian Orthodox, and Maronite Christians (a Roman Catholic sect) settled all around rural New South Wales as well as in Sydney's center. Many Lebanese restaurants still operate along Cleveland Street in Redfern. **Criterion** in the CBD serves Lebanese fare with a Modern Australian twist.

Thais The growth of Sydney's Thai community is a relatively recent (1970s and 1980s) occurrence. The city boasts a large number of Thai restaurants, found mainly in such areas as **Newtown, Kings Cross,** Darlinghurst, and **Surry Hills.** The Loy Krathong Festival, held annually in the western suburb of **Parramatta,** celebrates Thai culture and cuisine.

Vietnamese Most arrivals from Vietnam have settled in the western suburb of **Cabramatta** where many store signs are written in Vietnamese, and the spoken language is rarely English. The Vietnamese—many of whom were refugees—started coming to Australia in the early 1970s. There has been a great deal of debate about the Vietnamese immigration to Australia, including the alleged lack of assimilation by the Vietnamese into Sydney's mainstream, and its negative impact on the city (for example, gang warfare). At the same time, the population has contributed to Sydney's cultural life, particularly in the adaptation of its cuisine into the overall transformation of Australian cooking.

38 Downing Centre Now the location of the New South Wales Government law courts, this majestic late-Victorian building was formerly **Mark Foy's Piazza Store**—a department store now legendary in Sydney's retail history. In his structure designed by architects **McCredie and Anderson,** retailer Francis Foy opened the doors in 1908 of what was to become Sydney's most elegant store. In 1928, 10 years after Foy's death, the store was booming, and architects **Ross and Rowe** were commissioned to design an extension. Four stories were added, along with the mansard roof and terra-cotta moldings that suggest French Renaissance architecture.
♦ 143-47 Liverpool St (between Elizabeth and Castlereagh Sts)

Within Downing Centre:

Bambini Espresso Just around the corner from its parent, the **Bambini Cafe Bar** (see below), this small take-out cafe is a notch above the ordinary. The specialties are simple—take-out coffee, toast, and focaccia sandwiches—but the friendly staff takes extra care to make sure the customer is happy. A few seats are available. ♦ M-F. 299 Elizabeth St (entrance on Liverpool St). 9261.3331

39 Travel Book Shop What is it about travel bookstores? They tend to be both staffed by and filled with interesting people. Owner John Costelloe is happy to point out the right travel guide and map or talk about where you're headed next. Book and travel product launches and lectures are also held here.
♦ Daily. 175 Liverpool St (between Commonwealth and Nithsdale Sts), Shop 3. 9261.8200

40 Bambini Cafe Bar ★★$$ In answer to local business folks' yearning for an alternative to expense-account restaurants and quick-fix delis came this double deal—a popular cafe by day and bar by night. The space is designed in typical Sydney fashion—concrete floors, Jacobsen blond plywood chairs, communal tables, open kitchen, and spot lighting—and the food is standard Sydney fare: large salads, gourmet sandwiches, and fresh baked goods. The cafe closes 3-5PM for its transformation into an after-work bar. Good luck finding standing room on Thursday and Friday night. ♦ Cafe/Bar ♦ M-F 7AM-10PM. 262 Castlereagh St (between Liverpool and Bathurst Sts). 9264 9550

41 Grand Taverna ★$$ Don't be put off by the kitschy decor and the abrupt staff. They've been getting away with it for years, thanks to the good hearty food. This Spanish restaurant located in the Sir John Young Hotel is something of an institution with the local business crowd. The kitchen is busy and loud, and orders are placed at the counter. Seafood, accompanied by some sangria, is the way to go; try the barbecued prawns and any grilled fish special. ♦ Spanish ♦ M-Sa lunch and dinner. 557 George St (at Liverpool St). 9267.3608

42 Jackie's ★$ In an area full of pinball arcades, seedy pubs, and office buildings, this vaguely bohemian cafe is a blessing. With African masks on the walls and simple furnishings, it serves inexpensive coffees, tasty focaccia sandwiches, and such good desserts as sticky date pudding. Order from the blackboard menu and pay at the counter.
♦ Cafe ♦ Daily noon-midnight. 86 Liverpool St (between George and Kent Sts). 9261.1439

43 Judge's House Now named for its second occupant, Supreme Court Judge Justice Dowling, this house was originally built in 1822 for the family of a government surveyor, William Harper. As one of the last surviving Colonial Georgian houses in the Sydney city area, this is thought to be the second-oldest domestic dwelling still standing, after **Cadman's Cottage** in The Rocks. For over a century, it was used by the Sydney City Mission. In 1977, a threatened plan to demolish it to make way for a high-rise office development was stopped at the last minute by the state government. ♦ 531 Kent St (between Liverpool and Bathurst Sts)

44 Village Cinemas Part of cinema row, this theater screens the blockbusters and the odd foreign-language and local production.
♦ Discounts on Tuesday. Daily. 545 George St (between Liverpool and Bathurst Sts). 9264.6701

45 Planet Hollywood ★$$ Yes, Sydney has one too. Big on Hollywood memorabilia, this is the place to mingle with the local young people who love all things American.
♦ American ♦ Daily lunch and dinner until 2AM. 600 George St (at Wilmot St). 9267.7827

46 Hoyts Cinema This megacinema complex shows all the blockbusters, mainly imports from the United States. Beware of the hordes of teenagers on Saturday and Sunday and during school holidays. ♦ Discounts on Tuesday. Daily. 505 George St (between Liverpool and Bathurst Sts). 11680

Sydney Town Hall

47 Omni ★★$$ A cafe with a slick design, smooth service, and a commendable attention to detail is bound to be successful in this part of town. And this one is. The menu is diverse, offering everything from old Aussie standards like pumpkin soup and Irish stew to such modern interpretations of Asian food as tandoori chicken. There is a large selection of teas, all served in elegant diffuser teapots. If you can't live without the Dutch Piazza D'Oro coffee, apparently this is one of the only Sydney cafes to serve it. ♦ Cafe/Modern Australian ♦ M-F breakfast, lunch, and dinner. Reservations recommended. 125 Bathurst St (between Pitt and George Sts). 9267.4150

48 St. Andrew's Cathedral Today this cathedral represents the pinnacle of the Anglican church in Sydney, but its early history was rocky. Its construction was first planned in 1816 by Governor Macquarie, who chose the name St. Andrew after the patron saint of his Scottish homeland. Macquarie envisaged a grand church, which would be part of a whole complex of buildings, including a police watchtower, law courts, and a town hall. He laid the first stone in 1819. Not everyone, however, was impressed with his grand designs. Commissioner Bigge, sent to Australia by the Colonial Office in London to investigate complaints about Macquarie's big spending, halted the plans. Bigge directed the conversion of the Law Courts on King Street into a church—and this became **St. James**'s, now the oldest church in the city. But the

plans for the cathedral were not scrapped entirely and, despite funding crises and design disputes, the project was handed over to colonial architect **Edmund Thomas Blacket** in 1846. **Blacket** designed the cathedral in English Late Gothic style, the first faithful example of a large Gothic building in Australia. **Blacket**'s grasp of the Gothic style is said to be so impressive that the interior could be taken for a genuine product of the 15th century. The cathedral was opened officially in 1868, making it the oldest cathedral in Australia. The cathedral school, founded in 1885, is situated in nearby **St. Andrew's House.** The famed boys' choir is drawn from the 600 boys who attend the school. Visitors may enter from either George Street or Sydney Square via the north transept.♦ Services M-F 8AM; Su 8:30AM, 10:30AM, 6:30PM. Sydney Sq (just west of George St). 9265.1661

49 Sydney Town Hall Generations of Sydneysiders have met their friends at these steps. This building—and in particular its steps—is one of the city's most treasured landmarks, an outstanding example of High Victorian architecture (pictured above). Once the site of a colonial cemetery first used in 1793 (the remains of the early settlers and convicts interred at the site were relocated before construction began), the area has yielded relics over the years. A permanent marking of one grave site can be found in the southern corridor of the **Lower Town Hall.**The foundation stone was laid by Albert, Duke of

Edinburgh and son of Queen Victoria, on 4 April 1868. The building was constructed in stages, with the civic offices and magnificent vestibule built first, in 1869. The clocktower was completed in 1881, but it was not until 1884 that the clock itself was installed, and another year passed before the chimes were added. The **Centennial Hall**—the main body of the building—was completed in 1889, a year after Australia's Centenary Year, for which it was named. At that time, the 2,250-seat hall was the largest meeting hall in the world, and it remains one of the two grand surviving 19th-century halls in Australia (the other is the **Great Hall** of the **University of Sydney**). Its most important architectural features are the massive zinc molded ceiling, the 80-foot-wide grand organ, which spans the entire width of the western wall, and 21 stained glass windows featuring Australian flora.

The building and grounds encompass an area of approximately two acres. The marble steps and the terrace at the main entrance provide the setting for various ceremonial occasions and are a popular meeting place for Sydneysiders. Just north of the main entrance is one of the building's most intriguing details: Among the many lions' heads that are carved into the Pyrmont sandstone facade is one that's winking. Legend has it that the head stonemason "sighted" the course of sandstone being laid by closing one eye and looking along the line of new work. When the building was completed, it was found that one of the lions had been carved with one eye closed in imitation of the foreman. The many features inside the building worth seeing include the original mosaic tile floors; the 1906 "bird cage" lift, which was one of the first electric elevators in Sydney; and the vestibule—originally designed to be the **Town Hall** itself—which displays a stunning example of Victorian plaster work, elaborate stained glass, impressive parquetry, and joinery.

The Town Hall is the official home of the Sydney City Council (consisting of seven elected councilors, one of whom is the lord mayor of Sydney), and the building also houses the lord mayor's office, reception rooms, council chambers, and VIP rooms. Guided tours (reservations recommended) are offered by the **Centrepoint Touring Company** (9231.4629). ◆ M-Sa. 483 George St (at Sydney Sq)

50 EPT House One of the most striking features of this reinforced concrete office building is the facade made with tinted glass panels that form two merging diamond shapes. Completed in 1976, it was designed by **Mario Arnaboldi** and built with Italian materials. ◆ 263-73 Clarence St (at Druitt St)

ANTHONY HARVEY

51 Queen Victoria Building (QVB) This majestic building could be one the most elegant and historic shopping centers in the world. By the mid-1800s, Sydney had outgrown its markets and needed a grand central space to house both government and private enterprise (mainly produce stalls). This coincided with a desperate need to engage hundreds of stonemasons, stained-glass artists, craftsmen, and builders who had been thrown out of work by an economic recession. Erecting this monumental structure, designed by **George McRae** and completed in 1898, seemed like an ideal solution. Bounded by George, York, Druitt, and Market Streets, the building's four stories of opulent Byzantine architecture feature a copper-sheathed central dome, 20 smaller domes, a vaulted glass roof, colored-tile floors, and curved wooden staircases.

Its majestic looks belie the edifice's rather checkered history. Only a few decades after opening, when it housed the **City Concert Hall, City Library,** a coffee palace, and the Sydney City Council, it had become severely neglected. In 1959 it was nearly demolished. Then it sat empty for more than 20 years. It was not until the early 1980s, when the retail scene was again strong, that proposals were considered for redevelopment of the grand old building. A Malaysian company, Ipoh Gardens, won a 99-year lease and the right to overhaul the structure, transforming it into a retail center. It reopened in 1986 with 190 stores and concessions and a basement-level walkway connecting with **Town Hall Station.**

During the redevelopment, a worldwide search began to find a statue of **Queen Victoria** to adorn one of the building's entrances. One was finally found in Daingean, Ireland, a 1947 discard by the Irish Parliament. The pensive-looking statue was shipped to Sydney, reconditioned, and now sits at the Druitt Street entrance. Beside her is the **Royal Wishing Well,** which features a peculiar combination of a statue of the Queen's favorite dog, Islay, and a stone from Blarney Castle, Ireland. Note also the **Royal Clock,** which is 17 feet long and weighs more than a ton, suspended from the ceiling. At one minute before the hour, four mechanical heralds sound a trumpet voluntary from the top of the ramparts, replicas of those at Balmoral Castle, Scotland.

Hourlong guided tours of the building provide an education on the architecture and history of the late 19th century. Stores range from recognizable international labels to local names, plus great cafes, salons, elegant boutiques, and fine arts and jewelry stores. ♦ M-W, F-Su; Th 9AM-9PM. Tours: Daily 11:30AM, 2:30PM. 455 George St (between Druitt and Market Sts). Information 9264.9209, tours 9265.6864

Within the Queen Victoria Building:

Bar Cupola ★$ Good strong coffee and giant-size Italian sandwiches are the staples at this tiny cafe, which sits under the **QVB**'s stained-glass dome. There are a few tables and chairs outside, making it a popular place to meet someone before or after exploring the shops. ♦ Cafe/Takeout ♦ M-F 7:30AM-6PM; Sa-Su. 9283.3878

ABC Shop As one of the retail branches of the **Australian Broadcasting Corporation (ABC)**, this store offers rows of Australian music, videos, and literature, all related to television and radio programs. It's a great place to find classical music recordings from or videos of television programs you've fallen for while in Sydney. ♦ Gallery Level 1. 9333.1635

52 Gowing Bros. Ltd. Established in 1868, this menswear store is still run by the Gowing family. Window displays, with handwritten price tags and descriptions, give customers a taste of what's available inside this grand old retail outlet. The stock pleases both fathers looking for an Australian bush hat or business shirt and sons checking out the latest beachwear and hiking boots. A barber shop on the second floor has also helped make this place a Sydney institution; from shaved heads to conservative business cuts, the barbers are prepared for anything and charge very reasonable prices to cut your locks. Come here for a sense of how Sydney's men did and do like to shop; armchair shoppers can browse through the mail-order catalog. ♦ George and Market Sts. 9264.6321, catalog 008/803.304 (toll-free)

53 State Theatre This Baroque-style theater was opened as a movie house in 1929. Its lavish foyer, with marble columns, torchlights, and statues, is a hint of what's to come. Inside, a massive chandelier lights the 2,000-seat theater, which is outfitted in brass, red velvet, and more marble. These days it only functions as a cinema during the annual Sydney Film Festival in June. Otherwise, it's a

venue for live music and performances. Tours are offered during the day. ♦ 49 Market St (between Pitt and George Sts). Box office 9320.9050, tours 9231.4629

Within the State Theatre:

Retro Cafe ★$ Serving basic breakfast, lunch, and dinner fare, this cafe is popular for light (and inexpensive) pre-theater dinners. The staff is young but they try hard, so be nice to them. ♦ Cafe ♦ M-F 7:30AM-8PM; Sa 8AM-8PM. Reservations recommended during theater hours. 9261.3443

54 Grace Bros For more than 150 years, this store (once known as **Farmer's**) has been Australian for "let's go shopping." Detractors say that this place is less glamorous than newer emporiums, but fans note that it is also less expensive. Seven roomy floors are filled with domestic and imported clothing, cosmetics, homewares, and electronics. It's also possible to rent formal eveningwear here, if you've left your tux at home. ♦ Daily. 436 George St (at Market St). 9238.9111

55 Dymocks Booksellers James Forsyth, a descendant of William Dymock who founded this bookshop chain in 1879, recently bought back this flagship store from a public company that had been its owner. At press time he had plans to make it one of Sydney's most impressive book retailers. For the time being, this gigantic outlet sells books in every category, as well as CD-ROMs, computer equipment, and gifts. The Australian literature section is extensive; children's books and games are also well represented. ♦ M-Sa. 424 George St (between Market St and Strand Arcade). 9235.3144

56 R.M. Williams Based in Prospect, South Australia, R.M. Williams was originally a mail-order company calling itself the "bushman's outfitters." Although the more-than-60-year-old firm still offers sturdy leather boots, moleskin trousers, and Driza-bone coats by catalog, more recently it has opened retail stores in every major Australian city, as well as in New Zealand and London. The boots, in a range of styles and sizes for men and women, remain the best product. ♦ Daily. 389 George St (between Market and King Sts). 9262.2228

56 Soup Plus After years of presenting local jazz artists, this basement venue has become a required stop on the Sydney jazz scene. The food is hearty and affordable. ♦ Cover charge. Two shows nightly; call for times. 383 George St (between Market and King Sts). 9299.7728

57 American Express Tower Designed by **John Andrews** and completed in 1976, this structure is one of Sydney's modern architectural landmarks. Situated diagonally to George Street, the high-rise features an experimental method of external sunshades to protect the interior from the harsh afternoon sun. ♦ 388 George St (at King St)

58 Forbes Hotel After a number of renovations, this old four-story hotel has been converted into a drinking and eating multiplex. A simple pub occupies the ground floor, a quieter cocktail lounge is upstairs, and there are restaurants on the two top floors. The fourth-floor **Pasta Palace** specializes in big bowls of pasta accompanied by bread and salad; it's open Monday through Saturday for lunch and dinner. One floor down, **The Grill** is more sophisticated and sedate, offering great Italian-inspired seafood and poultry dishes for lunch and dinner. ♦ M-Sa 10AM-3AM; Su noon-10PM. 30 York St (at King St). 9299.3703

59 Restaurant CBD ★★$$$ Hotel CBD is a noisy city pub that's usually packed to the brim with thirsty nine-to-fivers looking for some after-work action. This classy little restaurant sits beside the bar and is worth visiting, particularly if you're in the CBD for business or a night of theater. Young chef Luke Mangan's modern yet mannered technique is a blessing for city diners. A pre-theater menu is available. Save room for dessert: The lemon tart is legendary. ♦ Modern Australian ♦ M-F lunch and dinner. Hotel CBD, 75 York St (at King St), Level 1. 9299.8911

60 Forum the Grace Hotel $$$ Originally headquarters of Australia department store moguls the Grace brothers, this 1930s art deco-style building was also the headquarters for US General Douglas MacArthur's South Pacific operations during World War II. Today, the beautiful stone facade is still perfectly intact, while the interior has been converted into a large (382-room) hotel in the middle of the city. Since the building was recently classified by the National Trust of Australia, utmost care has been paid to its renovation. And although remaining true to its heritage, all of its spacious rooms have modern conveniences including faxes, three phones per room, and in-room entertainment centers with CD players and cable TV. The furnishings are all new, but the warm yellow walls, dark wood beds, desks and tables, are very much in keeping with a 1930s style. In addition to a well-equipped gym with views of the city, the hotel also features a small wine bar, an open, airy cafe, and a brasserie for more formal dining, featuring Modern Australian cuisine. ♦ 77 York St (at King St). 9272.6888, fax 9299.8189

61 Bouillon Eatery ★★$$ This was one of the first restaurants to encourage the communal dining trend. The space is dominated by a long, all-dig-in communal table, although there are some individual tables. The menu is modeled on the "Bouillon" eating houses of 19th-century France, offering flavorful one-dish meals. Typical dishes are fish curry and leek bisque risotto. This is about as eclectic as Modern Australian cuisine gets. ♦ Modern Australian ♦ M-Th lunch and dinner; F dinner. Reservations recommended. City Hotel, 347 Kent St (at King St), Level 1. 9299.4981

62 Savoy Serviced Apartments $$$ If you're in town for a week or more, an apartment with maid service could be the way to go. The 70 one-bedroom apartments here are furnished with either a rustic style or a sleek contemporary one. All are outfitted with well-equipped kitchens and good-size living rooms with sofa beds. There's no restaurant on the premises, but the deli on the ground floor has provisions for cooking simple meals in the rooms. ♦ 37-43 King St (at Kent St). 9267.9211; fax 9262.2023

63 King Street Curry House ★★$ Offering some of the best Malaysian curry in town, this restaurant gets busy as soon as it opens its doors. The beef *rendang* (stewed with coconut milk and spices), lamb curries, and curry puffs are all popular. There's no liquor license, so bring your own wine or beer. ♦ Malaysian ♦ M lunch; Tu-F lunch and dinner. Reservations recommended. 29 King St (between Kent and Sussex Sts). 9299.7049

DA ADOLFO
RISTORANTE ITALIANO

64 Da Adolfo Ristorante Italiano ★★★ $$$ The southern Italian cuisine at this split-level restaurant has become extremely popular with the business crowd that comes for long lunches. The white walls, polished floorboards, and airy space on both levels set the scene for an equally uncomplicated menu. Local seafood features heavily—try the simple but delicious *spaghetti alle vongole* (with clams, garlic, and olive oil), or any of the daily specials written on blackboards posted around the dining rooms. Most of the other pasta dishes are Neapolitan in style, served with lots of rich tomato sauce. The lemon cream tarts get top billing. Italian wines are the way to go here. ♦ Italian ♦ M-Th lunch; F lunch and dinner. Reservations recommended. 115 Clarence St (between King and Erskine Sts). 9262.4406

65 General Post Office Survey the architecture of this grand Victorian post office (more commonly referred to as the "GPO") and pick up some stamps and aerograms while you're at it. The massive structure was designed by colonial architect **James Barnet;** construction began in 1866 and was completed in 1885. The realistic statues, sculpted by Tomaso Sani, are portraits of famous Australians of the day. ♦ Martin Pl (between Pitt and George Sts)

Within General Post Office:

The Westin Sydney $$$$ Slated to open at press time, this new hotel has all the right ingredients for a luxury city property. It is built within a carefully restored landmark building; it has 417 rooms (most of which are in one of the two towers that rise above the heritage-listed **GPO**); and it provides business, conference, and health club facilities (including a lap pool), a massive ballroom, a dining room, restaurant court, two bars, and 24-hour room service. For luxury with a capital "L," opt for one of the 51 large suites (known as the **Heritage Deluxe** rooms), some with 15-foot ceilings, that have been incorporated into the 19th-century sandstone building. And for the business traveler, the **Westin Guest Office** rooms have a separate area devoted exclusively to technological equipment. ♦ 1 Martin Pl. 8223.1111, 800.228.3000; fax 8223.1222

66 Emporio Armani What is there left to say about Mr. Armani and his hugely successful label? This boutique features some of Giorgio's more casual styles. ♦ M-Sa. Challis House, 4 Martin Pl (between Pitt and George Sts). 9231.3655

Within Emporio Armani:

Emporio Armani Express ★$$ This chic cafe is just the place to sip a Campari and soda while you contemplate the new additions to your wardrobe (and your credit card bill.) The menu, like the clothes, is simple yet stylish— prosciutto with Jerusalem artichoke, for example—and Mr. Armani himself approves it. ♦ Italian ♦ M-Sa. 9231.3655

67 Australia Square Tower When this 50-story structure (pictured at right) was completed in 1968, it was Australia's tallest building, dominating the Sydney skyline at 600 feet. The skyline has changed remarkably since then, and the height of the tower has been eclipsed

Australia Square Tower

several times over, but it remains a significant architectural landmark. When construction began in 1964, architect **Harry Seidler** announced his aim to create a focal point for Sydney, and he surely succeeded. Apart from its distinctive circular shape, this was the city's first office block incorporating public space into the design. The site, including indoor and outdoor areas for sitting and strolling, covers 1.5 acres, a whole city block. The office space is dominated by banking, financial, legal, and multinational companies. There is also a retail section underneath the building. **The Summit** restaurant (9247.9777) on the 47th floor is the largest revolving restaurant in the world and goes around once every 90 minutes. (On clear days it's possible to see the Blue Mountains 50 miles away.) The building also features several world-class art works, including a sculpture by Alexander Calder, and works by Joan Miró, Calder, Le Corbusier, and Australian artist John Olsen. ♦ 264-78 George St (between Curtin Pl and Bond St)

68 All Seasons Premier Menzies Hotel $$$ Named after a former prime minister, "The Menzies," as it is usually called, has a warm old-English charm, even though it was built in the early 1960s. Comfortable leather chairs grace the lobby and the décor features lots of dark wood and granite throughout the hotel. The 440 rooms and suites are large and surprisingly quiet considering that the hotel is built right on top of **Wynyard Railway Station** and is in the middle of the CBD buzz. There are two restaurants and three bars including **Sporters Bar** with a huge cluster of television screens. ♦ 14 Carrington St (between Wynyard and Margaret Sts). 9299.1000, 800/448.8355; fax 9299.5238

69 York Apartment Hotel $$$$ This 28-floor building has 130 elegant apartments with views of the city and **Darling Harbour.** All apartments have large bathrooms, kitchens, and balconies. Daily maid service and room service are also available. ♦ 5 York St (at Jamison St). 9210.5000; fax 9290.1487

70 Brooklyn Hotel ★★$$ Steak house and pub dining is a culinary trend that few expected to return. Here the offerings are a little more exciting than steak and chips. The menu features many different meats, including beef, lamb, buffalo, and kangaroo. Choose your own cut and sauce. Vegetarians may choose from a few meatless offerings. This is a popular spot with the local stockbroker crowd. ♦ Steak house ♦ M-Th lunch and dinner; F lunch. George and Grosvenor Sts. 9247.6744

Bests

Ben Hartley
Director of Corporate Communications and Sponsorship, Solomon R. Guggenheim Museum

Walking across the **Harbour Bridge** from **Milsons Point** to the city. The view is better on the pedestrian side, but if you walk over on the bike side it leads to **Observatory Hill,** a perfect place for a picnic and a view of the harbor. If you think you deserve a fancy meal after the walk try **Bel Mondo** restaurant just off the pedestrian exit of the bridge.

Go to **Sydney Fish Markets,** buy a pound of prawns, a dozen oysters, and a bottle of chilled Australian white wine, then take it all outside to one of the picnic tables. Try a Balmain Bug, an oversized local shellfish that tastes something like lobster.

The **Art Gallery of New South Wales** and the **Museum of Contemporary Art** offer the best of Australian art and touring exhibitions. Visit the **Art Gallery of New South Wales** if only to look at works by Australian artist Brett Whitely.

The **Belvoir Street Theatre** is always doing something interesting. It also offers a good after-performance bar scene.

The **Sydney Theatre Company** at the **Wharf Theatre** also offers good quality acting, if slightly more mainstream, and one of the best harbor views in town. Make sure you leave enough time for a pre-theater glass of Champagne on the outside seats and a view of the ever-smiling **Luna Park.**

You can't beat **Bar Coluzzi** in **Darlinghurst** for coffee and a scene. Also great for coffee, the best lemon gelati in town, and the bohemian crowd, is **Bar Italia** in **Leichhardt.**

Skip the organized cruise boats, just take the ferries with the Sydneysiders. The **Manly, Neutral Bay,** and **Mosman** ferry runs offer great views.

Try some windsurfing at **Balmoral Beach.** After you're done, buy fish and chips takeout and eat them on the benches by the beach. If you're feeling like spending more time and money, go to the **Bather's Pavilion** restaurant on Balmoral Beach. Balmoral Beach also offers fairly tame Sunday night jazz and the occasional performance of Shakespeare in the **Balmoral Rotunda.**

Take the **Cliff Walk** from **Bondi Beach** to **Tamarama** and stop for fruit smoothies at the cafes behind the beach.

No sampling of Australian cuisine is complete without trying a meat pie. Pass on the nouveau combinations and go straight for the plain variety.

Go and check out the latest in Australian fashion at the upper floor of the **Strand Arcade.** Make sure to visit **Dinosaur Design** for chunky plastic resin jewelry. Makes for unique gifts for the folks back home.

Put on your most casually cool clothes and go for a nonchalant stroll down **Oxford Street** on a Saturday morning. **Paddington Bazaar** on Saturday morning is worth a visit if only to see the latest fashions being paraded by your fellow shoppers.

If you want to look "fair dinkum" on the beach be sure to check out **Mambo** and **Hot Tuna** surf shops for board shorts and other beachwear on Oxford Street.

The **Powerhouse Museum** is a much-overlooked gem. If life-size models of trains and planes are not your thing, there's also some great design and popular culture exhibitions.

Put on your grungiest, hipster clothes and strut down **King Street** in **Newtown.** Stop for a Turkish pastry and coffee at any of the little cafes. Make sure to sneer and wear dark glasses.

For value and ingenious ingredient combinations, Sydney has to offer some of the best restaurants in the world. Try **Rockpool, MG Garage, Cicada,** and **Sailor's Thai** for starters.

Go to **Watsons Bay** for a sunset beer in the garden of **Watsons Bay Hotel** with its spectacular views of the harbor. Finish up with a walk up the hill to look over the cliffs out to the blue Pacific Ocean.

For a great jogging route start at the **Art Gallery of New South Wales,** wind down to **The Royal Botanic Gardens,** back past **Mrs. Macquarie's Chair.**

Australians love gambling. To get in the action avoid the sad new casino and off-track betting parlors and go to **Royal Randwick Racecourse** for the horses.

Peter Standring
Broadcast Journalist/Travel Writer, WTNH-TV (ABC) in Connecticut

Body surfing and people watching at the one and only **Bondi Beach.**

Visiting all the funny-faced denizens of **Taronga Zoo.**

Shopping for odd bargains at the **Paddington Bazaar.**

Crawling from one pub to the next along **Oxford Street.**

Finding a shady spot for a picnic in **Centennial Park.**

Catching a game of Aussie rules football at the **Sydney Cricket Ground.**

Watching the ebb and flow of ferries at **Circular Quay.**

Temporarily overcoming my fear of heights to enjoy 360° views of the harbor from the **Centrepoint Tower.**

Contemplating life—and death—at **The Gap** (not the clothes store, mind you!).

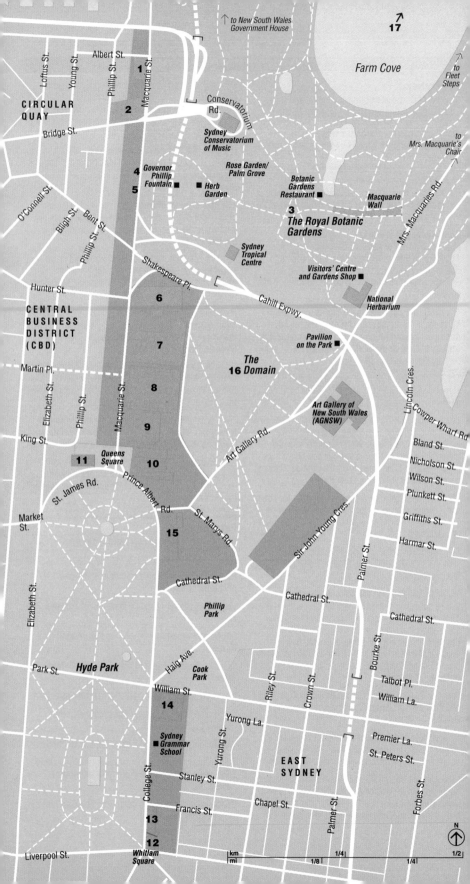

↑ to New South Wales
Government House

↗ 17

Farm Cove

↗ to Fleet Steps

Albert St.

Loftus St.

Young St.

Phillip St.

Macquarie St.

1

Conservatorium Rd.

CIRCULAR QUAY

2

Bridge St.

Sydney Conservatorium of Music

→ to Mrs. Macquarie's Chair

Governor Phillip Fountain ■

4

5

Rose Garden/ Palm Grove

Herb Garden ■

Botanic Gardens Restaurant ■

Macquarie Wall

Mrs. Macquaries Rd.

3

The Royal Botanic Gardens

O'Connell St.

Bligh St.

Bent St.

Phillip St.

Sydney Tropical Centre

Visitors' Centre and Gardens Shop ■

Hunter St.

Shakespeare Pl.

6

Cahill Expwy.

National Herbarium

CENTRAL BUSINESS DISTRICT (CBD)

7

Pavilion on the Park ■

Martin Pl.

Elizabeth St.

Phillip St.

Macquarie St.

8

The 16 Domain

Lincoln Cres.

Cowper Wharf Rd

King St.

9

Art Gallery of New South Wales (AGNSW)

Bland St.

Nicholson St.

11

Queens Square

10

Art Gallery Rd.

Wilson St.

Plunkett St.

St. James Rd.

Prince Albert Rd.

Griffiths St.

Market St.

15

St. Mary's Rd.

Sir John Young Cres.

Harmar St.

Elizabeth St.

Cathedral St.

Palmer St.

Cathedral St.

Phillip Park

Cathedral St.

Bourke St.

Cathedral St.

Hyde Park

Park St.

Haig Ave.

Cook Park

Riley St.

Crown St.

Talbot Pl.

William St.

William La.

14

William St.

Yurong La.

Premier La.

Sydney Grammar School ■

Yurong St.

St. Peters St.

EAST SYDNEY

Elizabeth St.

Stanley St.

Chapel St.

Palmer St.

Forbes St.

13

Francis St.

12

Whitlam Square

Liverpool St.

km
mi

1/8

1/4

1/4

1/2

N
↑

The Domain/The Royal Botanic Gardens

In the early 1800s Governor Lachlan Macquarie decided to leave untouched that green blanket of rolling parkland and vibrant gardens spreading out from the eastern border of today's Central Business District (CBD) and running down to the sparkling harbor at **Farm Cove.** Today this urban oasis, known as The Domain and **The Royal Botanic Gardens,** continues to be preserved as Macquarie intended. And thanks to the late–20th-century moves to maintain many of the buildings along **Macquarie Street,** it's easy to imagine the bygone years of Australia's refined Victorian era.

Stroll up Macquarie Street from **Sydney Harbour** and admire the elegant terrace homes built for the urban gentry that line the western side of the street. The view from these houses is of the beautifully kept 74-acre **Royal Botanic Gardens,** a living museum of exotic and indigenous plant life. Hidden behind these sculpted gardens is the Gothic-inspired **New South Wales Government House,** where the governor presided over the state until 1995. The governors clung to vestiges of Mother England throughout the 19th century, simulating and cultivating English gardens and society, and made this area of Sydney the most fashionable in the Southern Hemisphere at the time. And in the early 1900s medical professionals opened offices here, just down the street from **Sydney Hospital.** The strip still houses these practitioners.

At the southern end of **Macquarie Street** are the major public buildings built in the 19th century—**Parliament House, Sydney Hospital, Sydney Mint,** and **Hyde Park Barracks.** It is astounding how large these structures are, considering when they were constructed and how small the city was at the time. The huge **State Library of New South Wales,** which opened early in the 20th century and has had many additions since, is also here. It offers a labyrinth of research, archival, and exhibition facilities.

Farther afield on the edge of **Hyde Park,** but with a definitely separate feeling from the city, the country's foremost natural history museum, the **Australian Museum,** boldly sits overlooking both **Hyde Park** and the edge of **The Domain.** Across **Cook Park,** Australia's largest church, **St. Mary's Cathedral,** marks the entrance of the grassy **Domain**—the site of weekend preachers and poets and summer outdoor concerts. **The Domain,** developed as Governor Macquarie's private garden (or "domain"), is also now the home of the **Art Gallery of New South Wales.** The museum hosts major international art exhibitions and has a wing devoted exclusively to Aboriginal art. At the tip of **Farm Cove** at the end of **The Domain** is **Mrs. Macquarie's Chair,** arguably the city's best vantage point for views of Sydney and its harbor attractions. Thousands of visitors converge here daily for souvenir snapshots of the **Harbour Bridge, Opera House,** and **Fort Denison,** or just to inhale the sea breeze and marvel at it all.

---

1 The Ritz-Carlton Sydney $$$$

Nineteenth-century antiques, sparkling chandeliers, tons of beautiful marble, and an obliging staff make this 105-room hotel feel more like a luxurious club than a part of an international hotel chain. The sandstone and brick building that houses the hotel was constructed 1896-1898 as the headquarters of the New South Wales Board of Health. The Albert Street facade of the hotel still bears the metal plate depicting Hygeia, Greek mythology's goddess of health. The impeccable guest rooms are decorated with dark period pieces and Australian artwork. Simple elegance in the public rooms also reflects the hotel's attention to detail. Conveniently located just across from **The Royal Botanic Gardens,** the hostelry is also a relatively intimate place to stop for a post-opera drink or light meal at **The Bar.** The more formal **Dining Room** serves Modern Australian fare. It also offers a health spa, some meeting rooms, and business services. ♦ 93 Macquarie St (between Bridge and Albert Sts). 9252.4600, 800/241.3333; fax 9252.4286

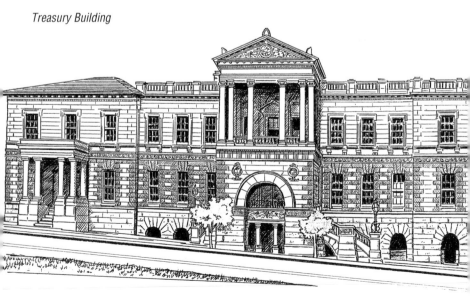

HOTEL INTER·CONTINENTAL

2 Hotel Inter-Continental $$$$ This luxury hotel's design is a tribute to honoring the past while realizing the needs of the present. The property incorporates the historic **Treasury Building** (pictured below) designed by **Mortimer Lewis,** and completed in 1851. After several additions and occupants, the New South Wales government sold the structure for redevelopment in 1982. In cooperation with Heritage New South Wales, **Kann Finch and Partners** designed a 28-story, 498-room addition to the old government building. The original sandstone facade is intact, along with interior sandstone and brick archways. The three-level, enclosed skylit lobby with exquisite white marble floors and colonial furniture is without a doubt one of Sydney's most elegant hotel lobbies. Two restaurants, two bars, and meeting rooms also occupy these floors, many of which are decorated with 19th-century furniture. The guest rooms, all in the modern tower, are simply decorated with Australian art and furnishings. Most overlook Sydney Harbour and **The Royal Botanic Gardens.** The hotel is conveniently located on the eastern edge of the CBD. ♦ 117 Macquarie St (at Bridge St). 9230.0200, 800/327.0200; fax 9240.1310

Within the Hotel Inter-Continental:

30 Something ★★$$$ The name of this restaurant has as much to do with its location on the 31st floor as with the age of its patrons. The food here is strictly wood-fired pizza and antipasto—with such exotic choices as Tandoori lamb pizza and Sydney rock lobster pizza. Formerly a formal piano bar, the place is now more relaxed and has a decent kitchen. The clientele is hip and happening, particularly on weeknights. The views of **The Royal Botanic Gardens** and the harbor make a stop here worthwhile. ♦ Modern Australian/ Pizza ♦ M-F lunch and dinner; Sa dinner. Reservations recommended. 31st floor. 9240.1275

3 The Royal Botanic Gardens This huge expanse of beautifully tended gardens on the eastern edge of the city runs right down to the harbor's edge at Farm Cove. Originally farmland for the first settlers, this area was later developed in 1816 into a living museum filled with plantings of Australian and exotic trees, shrubs, flowers, bird sanctuaries, fountains, and monuments. It is Australia's oldest scientific institution—there's a botany or biology lesson at every turn. All the plants are labeled, and the gardens and walkways are well signposted. Manicured stretches of shaded lawn make terrific picnic spots, while dozens of park benches are ideal reading and rest areas. This is also the place to enjoy some of the best views of the **Opera House** and the harbor. ♦ Daily 6:30AM-sunset. 9231.8111

Within The Royal Botanic Gardens:

Treasury Building

Sydney Conservatorium of Music

New South Wales Government House

Few buildings have sparked recent public debate as much as this structure, built 1837-1845 as the residence of the governor of New South Wales. It was home to a succession of these British governors until 1995 when the newly elected New South Wales Labor government made the controversial decision to eject the governor from the building and open it to the public on weekends. (The incumbent, Governor Gordon Deane, happily consented to the government decree and now carries out his duties from his home in suburban Sydney.) The decision was denounced by traditionalists and monarchists who considered the move a "change for change's sake" and a diluting of New South Wales's links with England. Others considered it a welcome departure from obsolete traditions.

Controversy aside, the building is well worth a visit, as it is the most sophisticated example of a Gothic Revival structure in New South Wales: It features a crenellated battlement, turrets, and detailed interiors. The building is surrounded by a stunning garden and lawn, and much of the grounds' 19th-century character remains.

The ground-floor state rooms include the dining, drawing, and ballrooms. These salons' outstanding collection of 19th- and 20th-century furnishings and decorations reflects both style changes over the years and the differing tastes of the governors and their wives. Following the English tradition, other ground-floor rooms display portraits of the governors and their coats of arms. The main hall features an impressive staircase leading to the private and guest apartments, which have been occupied by Queen Elizabeth II, members of her family, and other visiting heads of state. The building is still used by the governor for official receptions, dinners, and investitures. ♦ Free. Government House: F-Su 10AM-3PM. Garden: daily. Conservatorium Rd (just east of Cahill Expwy). 9931.5200

Sydney Conservatorium of Music

Just east of Macquarie Street is this white, fortress-style building (complete with turrets). Known to most locals as "the Con," the conservatory is Sydney's major music teaching center and was the training ground for some of Australia's leading singers and musicians.

The building (illustrated above) was originally constructed as a somewhat palatial compound for the governor's horses. It was designed by the famous pardoned convict architect **Francis Greenway**—who was sent to Australia from England in the early 1800s after he was found guilty of forgery—to accommodate 30 horses and an equal number of servants. Built under instruction from the then-governor, Lachlan Macquarie, the structure was completed in 1821. It soon became the object of criticism by those who said the governor had attended more to the comfort of his horses than to the well-being of most of his women convicts, who then had very unsatisfactory quarters in the western colonial settlement of Parramatta.

65

The stables were considered to be too big and too expensive for housing horses. But despite the reproofs, the structure housed horses until 1912, when it became a music conservatory.

In 1990 the conservatory became part of the **University of Sydney** as an academic college and was renamed the **Sydney Conservatorium of Music.** The **Henri Verbugghen Concert Hall** (named after the conservatory's first director) hosts free lunchtime concerts on Wednesday, and performances for a small fee at noontime on Friday. Occasional twilight productions are also offered for a small charge.
◆ Conservatorium Rd (just east of Macquarie St). Tickets: 9230.1222

Sydney Tropical Center

 Rose Garden The focal point of this elegant garden filled with dozens of varieties of roses is a sandstone and slate-roofed garden house that offers plenty of shade and seating. Some of the more unusual types include the orange Grey Chappel, named after one of Australia's most famous cricketers, and the thornless Banksia. No pesticides are used. Many of the benches have been dedicated to the memory of loved ones or come from community groups.

 Palm Grove Sydney's subtropical climate is ideal for this array of outdoor palms. The collection was started in 1862; today nearly 200 species flourish here.

Governor Phillip Fountain The Italian sculptor Achille Simonetti was commissioned to create this fountain to commemorate the Diamond Jubilee of Queen Victoria in 1896. The centerpiece is a statue of Governor Phillip, founder of the original colony.

Herb Garden In this garden, hundreds of herbs from around the world surround a flowing sensory fountain that begs to be touched and a traditional sundial. On a warm day the scent from these plants can be intoxicating.

One of the most disturbing events in Australian history occurred on 11 November 1974 when the Governor General (the Queen of England's representative) stood on the steps of Government House and announced the dismissal of Labor Prime Minister Gough Whitlam for allegedly trying to bankrupt the nation by engaging in dishonest business transactions. Even the most conservative monarchists were shocked at the queen's intervention.

Sydney Tropical Centre Two glass structures house tropical plants here—a pyramid contains native plants, while the arch-shaped building features exotic plants. ◆ Admission. Daily. 9231.8111

National Herbarium Plant specimens collected by the British First Fleet's botanist, Joseph Banks, and used to start these gardens, are displayed here, along with more than one million other plant samples. Botanists offer free identification of plants brought in by the public. ◆ M-F. 9231.8155

Macquarie Wall Only a small section of this early–19th-century wall, started in 1810 to protect the free settlers from the convicts, stands today.

BOTANIC GARDENS
R E S T A U R A N T

Botanic Gardens Restaurant ★★$$$
With its octagonal walls, steel-tube frame, vaulted skylight, and open windows, dining here feels more like eating at a garden pavilion than at a restaurant. Although the menu changes seasonally, the cuisine is normally influenced by North African and Middle Eastern flavors. It's a popular destination for tranquil business lunches. ◆ Modern Australian ◆ Daily lunch. Reservations recommended. 9241.2419

Sydney Harbour National Park

Hugging the foreshore of **Sydney Harbour, Sydney Harbour National Park** encompasses pockets of bushland, rugged sandstone cliffs, heath-covered headlands, secluded sandy beaches, and three small harbor islands. Hidden in the park's heaths and forests is a wealth of history, including ancient Aboriginal engravings, sandstone cottages, underground tunnels of the harbor's old forts, and the vaguely sinister disinfecting chambers of the old **Quarantine Station.** Wildlife abounds, especially water birds, and masses of brilliantly colored flowers are rampant in spring. Sunbathing and swimming are permitted at most beaches around the harbor (although it's debatable whether it is hygienic!), and there are netted (to prevent shark attacks) pools at many beaches, including **Nielsen Park** and **Shelly Beach.** Bushwalking trails feature spectacular views of the harbor at **North** and **South Heads, Blue Fish Point, Manly Scenic Walkway, Ashton Park, Gap Bluff,** and the **Hermitage Foreshore.**

The National Parks and Wildlife Service conducts "Bush Food" tours of **Bradleys Head** the second Sunday of the month at 1:30PM. During the two-hour tour, visitors discover how to make glue in the bush, and sample wattleseed biscuits, bush tomatoes, and lemon myrtle for a real "taste" of the bush. A four-hour guided walk around the **Manly Scenic Walkway** from **Spit Bridge** to **Manly** can be arranged in advance by calling 9977.6522. It offers spectacular views of Sydney Harbour, and a chance to view Aboriginal engravings and learn about the harbor's environment. A variety of tours of **Goat Island,** in the heart of the harbor off the shore of **Balmain** are also offered by the National Park Service. The island was the site of many historical moments. It was originally where the Gunpowder Magazine Complex (built by 200 convicts between 1833 and 1839) was located. The island became a quarantine zone for investigating the bubonic plague outbreak in 1900, and was used as a depot for the Port of Sydney in the 1920s. A tour to Goat Island is conducted Saturday 11AM-1PM and Sunday 11:30AM-1:30PM. It starts from the **Sydney Harbour National Park Information Centre, Cadman's Cottage.** For information about the walks, tours, Aboriginal culture, the **Quarantine Station,** or general information on **Sydney Harbour National Park,** call the **National Parks and Wildlife Service** (9247.5033).

Cliffs at North Head

KEELY EDWARDS

Visitors' Centre and Gardens Shop This shop offers what many consider to be the country's best selection of horticultural and botanical literature. Free, guided walks of the gardens leave from here daily at 10:30AM. ◆ Daily. 9231.8125

Fleet Steps Many wedding photos are shot on these sandstone stairs, with the picturesque backdrop of the harbor and **Opera House.** Ships used to dock here in the late 18th century. ◆ Mrs. Macquaries Rd (off Art Gallery Rd)

In 1880, the Garden Palace was built in the Botanic Gardens for the first international exposition held in the Southern Hemisphere. Tragically, this enormous, rambling structure was destroyed by fire in 1882.

4 Historic House This five-floor Victorian town house (illustrated below)—now the offices of the Royal Australian Historical Society—was built in 1856 for Dr. William Bland. It was sold soon thereafter, and over the next hundred years was everything from a parliamentarian's home to a gentlemen's club to a boarding house to doctors' offices. In 1952, a group of doctors purchased the property and named it **Wickham House.** But in 1968 it was again up for sale and under threat of being demolished. The Historical Society stepped in and bought it, and restored the building to its former grandeur. Today the edifice is filled with historic archives and research facilities, and is a venue for small functions. ♦ 133 Macquarie St (between Bent and Bridge Sts). 9247.8001

5 Royal Australian College of Physicians These two Macquarie Street buildings date back to the mid-1800s and are fine examples of Victorian town houses. The Royal Australian College of Physicians (RACP) purchased **No. 145** in 1937 after a long tenure as a gentlemen's club. Prior to that, it was the home of John Fairfax from the famous Sydney newspaper family. In 1959, the RACP bought **No. 147** from the Maitland family, and leased it until 1994 when the two buildings were renovated and joined by internal access. The building is not open to the public. ♦ 145-47 Macquarie St (between Bent and Bridge Sts)

6 State Library of New South Wales/ Mitchell Library Located next to the **Parliament House** (see below), these libraries are a testament to the determination of a group of 19th-century academics who wanted to have a grand building to house the state's growing collection of books. The concept can be traced back to 1826 when a group of 10 men started the **Australian Subscription Library and Reading Room.** The library moved many times and suffered repeated financial problems through to the 1890s, when David Scott Mitchell made an offer the government couldn't refuse. Mitchell, who had devoted 30 years to amassing the finest collection of Australasian material in the world, promised to hand over his treasures if the government erected a suitable building for a national library and made provision for keeping his collection separate. After many years of planning, the **Mitchell Library** finally opened in 1910. The **Dixson Gallery**—named after Sir William Dixson, who bequeathed his vast collection of books, manuscripts, and pictures to the library—was added in 1959.

A new general reference library wing (the **State Library**) was added on in 1988. This structure houses close to two million books and thousands of reels of microfilm, manuscripts, pictures, maps, and other documentary materials. The **Mitchell Library** now holds Australian research collections. Galleries in the **State Library** contain temporary exhibitions covering all aspects of Australian cultural history. The building itself is interesting, especially the foyer, which features an intricate terrazzo design of the world. The shop stocks the latest Australian literature and the **Glasshouse Cafe** offers light meals. ♦ Free. M-F 9AM-9PM; Sa-Su 11AM-5PM. Tours: Tu, Th 11AM, 2PM. Macquarie St and Shakespeare Pl. 9273.1414

Historic House

ANTHONY HARVEY

7 Parliament House When the New South Wales Legislative Council was formed in 1824, it held its first meetings in whatever place was available in the then-small town that boasted few government buildings. The council started convening in one of the rooms in **Sydney General Hospital's Surgeons' Wing** in 1829. Fourteen years later, the number of members was increased to 36, and a new meeting chamber was added to the northern end of the **Surgeons' Wing.** In 1879 the main building of **Sydney General Hospital** was demolished and replaced, but the old surgeons' wing stayed—reincarnated as the official central building of the Parliament. This original chamber became the home of the Legislative Assembly, established in 1856 when New South Wales gained responsible government. A second chamber was added for the Legislative Council. Like the Legislative Assembly chamber, the Legislative Council building was a prefabricated, cast-iron building originally sent from England to Melbourne for use on Victorian gold fields. The color schemes used for the Legislative Council (red) and Legislative Assembly (green) are derived from traditions inherited from the English Westminster system. The building also accommodates administrative offices and facilities for the 141 state ministers and their staff. It is one of the oldest surviving examples of Sydney's Early Colonial architecture. Visitors can observe the proceedings in the public galleries when the legislature is in session. One-hour tours of both the Legislative Council and the Legislative Assembly are given. ♦ Public areas: M-F. Tours M-F 10AM, 11AM, 2PM. Tour reservations required. Macquarie St (between Queens Sq and Shakespeare Pl). 9230.2111

8 Sydney Hospital There were no funds available to construct this much-needed hospital in 1811, so builders Blaxcell and Riley were paid with a three-year/45,000-gallon monopoly on the import of rum to the colony. Not surprisingly, the hospital became known as the "Rum Hospital." It originally had three two-story blocks comprising a main central building and two wings. But the builders must have been more concerned with their rum importation affairs than their construction business; in 1815 the colonial architect, **Francis Greenway,** issued a scathing report on the building's structure. Despite costly alterations to remedy its faulty construction, concerns remained, and in 1879, the long central block was demolished and replaced in

1894 by the present Victorian Classical Revival buildings designed by **Thomas Rowe.** The two outer wings of the original hospital were in a better condition and left as they were; today the **Sydney Mint Museum** and the **New South Wales Parliament House** are housed here.

Nurse training in Australia began here in 1868 when Florence Nightingale sent Lucy Osburn and five other English sisters to the colony. The brick and sandstone Gothic Revival **Nightingale Wing** of 1869, with its colorful fountain, was built according to Florence Nightingale's plans to house Sydney's first nursing school. One of the hospital's most interesting features is the bronze boar at the front of the building, near the Macquarie Street entrance, that was donated by an Italian family in 1968. *Il Porcellino* is a copy of the statue in Florence's Mercato Nuovo, and is supposed to bring good luck to those who rub its snout. Money thrown in the small pool near *Il Porcellino*'s trotters is used for the hospital. ♦ 8 Macquarie St (between Queens Sq and Shakespeare Pl). 9382.7111

9 Sydney Mint Museum This sprawling colonial building showcases a spectacular collection of gold coins, and gold and silver treasures from the past. Operated by the **Powerhouse Museum** (see page 84), this historic site, which dates back to 1816, tells the story of money and how the discovery of gold affected an emerging Australian society and changed it forever. One of the museum's highlights is a display of authentic and unique objects from early colonial Australia, including exquisite gold jewelry, mounted emu eggs, presentation cups, trophies and inkstands made of finely sculpted silver and gold—all crafted by Australian designers.

Another of the museum's features is the restored coining factory. Here visitors can mint their own souvenir coin, try to crack the combination lock of a safe, or use a touch-screen computer to explore the hidden architecture of this heritage building. ♦ Admission. Daily. Macquarie St (between Queens Sq and Shakespeare Pl). 9217.0311

10 Hyde Park Barracks Museum Erected 1817-1819 by convict workers, this elegant Georgian structure is part of the earliest group of public buildings to survive in Australia. It is one of the finest works of the accomplished convict architect **Francis Greenway** who designed this building, **St. James Church,** and the **Old Supreme Court** to be on a straight axis in the historic Macquarie Street precinct.

The barracks were originally created and built to provide accommodations for 600 convict men. It later became the **Immigration Women's Depot and Asylum;** and subsequently housed coroners, bankruptcy and industrial arbitration courts, and government offices. Today it is a museum displaying fragmentary evidence of the thousands of men and women who lived and worked there during the past 175 years. The lives of the convicts and orphans, the inmates and immigrants, and the judges and clerks are all brought to life through a combination of exhibitions and innovative soundscapes. Relics from the past, including aprons, pens, pipes, bones, and sewing materials uncovered from under the floorboards and in rats' nests, make up one of the exhibits. The life of the convict worker figures prominently in the museum's displays. Of equal import is a focus on the plight of the women who passed through here when it was an immigration depot. The museum also houses the **Greenway Gallery,** a modern gallery with changing exhibitions about history and culture. ♦ Admission. Daily. Queen's Sq (between Prince Albert Rd and Macquarie St). 9223.8922

Within Hyde Park Barracks:

The Barracks Cafe ★★$$ The wonderful ambience of this dining spot owes much to the contrast between the historic building that houses it and the modern decor and Mediterranean cuisine. Sit inside under cathedral-like ceilings or outdoors in the courtyard shaded by the barracks and market umbrellas. Soups of the day are always well prepared and the salads are more than a meal. The cheese plate with dates and walnut bread is a great way to finish a meal or to have with a pot of tea as an afternoon snack. With the courts nearby in Queens Square, this is a very popular lunch spot for the local legal community. There's a simple brunch menu on weekends. ♦ Modern Australian ♦ Daily. 9223.1155

11 St. James Church Built in 1824, this church is the oldest ecclesiastical edifice in Sydney. Governor Macquarie originally designated the site as a courthouse and the foundation stone was laid on 7 October 1819.

But the governor's plans for civic improvement were altered on the insistence of Commissioner Bigge, who had been sent by the British government to New South Wales to report on the workings of the convict system. Bigge ordered the building of a church (no major place of worship existed in the city) dedicated to St. James. **Francis Greenway** designed it, and Reverend Samuel Marsden consecrated the structure in February 1824. Extensive renovations and restoration projects have taken place since then, many of them around 1900. The majority of the stained-glass windows were manufactured in England in the 20th century. ♦ 173 King St (at Queens Sq). 9232.3022

12 Hyde Park Plaza Hotel $$$ The view of **Hyde Park,** close proximity to Oxford Street, and free parking are the draws at this relatively plain-looking, but affordable, hotel. Each of the 182 rooms has kitchen facilities, ironing boards, and other items useful for long-term guests. Two- and three-bedroom suites make this place ideal for families. A restaurant, bar, and room service provide refreshments. There are business facilities on the premises. The rooftop pool has views of **Hyde Park** and the Central Business District. ♦ 38 College St (between Whitlam Sq and Francis St). 9331.6933; fax 9331.6022

13 Sydney Marriot Hotel $$$ This 241-room (including 14 suites) hotel overlooking **Hyde Park** is on the fringe of hip and happening Oxford Street and also near restaurant- and cafe-filled Stanley Street. All the guest rooms are decorated in warm colors and have microwaves and refrigerators. The suites also have Jacuzzis and fax machines. Two restaurants, a bar, a business center, meeting facilities for 400, a pool with a view of the CBC, and a better-than-average gym are additional lures. ♦ 36 College St (between Whitlam Sq and Francis St). 9361.8400, 800/228.9290; fax 9361.8484

AUSTRALIAN MUSEUM

14 Australian Museum Botanists in the early colony of New South Wales were fascinated with the unknown species they discovered in the "new land," and voraciously collected, bottled, and documented their samples.

Hence the beginnings of taxonomy (classification of species) in Australia and the humble start of this museum, Australia's oldest. It was established in 1827, and today is one of the world's top five natural history museums. Its research scientists are considered to be at the forefront of biological and environmental sciences, archaeology, zoology, and anthropology.

Walking through the museum is like taking a journey through the social and natural history of Australia. While taxonomy is still practiced, the focus here is on contemporary exhibitions, social and environmental history, and "hands-on" experiences. It's a blend of the ancient and modern worlds—where fossils meet touch-screen computers, and dinosaur skeletons co-exist with CD-ROMs. The museum also actively promotes awareness and understanding of Aboriginal culture, and in 1997 installed *Indigenous Australians—Australia's First Peoples,* a permanent exhibition that offers insight into the contemporary culture, art, and spirituality of Australia's indigenous people. Another new addition is the *Albert Chapman Mineral Collection,* showcasing one of Australia's most stunning and historically important mineral collections. Other popular stops include the **Skeleton Room;** the *Planet of the Minerals,* and the birds and insects gallery. Dinosaur lovers shouldn't miss the *More Than Dinosaurs—Evolution of Life* exhibit. The museum's investigation center, **Search and Discover,** is equipped with CD-ROMs, computer data bases, the latest science journals and books, and a scientific staff ready to answer questions. Live theater lends a dramatic interpretation to the museum's exhibitions. A cafe serves basic fare. The shop features a huge selection of natural history books, authentic Aboriginal artifacts, jewelry, gifts, and cards. ♦ Admission. Daily. 6 College St (at William St). 9320.6000

15 St. Mary's Cathedral The first officially appointed Catholic chaplains to the colony of New South Wales were Fathers John Therry and Philip Conolly. Soon after their arrival in May 1820 the priests held a public meeting to raise funds to build a cathedral. But with half the Catholic population consisting of convicts, and the rest ticket-of-leave men (paroled prisoners), most of the gifts were small. **Francis Greenway,** the colony's most renowned architect, was initially asked to prepare the plans, but his design was rejected because he suggested a simple, inexpensive building. Father Therry had more ambitious ideas and the majority of Catholics—the colony's poorest community—agreed. They wanted a splendid symbol to demonstrate they were as good as their "betters."

The land Governor Macquarie allotted for the church was in an undesirable area near the convict barracks; ironically, the neighborhood later became one of Sydney's most sought-after locations. Macquarie laid the foundation stone on 29 October 1821 (the event is commemorated in one of the church's stained-glass windows), and the medieval-style building was completed in 1833. The church was elevated to cathedral status in 1835.

Thirty years later a fire completely destroyed the building and architect **William Wardell** was invited to design a new grand cathedral; work commenced on a Gothic-style structure in 1866. It opened in 1900, although work continued on it to 1928. The building (pictured below) is still not completely finished—spires were never added because of cost. At press time, plans were underway to finish the chuch and append the spires. Inside the cathedral is pure Gothic, with pointed arches, flying buttresses, and ribbed vaults. ♦ Cathedral and College Sts. 9220.0400

ANTHONY HARVEY

St. Mary's Cathedral

16 **The Domain** 1810 was a popular year for Governor Macquarie and his plans to introduce European-style parkland to fledgling Sydney. Apart from establishing **The Royal Botanic Gardens** and **Hyde Park,** Macquarie decided that he needed his own green "domain" for walks and entertaining. Today this vast space, stretching from **Mrs. Macquarie's Chair** past the **Art Gallery of New South Wales (AGNSW)** to **St. Mary's Cathedral,** is still a popular venue for soap-box philosophers in need of an audience, and the site of open-air free concerts in the summer months. It's also a terrific picnic spot—ignore the Cahill Expressway, which runs through it next to **AGNSW**—filled with a grand-old gum and Morton Bay fig trees.

Within The Domain:

THE ART GALLERY of NEW SOUTH WALES

Art Gallery of New South Wales (AGNSW)
This fine arts museum is located in a magnificent sandstone building. Established in 1874, it houses the nation's most comprehensive Australian art collection and an extensive selection of international art. The *Australian Art* permanent exhibit features sculpture and paintings from the early colonial period to the mid-20th century. The **Yiribana Gallery** boasts Australia's most comprehensive permanent exhibition of Aboriginal and Torres Strait Islander art. Other displays include an extensive collection of contemporary works by Australian and international artists, extending from the 1960s to the present, and an impressive selection of watercolors, prints, and drawings from Australia, Europe, and the US. The *Asian Art* exhibit showcases works from China, Korea, Japan, India, and Southeast Asia from prehistoric to modern times. The **James Fairfax Galleries** of Old Masters, adjoining the Victorian and Edwardian collections, feature European art from the 15th century to the end of the 18th century. French Impressionist and 20th-century British and European works (to about 1960) present the impact of modernism. Items from the gallery's collection of Melanesian art are on display next to the library. The photo collection includes works from the birth of photography to the present. Guided tours are available regularly throughout the day. The gift shop offers one of the most comprehensive ranges of art books in Australia, as well as souvenirs, posters, cards, and gifts. ◆ Free. Fee for major exhibitions. Daily. Art Gallery Rd (between Prince Albert and Mrs. Macquaries Rds). 9225 1744

Within the Art Gallery of New South Wales:

The Restaurant ★$$$ Perfect for the exhibitionist in everyone, diners feel on display in this minimal setting perched above the museum's foyer. The menu is simple, featuring grilled swordfish and tuna, some standard Australian desserts—pavlova (meringue and fruit) and sticky date pudding—and cappuccino. Be forewarned: The service is not quite as generous as the portions of food. ◆ Continental ◆ Daily lunch. Reservations recommended. First floor. 9232.5425

PAVILION

on the park

Pavilion on the Park ★★$$$ The Royal Botanic Gardens and Domain Trust supervised the renovation of this restaurant and cafe complex that sits opposite the **Art Gallery of New South Wales (AGNSW).** The restaurant is the best attraction, with the light and airy space featuring floor-to-ceiling glass windows that look out on **The Domain.** Such Mediterranean offerings as braised octopus with caponata, and hummus and pine nut salad are real treats, and the wine list is above average. The steak sandwich in the more low-key, less expensive cafe is well worth trying. ◆ Modern Australian ◆ Restaurant: M-F, Su lunch. Cafe: daily lunch and late-afternoon tea. Reservations recommended for restaurant. 1 Art Gallery Rd (between Prince Albert and Mrs. Macquaries Rds). 9232.1322

Mrs. Macquarie's Chair Be prepared for the constant sound of clicking camera shutters at this popular spot that boasts some of the best views of the harbor, **Opera House,** Harbour Bridge, and the headlands. The "chair" is actually a cut sandstone ledge that forms a firm bench. It gets its name from Governor Macquarie's wife, who considered this site on the eastern tip of Farm Cove to be one of the colony's most favorable vantage points. ◆ Mrs. Macquaries Rd (off Art Gallery Rd)

17 **Fort Denison** Perched on a small island in the middle of Sydney Harbour, this fort can be seen from almost any point along the harbor's foreshore. Come here for no other reason than because it's yet another place for superb photo opportunities, with fantastic views of Sydney Harbour.

The island was once a 25-meter-high (82-foot) rocky outcrop known to the local indigenous people as **Mattewai,** meaning "touch the sky." Soon after the arrival of the First Fleet in 1788, a convict was confined here for a week as punishment for taking biscuits from a fellow prisoner. The island was sometimes used to incarcerate people over the next eight years. It was nicknamed "Pinchgut Island," which referred to the meager rations that convicts received and to the nautical term describing the island's position in the harbor channel. The shark-infested waters were a sure bet to discourage any escape attempts by prisoners. In 1796, New South Wales's governor left a sobering warning for the colony by displaying an executed murderer, Francis Morgan, in gibbets from the highest point of the island.

The inadequacy of Sydney's defenses became apparent in 1839 after two American sloops and five warships entered Sydney Harbour unnoticed. The governor immediately ordered that convict labor be used to transform the island from a penal colony into a level gun battery.

The battery was completed by 1842 and remained unchanged for the next 14 years. After the outbreak of the Crimean War in 1856, and the potential threat from France and the United States, the government decided to strengthen the harbor's defense system and construct a fort here. Contract labor was used to move 8,000 tons of sandstone needed to build **Martello Tower,** a new gun battery, and barracks. All the work was completed one year later. The tower—a popular feature of early–19th-century European fortifications—was the last of its kind to be built in the world and is the only one in Australia.

The island was renamed **Fort Denison** in 1857 and outfitted for battle with cannons, a water tank, and thick stone walls. In the 1880s, with the introduction of improved weapons, the development of iron-clad warships, and the concentration of the Outer Harbour Defence Strategy, the fort was abandoned as a military installation.

In 1906, the "One O'Clock Gun" was transferred from Dawes Point to the fort to protect seagoing vessels that used the harbor. The gun was fired daily so sailors could set their ship's chronometers correctly. This practice ceased during World War II so as not to alarm residents; it was resumed in 1986 and continues to the present day. True to its name, the firing of the gun can be heard by visitors every day at 1PM.

Sydney's tide levels are also recorded here— a role the fort's staff has performed for almost 140 years—providing essential information for predicting future tide movements. ◆ Admission. Tours: daily at 10AM, noon, and 2PM. 9247.5033

The Sporting Life

With a warm and sunny climate, glorious beaches, an abundance of wide-open spaces, and a natural taste for the great outdoors, it's hardly surprising that Sydneysiders are sports lovers. And the city can easily cater to their needs, with surfing, swimming, basketball, tennis, sailing, riding, football, cricket, golf, and gyms in abundance at venues throughout Sydney. Below is a list of places where you can be a spectator or participate.

Centennial Park The city center's largest expanse of greenery, this park built in 1888 for Australia's centenary year is a perfect place for all of the outdoor sports. Cycling, horseback riding, jogging, walking, and in-line skating are all suited to this vast space. Nearby facilities have horses, in-line skates, and bicycles for rent. ◆ Oxford St (between York Rd and Centennial Sq)

Moore Park Golf Club This easily accessible golf club offers an 18-hole course, a day and night driving range, and all the standard equipment for very reasonable rates. ◆ Cleveland St (between Anzac Parade and S Dowling St). 9663.1064

North Sydney Olympic Pool Open-air in summer, covered by a "bubble" in the cooler months, this harborside pool has views of the **Harbour Bridge** and **Opera House.** ◆ Alfred St S and Northcliff St, Milsons Point. 9955.2309

Royal Randwick Racecourse There are over 50 horse meetings annually at this famous **Eastern Suburbs** track, including the famous Golden Slipper—Australia's richest horse race. And in true Sydney tradition, dress is fancy or casual. ◆ Alison Rd (between Wansey Rd and Doncaster Ave), Randwick. 9663.8425

Sydney Cricket Ground (SCG)/Football Stadium The legendary **SCG** is the home of Australian cricket. Test matches, or the more fast-moving one-day internationals under lights, are played in summer. In the winter months watch Sydney's Aussie Rules (football) team, the **Swans,** take the field at the adjacent stadium. This is becoming an increasingly popular event for Sydneysiders. Stop in the cricket museum or take a tour of the football grounds. ◆ Driver Ave (between Lang and Moore Park Rds). 9360.6601

ILLUSTRATIONS BY KEELY EDWARDS

Chinatown/ Darling Harbour

Chinatown and Darling Harbour, located side by side on the western fringe of the **Central Business District (CBD)**, seem like unlikely neighbors. Chinatown has had a long run, at a frantic pace, as a center of retail and culinary activity. Darling Harbour is newer and shinier—a pristine urban redevelopment area of exhibition centers and waterside tourist attractions. Identical they're not— but these two neighborhoods complement each other beautifully.

Chinatown (sometimes referred to as "The Haymarket") remains the hub of Sydney's Asian culture. Although many of the city's Asian residents now live in the North Shore and Western Suburbs, they still come to Chinatown—and for good reason. Restaurants along **Dixon, Sussex,** and **Hay Streets** serve the best shark's fin soup outside of Hong Kong; specialty supermarkets carry the freshest and most exotic Asian foodstuffs; Chinese herbalists mix vials of traditional natural remedies; and the bargain shopping for jewelry and trendy clothing can't be beat.

Chinese immigrants began arriving in New South Wales in the mid-1800s—the gold rush. During the next hundred years, Sydney's Asian population grew slowly and steadily. Then in the late 1980s and early 1990s, Australia experienced another big wave of Asian immigration. No longer the exclusive domain of the Chinese, Chinatown's shops and restaurants now reflect the tastes of their Vietnamese, Malaysian, Thai, Korean, and Japanese owners. Singaporean-style shopping malls line Sussex and Hay Streets, competing with old indoor marketplaces like **Paddy's Markets;** sushi bars jostle for space with noodle shops and fast-food franchises.

But some things endure. The chefs at the **Golden Century** and **Regal**

CENTRAL
BUSINESS
DISTRICT
(CBD)

Darling
Harbour

Casino

34

33

Pyrmont Bay

32

Pyrmont Bridge
(pedestrians only)

30

Darling Park

29

Market St.

Harbourside

31

Cockle
Bay

35

37

36

Convention
Square

38

Convention

42

26

Druitt St.

Park Plaza

Park St.

Bathurst St.

City
Centre

Day St.

28

27

25

1

Tumbalong
Park

24

Chinese
Garden

Liverpool St.

2

3

4

5

6 7

World Square

Goulburn St.

38

Pier St.

23

Little Pier St.

23

22

21

9

8

CHINATOWN

Little Hay St.

39

Haymarket

Haymarket

10

11

Hay St.

20

Campbell St.

14

12 13

Capitol
Square

Parker St.

Belmore
Park

Eddy Ave.

15

Central
Railway
Station

ULTIMO

40

41

19

18

17

16

CHIPPENDALE

Wentworth
Park

Fig St.

Exhibition
Centre

Western Distributor

Darling Dr.

Broadway

Lake
Northam

km   1/2   1

mi   1/2

N

prepare traditional Cantonese-style dishes with some of Australia's finest, freshest seafood. And at **East Ocean** and **Silver Spring**, *yum cha* (also known as dim sum, or simply brunch) is a chaotic and theatrical dining experience.

East meets west—literally and figuratively—down the hill toward **Harbour Street.** After the ornate streets of Chinatown, the massive concrete-and-glass **Sydney Entertainment Centre** comes as a bit of a culture shock. But just behind it, the lovely **Chinese Garden** in **Tumbalong Park** creates a visual link between traditional Chinatown and modern Darling Harbour.

Formerly known as **Cockle Bay**, Darling Harbour was named after Ralph Darling, seventh governor of New South Wales. This inlet was the center of Sydney's maritime industry, but by the 1960s the area had fallen into disrepair. The redevelopment of dilapidated docks and rail yards was completed in 1988. Now a commercial and recreational center with a nautical theme, Darling Harbour today attracts over 14 million visitors a year. Most of this area is closed to cars, and people are ferried around by the **TNT Monorail.**

Darling Harbour makes the most of its maritime past. The buildings, including the giant 200-store **Harbourside Festival Marketplace** and the grand **Novotel** and **Hotel Nikko** have sail-like canopies or arched roofing and lots of glass, giving views of the cove with its tall ships and cruise boats. Families come here to enjoy the outdoor performers, view the latest film at the **Panasonic IMAX Theatre,** marvel at the sharks and seals at the **Sydney Aquarium,** or walk across the pedestrian bridge to board the historic ships at the **National Maritime Museum** in **Pyrmont.**

Pyrmont, west of the bay, once was a busy commercial waterfront district. Now it's home to the **Sydney Convention and Exhibition Centre**, the quirky **Harris Street Motor Museum**, and Sydney's only casino, **Star City.** To the south is **Ultimo**, where an old power station has been converted to the **Powerhouse Museum,** with science, decorative arts, and social history exhibits.

A little farther west, on the shores of **Blackwattle Bay**, are the **Sydney Fish Markets.** The markets are a sight and smell to behold, especially at dawn when the catch of the day is being auctioned off to restaurants and seafood retailers. This area from Chinatown to Darling Harbour and beyond is generally a mob scene on weekends, but it's well worth braving the crush to sample its many attractions. Besides, the people watching is fun, too.

Harbourside Festival Marketplace

1 Marigold ★★$$ This restaurant on the outskirts of Chinatown was one of the first to introduce the concept of *yum cha* to Sydneysiders. Decorated with typical dragon motifs, the two-story, bustling eatery is well staffed, with fast and efficient service. It's popular for business lunches and weekend dinners, as well as for its banquet menus, which offer seemingly endless courses at modest prices. ♦ Chinese ♦ Daily lunch and dinner. 299-305 Sussex St (between Liverpool and Bathurst Sts). 9264.6744

2 Radisson Hotel and Suites $$$ This new 102-room property is relatively small for this leading hotel chain that tends to think big and generic is the way to go. In true cookie-cutter fashion, the rooms, though pleasant, are decorated in regulation pastels and light woods; but the real charm of this property is its terrific complimentary health spa which features an indoor swimming pool, gym, and sauna. Also on premises are conference facilities, plus a decent restaurant, **One on 1**, which incorporates a brasserie, a bar, and a small function center. Breakfast is complimentary and room service is available. ♦ 72 Liverpool St (between Kent and Sussex Sts). 9283.8707, 800/333.3333; fax 9268.8889

3 Waldorf Apartment Hotel $$$ Travelers who are planning an extended visit to the city will want to investigate this all-suite hotel. There are 70 large one- and two-bedroom apartments, with fully equipped kitchens, hairdryers and irons, and televisions and stereos. The decor runs toward generic dorm, but things are clean and well-maintained. Bonus: Most suites have nice views of the city. Although there's no restaurant, breakfast is available. ♦ 57 Liverpool St (between George and Sussex Sts). 9261.5355; fax 9261.3753

4 Regal ★★★$$ A favorite with the local Chinese community for both small dinners and large functions, this elegant restaurant is renowned for its prix-fixe banquets, which have at least six different dishes. (The à la carte menu is fine as well.) Seafood is the main attraction, but the roasted duck and chicken also earn raves. ♦ Chinese ♦ Daily brunch, lunch, and dinner. 347 Sussex St (between Goulburn and Liverpool Sts). 9261.8988

5 Kippo Hair Studio This hip hair salon caters to the Chinese community as well as others in need of a contemporary new do. If there isn't a line, you can be in and out in less than 20

minutes, and prices are very reasonable. ♦ M-Sa. 368 Sussex St (between Goulburn and Liverpool Sts), Shop 6. 9264.3639

6 The Changing Room Stocked with clothes from Gaultier to Catherine Hamnett, this trendy boutique is the place to buy cutting-edge women's fashions. If the clothing isn't enough to complete your look, pop into the well-run, in-house salon for a makeover. ♦ Daily 10:45AM-7:30PM. 16 Goulburn St (at Sussex St). 9267.5688

6 BBQ King ★★$ Sydney's food gurus would like to keep this spot to themselves. Food writers and local chefs come here on their night off or at the end of a long shift (the kitchen is open until 2AM). They definitely don't come for the decor—the lure is the menu, with suckling pig, chili prawns, and crisp roasted duck. Barbecuing is what they do best, so skip the westernized offerings like sweet-and-sour pork. ♦ Chinese ♦ Daily lunch and dinner. 18-20 Goulburn St (between George and Sussex Sts). 9267.2433

7 Morning Glory Visit this little store to pick up kitschy souvenirs, all Korean imports. Most of the T-shirts, tote bags, key chains, and the like are brightly colored and emblazoned with cute messages and popular Asian cartoon characters. ♦ Daily. 22 Goulburn St (between George and Sussex Sts). 9267.7899

8 Golden Century ★★★$$ At the entrance of this popular restaurant is a long, clean fish tank, full of healthy local fish, abalone, and lobsters. Nearby, patrons are greeted graciously by smiling staff. But the service is not speedy, so relax and order a crisp Australian white wine from the well-chosen wine list to sip while you wait. Seafood is the star of the menu. Try lobster with ginger and scallions, deep-fried chili abalone, or steamed Red Emperor—a local, meaty white fish. ♦ Chinese/Seafood ♦ Daily lunch and dinner. Reservations recommended. 393-99 Sussex St (between Little Hay and Goulburn Sts). 9212.3901

8 Thai-Kee Supermarket For amateur and professional cooks, this is the place to shop for the ingredients necessary for Chinese, Thai, Malaysian, or Vietnamese dishes. The exotic fresh fruits, vegetables, and meats are complemented by many varieties of rice, chili sauces and pastes, and hard-to-find herbs and spices. Look for the larger, newer version of this market at **Paddy's Markets** (see page 80). ◆ Daily. 393 Sussex St (between Little Hay and Goulburn Sts). 9281.2202

9 Golden Harbour ★★$$ Big and bustling, this Cantonese restaurant makes the most of Sydney's sensational seafood. Much of the fish goes directly from their fish tanks to the kitchen. Try the deep-fried king prawns with garlic, and the mud crab hot pot, an Asian-style stew. *Yum cha* is available all week, but on Saturday and Sunday the line of hungry patrons starts spilling into the street around noon. ◆ Chinese ◆ M-F lunch and dinner; Sa-Su breakfast, lunch, and dinner until 1AM. 31-33 Dixon St (between Little Hay and Goulburn Sts). 9211.5160

10 Hingara Chinese Restaurant ★★$ Don't be put off by the lackluster decor. This is one of the best choices in the area for a quick, hearty feed. Turn straight to the back of the menu for the house specials. One excellent option is the popular *jup wei won ton mien* (noodle soup with fat wonton and thin lo mein noodles). Order a dish by its Cantonese name, and the staff will remember you forever. ◆ Chinese ◆ Daily lunch and dinner. 82 Dixon St (between Hay and Little Hay Sts). 9212.2169

10 East Ocean ★★★$$ Although this Hong Kong–style eatery opens at 7AM, the best time to dine here is Saturday and Sunday between 11AM and 1PM, when the food on the restaurant's famous *yum cha* trolleys is at its peak. The hordes of locals and visitors generate a decibel level worthy of a sports stadium, which makes for great entertainment. Be sure to pick *gow choy* (steamed chives) and finish with *darn tart* (custard tart). The service is just like the crowd—loud and abrupt, but fun if you're in the mood for it. ◆ Chinese ◆ Daily breakfast, lunch, and dinner. 86-88 Dixon St (between Hay and Little Hay Sts). 9212.4198

11 Covent Garden Hotel Sydneysiders who are heading off to a rock concert at the **Sydney Entertainment Centre** often stop here for a quick beer. The music is loud at this traditional pub, but not as loud as the revelers spilling out onto the street. ◆ Daily 10AM-midnight. 102 Hay St (at Dixon St). 9211.1745

12 Bodhi ★★$$ A restaurant whose food is billed as "physically, ethically, and spiritually good for you" is bound to be distinctive. The menu is Asian-inspired and the food contains absolutely no preservatives. Tofu reigns supreme, so try the sticky rice wrapped in tofu skin, or the mango-and-tofu ice cream. The careful preparation hasn't raised prices; for the quality, this cafe remains one of the least expensive dining experiences in Sydney. ◆ Vegetarian/Takeout ◆ Daily lunch and dinner. 187 Hay St (at Parker St). 9212.2828

13 Silver Spring ★★★$$ Right behind the stately **Capitol Theatre** is a mammoth restaurant that serves what may be the best *yum cha* in Sydney. If the size of the place doesn't impress you (it seats up to 2,000), the variety and quality of the food will. Try the mouth-watering steamed dumplings or the fresh vegetables prepared tableside. The à la carte menu ranges from inexpensive pork spareribs and roasted duck to the "deluxe" shark's fin soup. Expect long lines. ◆ Chinese ◆ Daily brunch, lunch, and dinner. 191 Hay St (between Pitt and Parker Sts). 9211.2232, 9211.2213

14 Capitol Theatre Once known as the **New Belmore Markets,** this remarkable building now houses a 2,000-seat theater. In 1893, **George McRae** designed an indoor market for the wholesale selling of local produce; the market functioned only until 1909. In 1916, the building reopened as the **Hippodrome,** an arena for circus acts. In 1928, architect **Henry White** converted the space into a true theater, complete with classical statues and urns that gave it the atmosphere of a Florentine garden. Next came a long run as a cinema; that ended in 1973. By the early 1980s, the building was so severely dilapidated that it was nearly demolished. Luckily, it was saved by architecture and history buffs who recognized its historical value, and it was restored as a grand venue for major theatrical productions and concerts. ◆ 13 Campbell St (between Pitt and George Sts). 9320.5000

ANTHONY HARVEY

15 Central Railway Station At the edge of Chinatown and the southern end of the city is a massive railway station. "Central," as it's called, has been here for nearly a century. The sandstone facade, grand entrance, and large marble-and-wood waiting room impart an Old World charm. Despite its old-fashioned appearance, the station is a bustling hub for suburban railways and interstate trains. A **Countrylink Travel Centre** (9379.1808) inside the station books day- and long-distance trips. A number of interstate and local bus companies are based just outside the station on Eddy Avenue. ◆ Eddy Ave and Pitt St. 13.2232

Gone Fishing

Because of Sydney's coastal location, fresh fish and seafood figure prominently on the city's restaurant menus. Most dining spots have at least one daily special and the quality is almost guaranteed to be excellent. A good way to find out what's available is to visit the **Sydney Fish Markets** (see page 85) where the variety and colors of the creatures from the sea delight even carnivores. The following are some fish and crustaceans unique to Sydney's waters:

John Dory

Balmain Bug Although its name might sound like a pest, this delicious crustacean—usually 6-10 inches long—is related to the lobster and crayfish. The meat is tender and sweet and it's often served in the shells.

Barramundi The Aborigines have been catching and eating this popular, meaty white fish mainly found in the fresh waters in northern Australia for years. It's been on Sydney restaurant menus since the "let's-eat-anything-grown-in-Australia" trend began more than a decade ago.

Rainbow Trout

Blue-eyed Cod On the menu of nearly every Sydney bistro, this meaty, solid fish comes from Australia's ocean waters. It isn't a cod at all, but a fish very similar in texture to its Atlantic namesake. The best way to enjoy this delicacy is grilled.

Blue Swimmer The meat of this crab, prevalent all along Australia's coastline, has a mild flavor. The swimmer gets its name from the long periwinkle-blue claws; the shell is shiny brown.

Coral Trout This orange-red ocean fish is found around Sydney and up north in Queensland. It is a very bony, but delicious, fish.

John Dory Found on most Sydney restaurant menus, this odd-looking saltwater fish is similar in taste to its Atlantic counterpart. The extent of this fish's popularity is marked by the rhyming slang expression, "what's the John Dory?", which means "what's the story?" or "what's up?"

Leatherjacket Don't judge this ocean fish by its appearance: Although it has beautiful blue, yellow, and brown scales, the meat is rather bland. Some chefs are adept at preparing the fish in a tasty manner.

Murray Cod The Murray River is one of Australia's largest, and its shores have some of the country's prime grazing and farm land. This tan and white meaty fish comes from its waters.

Rainbow Trout This pink and gray freshwater fish is very popular in Sydney and throughout Australia. Much of it is farmed, smoked to perfection, and then packaged for specialty food shops.

Red Emperor Large, pink, and red-scaled, this ocean fish is well prepared at Asian restaurants and extremely flavorsome. It is usually relatively expensive.

Tiger Prawns These large striped shrimp are abundant along Australia's coastline, more commonly in the north.

16 Sydney Central YHA $ As the Youth Hostel Association of Australia's flagship property, this nine-story renovated 1930s building across from **Central Station** is arguably one of the best backpackers' accommodations in the world. With 530 beds, there are doubles and multi-share with shared, well-maintained bathrooms; other rooms for large families have en suite bathrooms. For quick meals, the property also boasts an in-house bistro, a supermarket, and kitchen facilities. For fun, there is a game and TV room and a rooftop swimming pool with a sauna and a barbecue area. All this, together with laundry facilities and a library and Internet access, will make you wonder why you have to bother venturing out for a day on the town. Surcharges apply for non-YHA members. ♦ 11 Rawson Pl (at Pitt St). 9281.9111; fax 9281.9199

17 Malaya ★★$ Located across the street from **Central Railway Station**, this Malaysian restaurant is popular with the employees of the nearby **Australian Broadcasting Corporation** and local print journalists. And with good reason. The dominant flavors in Malaysian cuisine are coconut, chili, curry, ginger, and peanuts. Try beef *rendang* (stewed with coconut milk), fish curry, or *laksa* (hot and spicy noodle soup). It's great food for such low prices. ♦ Malaysian ♦ M-F lunch and dinner; Sa dinner. 761 George St (between Quay St and Ultimo Rd). 9211.0946

18 Carlton Crest Hotel Sydney $$ In 1902 one section of this 251-room hotel was the **Infants' Hospital**. The overall style remains bland and institutional, but the accommodations are large and rooms have been renovated and outfitted with new fixtures and baths. There's a well-equipped business center, swimming pool, spa, garden area, putting green, restaurants, and cocktail lounge. ♦ 169-79 Thomas St (just west of Quay St). 9281.6888; fax 9281.2213

19 Aarons Hotel $ The most outstanding feature of this 94-room no-frills hotel is its incredible location at a bargain rate. Although it feels as if it's off the beaten track, the hotel is within easy walking distance of Darling Harbour and the CBD, and just moments from the **Powerhouse Museum**. Standard rooms have private baths; budget rooms share facilities. A few rooms have efficiency kitchens. A free airport shuttle bus for guests is a welcome amenity. ♦ 37 Ultimo Rd (at Quay St). 9281.5555; fax 9281.2666

20 Paddy's Markets One of Sydney's great marketplaces has operated for over 100 years in the Haymarket area at the southwestern edge of Chinatown. No one knows how it got its name, but the management has adopted the shamrock as its logo and the leprechaun as its mascot. With more than 1,000 stalls, Sydney's biggest indoor market offers everything from souvenirs, clothing, jewelry, and furnishings to fresh flowers and produce. Spend a few hours here if you're in the mood to rummage around in the maze of stalls. ♦ F-Su. Hay and Thomas Sts. 9325.6294

21 Furama Hotel Sydney $$ Located just opposite the **Sydney Entertainment Centre**, this 226-room heritage-listed hotel is a convenient place to stay after late-night concerts. The decor is standard hotel style, but rooms are ample and comfortably furnished. There are small meeting and function facilities for business travelers. A brasserie and bar offer light snacks and libations. ♦ 68 Harbour St (between Little Hay and Goulburn Sts). 9281.0400; fax 9281.1212

22 Sydney Entertainment Centre This concrete monolith on the fringe of Chinatown was completed in the early 1980s—when Sydney was in dire need of a venue big enough to attract touring international stars. It remains the city's largest indoor entertainment arena, and plays host to visiting musicians such as Elton John, Tina Turner, Midnight Oil—the list goes on and on. The **Sydney Kings,** Sydney's home team, play all their basketball games here. A variety of other attractions—from indoor tennis matches to musicals—are also staged here. When the pubs and restaurants of Chinatown and Darling Harbour are jam-packed, you can be certain a big concert is on here. ♦ Harbour St (between Hay and Little Pier Sts). Bookings and show information 9266.4800

23 Pumphouse Brewery Tavern As the name suggests, this lively brewpub built in 1891 was once the city pumphouse. Today crowds of locals frequent the Darling Harbour spot for its housemade beers and other Aussie brews. The selection is vast—from light, refreshing Golden Wheat beer to Thunderbolt Ale, which is definitely not for the faint of heart. This is also a great place for a basic pub lunch or dinner. ♦ Daily. 17 Little Pier St (west of Harbour St). 9281.3967

24 Tumbalong Park A major public space in Darling Harbour, this park is the setting for various community events, concerts, shows, and entertainment. ♦ Harbour and Pier Sts

Within Tumbalong Park:

Chinese Garden of Friendship A gift from the Guangdong Province in China (New South Wales's sister state), this lovely garden was opened on 17 January 1988 in honor of Australia's Bicentennial. The landscape artists,

Chinese Garden of Friendship

trained in the ancient traditions of Chinese landscape design, created a tranquil world where pathways thread past waterfalls, lakes, and quiet courtyards, providing respite from the urban din. The **Tea House,** open daily for traditional Chinese tea and cakes, is a popular site for weddings and photographs for Sydney's Asian community. ◆ 9281.6863

Children's Playground This carefully designed and shaded enclosure has a big sandbox and plenty of playground equipment to keep the kids busy for hours. The equipment is designed to be safe, and the park has its own security staff, so adult companions can take a breather.

25 Sega World Perfect for both kids and adults who never grew up, this 10,000-square-meter (33,000 square feet) video arcade has all imaginable high-tech entertainment. Features include virtual reality rides and games; the **Magic Motion Theatre,** where the seats move in sync with images on the screen; and **Ghost Hunters,** a train ride that lets you fire foam balls at monsters. ◆ Admission. M-Th, Su 10AM-10PM; F-Sa 10AM-midnight. 1-25 Harbour St (at Day St). 9273.9273

25 National Aboriginal Cultural Centre In the middle of what has to be Sydney's most tourist-happy commercial park, this center has been developed to provide visitors with a taste of

Aboriginal culture. Different Aboriginal tribes and communities from around Australia are invited here to give dance and music performances and to demonstrate their arts and crafts to those who want to learn more about the diverse, rich culture of Australia's indigenous people. On any day you'll find a woman telling her "Dreamtime" stories or a man making a boomerang or *didgeridoo* (a traditional musical instrument). The center also offers art exhibits, and art, musical instruments, and other memorabilia are for sale. ◆ Admission; no fee if purchase is made. Daily 9:30AM-8PM; performances at 11AM, 1PM, 4PM, and 6PM. 1-5 Harbour St (at Day St). 9283.7477

26 Panasonic IMAX Theatre IMAX—with its eight-story screen—may be the world's most exciting film format. But this distinctive, eye-shaped building offers much more than a gigantic movie screen. You can take in the scenic view overlooking Cockle Bay while enjoying a gourmet meal in the **Wockpool** (see below). A visit to the well-stocked gift shop yields good movie and Sydney souvenirs. ◆ Shows daily on the hour from 10AM-10PM. Cockle Bay Promenade. 13.3462

Within the Panasonic IMAX Theatre:

Wockpool ★★★$$$ An outpost of the empire of Sydney superchef Neil Perry, this restaurant lends a touch of much-needed style to touristy Darling Harbour. The modern Asian-inspired menu is as outstanding as the one at **Wockpool** in Potts Point (see page 108), but the ambience is very different. The restaurant caters mainly to a bustling crowd moviegoers and sightseers, for whom Perry maintains his high standards of elegant simplicity and smart service. A nice touch: the restaurant's glass walls bring the outdoors in even on the gloomiest days. ◆ Asian ◆ Daily lunch and dinner until 11PM. 9211.9888. Also at: 155 Victoria St (between Brougham La and Horderns Pl). 9368.1771

27 Mori Gallery Operating for over 20 years, this gallery has earned its reputation as one of Sydney's outstanding venues for brave new art. Although Stephen Mori opened his gallery in a rather unlikely location on the fringe of Chinatown and Darling Harbour, he still attracts huge crowds of art lovers to his show openings. The gallery exhibits works that span a full range of media—from photography to textiles, painting to sculpture—and while its primary focus is on Australian and New Zealand artists, the gallery also represents some international artists. ◆ W-Sa. 168 Day St (between Liverpool and Bathurst Sts). 9283.2903

Dreamtime Sign Language

These symbols appear in Aboriginal representations from petroglyphs to contemporary art and design:

◎ Campsite, hill, digging hole, waterhole

∪ Person sitting, windbreak

)) Boomerang, clouds, rainbow

| Spear, diggingstick

~ Snake, smoke, water flow, lightening

〰 River, bushfire

⦂⦂⦂ Rain, ants, eggs

‖‖‖‖ Rain

⌇ Path, track, bodypaint

↓↓ Footprints ᗶᗰ

● Coolamon (carrying dish), shield

∫ Spear thrower

PARKROYAL
AT DARLING HARBOUR

28 Parkroyal at Darling Harbour $$$ The lofty lobby of this modern 295-room hotel is the perfect stage for a grand entrance—even if you're not a celebrity. The lavishly decorated rooms, which have views of Cockle Bay, are fully equipped with all the amenities of a top-notch hotel, plus spacious marble bathrooms, large closets, and well-stocked bars. Chinatown, the **Sydney Entertainment Centre,** and the **Sydney Convention and Exhibition Centre** are all nearby. There's a restaurant and two busy bars on the premises. ◆ 150 Day St (between Bathurst and Sussex Sts). 9261.1188; fax 9261.8766

29 Hotel Nikko Darling Harbour $$$$ With 645 rooms, including 56 luxury suites, this is Australia's largest hotel and one of its grandest as well. The decor of both the public spaces and guest rooms is stylishly modern—glass, marble, and state-of-the-art facilities throughout. Still, historic elements have been retained: The **Corn Exchange Building** was incorporated into the hotel's lobby and houses the Japanese department store **Takashimaya** (see below). Most rooms have views overlooking Darling Harbour and the CBD. There are three restaurants and two bars on the premises. The location can't be beat—with the **Sydney Convention and Exhibition Centre** only a few minutes' walk in one direction and the heart of the CBD a short walk in the other. ◆ 161 Sussex St (between Market and King Sts). 9299.1231; fax 9299.3340

Within the Hotel Nikko Darling Harbour:

Takashimaya Complex Formerly the **Corn Exchange Building,** this two-story complex has a unique curved facade. It was constructed in 1887 using a German method of fire-resistant cast-iron columns and floor beams. The building functioned as a market for only a few years until the giant **Queen Victoria Building** (see page 57) was finished nearby. Since its early days, it has been everything from a parking garage to a theater. In 1990 it was made over into a retail and restaurant complex geared toward Japanese tourists. ◆ 173-85 Sussex St

30 Pyrmont Bridge Built in the 1920s, the world's oldest electrically operated swing-span bridge is now the primary pedestrian pathway between the city and Darling Harbour. It also supports the track for the **TNT Monorail.** The bridge swings open when large ships need to enter Cockle Bay. ◆ Access from Market St (just east of Sussex St)

31 & (Ampersand) ★★★$$$$ Tony Bilson, the executive chef of this ultramodern and ultrapopular restaurant, has been a major force on Australia's culinary scene for decades. At his new dining spot he continues to offer first-rate Modern Australian fare. The decor is minimal, but warm—simple white walls, touches of warm yellows and reds, sweeping black banquettes, and grand floor-to-ceiling windows with translucent shades to filter in the light and view of Darling Harbour. But the food is the ultimate main attraction. The menu changes seasonally, but is predominantly influenced by the cuisines of France and Japan. Some examples of wonders from the kitchen include poached baby leeks with a tangy vinaigrette, rack of veal with a purée of fresh anchovies and almonds, and baked free-range chicken breast stuffed with imported truffles. The homemade smooth-as-silk sorbets are a refreshing way to end the meal. As the place is new, expect some kinks in the service. The staff, however, is very well-informed, especially about the excellent wine selection. ◆ Modern Australian ◆ Daily lunch and dinner. Reservations recommended. Wharf 2000, Wheat Rd (west of the Western Distributor), Roof terrace. 9264.6666

32 Sydney Aquarium More than 5,000 living and preserved sea creatures (representing over 600 species) populate this watery wonder, one of the most spectacular aquariums in the world. The huge complex is composed of a hangarlike building on the harborfront and three oceanariums that float on pontoons. Underneath them is a 150-meter (492-foot) underwater tunnel that allows face-to-fin viewing of sharks, stingrays, and schools of fish—creating the sensation that you're actually part of the underwater world. The **Sydney Harbour Oceanarium** features living examples of sea life found in and around Sydney Harbour. And if a trek to the Great Barrier Reef is not on your itinerary, be sure to see the aquarium's array of corals, tropical fish, and marine turtles from this region. Children enjoy exploring the "Touch Pool," a rock pool brimming with crabs, shells, and creatures found along the Australian coast. Other highlights of the aquarium include a habitat for saltwater crocodiles and the seal sanctuary. Try not to be deterred from swimming at Sydney's beaches after seeing the size of the sharks in the tanks here. Although many of these ferocious specimens are found off the coast of Sydney, the aquarium's staff maintain that there is little to worry about. Stop in the gift shop for marine-related items, including CD-ROMs, books, music, and toys. ◆ Admission. Daily 9:30AM-9PM. Wheat Rd (west of the Western Distributor). 9262.2300

National Maritime Museum

Adjacent to the Sydney Aquarium:

Sydney Harbour Cruise Centre Here is the place to board any one of a number of excellent floating excursions. **Matilda Cruise** (9264.7377) and **Harbour Days Sailing Experience** (9968.1578) offer visitors a chance to see Sydney in the very best possible way—from the water.

33 National Maritime Museum Fittingly located in the heart of Darling Harbour, this museum (illustrated above) explores the role that the sea and ships have played in Australia's history. Permanent exhibits investigate Aboriginal culture, successive waves of European and Asian immigration, development of coastal commerce and industry, naval defenses, aquatic sport, and seaside recreation. One gallery—a bicentennial gift from the United States— explores two centuries of maritime contact between the US and Australia. A program of rotating exhibitions offers a chance to see a variety of Australian and international marine artifacts. Moored at the wharves outside the museum are 12 historic vessels—ranging from a Vietnamese refugee boat to a former Royal Australian Navy destroyer—to inspect. Grab a waterside snack from the kiosk at the front of the museum and stop at the gift shop for maritime gifts and books. ♦Admission. Daily. 2 Murray St (at Pirrama Rd). 9552.7777

At the National Maritime Museum:

Guided Walks of Pyrmont A joint venture of the museum and City West Development Corporation, this organization offers guided walking tours through the winding streets of the surrounding Pyrmont neighborhood. Once a busy commercial maritime hub, this historic area boasts 100-year-old terrace houses, wharves, wool stores, and pubs, many of which are still in use today. Guides meet walkers in the foyer of the museum.
♦ Admission. Tours: First Tu of the month at

10:30 AM, or by special arrangement. Reservations required. 9552.7555

34 Star City Sydney's answer to Las Vegas, this harbourside casino complex offers countless opportunities for an adrenaline rush. From the ceiling murals with Aboriginal motifs in theaters and gaming rooms to earth tones and native flowers in guest rooms, this whole joint is decked out in Australiana. To add to the frenzy, there are six restaurants and bars serving everything from burgers to Bollinger; a 491-room hotel (4657.7687, fax 9657.7691); a 2,000-seat theater for show-stopping extravaganzas and a smaller 900-seat venue; 13 various retail outlets; and plenty of ATM machines—just in case. If you're not short of cash, try your hand at the gaming tables where the play consists of blackjack and roulette, *Pai Gow* and *Sic Bo* for the Asian clientele, or the old Aussie pub game of Two Up. The more cautious may try the 1,500 slot machines.
♦ Daily 24 hours. 80 Pyrmont St (between Union St and Jones Bay Rd). 9657.8393

35 Ibis Hotel Darling Harbour $$ Another of the big international hotels clustered at Darling Harbour, this 256-room property offers all the standard amenities. The comfortable guest rooms, room service, and the two restaurants and two bars help maintain the hotel's popularity with business travelers. The hotel is only a five-minute taxi ride to the CBD. ♦ 70 Murray St (south of Darling Dr). 9563.0888; fax 9563.0899

36 Novotel Sydney on Darling Harbour $$$ It's impossible to miss the silhouette of this imposing terraced hotel sitting high up on the Darling Harbour skyline. Adjacent to the **Sydney Convention and Exhibition Centre,** with a monorail stop right outside the door, the hotel is in easy reach of virtually anywhere in the city. The 527 guest rooms boast terrific city views, and the large swimming pool, tennis courts, and fully equipped gym help keep guests fit. Other amenities include a restaurant, 24-hour room service, free guest parking, and what some say is the best service staff in the city. ◆ 100 Murray St (south of Darling Dr). 9934.0000; fax 9934.0034. Show information 1.300.300.711

37 Harbourside Festival Marketplace
Here's the place to get down to serious souvenir shopping. This sprawling glass, steel, and concrete complex (pictured on page 76) houses more than 200 specialty stores and 40 fast-food outlets. Whether you're looking for duty-free bargains, jewelry, novelty gifts, your photo on a T-shirt, or Australian brand names such as Country Road and Sportsgirl, you'll find it here. ◆ Daily 10AM-6PM. Darling Dr (between Pier and Murray Sts). 9281.3999

Within Harbourside Festival Marketplace:

Jordon's ★$$$ Located at the entrance of Harbourside, this large seafood restaurant is popular with tourists as well as shopping Sydneysiders. There's both inside and outdoor seating with excellent views across the bay to the CBD skyscrapers. Australia's most popular seafood—including fresh mud crabs, Balmain bugs, and barramundi—is on the menu, prepared in every way imaginable. This is a good place to come with a group: the seafood platter is enough for a crowd, and the selection of domestic wines is stellar. ◆ Seafood ◆ Daily lunch and dinner. 9281.3711

38 Sydney Convention and Exhibition Centre Built in 1988, the glass and exposed steel convention, seminar, exhibition, and conference complex blends neatly into the harborside. The structure is topped with a series of innovative masts that reflect the maritime theme of this harbor area. Inside, the building features five separate meeting halls, each free of vision-obstructing pillars. Throughout the year, the center plays host to a variety of international and domestic trade shows and conventions weekly, including the annual Australian Motor Show. The ballrooms and banquet halls, with food catered by executive chef Detlef Haupt, are the venues for a variety of glittering galas. ◆ Darling Dr (between Pier and Murray Sts). 9282.5000

At the entrance to the Sydney Convention and Exhibition Centre:

Tidal Cascades On warm days droves of children can be found in and around this public fountain designed by **Robert Woodward.** The fountain features a double spiral of water, reflecting the circles and spirals of the **Sydney Convention and Exhibition Centre.**

39 Powerhouse Museum In 1879, Sydney hosted an international exhibition to showcase the colony's greatest achievements. Unfortunately, a fire swept through the collection, destroying virtually everything in it. Some items, however, were saved and set aside to form the basis of a permanent museum. As it grew, the establishment changed sites several times, finally ending up in the old Ultimo power station on the edge of Sydney's CBD. The building, which dates back

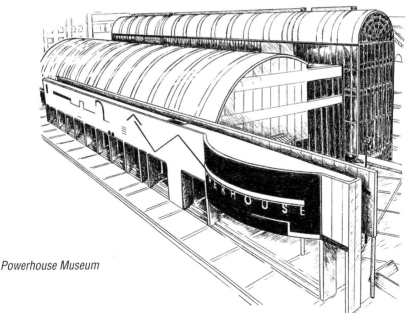

Powerhouse Museum

to 1899, functioned as the power station for Sydney's tram system until 1963, when the trams were retired. The museum took up residence here in 1988, Australia's bicentennial year.

This vibrant center explores the rich and diverse nature of science and technology, decorative arts and design, and social history. The spacious layout showcases more than 30,000 objects in 25 different displays; there are planes, trains, ceramics, furniture, and steam engines. Each exhibition tells a story—from the history of steam technology (featuring 12 operating steam engines) to the harsh living conditions of the 19th-century bush squatters. Visitors can explore the frontier of space in the world's only combined display of Soviet, Chinese, American, and Australian space technology. NASA's life-size space habitation module shows what future life in space might be like. The museum's many interactive tools include touch-screen computers, audio phones, and hands-on science experiments. The collection of decorative arts contains Thomas Hope's Egyptian suite (circa 1700), clothing from different eras, and a stunning Wedgwood collection. The museum's restaurant (see below) is enlivened by colorful Impressionist-style murals by Australian artist Ken Done. There's also a courtyard cafe and shops specializing in innovative games, books, and gifts. ◆ Admission. Free the first Saturday of every month. Children under age five and Australian seniors free. Daily. 500 Harris St (at William Henry St). 9217.0111

Within the Powerhouse Museum:

Powerhouse Garden Restaurant ★$$
With its high ceiling and brightly painted walls, this large cafe provides a welcome respite to weary museum visitors in need of a quick break and light meal. The pasta dishes, focaccia, french fries, and homemade scones are the most popular items, and a children's menu is available. Morning and afternoon teas are the best bets. ◆ Cafe ◆ Daily. Level 1. 9217.0111

40 Macarthur Take-Away Cafe ★★$ Take your pick from an enormous selection of gourmet sandwiches and focaccias. Students and tourists alike are drawn to this little spot for its big Australian breakfast and locally famous egg-and-bacon rolls. There is a sweet, sunny outdoor patio with a few tables if you choose to eat in, but most folks get their grub to take out ("take away" in local parlance). ◆ Cafe ◆ M-Sa breakfast, lunch, and afternoon snacks. 373-75 Bulwara Rd (at Macarthur St). 9211.5736

41 Mercure Hotel Lawson $$ Just two blocks away from the **Powerhouse Museum** and within walking distance of the CBD and

Darling Harbour, this 96-room, reasonably priced hotel is a great find. The rooms are spacious, and each has a private bath and its own small balcony. There is 24-hour room service and a lobby restaurant that serves breakfast, lunch, and dinner. A complimentary airport shuttle bus is available to guests with hotel reservations. ◆ 383-89 Bulwara Rd (between Mary Ann and Macarthur Sts). 9211.1499; fax 9281.3764

42 Harris Street Motor Museum With a spectacular display of more than 150 classic motor cars, bikes, and commercial vehicles, this museum is a must-see for auto fans. Unique and exotic cars as well as everyday vehicles provide a well-organized trip down memory lane. A number of cars are on display courtesy of their Australian owners. The museum is also home to Australia's largest international standard slot-car track. ◆ Admission. W-Su; daily during school holidays. Goldsborough Mort Bldg, 320 Harris St (at Allen St). 9552.3375

43 Simon Johnson No gourmet should miss a stop at this classic purveyor of quality foods. Fresh, traditional and modern ingredients, and fancy prepared foods are all available at one of the best delis in Sydney. Ask for the elaborate mail-order catalog for future purchases of these stylishly packaged foods. ◆ 181 Harris St (between Pyrmont Bridge Rd and Miller St). 9552.2522

44 Sydney Fish Markets Big trawlers and little boats alike chug into Blackwattle Bay at dawn every day to offload their catches at the fish markets. Around 7AM, local restaurateurs and members of the general public start rolling in to examine the best and freshest seafood Sydney has to offer. Before 8AM, the top-of-the-line stuff has been auctioned off to the highest bidders. These markets were once a little rowdier and ranker, but the area has been spruced up by the seafood restaurants, take-out joints, and sushi bars that have opened here. Try the **Oyster Bar** or one of the many cafes for a quick lunch. Buyers of fresh fish can also pick up cooking supplies at the supermarket or a bottle or two of Australian wine at the liquor store. ◆ Daily 7AM-4PM. Pyrmont Bridge Rd (just southwest of Bank St). 9660.1611

Restaurants/Clubs: Red	**Hotels:** Blue
Shops/ ☂ Outdoors: Green	**Sights/Culture:** Black

East Sydney/Surry Hills/ Darlinghurst

Just on the eastern fringe of the Central Business District (CBD) is Sydney's epicenter of youthful, streetwise, club-going, artsy cafe culture. But within the area are three neighborhoods, each with its own distinctive character. East Sydney attracts people from all over the city who love to show off their new designer apparel as much as they go for a caffe latte. Darlinghurst draws a more international group, who like to display the latest fashions while they nibble focaccia and sip bottled water. On the southern side of **Oxford Street**, the people in Surry Hills have a cafe culture of their own—less showy but nevertheless very style-conscious.

This young cafe culture begins just south of the **Australian Museum**, parallel to lower Oxford Street on **Stanley Street.** More than 20 restaurants and cafes are clustered on a small stretch of Stanley Street, between **Yurong** and **Riley Streets,** creating a wonderful culinary enclave. Here, evening finds the street-front verandas of cafes packed with young, boisterous, well-to-do Eastern Suburbs residents who drive up in their hot sports cars for cappuccino and cake at such places as **San Siro.** Slightly older patrons and businesspeople seem to prefer long lunches at **Mario's** on Yurong or dinner at **The Edge** on Riley.

Long before trendy Sydneysiders made East Sydney fashionable cafe territory, the area was covered with rich and fertile farmland that provided the city's dairy products and other foods until the mid-1800s. When the **Australian Museum** was built in 1849 and the **Sydney Grammar School** was established ten years later, light industry and row houses (known in Australia as terrace homes) soon followed, transforming East Sydney into a suburb within the city. The Stanley Street restaurants did not appear until much later, after World War II, when the city had expanded and many Italian immigrants moved in and gave the area a more pronounced sense of community.

Just up the hill from the CBD is **Lower Oxford Street** and the beginning of Darlinghurst. Here you'll find a mix of clubs, pubs, small hotels, hip clothing stores, and little cafes, all of which attract a lively and diverse crowd. The entertainment seems to continue even after the clubs close: You are just as likely to see a transvestite shopping for high heels here as you are a young student looking for a book or a pair of army boots. This first stretch of Oxford Street is also where the annual Gay and Lesbian Mardi Gras celebration has started since the 1970s. The participants parade past throngs of curious spectators, many of whom have staked out good viewing spots long before any of the sequined drag queens, marching bands, and colorful floats arrive on the scene.

The party continues every Friday and Saturday night in Darlinghurst around **Taylor Square**—Sydney's undisputed gay epicenter and the weekend hot spot for outlandishly clad and coifed Sydneysiders and visitors in search of a night of disco and drink. The pubs and bars around Taylor Square, such as the **Oxford Hotel** and **Flinders Hotel**, serve mostly a gay clientele, while the cafes and clubs are generally mixed and welcome anyone who looks fashionable. The modestly priced accommodations in the vicinity, still close to the CBD, are fine for those who don't mind the weekend frenzy.

Victoria Street and **Darlinghurst Road**, between Oxford and **William** Streets in Darlinghurst, are the *ne plus ultra* of Sydney's cafe culture, as well as the city's creative nucleus. Along these two streets, small groups of stylishly dressed and body-conscious fashion mavens, musicians, and designers, most in their twenties and thirties, huddle together to discuss such critical issues as the state of their respective industries and who was with whom at which club the night before. The cafes **Parmalat, Bar Coluzzi,** and **Le Petit Creme** have made this Sydney's caffeine alley, while boutique hotels such as **L'otel** and **Morgan's of Sydney** are equally chic.

Darlinghurst has come a long way from its origins. In the early 1800s, several large windmills dotted the area, providing power for the colony's grain mill. The Aboriginal reserve here was soon cleared for the free (and thus relatively well-to-do) settlers who had colonial land grants. The area lost its aristocratic edge in 1841, when the **Darlinghurst Gaol** was built at **Forbes** and Oxford Streets. Toward the end of the 19th century, the area became strictly working class, and rows of narrow brick homes began to fill the streets. The grim presence of the jail was lost in 1921, when the building became the **East Sydney College of the Arts** (today it is the **Sydney Institute of Technology**). Artists and bohemians moved in to the area, and a gay population soon followed. By the 1970s, many of Darlinghurst's residents had mounted a massive modernization campaign and renovated their homes. Today this mixed population gives the neighborhood an easygoing sophistication.

The main streets of Surry Hills are **Crown** and **Bourke Streets,** south of Oxford Street, is where a different scene unfolds. There's a mix of commercial and residential, with factories and studios standing next to rows of three-story Victorian row houses. Among the residents, Surry Hills appears to have one fashion maverick for every fashion follower in Darlinghurst. The cafes on Crown Street and its side streets are full of artists, painters, and poets, whereas the population of Darlinghurst is more stable and slightly more upscale.

Like Darlinghurst and East Sydney, Surry Hills was mostly farmland until it became a working-class residential area in the 1850s. The 1855 opening of the **Central Railway Station,** Sydney's main train station, made it possible for the garment and other light industries to establish factories. After World War II, many Lebanese and other Mediterranean immigrants moved in to Surry Hills and neighboring **Redfern,** working in the factories and establishing small Lebanese restaurants and cafes where Crown and **Cleveland** Streets meet.

Close to but not in the CBD, Surry Hills is a great place to find affordable accommodations. The **Medina on Crown,** which houses **bills 2** cafe, is one such hotel for those who don't need to be right in the middle of the CBD. Closer to the **Central Railway Station** is the **Furama Hotel Central,** which caters to business travelers. Nearby are the **Brett Whitely Studio,** the workplace of the late artist, and the **Belvoir Street Theatre,** which might be showing a new Australian play.

The brothels, boardinghouses, and dilapidated row houses within East Sydney, Darlinghurst, and Surry Hills remind visitors that this area was once a lot less glamorous. At the same time, these buildings also lend authenticity to the bohemian chic that these neighborhoods offer.

East Sydney

1 Mario's ★★$$$ The long lunch is enjoying a renaissance at this large, fashionable restaurant, where some of the most important deals in Sydney are closed. Here is a place where divorces are finalized, affairs begun, executives hired, and stars are born. The handy East Sydney location—just five minutes' walk from the city center—makes it a great lunch spot. Besides, you'll be surprised by how much networking you can do during the course of an hour. The food is contemporary Italian, nothing terribly innovative, but you don't come here for the food. Wine is served by the glass. ♦ Italian ♦ M-F lunch and dinner; Sa dinner. Reservations recommended. 38 Yurong St (at Stanley La). 9331.4945

2 Beppi's ★★$$$ While even the old Sydney dining establishments are jumping on the modern cuisine bandwagon, restaurateur Beppi Polese continues his more-than-40-year tradition of offering old-fashioned Italian food with friendly service. The decor is basic, with an Old World charm. Classic pasta and seafood dishes are specialties of the house. Try the osso buco if it's on the menu (which changes seasonally); it's one of the best in town. ♦ Italian ♦ M-F lunch and dinner; Sa dinner. Reservations recommended. Yurong and Stanley Sts. 9360.4558

TWO
C H E F S

3 Two Chefs on Stanley ★★$$ Food is the focus here, not the overly plush decor or the extremely attentive service. The two chefs who run this busy place work in tandem to deliver modern French-Italian cuisine using native Australian fish, products, and herbs. The handwritten menus are a nice touch. Let the well-versed waiters pick the wine; the impressive but enormous wine list may overwhelm those not in the know. ♦ Modern Australian ♦ M-F lunch and dinner; Sa dinner. Reservations recommended. 111 Riley St (at Stanley La). 9331.1559

4 Watters Gallery Visit this gallery, one of Sydney's most established, if you want to keep your finger on the pulse of the city's contemporary art scene. Founded in 1964, the gallery showcases a wide spectrum of Australian art, from the work of the renowned sculptor Robert Klippel to James Gleeson (one of Australia's most important surrealist painters) and Tony Tuckson (widely considered one of the greatest Australian painters of the 20th century). ♦ Free. Tu, Sa; W-F 10AM-8PM. 109 Riley St (at Stanley La). 9331.2556

5 San Siro Coffee Lounge ★★$ For more than 25 years, this busy Italian cafe has been attracting Sydneysiders in search of a *real* caffe latte, cappuccino, or espresso. Drawing a diverse crowd, this place serves terrific strong coffee, fresh pastries and cakes, focaccia sandwiches, and gelati. The decor is as old as the cafe, but the food is always fresh and delicious. ♦ Cafe ♦ Daily. 72-74 Stanley St (between Crown and Riley Sts). 9331.3497

Above San Siro:

Bill and Toni's ★$ For 20 years, this no-frills restaurant has been pleasing budget-conscious diners and those in the market for a quick Italian-style meal. As soon as you place your order, a server brings a large salad, a basket of bread, and a jug of orange drink to take the edge off your hunger while you wait for your main course. Old Italian standards like *spaghetti bolognese* and fettuccine with chunks of bacon, mushrooms, and cream are staples here, along with a few meat dishes such as osso buco and Wiener schnitzel (yes—in an Italian restaurant). ♦ Italian ♦ Daily dinner. 9360.4702

6 Liago ★★★$$$ Although the chic crowd at this recent addition to the Stanley Street restaurant scene appears more interested in the terrific 1950s-style cocktail bar than what is coming out of the kitchen, the food here is splendid. The terrazzo floors, curved wood walls, and faux fish tank create a wonderful minimalist setting for the Mediterranean-style pasta and seafood dishes and generous salads. Start with a dozen oysters (always the freshest), then try the seafood ravioli drizzled with shellfish oil, whole baby snapper with lemon and olives, or blue swimmer crab tart with a rich saffron broth. Save room for the fabulous tarte tatin for dessert. The selection of wines by the glass is outstanding. ♦ Modern Australian ♦ M-F lunch and dinner; Sa dinner. Reservations recommended. 73 Stanley St (between Crown and Riley Sts). 9360.4640

7 The Edge ★★$$$ Large and open, this restaurant has become very popular with Sydneysiders who love good food. One of the owners, Carol Jaggard, is often on hand to make sure everyone gets seated promptly and is well served. The antipasto plates are deservedly popular, and the barbecued sea-food pizza is one of the best variations on a popular theme. Try one of the many charcoal-grilled dishes and scrumptious side orders of vegetables and salads. The wine list features Australian selections, which may be ordered by the glass. ♦ Modern Australian ♦ Daily dinner. 60 Riley St (between Stanley St and Yurong La). 9360.1372

Australia is the only English-speaking nation that has made voting compulsory by all citizens over the age of 18 in federal and state elections.

Between 1788 and 1856, 157,000 convicts were sent to Sydney. This is only one-third of the total shipped by the British to its North American colonies.

Restaurants/Clubs: Red   **Hotels:** Blue
Shops/ Outdoors: Green   **Sights/Culture:** Black

THE SYDNEY BOULEVARD

8 Sydney Boulevard $$$ This 270-room hotel was extremely popular, even a bit glamorous, when it opened in the 1960s. Today it has been eclipsed by the big city hotels, but it is still a popular alternative for those who want a midway point between the sometimes international style of the CBD and the around-the-clock activity of Kings Cross and Darlinghurst. Many of the basic, pastel-colored rooms have views of the harbor and city. Business and secretarial services are available, along with 8 meeting rooms, which can hold between 10 and 600 people. There are 2 restaurants, 3 bars, and a nightclub, including the 25th-floor restaurant and cocktail bar with panoramic city and harbor views—or head around the block to the row of cafes and restaurants on Stanley Street. ♦ 90 William St (at Crown St). 9357.2277; fax 9356.2115

9 Hard Rock Cafe ★$$ The successful Hard Rock formula—burgers, salads, and loud music—has crowds forming each night on Crown Street (particularly on Friday and Saturday). They come not so much for the unremarkable food as for the chance to sit next to some authentic, heavy-duty rock memorabilia from both Australia and the US. ♦ American ♦ Daily lunch and dinner. 127 Crown St (between Stanley St and Yurong La). 9331.1116

10 Yutaka ★★$$ Sitting next to you at the sushi bar here could be a famous supermodel, an actor, singer, cluster of Tokyo tourists, or a smattering of Eastern Suburbs socialites. All of which is fun, but you don't come here to rub shoulders, you come for great-value Japanese cuisine. The extensive menu never changes and covers all the traditional favorites—yakitori, sukiyaki, and *udon* (Japanese noodles), to name a few—but the sushi bar is where it all happens. With the Formica tables and the piped-in pop music, it's definitely a special atmosphere. This restaurant is so popular that it now has a younger sibling, **Yutaka 2,** just up the road at 234 Crown Street (9361.4804). ♦ Japanese ♦ M-F lunch and dinner; Sa-Su dinner. Reservations required for sushi bar. 200 Crown St (between Liverpool and Chapel Sts). 9361.3818

11 Phat Boys ★★★$$ This long, narrow white-walled restaurant with its trendy Formica tables and comfy plastic chairs provides a stark, theatrical setting for terrific Thai food. The open kitchen literally turns out hundreds of different dishes listed on the huge menu. The Thai salad plate makes a great starter for two, while the chicken and snake bean green curry is a favorite entrée

with the local hipsters who frequent the place. Other standouts are the traditional pad thai and the more Australian-influenced barramundi (local fish) with eggplant, paprika, red curry, and dry basil. The wine list is not too exciting, but desserts—like the simple sticky rice with fresh mango—make up for this. Service comes with many smiles. ♦ Thai ♦ M-F lunch and dinner; Sa-Su dinner. Reservations recommended for dinner. 118 Crown St (at Barnett La). 9332.3284

12 Eleni's ★★$$ Many frequent visitors to Sydney will remember this relatively small place as the modern Greek restaurant **Cosmos.** Peter Conisitis, the chef who used to run it, decided to take a sabbatical in Greece to brush up on culinary trends there. At that point, his mother, Eleni, stepped in, renamed the place, added a few modern touches to the decor, and started serving her more traditional version of Greek food. In 1998 Peter returned and is now working beside Eleni, creating such Mediterranean treats as grilled octopus and tomato on grilled olive bread, moussaka with sea scallops and *taramasalata,* and phyllo-wrapped lamb on a bed of Greek salad. Leave room for one of their delicious desserts, such as the frozen chocolate-and-orange torte. ♦ Greek ♦ Tu-Th dinner; F lunch and dinner; Sa brunch and dinner; Su brunch. 185A Bourke St (between Barnett La and William St). 9331.5306

13 Kings Cross Holiday Apartments $$ Florida-style family vacation apartments meet the red-light district at these modern, self-contained accommodations. Facilities in each of the nine apartments include a fully equipped kitchen and a washing machine, dryer, iron, and ironing board. There's also guest parking—a blessing in this neighborhood. ♦ 169 William St (at Forbes St). 9361.0637; fax 9331.1366

Darlinghurst

14 Robin Gibson Galleries Renowned for its chic openings, this gallery features some Australian artists but is mostly international, representing both relatively unknown and mid-career contemporary artists. ♦ Tu-Sa. 278 Liverpool St (between Darley and Forbes Sts). 9331.6692

15 Dov ★$ The old sandstone walls of this cafe are a pleasant contrast to its stainless-steel countertops and modern furniture. Located across from the **Sydney Institute of Technology, Dov** attracts a mix of artsy students and corporate types. The blackboard menu with specials changes daily, but regular items such as the mixed plate (the chef's selection of six items from the menu) and the breaded chicken with mashed potatoes are usually available. Breakfasts here are as simple as toasted Italian bread, made in a wood-fired oven, served with homemade jam and a boiled egg on the side. The coffee is as consistently good as the service. ◆ Cafe ◆ M-Sa breakfast, lunch, and dinner. Forbes and Burton Sts. 9360.9594

16 Darlinghurst Gaol/East Sydney Campus for Sydney Institute of Technology This complex, once called the **Woolloomooloo Stockade,** is now the art school for the **Sydney Institute of Technology.** Construction of the sandstone-and-rock jail complex began in 1822 and took nearly 20 years to complete. The walls that surround the complex, which are 7 meters (23 feet) high, imprisoned some of Australia's most notorious felons in the late 1800s. In 1921, the jail was converted to the art school, where many of Australia's most famous visual artists have studied and lectured. ◆ Free. M-F 7:30AM-10PM. Forbes St (between Bourke and Burton Sts). 9339.8666

Adjacent to the Darlinghurst Gaol:

Darlinghurst Court House Built in 1835, this dark, old Greek Revival–style courthouse was designed by colonial architect **Mortimer Lewis.** Today the New South Wales Supreme Court occupies the building, which is connected via underground passageways to the jail complex. ◆ M-F; closed in January. 9368.2947

17 Sydney Jewish Museum Dedicated to "documenting and teaching the history of the Holocaust so that these events will never be repeated," this museum presents visitors with an elaborate critique of the best and worst of humanity. Its two permanent exhibitions, *Culture and Continuity* and *The Holocaust,* explore the issues of democracy, morality, social justice, and human rights. The museum combines unforgettable images of the past and a window on the contemporary Australian Jewish experience. Visitors can hear the stories of Holocaust survivors and view archival and contemporary videos during the daily film screenings. A resource center is open to the

public and offers more than 2,500 books, audiotapes, and videotapes. The on-site kosher eatery, **Cafe Macc,** offers both traditional and contemporary Jewish food. ◆ Admission. M-Th, Su; F 10AM-2PM. 146 Darlinghurst Rd (at Burton St). 9360.7999

18 Fishface ★★$ One of Sydney's more chic, well-decorated fish-and-chip shops, this restaurant also offers takeout from its simple, short menu. All seafood plates come with the place's famed golden chips and a side salad. The barbecued Cajun octopus is lip-smacking good. Those who prefer to prepare their fish at home may choose from the selection of fresh fish. ◆ Seafood ◆ M-F lunch and dinner; Sa-Su breakfast, lunch, and dinner. No credit cards accepted. 132 Darlinghurst Rd (between Burton and Liverpool Sts). 9332.4803

19 Eca Bar ★★$ This corner cafe caters to all types and all tastes. From scrambled eggs on toast with prosciutto to big servings of children's cereals, the menu at this wedge-

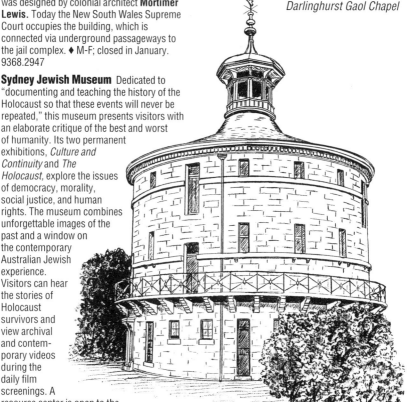

Darlinghurst Gaol Chapel

shaped eatery is about as eclectic as its customers. The simple street-side seating is the best vantage point for checking out the regulars, including suits, artists in pursuit of a good feed, and nurses from the nearby St. Vincent's Hospital. The homemade ice cream is a good reason to linger after indulging in a large sandwich. ♦ Cafe ♦M-W 7AM-5PM; Th-Su 7AM-11PM. 128 Darlinghurst Rd (at Liverpool St). 9332.1433

20 Medusa $$ Inspired by Caravaggio's *Medusa*, local interior designer Scott Weston transformed this old Victorian row house into a hip 18-room boutique hotel. Very minimalist rooms and furnishings are softened with the liberal use of color and texture. A quaint little reflecting pool in the courtyard seems to attract body-beautiful men and women who aren't afraid of potential voyeurs from the rooms above. Room service is available for breakfast only. ♦ 267 Darlinghurst Rd (between Liverpool St and Tewkesbury Ave). 9331.1000; fax 9380.6901

21 Le Petit Creme ★★$ This French cafe run by two busy brothers, Andrew and Paul Ryder, seems even busier than it is because of its small terrace, cramped main room, and open kitchen. Breakfast is the best bet here: Order a big bowl of coffee, a giant omelette, and a homemade pastry. The cafe attracts a mixed crowd during the week and lines of brunching locals on weekends. ♦ Cafe ♦ Daily breakfast and lunch. No credit cards accepted. 118 Darlinghurst Rd (between Hardie and Craigend Sts; rear entrance on Victoria St, between Liverpool and Craigend Sts). 9361.4738

21 Zen—The Art of Body Maintenance Just when you thought the New Age movement had come and gone, you find this holistic health clinic apparently doing very well. A full range of healing services using  nontraditional, natural methods, including acupuncture, aromatherapy, reflexology, shiatsu, and Swedish massage, are here for the asking. ♦ M-Sa. Appointments required. 116-18 Darlinghurst Rd (between Hardie and Craigend Sts). 9361.4200

21 L'otel $$ With only 16 rooms, this hotel is situated smack-dab in the middle of Sydney's cafe culture. Each room is a carefully styled suite—some are quasi-French provincial, others have a more modernist look. The hallways are lined with the work of young local artists, giving the hotel a residential feel. Room service is available. ♦ 114 Darlinghurst Rd (between Hardie and Craigend Sts). 9360.6868; fax 9331.4536

Within L'otel:

L'otel Cafe ★$$ Breakfast here is a serious matter. If the patrons and the substantial food (omelettes, eggs Benedict, and sausages) are any indication, this is a good place to come after a long night of dining and dancing. The menu changes daily for lunch and dinner and has a definite Southeast Asian bent. ♦ Cafe ♦ Daily 4PM-3AM. 9360.6868

22 The Movie Room This tiny, popular movie theater with comfortable armchairs doesn't advertise, so phone ahead or come early to find out what's showing and to get a seat. Alternative, independent films are usually featured. ♦ Daily. 112 Darlinghurst Rd (between Hardie and Craigend Sts). 9360.7853

23 The Cauldron For years, this nightclub has been catering to a well-dressed, well-to-do crowd. From rich university students to executives in business suits, a sophisticated mix of people comes to dance, flirt, drink, and eat supper. ♦ Daily 8PM-3AM. 207 Darlinghurst Rd (at Farrell Ave). 9331.1523

24 International ★★★$$$ Top of the Town Hotel is more famous these days for housing this popular modern restaurant and bar than the tired, funky accommodations that were popular in the 1970s. Take the large lift to the 14th floor and enter the place where Sydney's Gucci-loving, air-kissing twenty- and thirtysomethings dine in style. Those lucky enough to get a reservation (if not, be sure to stop in and have a drink at the bar) should ask to sit at one of the three dark-wood–paneled booths or a table by the window with a splendid view of the CBD. Chef Brian Duncan changes the menu every other week, but consistently produces some amazing meals. Don't miss the poached blue-eye cod with tomato-lime broth or the passionfruit soufflé if they're on the menu. The bar menu is also promising for those looking for a drink, snack, and view. Many wines are available by the glass. The service, however, is sometimes harried. ♦ Modern Australian ♦ Tu-Sa dinner. Reservations recommended. 227 Victoria St (between Liverpool and Craigend Sts), 14th Floor. 9360.9080

24 Tropicana Espresso Bar ★$ The worn-out tile floor, plastic chairs, and laminated tabletops don't seem to deter the people who flock here for the superb coffee. The story is that this is where the whole Victoria Street cafe culture was born. Table service is limited—it's best to pay and order at the counter. Simple salads, focaccia, and cakes are all listed on the blackboard menu.The cafe hosts an annual alternative film festival. ♦ Cafe ♦ Daily 5AM-midnight. 227B Victoria St (between Liverpool and Craigend Sts). 9360.9809

Gay Sydney

Sydney boasts the world's largest gay and lesbian population after San Francisco, its sister city. The heart of the community is **Oxford Street** and the area around **Taylor Square,** both in **Darlinghurst.** (There are also clusters in **Paddington, Surry Hills,** and **Newtown**). Sydney's gays and lesbians have gravitated to these spots over the years, opening bars, cafes, restaurants, shops, and bookstores.

The city has had a conspicuous gay and lesbian presence since the 1950s, but it wasn't until the 1970s that antidiscrimination legislation was passed declaring that homosexual activity was not a criminal offense. Soon after, in 1978, Sydney had its first Mardi Gras Parade. This small affair was originally held to commemorate the Stonewall Inn uprising in New York City, but it has grown into one of the world's largest gay and lesbian celebrations, attracting thousands of international and regional visitors each year.

A month before the big night, the Gay and Lesbian Mardi Gras Festival is held at different venues around the city, featuring performing and visual arts events related to the gay and lesbian community. All this culminates in the often-outrageous Mardi Gras Parade that takes place on the Saturday evening before Lent. The crowds that line Oxford Street to watch the parade can be as eclectic as the floats that make this celebration so spectacular. Expect to see parents with their children jostling for room along the jam-packed streets, alongside leather-clad bikers who are buffed and polished and ready to rev up the crowd. **Lower Oxford Street** in Darlinghurst is the hub of activity, before, during, and after the street extravaganza. All the major gay and lesbian pubs teem with revelers for the entire weekend.

The other major event on the gay and lesbian calendar is Sleaze Ball, usually held on the first Saturday night in October at the **Old Sydney Showground.** Sydney's party-hearty crowd dresses up in outrageous club gear, and as the night wears on, dresses down to virtually no clothes. This long-running gala used to raise money for the Mardi Gras celebration, but these days it benefits a number of charities, including AIDS and legal defense organizations.

It's no surprise that with Sydney's enormous gay and lesbian population and lavish celebrations come a bevy of great hotels, bars, and publications for the traveler to enjoy.

Accommodations

Try the smaller places in Darlinghurst (for example, **L'otel, Medusa, Morgan's of Sydney,** and **Oxford Koala Hotel Apartments**), Surry Hills, Paddington, **Kings Cross,** and Elizabeth Bay (**Sebel of Sydney** offers a more upscale experience in a larger hotel). Generally, these are the city's most gay-friendly neighborhoods and the hotels here are geared to making gay and lesbian travelers feel comfortable. *Note:* Be sure to book at least six months ahead for Mardi Gras as there's a scarcity of rooms in even the major hotels. For long-term accommodations, try **Share Space** (9360.7744; fax 9360.4818). It has an extensive database and tries to match personalities.

Bars/Clubs

Most bars are open daily and until very late. Some have special theme nights and shows. These are the main establishments:

Albury Hotel ◆ 6 Oxford St (between West St and Barcom Ave), Paddington. 9361.6555

Beresford ◆ 354 Bourke St (at Hill St), Darlinghurst. 9331.1045

Imperial Hotel ◆ 35 Erskineville Rd (between Union and Gowrie Sts), Erskineville. 9519.9899

Newtown Hotel ◆ 174 King St (at Watkin St), Newtown. 9557.1329

Oxford Hotel/Gilligan's ◆ 134 Oxford St (at Taylor Sq), Darlinghurst. 9331.3467

Publications

The *Sydney Star Observer* and *Capital Q Weekly* are Sydney's two main gay and lesbian publications. Both are free weeklies and are available in gay pubs and some bookstores in Darlinghurst, Newtown, and **Glebe.** They feature guides to community events, the arts, and sometimes deal with political issues.

Resources

The **Gay and Lesbian Information Line** (9361.0655) has up-to-date information on events in the city. Offering phone consultations and referrals from trained counselors, the **Gay and Lesbian Counselling Service of New South Wales** (9360.2211) operates daily from 4PM to midnight. The police stations in Kings Cross, Darlinghurst, and Newtown have gay/lesbian liaison officers for emergencies (dial 000 for assistance). For information on legal issues, call the **Gay and Lesbian Rights Lobby** (9360.6650).

25 Morgan's of Sydney $$$ With 26 roomy suites, this relatively small hotel has many of the amenities of a larger establishment. All suites have queen-size beds and bay windows or balconies. The fully equipped kitchens include microwaves, which come in handy for reheating take-out food. The location is superb, with some of the best cafes and restaurants right on the doorstep. There is a restaurant/cafe on the premises, and room service is also available. ◆ 304 Victoria St (between Surrey and Craigend Sts). 9360.7955; fax 9360.9217

Within Morgan's of Sydney:

Morgan's Restaurant ★$$ Perhaps this split-level restaurant/cafe would be more impressive if it weren't surrounded by so many other exceptional places. The menu is uncomplicated, the ingredients are very fresh, and the dishes are presented simply. The big Australian-style breakfasts of bacon, eggs, tomato, and hefty slices of toast are a great way to start the day. ◆ Modern Australian ◆ Daily breakfast, lunch, and dinner. Reservations recommended on Friday and Saturday. 9360.7955

26 Parmalat ★★$ This small, narrow, extremely hip cafe features hard seats and tiny tables that discourage people from stopping too long. Don't expect fabulous service, as there are no menus and you get to pick out your drinks and pastries from the shelves and the refrigerated cases. The coffee and focaccia, however, are arguably some of the best in Sydney. ◆ Cafe ◆ Daily 6AM-8PM. 320B Victoria St (between Surrey and Craigend Sts). 9331.2914

26 Bar Coluzzi ★★$ In Sydney, the Coluzzi name has been associated with great cafes and Italian food for years. This relaxed coffee bar was one of the first on the strip and continues to attract a devoted band of patrons. Young Euro-chic types mix with older locals who have long made this place their canteen. The menu includes simple Italian sandwiches and salads, although coffee is the main attraction. ◆ Cafe ◆ Daily 5:30AM-7:30PM. 322 Victoria St (between Surrey and Craigend Sts). 9380.5420 Also at: 99 Elizabeth St (between Market and King Sts). 9233.1651.

Burgerman

27 Burgerman ★★$ Tempting the waiflike people who inhabit the streets and cafes of Darlinghurst is this great little restaurant serving big juicy hamburgers. Order one of the ten varieties of burgers at the stainless-steel counter and take a seat at one of the tables in the futuristic dining room, decorated in red-and-white plastic. (You can also order your burger to take out.) From ground lamb fillet with garlic-and-basil mayonnaise to the vegetarian variety, there's a burger for everyone. Wash it down with one of the fresh-squeezed juices or homemade lemonade. ◆ Modern Australian ◆ Daily noon-10PM. 116 Surrey St (at Victoria St). 9361.0268

28 bills ★★$$ Everything is gorgeous here—the customers, the staff, and, perhaps most important, the food. This was one of the first cafes in Sydney to follow the communal dining table trend. The huge blond-wood tables always have splendid floral and fruit displays to admire and are covered with glossy magazines to read. Sit down and dig into a mound of creamy scrambled eggs for breakfast or try the huge sandwiches and delicious salads at lunchtime. **bills 2,** a branch of this cafe, is in Surry Hills (see page 97). ◆ Cafe ◆ M-Sa breakfast and lunch. No credit cards accepted. 433 Liverpool St (between West and Victoria Sts). 9360.9631

29 Green Park Hotel Most nights this friendly pub, with its bar and big lounge area, caters to a mixed crowd of younger trendsetters and older residents. The pub's bottle shop (liquor store) is always buzzing on the weekend as locals grab a bottle of wine on their way to dinner. ◆ Daily. 360 Victoria St (at Liverpool St). 9380.5311

30 Fez Cafe ★★★$$ The Middle Eastern menu and music and the glamorous crowd make a stop at this cafe an intoxicating experience. The decor is Moorish-meets-modern, with lots of color, cushions, and tile. The menu is a fairly Westernized version of North African/Middle Eastern cuisine, and, in the Arab tradition, the portions are generous. The *meze* plate is full of dips, olives, and pickled goodies, and the vegetable *tagine* (a North African stew) is both spicy and fragrant. Iced Moroccan mint tea, and the lemon, pineapple, and mint frappés are all delicious. When the weather is fine, the outdoor tables and cushions on the windows are full of patrons in need of a quick coffee. ◆ Middle Eastern ◆ Daily breakfast, lunch, and dinner. 247 Victoria St (at Liverpool St). 9360.9581

30 Fu Manchu ★★$ Terrific contemporary Asian food for next to nothing is the draw at this funky little noodle bar. The narrow but stylish dining space has bright red punching-bag stools and matching red chopsticks, and is accented with just the right amount of stainless steel. The place is forever busy but well worth the wait for a table. Be sure to try the steamed dumplings. ◆ Asian ◆ M-Sa lunch and dinner; Su dinner. 249 Victoria St (between Burton and Liverpool Sts). 9360.9424

30 Oh! Calcutta! ★★$$ The thoughtful range of dishes at this not-so-typical Indian restaurant—from traditional to modern—provides plenty of options, including vegetarian. This is Indian food at its most contemporary and most interesting. If you're looking for an intimate dining experience, though, you'll be disappointed—tables are very close together. Outdoor seating is available. ◆ Indian ◆ M-Th, Sa-Su dinner; F lunch and dinner. Reservations recommended. 251 Victoria St (between Burton and Liverpool Sts). 9360.3650

31 Rockerfellers ★$$ It's unlikely that you'll find a real Rockefeller at this hamburger restaurant and diner, but plenty of Sydneysiders and out-of-towners make it their business to chow down here. The all-American menu includes lots of french fries, pickles, and creative burger toppings. ◆ American ◆ Daily dinner. 225 Oxford St (between S Dowling St and Taylor Sq). 9361.6968

32 Taylor Square Restaurant ★$$ Climb the steep, long staircase here and enter one of Sydney's most colorful dining rooms. The walls are blue, lavender, and lime, and the mirrors on the wall reflect everything that's going on. The food is good and relatively inexpensive. Try the Peking duck on a bed of risotto, or the Atlantic salmon with potato-and-chervil salad. The rhubarb brûlée with orange-cinnamon salad is a popular signature dessert. The service here can sometimes be less than friendly, but the diners seem unperturbed. ◆ Modern Australian ◆ Tu-Su dinner. Reservations recommended. 191-95 Oxford St (between S Dowling St and Taylor Sq). 9360.5828

32 Cafe 191 ★$ Dance music pulses here morning, noon, and night as the staff, clad in tight clothing, serves coffee and simple, light, cafe food. Whether seated inside or outdoors, you always have a view of the goings-on

around Oxford Street and Taylor Square—and people watching is a popular pastime. ◆ Cafe ◆ Daily breakfast, lunch, and dinner. 191 Oxford St (at Taylor Sq). 9360.4295

33 Taxi Club A Sydney institution, this formerly seedy bar has undergone a face-lift, but still attracts the same collection of drag queens, serious drinkers, and those in need of a bizarre after-hours experience. On some nights, DJs spin the latest music until the wee hours, when performers in heavy-duty drag take center stage for some hair-raising performances. ◆ Admission. W 9AM-11:30PM; F-Su midnight-5PM. 40 Flinders St (between Hannam and Taylor Sts). 9331.4256

34 Flinders Hotel A predominantly gay male crowd, which doesn't really like to fill the place until after midnight, gather at this, one of the area's oldest gay pubs. It's generally a very laid-back, unpretentious, come-as-you-are establishment. The early-morning "recovery" parties here are notorious. ◆ M-Th 8PM-3AM; F-Sa 10PM-7AM; Su 8PM-midnight. 63 Flinders St (at Hill St). 9360.4929

35 The Palace ★★$$ This wedge-shaped pub got the royal treatment and was transformed into a smart restaurant serving Modern Australian cuisine. With lots of wood details and native flowers, the decor here is contemporary, a cut above every other converted city pub. Some very creative dishes are served, including variations on such old bistro favorites as pasta, roasted meats, and salads. Desserts, such as the raspberry soufflé with mint pesto, are too good to pass up. ◆ Modern Australian ◆ Daily dinner. Reservations recommended. 122 Flinders St (between S Dowling St and Fleming La). 9361.5170

36 Kinselas Spread over three floors, this club used to be a funeral parlor. The interior features some great Art Deco detailing, especially in the lovely ground-floor bar, which often has live entertainment. On the middle floor is a small bar, which is often open to "members only," while the dance floor is located on the top level. Officially, there is no dress code—the secret here is to avoid being either too casual or too formal. ◆ M-Tu, Su 8PM-midnight; F-Sa 8PM-3AM. 383 Bourke St (between Campbell St and Taylor Sq). 9331.1600

China is Sydney's major trading partner. Nonferrous metals—aluminum, zinc, and lead—are the leading exports.

Restaurants/Clubs: Red   **Hotels:** Blue
Shops/❦ **Outdoors:** Green   **Sights/Culture:** Black

37 Court House When a pub in the middle of Sydney's most exciting and outrageous street scene is open 24 hours a day, seven days a week, then it's sure to attract a pretty unusual crowd. This pub caters to both gay and straight patrons, and the music can get loud as the night passes. All in all, it is a singular Sydney experience. ◆ Daily 24 hours. 189 Oxford St (at Taylor Sq). 9360.4831

38 Oxford Hotel The ground floor of this pub seems to be strictly a gay men's domain, but upstairs, at **Gilligan's,** anything goes. Transvestites, young clubgoers, and businesspeople all converge to sample the latest cocktail creations from the bar. When things quiet down, table service is available. ◆ M-Sa 3PM-2AM; Su 3PM-midnight. 134 Oxford St (at Taylor Sq). 9331.3467

39 S(a)x Leather This heavy-duty leather store— not for the fainthearted— is worth a visit, even if you have no intention of purchasing the kinky outfits and accessories for sale. This place leaves many asking, "What's that for?" If you're too shy to browse, grab the catalog and depart discreetly. ◆ M-Sa. 110A Oxford St (between Bourke and Palmer Sts). 9331.6105

40 Aussie Boys Offering the latest in casual clothing for clubbing and the gym, this store is popular with gay men in search of just the right outfit. The long racks of stock include relatively inexpensive locally made items. ◆ M-Sa. 102 Oxford St (between Palmer and Crown Sts). 9360.7011

MERCURY TOBACCO

41 Mercury Tobacco Virtually any brand of tobacco product is available here, along with related paraphernalia. The place isn't much for atmosphere, but the selection can't be beat. ◆ Daily. 133 Oxford St (between Taylor Sq and Crown St). 9360.1276

42 Gitte Weise Gallery Although this contemporary photo gallery is new on the art scene, it has already attracted crowds to its openings. Exhibitions change every couple of months, and an annex displays the work of photographers not in the gallery's regular roster of artists. ◆ Tu-Sa 11AM-6PM; closed in January. 94 Oxford St (between Palmer and Crown Sts), Level 2. 9360.2659

43 Reach'n Records For those interested in the latest in disco and rave music, this underground (literally) store sells it, samples it, and mixes it. Young clubgoers come to browse, while older patrons enjoy thumbing through the selection of retro music. ◆ M-Sa. 80 Oxford St (at Crown St). 9380.5378

44 Midnight Shift Something of a legend in the gay men's nightclub scene, "The Shift" (as locals call it) features a modern bar downstairs, while upstairs a busy dance party is in progress nightly. On the third Thursday of each month, when it welcomes a lesbian crowd, the place is women-only territory. ◆ M-Th 9PM-3AM; F-Sa 10PM-6AM; Su 11PM-6AM. 85 Oxford St (between Crown St and Oxford Sq). 9360.4463

45 Darlinghurst Health Products The motto of this store is "Health, sport, and thought." From vitamins and power drinks to health-oriented literature—food for the mind—this is one of the most well-stocked health food stores in Sydney. Come in and enjoy the faint aroma of incense and essential oils. ◆ M-Sa. 62-64 Oxford St (between Crown St and Oxford Sq). 9360.9600

46 Oxford Koala Hotel Apartments $$ This plain 330-room hotel is only a few minutes from the center of the city and the neighborhood's good restaurants. It also features a visitors' information service, restaurant, and 24-hour room service. The rooms haven't been refurbished since the 1970s, so they look a little tattered and tired. The decor—rather gray and institutional—is equally lackluster, but in general this hotel offers an excellent value for the money. ◆ 55 Oxford St (at Pelican St). 9269.0645; fax 9283.2741

47 Cash Palace From wedding dresses to simple streetwear, this boutique that sells some local designer labels has been part of the alternative clothing scene for years. Drag performers, clubgoers, and suburban mothers all shop here in happy harmony. It's best to know what you're looking for, as the service leaves something to be desired. ◆ M-Sa. 42 Oxford St (between Oxford Sq and Liverpool St). 9360.1565

48 Oxford Street Camping and Disposal This store was a place where you could buy surplus army and navy gear. Now, however, like many similar stores in Sydney, this one sells everything from backpacks and tents to work boots and slippers. The store is crammed with goods and carries countless pairs of the famous Australian Blundstone boots. ◆ M-Sa. 43 Oxford St (between Pelican and Brisbane Sts). 9261.8775

49 Holiday Inn Park Suites $$$ Each of the 135 one- and two-bedroom apartments at this hotel offers a separate lounge/dining room, fully equipped kitchen, laundry facilities, and private balcony. Rooms are furnished with simple blond wood and lots of Formica. The restaurant, bar, swimming pool, spa, and sauna are all basic, no-frills amenities. Conference rooms and some business services are also available. ◆ 16-32 Oxford St (between Oxford Sq and Liverpool St). 9331.7728; fax 9360.6649

Within the Holiday Inn Park Suites:

Open 'N' Shut Case It's not a bad idea to know about this store when in need of an extra suitcase or carry-on bag to bring home the fruits of all that shopping. Luggage, briefcases, handbags, corporate-style gifts— it's all here. The merchandise is mostly utilitarian, but the store does carry some luxury brands. ◆ M-Sa. 9360.3939

50 D.C.M. This large space is primarily a gay male club, yet it welcomes everybody who comes in with the right attitude and the urge to bump and grind on the dance floor. It's always noisy, with a very young, very extroverted crowd dancing to disco and contemporary club favorites. ◆ Daily 9PM-3AM. 33 Oxford St (between Pelican and Brisbane Sts). 9267.7380

51 Burdekin Hotel A heavily remodeled old pub that now has the look of a sleek, modern bar, this place serves a young and suave clientele who look as though they go to art college—or at least aspire to do so. Downstairs at the **Dug Out Bar,** the older patrons appreciate the selections from the cocktail menu. ◆ M-Sa 11AM-2AM; Su noon-midnight. 2 Oxford St (at Liverpool St). 9331.3066

Surry Hills

52 Pepe Mejia About 20 young Australian fashion designers are represented at this wonderful boutique. Take the time to search through the stock, and you might just unearth an item made by the next Donna Karan or Richard Tyler. ◆ M-Sa. 318 Crown St (at Campbell St). 9360.2463

53 Bentley Bar This harmless-looking corner pub hosts a dance and music extravaganza every night after 9PM. The place attracts a relatively young, beer-drinking crowd, from urbane local clubgoers to traveling backpackers. The overall scene is lots of fun for those young enough (in years or at heart) to enjoy its intensity. ◆ M-Tu noon-2AM; W-Th noon-3AM; F-Sa noon-5AM; Su 10AM-10PM. 320 Crown St (at Campbell St). 9331.1186

54 Medina on Crown $$ Right in the middle of funky Surry Hills sits this more refined-looking apartment hotel, which opened in 1994. With 85 large one- and two-bedroom suites—complete with full kitchens and separate sitting rooms—this place is ideal for visitors on an extended stay and families who need to spread out. The decor is strictly modern and very functional. The meeting rooms, rooftop tennis court, gym, and

business services make this a good place for business travelers. There is no room service, but the concierge will arrange the delivery of groceries or food, and there is daily maid service. Plenty of restaurants and cafes are within walking distance. ◆ 359 Crown St (between Fitzroy and Albion Sts). 9360.6666; fax 9361.5965

Within Medina on Crown:

bills 2 ★★★$$ Bill Granger, the owner of **bills** in Darlinghurst (see page 94), has put his name and stamp on this truly stylish cafe. By day it's perfect for a casual, quick breakfast or lunch. At night, the white tablecloths come out for a relatively formal dining experience. The menu is fabulous and puts this cafe in a class of its own—ricotta hotcakes with fresh banana-and-honeycomb butter for breakfast, or a warm chicken salad for lunch. The dinner menu changes daily and features Modern Australian cooking. ◆ Cafe ◆ M-Sa breakfast, lunch, and dinner; Su breakfast and lunch. 355 Crown St. 9360.4762

55 Dolphin Hotel ★★$$ In its former incarnation, this place was a rugged ◆ neighborhood pub. Today it is one of a successful new breed of Sydney pubs that have been converted into casual restaurants. The downstairs area is essentially a large pub and cafe with a communal table. Upstairs is a contemporary cocktail bar and dining room. Seafood stands out on this menu, with daily specials and such regular items as barbecued Yamba king prawns and tuna steaks with Asian spices. The wine list is outstanding. ◆ Modern Australian ◆ Restaurant: daily lunch and dinner. Cafe: daily breakfast, lunch, and dinner. Reservations recommended. 412 Crown St (at Fitzroy St). 9331.4800

In the early 1800s Spanish dollars were imported from India to provide much-needed currency. Holes were cut in them to prevent exportation. The resulting hollow coin, and the piece cut from the middle were called, respectively, the Holey Dollar and the Dump. The Holey Dollar was valued at 5 shillings, while the Dump was worth about 15 pence.

56 Vegas ★$ For a break from Sydney's slick, minimalist cafes, try this retro American-style cafe, where you'll feel right at home in your Hawaiian shirt. Locals come for the enormous breakfasts and laid-back service. It's a small space, but you feel as though you could sit here all day and not be bothered. ♦ Cafe ♦ Daily breakfast, lunch, and dinner. 393 Crown St (between Withers La and Foveaux St). 9380.5242

57 Prasit's Northside on Crown ★★★$$ Those who can't handle their chilies need not read further. Owner/chef Prasit Prateeprasen is as obsessed with chilies as he is with the color purple, a fondness reflected in the walls, tables, and even the waiters' aprons. A mainly local crowd of die-hard fans sits on the bright, padded banquettes of this warm, lively restaurant, tucking into the *masaman* (lamb curry, Asian style) or a pretty dish of crisp, smoked fish salad. Grab a bottle of wine from the pub up the road and sit back and enjoy the slow chili afterburn. ♦ Thai ♦ M-Sa dinner; Th-F lunch and dinner. 415 Crown St (between Withers La and Foveaux St). 9319.0748

58 MG Garage Restaurant ★★★$$$ You may come here to see the three sleek MGs parked on the main floor, the fashionable patrons, or the Philippe Starck–designed furnishings, but you'll soon forget them once you start eating. Chef Janni Kyritsis, of **Bennelong** fame (see page 22), ensures that his kitchen is the star attraction, serving some of the best seafood and poultry dishes in town. Two can share a guinea fowl wrapped in salty pancetta and roasted to perfection; another favorite is the delicate squid, mussel, and snapper stew. Finish with the delicious fig tart. The terrific wine list features many European vineyards. The waiters are so articulate when describing the dishes, they might all have apprenticed in the kitchen. The lower-priced **Fuel** serves somewhat less elaborate fare. ♦ Modern Australian ♦ M-Sa lunch and dinner; Su lunch. Reservations required. 490 Crown St (at Arthur St). 9383.9383

Almost one-quarter of New South Wales's population emigrated from other countries, with the majority coming from China, New Zealand, and the United Kingdom.

59 Melograno ★$ The open kitchen lends a homelike air to this comfortable cafe. There is nothing ordinary about the blackboard menu, however, which changes weekly. Sample the delicious baked eggs for breakfast, or the big cookies and other homemade desserts, which go perfectly with one of Melograno's strong coffees. The service is excellent. ♦ Cafe ♦ Tu-Su breakfast and lunch. 572 Crown St (between Cleveland and Devonshire Sts). 9698.9131

60 La Passion du Fruit ★★$ Decorated with bright colors, African masks, and little potted plants, this popular cafe also has an open kitchen to add to its welcoming atmosphere. All items on the blackboard menu are moderately priced. The croissants and *croque monsieur* (grilled, batter-dipped ham-and-cheese sandwich) are the best bets for breakfast, while the mixed plate for lunch is enough for two. The service is very casual. ♦ Cafe ♦ Daily breakfast and lunch. 633 Bourke St (at Devonshire St). 9690.1894

61 Cafe Niki ★$ All the Sydney cafe standards are served here, as well as extra touches like homemade bagels and enormous cakes. Sit outside on one of the comfortable wicker chairs or inside at the old hardwood bar. Jazz music fills the room as a mostly local crowd files in and out. ♦ Cafe ♦ M-Sa breakfast, lunch, and dinner. 544 Bourke St (at Nobbs St). 9319.7517

62 Brett Whitely Studio Until his death in 1992, Brett Whitely was one of Australia's most flamboyant and provocative contemporary artists, and intense public interest in his life continues unabated. During his controversial career, he was a painter of passionate extremes, who explored the dualistic themes of heaven and hell, good and evil, and east and west. He had an ardent love of the landscape, the female figure, and the heroes of art and literature—all regular motifs in his works. In 1985, the artist purchased this building that was previously a factory and made it his studio and residence. After his death, the studio became a public museum and art gallery, featuring his work and that of other artists. Walking into the studio gives you an intimate feeling for Whitely's life and work: Much of the studio remains just as he kept it—scattered with his notebooks, personal effects, and memorabilia. Operated as an annex of the **Art Gallery of New South Wales** (see page 72), the space also features a program of changing exhibitions of contemporary works. ◆ Free. Sa-Su. 2 Raper St (at Davies St). Information 9225.1744

63 Mohr Fish ★★$$ Once a local butcher shop, this place is now a tiny, well-run seafood restaurant. If there were such a thing as a seafood bar, then this would be it—although there is no liquor license (you can bring your own), customers order at the counter and sit on stools at small round tables in a tile-covered room. The catch of the day determines the offerings on the blackboard menu. When it's available, try the blue-eyed cod with *salsa verde* for a hearty meal. The steamed mussels *Provençale* and regular beer-batter fish-and-chips will tempt you to pay another visit. The smoked-salmon breakfasts are also a treat. ◆ Seafood ◆ Daily breakfast, lunch, and dinner. 202 Devonshire St (between Little Riley and Steel Sts). 9318.1326

64 O Bar ★★$$ The **Clarendon Hotel**'s makeover transformed this old Sydney pub from a dark, dingy watering hole to a happening new bar with a happening new restaurant. Resist the call of the O-shaped bar and walk through to the dining room at the back of the pub. A cozy little courtyard is the best place to sit in good weather to avoid the big rowdy tables and the flow of smoke from inside. An ever-changing blackboard menu and wine list keep the crowd guessing and coming back for more. Asian flavors are popular here, fused with touches of good, old-fashioned home cooking. ◆ Modern Australian ◆ Daily lunch and dinner. Reservations recommended. 156 Devonshire St (at Waterloo St). 9319.6881

65 Belvoir Street Theatre This alternative theater space was once a tomato-sauce (ketchup) factory. Two stages are housed in the complex—the downstairs space presents more experimental plays and performances, while the upstairs theater is home to the **Belvoir Theatre Company** productions. ◆ Call for performance schedule. 25 Belvoir St (between Wilton and Elizabeth Sts). 9699.3444

66 Furama Hotel Central $$$ Centrally located, this international-style hotel has 270 rooms and amenities that include a sparkling 20-meter (65-foot) indoor pool, Jacuzzi, spa, sauna, gym, and irons and ironing boards in the rooms. The 100-seat restaurant, a bar and bistro, conference facilities, and catering for up to 600 people make this a popular choice with business travelers. The decor is nondescript—perhaps because it is so new—with neutral colors and standard Australian prints on the walls. ◆ 28 Albion St (between Mary and Elizabeth Sts). 9281.0333; fax 9281.0222

Bests

Deborah Hutton

Fashion Editor, *Australian Women's Weekly*/Fashion Commentator and Host, Channel 9 Network/ Promotion Consultant, Myer Grace Bros. Department Stores

Having lunch at **Pier** restaurant at **Rose Bay,** overlooking the harbor on a sunny day with the best fish and chips!

Walking the foreshore cliffs between **Bondi Beach** and **Tamarama.**

Watching the first light break as the sun rises at Bondi.

Flying into Sydney on a sunny day and admiring the tremendous beauty of it.

Enjoying the scenic drive from the city to **Palm Beach** with the roof down in my convertible.

Having dinner at **Hugo's** at Bondi while watching the passing parade of gorgeous tanned bodies.

Taking a friend's speed boat out and doing a "Lifestyles of the Rich and Famous" tour of the foreshores of the **Eastern Suburbs** harbor homes.

Having coffee with friends at any one of the cafes on **Victoria Street** in **Darlinghurst**. A particular favorite is **Morgan's.**

Ordering the world's best scrambled eggs at **bills** cafe.

Enjoying open-air night concerts at the **Sydney Cricket Ground (SCG).**

Taking an early morning brisk walk around **Mrs. Macquarie's Chair,** on the foreshore near the **Opera House.**

Staying a night at the **Park Hyatt** on **Sydney Cove,** overlooking the **Opera House,** the **Harbour Bridge,** and the passing ferry traffic.

Enjoy seeing the **Sydney Dance Company.**

Doing the **Oxford Street** markets in **Paddington** on a busy Saturday.

Shopping at **Tiffany's** in the beautiful **Chifley Tower** building.

The Gay and Lesbian Mardi Gras parade is a sight to be seen.

Kings Cross/Elizabeth Bay/ Potts Point/Woolloomooloo

Sydney's seedier side sits next to one of the city's most elegant in the area encompassing Kings Cross, and its neighbors, Elizabeth Bay, Potts Point, and Woolloomooloo. Sleazy bars are just moments from some of Sydney's finest restaurants; brothels operate next to luxury apartment blocks and hotels; and armies of pub crawlers from the suburbs mingle with ultrachic locals.

At the top of **William Street** just under the huge red-and-white Coca-Cola sign, Kings Cross is replete with prostitutes, strip joints, all-night bars, and clubs. Groups of foreign sailors in need of R&R come here, and busloads of tourists arrive in search of a 24-hour buzz. First named Queens Cross (after Queen Victoria) until King Edward became its namesake, "The Cross" (as it is commonly called today) was originally a bohemian enclave for poets, artists, and those who liked to live on the fringe of mainstream Sydney life. This

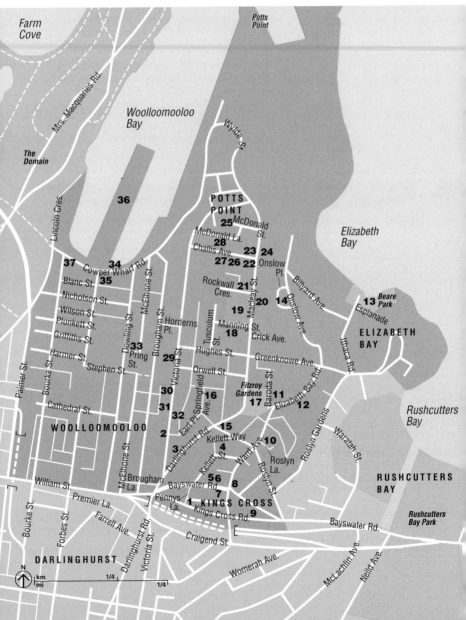

scene changed in the 1940s when sailors from the US hit the shores, World War II brought an influx of more Europeans, and strip joints and bars started popping up in this avant-garde neighborhood.

Unlike other red-light districts around the world, The Cross does not emit particularly threatening vibes. The area may have its share of drunken street brawls, but it is well policed, and some of its cafes, small hotels, and fashionable clubs help refine and define what would otherwise be a shabby neighborhood. Along **Kellett Street** and **Bayswater Road**, such restaurants as **Darley Street Thai** and **Bayswater Brasserie** serve some of Australia's more innovative food. And while the **Victoria Street** area may also have its share of drug addicts and desperate backpackers, it is also home to such extraordinary boutique properties as the **Regents Court Hotel** and fine dining spots like **Wockpool** and **Mezzaluna**.

On the borders of The Cross are the more residential enclaves of Elizabeth Bay and Potts Point. These areas boast some of Sydney's most prized real estate, thanks to their harbor views, the monied fashionable community who lives here, and their proximity to the Central Business District (CBD). The streets of Elizabeth Bay twist and turn, running down to the harbor to meet **Beare Park.** Elizabeth Bay (or "Betty Bay," as some locals call it) also features grand old apartment buildings from the 1920s and 1930s, rows of Victorian terrace mansions on **Roslyn Gardens,** and the historic **Elizabeth Bay House.**

Potts Point is equally impressive, with its Victorian terrace homes, Art Deco apartment blocks, and celebrated restaurants. It was originally developed in the early 1800s for free settlers. The main thoroughfare is **Macleay Street** (named after Alexander Macleay, colonial secretary of New South Wales from 1826 to 1837), a street lined with major hotels, such restaurants as **Paramount** and **Cicada,** and a cluster of chic cafes. Victoria Street has an odd mix of both the rowdy backpacker crowd who hangs out at the Laundromats, cafes, and inexpensive eateries, and the more refined upwardly mobile who linger at restaurants and reside in the rows of well-kept terrace homes.

Near the harbor and **The Domain** is the old wharf area of **Woolloomooloo.** The pubs here are regular haunts for Sydneysiders and sailors searching for a beer or two or three. At press time plans were underway for a complete facelift and development of this wharfside stretch into residential properties.

Chaos and order comfortably coexist in the Kings Cross and Potts Point areas. Whether it's the thrill of a nightclub or the comfort and tranquillity of a fine restaurant, this urban neighborhood always has its lights on.

1 Millennium $$$ This octagonal 390-room hotel sits at the top of William Street, right behind the famous flashing red-and-white Coca-Cola sign. The standard contemporary guest rooms have spectacular views of Sydney Harbour, the CBD, and/or the eastern suburbs. A business center, a large four-floor conference center, a swimming pool, fitness center, and bar/bistro are among the amenities. ♦ 2-14 Kings Cross Rd (at Pennys La). 9356.1234; 9356.4150

2 Holiday Inn Potts Point $$$ All the basic services and 278 well-decorated rooms can be enjoyed at this hotel just on the fringe of rowdy Kings Cross and the more sedate Potts Point. The **Harbour View Lounge and Bar** on the top floor lives up to its name, while the **Bistro Victoria** serves simple meals. Well-organized, theater-style meeting rooms are available, as are some business services. ♦ 203 Victoria St (between Brougham La and Horderns Pl). 9368.4000, 800/835.7742; fax 9267.4119

3 Hotel Capital $$ With 227 rooms, this hotel is more popular for its location and views than for its undistinguished, standard decor and service. All rooms have air-conditioning, mini-bars, and coffee-making facilities. Nonsmoking rooms, connecting rooms, and suites are all available. There are two restaurants and a cafe and decent room service. The swimming pool, gym, and "Relaxation Centre"—with a wonderful ginseng bath and wet and dry saunas—are all very popular with guests and locals. Weekend packages are available. ♦ 111 Darlinghurst Rd (between Victoria St and Springfield Ave). 9358.2755; fax 9358.2888

4 Lime & Lemongrass ★★$$$ Housed in an old Victorian terrace house, this Thai restaurant has an elegant atmosphere with Asian antiques and warm-colored walls and trims. The food is just as fine, with such basic dishes as pad thai, *larb* chicken (Thai-style curry), and steamed spring rolls on the menu next to the more innovative daily specials. Leave room for the coconut and banana pudding, or one of the other Thai-inspired desserts. On warm nights ask to sit in the courtyard or at one of the balcony tables and enjoy the local street life. ♦ Thai ♦ Daily dinner. 32 Kellett St (between Ward Ave and Kellett Way). 9358.5577

5 Rhino Bar It's hard to believe that this beautiful old terrace with an unassuming front houses a happening nightclub. If you're decked out in the latest Sydney fashions and have a marching attitude, then this is the place to flaunt your stuff. The crowd is young and hip with a need to be noticed as everyone grooves to the DJ's mixes. It's lots of fun if you're in the right mood. ♦ M-W 3PM-1AM; Th 3PM-3AM; F 3PM-5AM; Sa 5PM-5AM; Su 4PM-11PM. 24 Bayswater Rd (between Ward Ave and Kellett St). 9357.7700

6 Box ★★$ From a stainless-steel floor to the tiny scratched name on the door, this narrow cafe's decor is sheer simplicity. Patrons sit on tiny boxes at plastic tables while waiting to be served extra-strong coffee and uncomplicated food. This place is an experience-and-a-half—arriving customers are given the once-over by fellow habitués as they enter. ♦ Cafe ♦ M-F 7:30AM-4:30PM; Sa-Su. 28A Bayswater Rd (between Ward Ave and Kellett St). 9358.6418

Restaurants/Clubs: Red   **Hotels:** Blue
Shops/ Outdoors: Green   **Sights/Culture:** Black

6 Darley Street Thai ★★★$$$ This is quite possibly Sydney's only Thai restaurant that boasts a truly glamorous interior, with watermelon-pink walls and a scattering of colorful, Thai silk cushions that help the well-clad clientele get comfortable. Forget every preconceived notion about Thai food when dining here—co-owner and chef David Thompson studies ancient Thai recipes to uncover wildly different flavor combinations. Order à la carte or from the eight-course, prix-fixe menu, and enjoy a unique culinary experience. The grilled trout with sweet fish sauce and spicy salads with seafood are two recommended dishes. Sister restaurant **Sailor's Thai** (see page 33) offers the same fare. ♦ Thai ♦ M dinner; Tu-Su lunch and dinner. Reservations recommended. 28-30 Bayswater Rd (between Ward Ave and Kellett St). 9358.6530

6 Bayswater Brasserie ★★$$$ "The Bayz," as this place is affectionately known to some, has never lost favor with Sydney's style mongers. In fact, they've made a tradition of meeting friends in the dimly lit bar out back while waiting for a table. This is a spot that's equally good during the day for an intimate lazy brunch in the front conservatory as it is at night for a rowdy dinner for 10 in the courtyard. The conventional Modern Australian seafood menu (with a few meat dishes) is supplemented by more interesting offerings on the changing specials board. Fresh oysters are always available. Service is snappy with a little bit of attitude on the side. The wine list is extensive and diverse. ♦ Modern Australian ♦ M-Sa lunch and dinner; Su brunch and dinner. 32 Bayswater Rd (between Ward Ave and Kellett St). 9357.2177

7 The Crescent on Bayswater $$$ With all the noise and partying on Bayswater Road, guests are grateful for the soundproof windows at this stylish hotel. There are 68 guest rooms and several one-bedroom suites and family-size suites—all with private balconies, fully equipped kitchenettes, mini-bars, and in-house movies. The swimming pool is a decent size and the gym on the building's first floor is open to guests. Room service is available. ♦ 33 Bayswater Rd (between Ward Ave and Pennys La). 9357.7266, 800/257.327; fax 9357.7418

Within Crescent on Bayswater:

Sydney in Print

A good way to explore Sydney before visiting the city is to read one of the many books and plays that either talk about the town or that use it as a setting for a broader tale. The following selection should help launch a literary tour.

Antipodes by David Malouf (Penguin Australia, 1986) This collection of short stories is one of the many works written by an Australian poet and novelist about the country and its relationship to the world. Some of the stories refer to Sydney and also provide an insightful look at Australia's complex culture.

Bliss by Peter Carey (Picador, 1984) A Sydney advertising executive goes on a search for the meaning of life. Along the way he gets in touch with nature and himself. Like many of Carey's early works, this novel is set in Sydney.

Bloody Delicious by Joan Campbell (Allen & Unwin, 1997) This Australian food reference and cookbook explores nearly a hundred years of Australian cuisine. From the basic roast to the infusion of Asian and Mediterranean flavors, Campbell offers a witty, detailed account of what Aussie food is all about and how to prepare some of the country's favorite feasts.

Damned Whores and God's Police by Anne Summers (Penguin Australia, 1975) Summers, a magazine editor (including the US-based *Ms*) and the former prime minister's advisor on women, wrote this compelling and previously untold history of women in the early colony.

Emerald City by David Williamson (Currency Press, 1987) Set in Sydney, this play (which was also made into a film) by the Australian playwright who also wrote the film script *Gallipoli,* deals with the politics of the publishing industry.

The Fatal Shore by Robert Hughes (Vintage, 1989) This renowned expatriate Australian (and art critic) details a stimulating fiction-based-on-fact account of Australia's humble and harsh beginning as a British penal colony. It takes place mostly in Sydney.

A Fortunate Life by A.B. Facey (Fremantle Arts Centre Press, 1981) From rags to ruins, this \account of a man's struggle to survive in the face of personal tragedy and economic hardship has become an allegory for the Australian battler.

Good Food Guide by Terry Durack and Jill Dupleix (Anne O'Donovan Pty. Ltd., 1984) Considered the king and queen of food writing and criticism in Australia, Durack and Dupleix have been penning witty reviews for the *Sydney Morning Herald* and Melbourne's *The Age* for two decades. This annual opus provides well-written critiques of Sydney's cafes and restaurants.

Homebush Boy by Thomas Keneally (Minerva/Heinemann, 1996) The author of *Schindler's List* wrote this autobiographical account of his school days at **St. Patrick's College** in Sydney's western suburbs.

Kangaroo by D.H. Lawrence (Thomas Seltzer, 1923) Colonial impressions of the British author's 1922 visit to Sydney and its countryside form the basis of this novel.

Lillian's Story by Kate Grenville (Allen & Unwin, 1985) The life of Bea Miles, a colorful street character and one of Sydney's most eccentric urban legends, is explored in this book. Miles was a part of Sydney's street life until the 1980s. The story was also made into a successful feature film of the same title.

The Lucky Country by Donald Horne (Penguin Books, 1971) Horne is one of Australia's most famous political and social commentators. The expression "The Lucky Country" is part of the Australian vernacular and describes the nation's remarkable quality of life and wealth of natural resources. Much of the book focuses on social dynamics in Sydney.

No Safe Harbor by Peter Corris (Dell Publishing, 1991) While searching for a missing man, a private detective uncovers some suspicious deaths connected with the building of the **Sydney Harbour Bridge** some 60 years earlier.

The Oxford Anthology of Australian Literature by Stan Arnell (Oxford University Press, 1978) This popular academic and consumer resource tool to assist in searching for books on Sydney and Australia is regularly updated.

Patrick White—A Life by David Marr (Random House, 1991) One of Australia's most famous novelists, Patrick White won the 1973 Nobel Prize for Literature. Marr's biography offers insight into White's complicated life and both Sydney and Australia's literary scene from World War II through the 1980s.

Sydney by Jan Morris (Penguin, 1992) This social and cultural portrait of Sydney by the British travel writer focuses on the city center and harbor life of the city from its early days to the present.

Sydney Beach Guide by David Crowe (Reed Books, Australia, 1996). For beach bums, this book gives a full rundown on the city's and Greater Sydney's beaches (all within a two-hour drive of the city), including many of the smaller harbor beaches. Also here are the contact numbers for **Surf Life Saving Clubs,** safety tips, water quality information, and maps.

Unreliable Memoirs by Clive James (Pan Picador, 1980) One of Australia's more famous expatriate writers and social commentators, James has been based in London for decades. This humorous autobiography recounts his early years growing up in Sydney's southern suburbs.

Bayswater Fitness This gym is full of local hard bodies (mainly male) who have come to pump iron, sweat on the aerobic equipment, or take one of the many exercise classes. Day passes are available. ◆ Daily 6:30AM-11PM. 9356.2555

8 Metro Motor Inn $$ Each of the 37 basic rooms at this motel offers air-conditioning, fully equipped kitchens, and in-house movies. The only problem is that the off-street parking for guests is very limited. Breakfast is available in the room or in the small dining room for guests. ◆ 40 Bayswater Rd (at Ward Ave). 9356.3511; fax 9357.1426

9 Cafe Hernandez ★★$ For decades this old Spanish cafe with old paintings and mismatched tables and chairs has been something of a drop-in center for those in need of a caffeine boost in the wee hours of the morning. Because it's open round-the-clock, it attracts everyone from those recovering from a big night out to taxi drivers and locals who come for a quick empanada and "long black" to keep them revved up. The staff is as quirky as the patrons. ◆ Cafe ◆ Daily 24 hours. 60 Kings Cross Rd (between Roslyn St and Ward Ave). 9331.2343

10 Madison's $$ The tropical garden that divides the two sides of this 40-room motel-style property is the main feature here. Guest rooms are small but clean, and the facilities and furniture are purely functional. It's a short stroll down the street to the bustle of Kings Cross. Enjoy breakfast in the room or in the dining room. ◆ 6-8 Ward Ave (at Bayswater Rd). 9357.1155; fax 9357.1193

11 Gazebo Sydney $$$ A standard international-style hotel, this cylindrical-shaped hotel has 385 rooms and 6 suites. Two of its best features are a rooftop swimming pool and spectacular views of the city and the northern harbor. A complimentary bus shuttles guests to the city center every morning. There are also two restaurants and two bars. ◆ 2 Elizabeth Bay Rd (at Baroda St). 9358.1999; fax 9356.2951

12 Sebel of Sydney $$$ Although Sydney has many larger, more luxurious hotels, this 166-room property still attracts local and international celebrities—Elton John has stayed here—who favor its large rooms, clublike ambience, attention to detail, and outstanding service. Some guest rooms have balconies and/or views of the city and Rushcutters Bay. There's a restaurant, room service, a rooftop pool, meeting rooms, a grand ballroom, and business services.

◆ 23 Elizabeth Bay Rd (between Ward Ave and Roslyn Gardens). 9358.3244; fax 9357.1926

13 Beare Park A grassy oasis among the dense high-rises of Elizabeth Bay, this harborfront public park was once part of the **Alexander Macleay Estate.** Today it's a popular spot for picnics, short walks, and views of Elizabeth Bay. ◆ Ithaca Rd and Esplanade

14 Elizabeth Bay House This residence (illustrated on page 105) was built 1835-1839 for Colonial Secretary Alexander Macleay, and is now a part of the Historic Houses Trust of New South Wales. Macleay and his wife, Eliza, commissioned **John Verge,** the most fashionable and accomplished architect of the day, to design a "Grecian villa" for their harborside 54-acre land grant. Some considered the house "the finest in the colony" because of its sophisticated design and quality handiwork (seen in the joinery, and stone- and plasterwork) that has rarely been matched in Australia. Some examples are the sweeping ascent leading to the first-floor gallery—considered one of the country's finest colonial staircases—and the domed oval saloon symmetrically placed in the center of the house. The Macleays lived here for only six years before their lifestyle sent them into bankruptcy. Macleay was also a renowned scientist with an interest in botany. He had a significant library and an entomology collection. The entire family was involved in scientific activities, from collection to illustration.

The interior was carefully reconstructed in 1977 by the Historic Houses Trust, using the content and furniture inventories prepared by Macleay before he left the house. Furniture, wallpaper, carpets, soft furnishings, and fittings of the mid-19th century were put in place. The original paint schemes, with stipple finishes and framed by the renowned cedar joinery, were recreated. ◆ Admission. Tu-Su. 7 Onslow Ave (at Onslow Pl). 9356.3022

15 Round Midnight Intimate and smoky, this nightclub is a good venue for live jazz and blues. The house band, Umbrella Red, does its distinctive Latin-meets-funk repertoire on Friday and Saturday nights. Call for the schedule of other performers. ◆ Admission. Tu-Su 8PM-3AM. 2 Roslyn St (at Darlinghurst Rd). 9356.4045

15 Bourbon and Beefsteak ★$$ Be prepared to party hard at this seedy, New Orleans–style bar and restaurant that's a Sydney institution. It's open around the clock, and although diner-type food is offered, the focus is on serving drinks to the late-night revelers who come to finish off the evening. The interior is something to behold—dark wood, brass, kitsch, and walls covered with signed photos and caricatures of local and international celebrities. ◆ Daily 24 hours. 24 Darlinghurst Rd (between Macleay and Roslyn Sts). 9358.1144

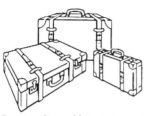

16 Regents Court $$ Tucked away behind the main drag of "The Cross" is one of Sydney's most stylish and innovative boutique hotels. The 5 floors of this Art Deco building house 30 large suites, each with a fully equipped kitchen and dining alcove, and contemporary furnishings. Every detail—from the bathroom lighting to the fine linens—has been well thought out. One of the hostelry's most special aspects is the staff—they take genuine pride in catering to guests' needs, making them feel as if they are staying at a well-managed home rather than a hotel. Another feature that sets this place apart from other boutique properties is the well-groomed, leafy rooftop garden, a perfect place for morning tea or a sunset drink. There's no restaurant, but hearty breakfasts are offered in the room or on the roof. Parking is available in a neighborhood hotel. ♦ 18 Springfield Ave (between Darlinghurst Rd and Springfield La). 9358.1533; fax 9358.1833

17 El Alamein Fountain Built in 1961, this fountain marks the heart of Kings Cross and commemorates the Australian role in the battle of El Alamein in Egypt during World War II. When the water is turned on, the fountain looks like a huge dandelion. This is a popular place for Sydneysiders to gather before they start their big nights out. Backpackers also congregate here to swap stories, and some of

Sydney's more colorful street characters have made it their home. ♦ Fitzroy Gardens, Macleay St (between Darlinghurst Rd and Greenknowe Ave)

18 New South Wales Institute of Architecture Housed in an old colonial sandstone home with a grand courtyard, this small but well-planned institute offers a tranquil oasis from the traffic along Macleay Street. There's a program of exhibitions and a terrific bookstore with architecture books, periodicals, and greeting cards. ♦ M-F. 3 Manning St (between Macleay and Tusculum Sts). 9356.2640

19 Landmark Parkroyal $$$ Many of the 470 rooms of this modern hotel have views of Sydney Harbour, the CBD, or both. All the guest rooms are large and are furnished in pastels and blond wood. There are two restaurants, three cocktail lounges, meeting facilities, an outdoor swimming pool, and a beautiful terrace garden. Complimentary parking for guests is a plus in this residential neighborhood. ♦ 81 Macleay St (between Manning St and Rockwall Crescent). 9368.3000, 800/835.7742; fax 9357.7600

20 Dorchester Inn $$ This 1886 hotel located on a tree-lined, tranquil part of Macleay Street on the fringe of Kings Cross noise has 15 large apartments with modern facilities. The original Victorian features and moldings were preserved, making guests feel as if they're experiencing turn-of-the-century Sydney. There's no restaurant, but room service and breakfast (either in the room or in the small dining room) are available. ♦ 38 Macleay St (between Crick Ave and Wylde St). 9358.2400; fax 9257.7579

Elizabeth Bay House

Child's Play

After the requisite trip on the monorail, what's a parent to do to keep the kids entertained in Sydney? The following are some ideas:

1 **Australia's Wonderland** Just on the fringe of Sydney, this vast theme park was built with children in mind (though kids of all ages seem to love it). The **Beach, International Village,** and the **Goldrush** are just three of the areas that feature the numerous rides and displays.

2 **The Rocks Puppet Cottage** Colorful puppets and toys from Australia and around the world are found in this restored sandstone cottage. Free puppet shows are given regularly.

3 **Sydney Aquarium** This beautiful aquatic habitat features some 5,000 sea creatures. Walk through a giant Plexiglas tunnel and come face to face with enormous sharks, stingrays, and many other water beings. Tropical fish, marine turtles, and an enormous array of corals are the draw in the **Australian Great Barrier Reef** display. Children love the **Touch and Learn Pool,** where they can handle sea urchins, starfish, and shellfish. There's also a well-organized seal pool. Take a ferry from **Circular Quay** and enjoy spectacular views of the city's best-known landmarks.

4 **Waratah Park** Get up close to Australia's unique wildlife at this park. You can even have a photograph taken while cuddling a koala. Dingos, cockatoos, rosellas, emus, kangaroos, and tree-climbing kangaroos are just some of the many animals living here. A **Bush Railway** takes those inclined to be less "hands-on" around the park.

5 **Koala Park Sanctuary** Although there seem to be more adults here than children, this koala and kangaroo zoo is a real kid pleaser. The daily sheep-shearing demonstration is popular, as is the boomerang exhibition.

6 **Taronga Zoo** This zoo, with the pleasant backdrop of **Sydney Harbour,** has long been a pioneer in keeping animals in fairly unrestricted enclosures. It's another great place to come into close contact with Australia's wild native animals. Highlights include seal shows; **Discovery Park,** where visitors meet feathered and furry inhabitants; the **Orangutan Rainforest;** and **Cats of Asia,** where a white Sumatran tiger roams in the wild.

7 **Powerhouse Museum** Formally a station that was used to power Sydney's tramway system in 1902, this museum places emphasis on Australian innovations and achievements. Here both the extraordinary and the everyday are celebrated—from computer technology and space travel to the decorative and domestic arts. Kids are more often than not spellbound by the hundred interactive science units.

8 **Beach Life** A visit to one of the city beaches is mandatory to really experience Sydney. Many city beaches have rock pools and swimming areas ("baths") that are safe for children. There are also plenty of cafes for refreshments. Two of the better beaches for kids are **Bondi** and **Bronte.** Both have clean saltwater baths and large grassy areas. **Nielsen Park** at **Vaucluse** is another harbor beach and is a great picnic spot.

9 **Darling Harbour** If the harborside festivals and street performers don't captivate the kids here on weekends, then the **Panasonic IMAX Theatre** and **Sega World** will keep them busy. These two spots are perfect for the media-savvy and game-addicted child. Don't miss the children's play center near the **Sydney Exhibition Centre.**

10 **Centennial Park** This is a favorite weekend retreat for Sydneysiders in search of a picnic spot, an in-line skating and bicycling track, or just a breather from the city. Bicycles and skates may be rented along Oxford Street and Clovelly Road.

KEELY EDWARDS

21 Macleay Street Bistro ★★$$$ A fair share of French standards, including steak tartare and some duck dishes, are on the menu at this dining spot that's touted as serving Modern Australian cuisine. But the fish specials, prepared in "Down Under" style, are some of the chef's best creations. The main dining room features wooden tables and chairs, linen tablecloths, and warm white walls. Arrive early on weekend nights to avoid waiting on line. ♦ Modern Australian ♦ M-Th dinner; F-Su lunch and dinner. 73A Macleay St (between Rockwall Crescent and Challis Ave). 9358.4891

THE PARAMOUNT
RESTAURANT

21 Paramount Restaurant ★★★$$$$ Chef Christine Manfield delivers classic dishes with many modern twists and turns at this restaurant with an ultraminimalist decor and excellent service. The menu changes monthly, but expect to see items like pepper steak made with kangaroo meat and seafood dishes that have both Asian and Mediterranean flavors. The menu of delicious elaborate desserts changes frequently, and the wine list is extensive. A six-course tasting menu is perfect for those who want to try a little of everything. Be forewarned: The decibel level gets rather high after 9PM. The restaurant's eponymous cookbook has been a popular addition to many Australian kitchens for several years. ♦ Modern Australian ♦ Daily dinner. Reservations required. 73 Macleay St (between Rockwall Crescent and Challis Ave). 9358.1652

21 The Pig and the Olive ★★$$ Although this place's name sounds like a children's book, it's actually a wonderful grown-up gourmet pizza restaurant. The wooden chairs and tables are constantly filled with locals sharing thin-crusted pizza—offered in three generous sizes—with such toppings as marinated lamb with feta and crispy prosciutto with gorgonzola. Try one of the Italian-inspired appetizers before inhaling one of the delicious pies. Wines may be ordered by the glass. ♦ Italian/Modern Australian ♦ Daily dinner. 71A Macleay St (between Rockwell Crescent and Challis Ave). 9357.3745

22 La Buvette ★★★$ Virginia Kerridge designed this beautiful, Art Deco–style cafe that's a breakfast and brunch hangout for Potts Point and Elizabeth Bay residents who come here to munch on scrumptious sandwiches and homemade pastries. Like its Darlinghurst cousin, **Parmalat** (see page 94) this place prepares and delivers great simple meals that don't require utensils. Takeout is a better option on the weekend, as the outdoor and indoor seating is usually filled. ♦ Cafe/ Takeout ♦ Tu-F 7AM-6PM; Sa-Su. 65 Macleay St (at Challis Ave), Shop 2. 9358.5113

Morans
RESTAURANT AND CAFE

23 Morans ★★★$$$ Restaurants and cafes seem to spring up every few weeks in the buzzing heart of Potts Point, the owners perhaps hoping for some of the good luck that this dining spot has enjoyed. The interior is modern yet comfortable, the service friendly yet professional, and the food comforting yet intriguing. The menu is seasonally based and the flavors are a thoughtful mix of Asian, French, Moroccan, and Italian cuisines—the lamb with eggplant relish is a delight, as are any of the several daily specials. Add an enticing wine list and the sum total is a wonderful dining experience. ♦ Modern Australian ♦ M-Tu dinner; W-F lunch and dinner; Sa dinner; Su brunch and dinner. 61-63 Macleay St (at Challis Ave). 9356.2223

23 Morans Cafe ★★$ Connected to the popular restaurant next door, this cafe is a good place to rest weary feet. The food and ambience lack some of the pretentious style of its neighboring cafes, plus the room is large and relatively quiet—even on the busiest of days. The coffee here always gets a mention. ♦ Cafe ♦ Daily 8AM-11PM. 61-63 Macleay St (at Challis Ave). 9358.2194

24 Chateau Sydney Hotel $$$ For those who like to be in the heart of the action, this simple, 94-room hotel is the place to stay. There are mini-bars in every room, 24-hour room service, a bar, restaurant, and pool, and complimentary parking for guests. It's a little pricey considering the facilities are fairly basic. ♦ 14 Macleay St (between Crick Ave and Wylde St). 9358.2500; fax 9358.1959

25 Florida Motor Inn $$ A wall of greenery hides this 91-room motel at the end of a dead-end street. There's an American 1950s retro feeling here, especially around the swimming pool that's surrounded by palm trees. Rooms come in three sizes: studios, one-bedroom apartments, and two-bedroom apartments that can sleep six comfortably. All the accommodations come with kitchens. There are no dining facilities, but breakfast is available from the inn's kitchen. ♦ 1 McDonald St (west of McDonald La). 9358.6811; fax 9358.5951

26 Cicada Restaurant ★★★$$$ This Modern Australian restaurant remains one of the city's best dining experiences, thanks to owner/chef Peter Doyle and his diligent staff. The menu changes seasonally, but always features Mediterranean and Asian flavors. Try the crab cakes or braised lamb if they're on the menu. Order by the glass or bottle from the excellent wine list. The beautiful vine-covered terrace is many patrons' favorite place to sit. ♦ Modern Australian ♦ M-Tu, Sa dinner; W-F lunch and dinner. Reservations required. 29 Challis Ave (between Macleay and Victoria Sts). 9358.1255

27 Challis Lodge $ Inside this peach-and-white Victorian terrace building are 62 large rooms with refrigerators and private baths; some feature balconies. A quiet oasis in a noisy neighborhood, this hotel usually offers special weekend rates. Breakfast is available. ♦ 21 Challis Ave (between Macleay and Victoria Sts). 9358.5422; fax 9357.4742

28 Simpsons of Potts Point $$ Built as a stately family residence in 1892, this boutique bed-and-breakfast was renovated in the late 1980s to retain the charm of the late 19th century. The 14 guest rooms are large and airy, furnished with antiques, painted and wallpapered in the colors of the Victorian era, and outfitted with modern amenities. The hallways feature stained-glass windows, and prints and friezes of Australian flora. The breakfast room at the back of the building is a converted conservatory, with lovely views into the beautiful kept gardens. ♦ 8 Challis Ave (between Macleay and Victoria Sts). 9356.2572; fax 9356.4476

29 Mezzaluna ★★$$$ A wonderful view of the city skyline is revealed on the other side of this restaurant's plain terra-cotta–colored facade. There's a touch of Los Angeles here, especially when the staff turns on the outdoor heaters to warm those patrons who choose to dine alfresco. The menu offers classic Northern Italian dishes with a modern flair. Start with the antipasto plate, follow with one of the polenta or pasta dishes, and either the Australian lamb or venison. ♦ Northern Italian ♦ Tu-F, Su lunch and dinner; Sa dinner. 123 Victoria St (between Brougham La and Horderns Pl). 9357.1988

30 Wockpool ★★$$$ This modern two-floor restaurant run by Neil Perry of **Rockpool** fame (see page 28) has something for everyone: The casual noodle bar is always hopping with those in the mood for a quick, large bowl of *laksa* (a kind of soup), stir-fry, or rice noodle dish; while on the main dining floors, Perry has introduced fine Australian products to Asian cooking methods. The Thai pork and seafood sausages are very popular, along with the lamb and seafood dishes that are presented with elegant simplicity. The service here is more laid-back than its sister restaurant. ♦ Asian/Modern Australian ♦ M-Sa dinner. Reservations recommended for restaurant. 155 Victoria St (between Brougham La and Horderns Pl). 9368.1771. Also at: Panasonic IMAX Theatre, Cockle Bay Promenade. 9211.9888

31 Soho Bar & Lounge From the wild curve of the bar to the black-and-white checkered floor, this place is as cool as the crowd it attracts through the night. It's just far enough off the beaten track of Kings Cross to make it feel more like an upmarket local pub than a tourist attraction. The bartenders pride themselves on concocting exotic and inevitably potent cocktails. ♦ Daily noon-5AM. 171 Victoria St (between Brougham La and Horderns Pl). 9358.6511

32 Roys Famous ★★$ This comfortable cafe with an eclectic American-type menu attracts a stylish local crowd. There are blackboard specials, along with such popular snacks as caramel shortbread that goes well with coffee. Sit inside for a relaxing ambience, or outside if you want to be a part of the scene. ♦ Cafe ♦ Daily 9AM-11:30PM. 176 Victoria St (between Earl Pl and Orwell St). 9357.3579

33 Woolloomooloo Waters Apartments $$$ This modern 80-apartment hotel was once a huge warehouse near the Woolloomooloo dockyards. Ideally located within walking distance of the CBD and the harborfront, this hotel is a good place for business travelers and for enjoying the views from the foreshores. The studios and one-bedroom apartments are large and decorated in pastel colors; all have kitchen and laundry facilities. There's also an indoor pool, a rarity in Sydney. Breakfast is available from the hotel's kitchen. ♦ 88 Dowling St (at Pring St). 9358.3100; fax 9356.4839

34 Harry's Cafe de Wheels This caravan diner that's open round the clock is a Sydney icon that's frequented by everyone from local sailors to families in search of a midnight greasy food fix. The take-out menu features such Aussie standards as meat pies and sausage rolls. No tables and chairs here, so customers eat roadside or in their cars. ♦ Daily 24 hours. Cowper Wharf Rd (between Dowling and Forbes Sts). 9357.3074

35 Artspace Nationally and internationally recognized as an exhibition venue devoted to promoting contemporary arts, this institute is also an educational resource that receives funding to research and develop cutting-edge art. It combines its exhibition programs with lectures, workshops, performances, conferences, and studio residencies. According to its own mission statement, the establishment "strives to ask the difficult questions implicit in the evolution of art, culture and society, questioning the status of art itself within the practices of contemporary visual art." The exhibition program demonstrates the extraordinary diversity of the contemporary arts—including film, video, installation, and interactive and multimedia artworks. There are three spacious galleries, four studios in the so-called "Gunnery Studios complex" (a converted old Gunnery building), and a 24-hour exhibition space on the street level of the Gunnery. ♦ Free. Tu-Sa 11AM-6PM. 43-51 Cowper Wharf Rd (between Dowling and Forbes Sts). 9368.1899

36 Woolloomooloo Finger Wharf Built in 1914, this dilapidated old wharf on the harbor was a major departure port for soldiers being shipped off to fight in the Pacific during World War II. After the war, and up until the 1960s, it was a debarkation point for immigrants flocking to Australia. Conservation groups blocked plans to demolish the wharf in the 1980s, and at press time there were plans to redevelop the dock as an apartment block with harbor views. ♦ Cowper Wharf Rd and Forbes St

37 Woolloomooloo Bay Hotel Pubs in Sydney don't get more popular than this well-run place. On a warm day, it's teeming inside or out with crowds looking for a cold beer or two. This is particularly true on Saturday and Sunday afternoon when everyone is in weekend party mode. Its bottle shop (liquor store) offers one of the best wine selections in town. ♦ Daily. 2 Bourke St (at Cowper Wharf Rd). 9357.1177

Bests

Robyn Nevin
Artistic Director, Queensland Theatre Company

An elegant oasis in the part rustic, part Oz bush, part European landscape environs, fabulous **Centennial Park** is the perfect place to lunch on Sunday. It is not too elegant for the kids to join the grownups. The food is tops and the equestrians riding by and the cricket match yonder add to a sense of community at play. (Also recommended for a first date . . . it is pretty, casual, and romantic.)

Pre- or post-theater suppers at the ideally located **Bennelong,** almost atop the **Sydney Opera House,** competes with the already famous sails for status as the world's Seventh Wonder. Sophisticated food and ambience add immeasurably to an evening of opera, music, or drama. Performers like it too, and have been known to linger over post-performance Billecart salmon, nonvintage Champagne and lemon confit, candied citron, pastry cream, and biscuit.

Book to see anything at the **Wharf Theatre** because the building is surrounded on three sides by water. From the restaurant you can see the **Sydney Harbour Bridge** and the famous fat **Luna Park** face, plus ferries and tugs and cargo ships. But you need the sustenance of theater to add to the chic foodstuffs served at the small, smart **Wharf Restaurant.** It is the world's best situated theater complex. Trust me. (You will also feel the wharf itself move at high points in the drama . . . or if a big ship nudges it.)

Pam Burridge
Professional Surfer

Bradleys Head, Sydney Harbour. Watch the 18-foot skiffs race on a Saturday afternoon in summer. Great view of Sydney. Close to the action.

Manly Beach. Walk the promenade, take a swim or surf, meet for a coffee at many great cafes, watch the people, then catch the ferry to **Circular Quay,** where workers and tourists feel the same calm on the gentle (sometime rough and exciting) 30-minute visual feast commute.

Nick Greiner
Former Premier, New South Wales

The cliff walk between **Bondi** and **Coogee,** or any part of it, followed by brunch.

Mozart in **The Royal Botanic Gardens** in late November.

Watsons Bay Hotel after a water taxi trip from the city.

Watch the **Sydney Swans** play at the **Sydney Cricket Ground** on a balmy Saturday night.

The Australian gold rush in the 1850s brought major waves of foreign immigration to Sydney.

Paddington/ Woollahra/ Centennial Park

Just east of Darlinghurst and Surry Hills are Paddington and Woollahra—two cool urban neighborhoods known for their chic clothing boutiques, well-known art and antiques dealers, popular cafes, swanky bars and pubs, and rows of beautifully renovated Victorian terrace homes. And right in the middle of it all is a vast expanse of greenery known as **Centennial Park**—a tranquil haven from the urban din.

Named after the London borough, Paddington (or "Paddo") is only 4 kilometers (2.5 miles) away from the CBD, but more distant in style. **Oxford Street**, from **South Dowling Street** east to **Queen Street**, is its center. Here, both well-dressed mothers pushing strollers and some of Sydney's most prominent artisans lunch and shop. Oxford Street, and its side streets **Glenmore Road** and **William Street**, are lined with boutiques of younger Australians, including the popular **Jodie Boffa**, **Collette Dinnigan**, and **Bracewell**. This stretch of Oxford Street is also the site of **Paddington Bazaar**, a jam-packed outdoor market held Saturday on the grounds of the local United Church. Beyond the shops are such cafes as **La Mensa** and **Sloan Rangers**, usually full of Sydneysiders and visitors who stop in to rest and sip "long flat whites" (warm milk with espresso). Those who don't want to take the time to sit at a cafe can stop by the local bottled-water store, **Thirst For Life.**

All of Paddington, including **Centennial Park,** was once the paddock for **Victoria Barracks,** built in 1838 and still standing as the headquarters for the Eastern Command of the Australian Army. In the 1840s the government began to

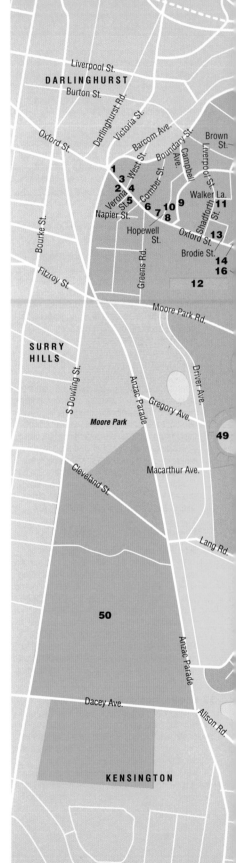

build terrace homes for men working on the barracks. Once the soldiers and their families moved in, businesses followed, and the area developed quickly.

Although much of Paddington was working class throughout the 1800s, the gentry took possession of streets facing the harbor along the steep northeastern hills. Their grand homes continue to grace **Five Ways**, **Glenmore Road**, and **Goodhope** and William Streets. These houses, some five or six stories tall, feature stone details and lacy wrought-iron work. Another reminder of 19th-century Sydney is merchant Robert Cooper's mansion, **Juniper Hall**, an Oxford Street landmark since 1822, that is cared for by the National Trust today.

At the top of Oxford Street, across from **Centennial Park**, is the beginning of Queen Street, the main commercial and residential thoroughfare for Woollahra. The antiques stores, art galleries, and home furnishings shops on this street, along with the gracious terrace homes and well-kept gardens, evoke a Victorian English village. But the name, "Woollahra," is an Aboriginal word that means "camp" or "meeting ground." In 1856, the area was given the name by Sir Daniel Cooper, a speaker of the New South Wales Legislative Assembly, who built his family home here. The Aboriginal names didn't catch on further; soon the whole suburb had streets named after English towns, governors, and early settlers—Queen, James, Smith, Jersey, and Victoria among them.

At the junction of Queen and **Moncur** Streets, the shops thin out, and stylish cafes, pubs, and restaurants take over. **Bistro Moncur** (within the **Woollahra Hotel**) is perhaps the best known, while **Caffe Agostini** and **Nostimo** are favored by those with time for long leisurely lunches. If a picnic in the park sounds appealing, make a stop at **Jones the Grocer** for gourmet foodstuffs that look almost as good as they taste.

Centennial Park was established in 1888 to honor the colony's first hundred years, and it still serves the city well more than a century later. When the park

Paddington Residences

was built, its great green expanse and horse-riding facilities encouraged Sydney's wealthy families to build stately abodes around its perimeter. **Lang Road**, along the western edge, is lined with many fine examples of late–19th- and early–20th-century sandstone and brick mansions whose ballrooms and large shaded verandas feature views of the park.

Just behind the stately homes of Paddington and the tranquil expanse of **Centennial Park** lies the giant sporting complex of the **Sydney Football Stadium** and the **Sydney Cricket Ground.** On some Sunday afternoons, when the neighborhood is quietly recovering from the previous night's revelry, the roar of sports fans may be heard through the streets, and golfers playing nine holes at **Moore Park Golf Club** have been known to stop in mid-swing in an attempt to hear the latest scores first hand.

Paddington

1 Albury Hotel The drag shows here run rings around the performances in *Priscilla, Queen of the Desert*. On Friday and Saturday, it's standing room only as crowds spill into the streets, clutching their drinks, as they try to catch a glimpse of the bar-top performances inside. Once a gay speakeasy, the club is now a mainstream tourist attraction. ♦ M-Sa noon-2AM; Su noon-midnight. 6 Oxford St (between West St and Barcom Ave). 9361.6555

2 Mr. Goodbar Whatever its incarnation of the moment (and there have been many), this long-established club always manages to attract a crowd of hip young things who love the latest dance tunes. On Friday and Saturday, when the dance floor is usually full, the fashion police at the door decide who looks cool enough to be admitted. ♦ Admission. M-Sa 6PM-3AM; Su 6PM-4AM. 11A Oxford St (between Verona and S Dowling Sts). 9360.6759

2 Verona Cinema They entertain you, feed you, and will even clothe you at this cinema complex. In addition to the four screens that mostly show independent feature films, there's a yoga center, a health-food store, and a cafe serving organic foods, as well as a beachwear boutique and a day spa (see below). If the movies are the main draw and you're going to be in town for a while, buy a discount pass good for six films. ♦ Daily 10AM-midnight. 17 Oxford St (between Verona and S Dowling Sts). 9360.6099

Within the Verona Cinema:

Verona Cafe Bar ★★$$ Whether it's a quick snack before a movie, a lunch break between shopping, or a drink after work, this is the place to be. The restaurant boasts a neat, clean design: white walls, a long slatted bench seat along the main window, and small stainless steel tables. The menu is conventional, but there's something for everyone in the list of pizza, pasta, and risotto. Jazzier specials are featured on Friday and Saturday when the crowd gets bigger and the bar gets busy. ♦ Cafe ♦ Daily lunch and dinner. No reservations accepted. 9360.3266

Mambo Taking surf culture all the way, this concept store by one of Australia's leading surfwear labels is a knockout, with a mind-boggling, huge range of colorful and bizarre surfer creations. The line includes clothing, surfboards, watches, rugs, ceramics, bags, recordings, kidswear, and a lot more. For a uniquely Australian souvenir, forget those stuffed koalas and boomerangs, and do some shopping here. ♦ M-F 10AM-8PM; Sa-Su. 9331.8034

Aveda In addition to the shampoos, conditioners, and bath and skin-care products sold here, this branch of the American chain of body-care stores also offers spa services. All cosmetics are created with pure flower and plant essences, and the spa provides a wide range of body treatments, including various varieties of massage and facials. ♦ M-F 10AM-8PM; Th 9AM-9PM; Sa-Su. Appointments required for spa services. 9380.5550

3 Oz on Sports Get buff before shopping at this sports- and gymwear store. You'll need to be, to fit into the slinky Australian-made items that are so popular with the men who shop in the neighborhood. ♦ M-W, F-Sa; Th 10AM-8PM. 26 Oxford St (between West St and Barcom Ave). 9331.1783

Where to Enjoy the Harbor

Sydney Harbour is one of the world's most stunning sights, a delight to visitors and residents alike, a joy to behold. From ferries to water taxis, cruisers to yachts, every mode of water transport glides across the harbor—even a Mississippi paddlewheeler! For more information on transportation options and tours, see "Getting Around Sydney" on pages 8 to 10.

Over 140 harbor inlets and coves, including some sandy harborside bays, tiny beaches, and islands, lie just beyond **Darling Harbour** and **Circular Quay.** The tour companies have their designated routes, but Sydneysiders have their own special places to picnic near the harbor, moor their yachts, or take a leisurely stroll. The following is a list of some of the spots popular with the locals:

East/South

Watsons Bay This villagelike suburb at the southern mouth of the harbor is famous for its seafood restaurants, cafes, and scenic walks. After a lunch at **Watsons Bay Hotel,** wander up to the cliffs of **The Gap** (pictured at right) and see the beautiful bottle and glass rock formation and the **Macquarie Lighthouse.**

Nielsen Park At the northern end of **Vaucluse** is this expanse of national parkland that's a favorite walking, picnic, and swimming spot for families. **Nielsen Park Kiosk** is a good place for Italian fare. **Shark Beach** is a lovely stretch of sand, and despite its name, a popular place to swim. (Nets keep the toothy sea predators away.)

Rose Bay Known for its yachting life, golf club, and fine restaurants, this suburb is a perfect example of harborfront living. Take a seaplane for a joy ride around Sydney, then have lunch or dinner at the sleek-looking **Catalina** or **Pier.**

Darling Point McKell Park at the end of this well-to-do community is one of Sydney's hidden treasures just minutes from the **Central Business District (CBD).** Take the ferry from Circular Quay or a cab from the city center. Bring along a picnic and enjoy the view of the city, **Opera House, Harbour Bridge,** and harbor traffic. No swimming is allowed.

Rushcutters Bay From the number of sailing craft moored here, it's no surprise that this is where sailors gather before the annual Sydney-to-Hobart Yacht race on Boxing Day (26 December). Power walkers and joggers also use the shoreline as their track in the early morning and evening. **Rushcutters Bay Kiosk,** a small cafe with outdoor seating, is swarming on the weekend with fashionable locals with children and pets in tow.

Shark and **Clarke Islands** These harbor islands are managed by the **National Parks and Wildlife Service** (**NPWS;** 9247.8861). Contact them for information and using the islands' facilities. Many harbor tours cruise past, but it's quite an experience to linger awhile on one of these green sanctuaries out in the middle of the harbor.

North

McMahons Point Picnic in this residential area and a enjoy an excellent vista of the city, or stroll up the hill to a local cafe.

Lavender Bay Once the domain of artists and poets who were looking to escape the more ostentatious **Eastern Suburbs,** this northern cove is a popular mooring place for small sailing boats. This area has resisted major development, making it a truly tranquil harborside village.

Mosman Bay Ferries chug in and out of this leafy cove, transporting commuters to and from the city to the beautiful northern suburb of **Mosman.** The old wharf and the historic sailing and rowing clubs add to its Old World charm.

Balmoral Beach A far cry from its Scottish namesake, this beach (which looks more like a bay) has some famous dining venues, such as **Bather's Pavilion,** and a wonderful promenade that winds around the well-protected shore. Don't expect any waves here, just gentle breezes, green parkland, and North Shore cafe society. Ferry service is available on the weekend.

The Gap

4 Ariel Booksellers At this contemporary bookstore, readers can find the hottest titles from Australia and elsewhere around the globe. The best sections are photography, design, architecture, and cooking. International film and art magazines are stocked, as are copies of the local free press. New Yorkers yearning for a taste of home can even pick up a copy of the *Village Voice*. Check listings for the well-organized program of author readings and signings. ◆ Daily 10AM-midnight. 42 Oxford St (at West St). 9332.4581

beyond flowers

4 Beyond Flowers The sweet fragrance of flowers fills the air here. This florist specializes in pretty bouquets and gorgeous arrangements of native flora. The prices are reasonable—for one of Sydney's more expensive neighborhoods. ◆ M-Sa. 56 Oxford St (between Comber and West Sts). 9361.3277

5 Berkelouw This bookshop, with a large selection of both new and second-hand volumes, has been in business since 1812. Thousands of used books are in stock, ranging from contemporary paperback fiction to antique Australiana volumes; collectors should check out the extensive rare book selections. The cafe on the second floor is a perfect spot to sit and sip a cup of freshly brewed coffee, while thumbing through your purchases. ◆ Daily 10AM-midnight. 19 Oxford St (at Verona St). 9360.3200

6 Jewels of the Earth New Age and spiritually enlightened residents of the city come here to stock up on incense, crystals, books, and other paraphernalia. Enthusiastic staff share their wisdom and knowledge. ◆ M-Sa. 84 Oxford St (between Hopewell and Comber Sts). 9331.8411

Sweet Art

7 Sweet Art You can get a sugar rush just breathing in the air of this bakery. How about a birthday cake modeled on your dog? Or your favorite hobby? From weddings and birthdays to corporate functions and product promotions, the bakers bake delicious rich fruit, chocolate, and banana cakes and tortes, and craft them in any shape or size. Kosher cakes are also available. ◆ M-Sa. 96 Oxford St (between Hopewell St and Kidman La). 9361.6617

8 Gamla Lan Interiors Two floors of antique and 20th-century furniture and *objets d'art* from Sweden fill this plush store. These fine furnishings are a far cry from IKEA. ◆ M-Sa. 114 Oxford St (between Glenmore Rd and Hopewell St). 9360.2217

9 Barry Stern Gallery Fine art, particularly paintings by modern Australian artists, fills the two floors of this gallery. Check newspaper listings for special exhibitions. ◆ Tu-Sa; Su 1PM-5PM. 19 Glenmore Rd (between Oxford and Liverpool Sts). 9331.4676

JODIE BOFFA

10 Jodie Boffa The simple and classic tailoring of this line of womenswear seems perfectly suited to Sydney's young executives who shop here in packs. The stock includes understated smart suits and eveningwear plus the latest shoes and handbags by Robert Clergerie. ◆ M-Sa. 26 Glenmore Rd (between Oxford St and Campbell Ave). 9361.5867

10 Louella Kerr/Lorraine Reed A classic-looking bookstore with old-world English charm, this cozy spot is filled with antique, fine, and rare books for serious collectors. It may look a little stuffy, but the staff is friendly and helpful. ◆ M-Sa . 30 Glenmore Rd (between Oxford St and Campbell Ave). 9361.4664

11 Hogarth Galleries Aboriginal Art Centre Sydney's first Aboriginal art gallery represents some of Australia's finest Aboriginal artists, including Emily Kame Kngwarreye and Clifford Possum Tjapaltjarri. Works include paintings on bark and canvas; prints, drawings, and paintings on paper; and photographs. In addition to an impressive program of changing exhibitions, private and group lectures on Aboriginal art and culture are offered. ◆ Tu-Sa. 7 Walker La (between Brown and Liverpool Sts). 9360.6839

The expression "shoot through like a Bondi tram," which is still heard occasionally, refers to the express streetcars that ran through Paddington until 1960.

Arthur Stace (1885-1967) chalked the word "Eternity" in copperplate script throughout the streets of Sydeny over a 30-year period. He is said to have done this nearly 50 times a day, claiming that it was a divine calling from God. A memorial plaque with the word "Eternity" has been placed in Sydney Square.

Restaurants/Clubs: Red   **Hotels:** Blue
Shops/🌳 **Outdoors:** Green   **Sights/Culture:** Black

Victoria Barracks

KEELY EDWARDS

12 Victoria Barracks Some architectural historians call this one of the finest Victorian barracks built by the British Empire and some of the best-preserved Georgian architecture in Australia. The sandstone buildings (pictured above) were designed by Lieutenant Colonel **George Barney** and constructed between 1841 and 1848. The walls are 10 meters (33 feet) thick in places to withstand attacks, and the main two-story building has beautiful cast-iron verandas. Originally housing 800 soldiers, the barracks is still a functioning military facility. (It's a peculiar sight to see packs of soldiers walking along ultrahip Oxford Street.) While it's not possible to tour the barracks, a visit to the **Army Museum,** located in the old jail block, offers a chance to see some interesting military memorabilia. ♦ Free. Museum: Th 10AM-12:30PM; Su 10AM-3PM. Changing of the guard with a military band: Th 10AM. Oxford St (between Oatley and Greens Rds). 9339.3000

13 Byron Mapp Galleries This commercial gallery represents both modern and contemporary Australian photographers. It is also one of the best places in Sydney to find photography books—and grab a cappuccino while you're at it. ♦ M-Sa. 178 Oxford St (at Brodie St). 9331.2926

Australia has over 900 wineries.

Sydney's major source of fresh water is Lake Burragorang, formed by the Warragamba Dam, completed in 1960. It is about 70 kilometers (43 miles) west of the CBD.

14 Hot Tuna Both wannabes and genuine surf-and-skate dudes and dudettes own at least one item of this label. From splashy Hawaiian-print shirts to colorful backpacks, the designs are mainly inspired by Aussie beach culture. ♦ M-Sa. 180 Oxford St (at Young St). 9361.5049

15 Royal Bar and Grill ★★$$ The old **Royal Hotel** at Five Ways (an old Victorian junction of roads and stores) has been given new life as a popular Sydney bistro. The first-floor restaurant is a noisy spot, best described as well-managed chaos. The colonial-style veranda provides a perfect setting for a twilight dinner of Caesar salad, beef fillet with béarnaise sauce, and a big bowl of chips. Portions are large, and appetizers often will do the job of a main course. Upstairs, the **Elephant Bar** is popular for its merry cocktail hour and comfy armchairs. ♦ Modern Australian ♦ Daily lunch and dinner. 237 Glenmore Rd (at Broughton St). 9331.2604

16 Paddington Town Hall/Chauvel Cinema Built in grand Classic Revival style and opened in 1891, the 32-meter-high (104 feet) clocktower is visible for miles. The building's large and well-preserved interior houses the **Chauvel Cinema** (run by the Australian Film Institute), the **Paddington Library,** a video studies unit, a ballroom, and various meeting rooms. ♦ Daily 10AM-midnight. Oxford St and Oatley Rd. Cinema information 9361.5398

17 Wilson Stuart Everyone from club kids to those who want to look terribly groovy when they strut their stuff down Oxford Street comes to this menswear store. The clothing line is casual with some beautifully tailored jackets and slacks. No extra-large sizes to be found here, as most of the customers are fairly buffed. The selection of belts and shoes is small, yet is in keeping with the up-to-the minute street styles. The staff is equally as stylish and helpful, too—without putting on too much pressure. ♦ M-Sa. 238 Oxford St (between Ormond and Young Sts). 9360.6187

18 Juniper Hall This Colonial Georgian mansion (pictured below) was built in 1824 for Robert Cooper, a champion of convicts and distiller of spirits. The mansion was named for the juniper berry, the basis of gin—and the basis of the wealth earned by Cooper and his partners. Cooper (who fathered 28 children) and his third wife Sarah raised 8 daughters and 6 sons here. After the Coopers left the house, it was briefly renamed **Ormond House** in an effort to mask its alcohol-based past. Restored for the 1988 Bicentennial celebrations, the building is now open to the public under the stewardship of the National Trust of Australia. Modern additions include a comfortable cafe and a good book-and-gift shop. ♦ Free. M-Sa. 250 Oxford St (at Underwood St). 9258.0123

19 Bracewell European designers such as **Ghost, Costume National,** and **Patrick Cox** are all featured in this womenswear store, along with this Paddington institution's own ultrafashionable line. Black dominates, and mixes well with unusual jewelry, chic sunglasses, and very high-quality footwear. **Bracewell for Men** is just a few doors up the road (274 Oxford St, between Underwood and William Sts, 9331.5844). ♦ M-W, Sa-Su; Th 10AM-8:30PM. 264 Oxford St (between William and Underwood Sts). 9360.6192

19 Micky's Cafe ★$$ With all the see-and-be-seen cafes in Paddington, it's a relief to walk into this laid-back, colorful eatery. The menu, primarily burgers and simple sandwiches, is extensive enough to please most palates. A big, brightly decorated chalkboard advertises daily specials and desserts. There's a kids' menu and free delivery. ♦ Cafe ♦ Daily breakfast, lunch, and dinner until midnight. 268 Oxford St (between William and Underwood Sts). 9361.5157

20 Saba for Men This Melbourne-based clothing line is popular with urban, style-conscious young men. Prices are high, but the quality is good. ♦ M-Sa. 270 Oxford St between William and Underwood Sts). 9331.2685

20 Museum There's nothing archaic about this clothing store, which is usually filled with shoppers whose attire suggests that they're ready to head off to a nightclub at a moment's notice. This is the place to shop for those hip international labels. ♦ M-W, F-Sa; Th 10AM-8PM; Su noon-5PM. 296 Oxford St (between William and Underwood Sts). 9332.2030

Juniper Hall

21 Australian Centre for Photography (ACP) Fans of photography will want to spend some time here. Programs feature both Australian and international photography exhibitions, plus a photographic education program incorporating a workshop, darkrooms, studios, and state-of-the-art imaging facilities for public access. ♦ Gallery: Free. Workshop: fee. Tu-Sa. 257 Oxford St (between Newcombe St and Oatley Rd). 9332.1455

la mensa

21 La Mensa ★★$$ Stark and stylish, this very popular cafe was set up by renowned Sydney chef Steve Manfredi and friends. The attention to detail is extraordinary—down to the staff wearing 1940s-style white waiter jackets. Make up your own plate from the antipasto bar or choose a pasta or meat entrée from the full blackboard menu. The servings are generous enough to share. Sit either on the long parklike benches and tables, at the high communal table, or in the small courtyard. The shelves of the main floor are stacked with take-out items—fresh produce and the restaurant's own brand of packaged foods, including candy, sauces, salad dressings, oils, vinegars, jams, and pastas. ♦ Cafe ♦ M-F lunch and dinner; Sa-Su breakfast, lunch, and dinner. 257 Oxford St (between Newcombe St and Oatley Rd). 9332.2963

SLOANE RANGERS
CAFE

22 Sloane Rangers $ This joint jumps on Saturday when **Paddington Bazaar** (see page 119) up the street is in full swing and shoppers drop in here for a jolt of caffeine. It's a little more sedate at breakfast time, when the potato *rosti* is an excellent, filling way to start the day. ♦ Cafe/Takeout ♦ Daily breakfast, lunch, and early dinner. 312 Oxford St (between William and Underwood Sts). 9331.6717

30.5 percent of Sydneysiders speak a language other than English at home.

Restaurants/Clubs: Red   **Hotels:** Blue
Shops/ Outdoors: Green   **Sights/Culture:** Black

22 Holy Sheet! Affordable and attractive bed linens and homewares are the blessings to be found here. Other outposts of these handy stores are located in Newtown and Balmain. ♦ M-W, F-Sa; Th 10AM-8PM. 320 Oxford St (between William and Underwood Sts). 9360.3111. Also at: 270 Darling St (between Booth St and Loyalty Sq). 9810.3091

22 Derek Scott The luxurious bed linens, cotton sheets, and bath towels are all elegantly packaged and presented in this minimalist store. The store is also renowned for its bathrobes, with selections ranging from thick waffle weave and toweling to fine cotton. ♦ Daily. 336 Oxford St (at William St). 9360.4879

23 Thirst For Life Premium Waters In a world of increasing environmental pollution and a lust for fads, it had to happen—a store that specializes in water. Stocking more than 100 waters from around the globe, this is virtually a shrine for bottled-water fanciers. Labels range from the obscure to the everyday, and there is a Water Club (a different offering each month) for the really serious drinker. Ask for a taste of the latest *acqua minerale*. ♦ M-Sa. 37 William St (between Victoria and Underwood Sts). 9331.6424

23 Collette Dinnigan The high priestess of Australian haute couture, Collette Dinnigan is known for her use of exquisite fabrics from around the world. Dinnigan's personal touch is evident in all her designs, from delicate silk and lace lingerie to stunning eveningwear. Sydney's young socialites have favored these innovative yet highly wearable designs for years. ♦ M-Sa; Su noon-5PM. 39 William St (between Victoria and Underwood Sts). 9360.6691

24 Sherman Galleries For insight into the latest direction of Australia's contemporary art scene, visit these galleries, which specialize in progressive Australian and international art. The original gallery opened in Glebe in 1981, and was dedicated exclusively to the promotion of contemporary sculpture. In 1989, the gallery moved to Paddington, where it now has two locations—this one, and another on Goodhope Street. The Goodhope Street gallery (16-18 Goodhope St, between Glenmore Rd and Glen St, 9331.1112), transformed from a gallery warehouse into a large exhibition space, overlooks a huge outdoor sculpture garden. The Hargrave Street gallery was designed specifically to accommodate contemporary sculpture and paintings although, since 1990, it has focused on exhibitions of prints, some textiles, and the decorative arts. ♦ Tu-Sa. 1 Hargrave St (at Cascade St). 9360.5566

25 Roslyn Oxley Gallery Founded in 1982, this is one of Sydney's top commercial contemporary art galleries. The exhibition program in this large warehouse-style space features challenging works that are at the forefront of contemporary art, encompassing a wide range of media—from painting and sculpture to performance and installation art, and video and other electronic media. ♦ Tu-Sa. Soudan La (just south of Hampden St). 9331.1919

26 Platypus Shoes Those in the know buy their Aussie R.M. Williams and Blundstone boots at this discount store. Students in need of heavy-duty work boots to look the part for their favorite club stop here first. The staff is sometimes overly enthusiastic, but remain patient even after you've tried on your tenth pair of shoes. ♦ Daily. 385 Oxford St (between Newcombe St and Oatley Rd). 9360.1218

26 Paddington Bazaar What began in 1973 with a handful of makeshift stalls has become Sydney's most famous art, fashion, and crafts market, now boasting more than 250 vendors. Although a bit of a hippie/New Age element still clings to the market, the clientele is primarily young, fashionable, and bargain-conscious, there to check out the new designers and jewelry stalls. People watching is often as much fun as shopping. The bazaar, which is open Saturday year-round, is held on the grounds of the United Church. ♦ Sa. 395 Oxford St (at Newcombe St). 9331.2646

27 Reject Shop In the 1980s, this store began selling damaged or "rejected" china and kitchenware to those who wanted good stuff but were prepared to accept slightly damaged items at discounted prices. Today, in addition to the "rejects," barrels of brand new stock are also available. Locals come here to outfit their entire kitchen for a fraction of what it would normally cost. ♦ Daily. 380 Oxford St (between Elizabeth and William Sts). 9332.1003

28 Chocolate Factory ★★$ A Russian immigrant named Wladyslaw Pulkownik started making chocolates in this space in the 1930s during the Depression. Today his rich, creamy chocolates are more popular than ever and are now known as Paddington Chocolates. The main factory has moved to larger premises in Camperdown, and this space is now something of a shrine to the old one—as a cute cafe on a quiet tree-lined street. Nestled between old Paddington terrace houses, it's a

well-kept secret among locals who want to avoid the trendiness of Oxford Street. The dark wooden shelves are stacked with coffee and mineral water as well as the colorfully wrapped chocolates. Come for the live music on Sunday starting at 2PM. ♦ Cafe ♦ Daily. 8 Elizabeth St (at Victoria St). 9331.3785

29 Lucio's ★★★$$$ If it weren't for the occasionally rowdy pub scene across the road, you'd swear you were in Italy. This Italian restaurant is adored by locals for many reasons; from the Tuscan conservatory with its butter-colored walls and Australian art, to the fine fresh dishes turned out by the kitchen, to the professionalism and charm of its owners and staff. A popular choice for long lunches in the economic boom of the 1980s, this spot has retained its strong following. After a morning of gallery-hopping or a tough day of shopping, this is the spot for a bowl of tagliolini with blue swimmer crab, a glass of wine, and a slice of *la dolce vita*. ♦ Italian ♦ M-Sa lunch and dinner. Reservations recommended. 47 Windsor St (at Elizabeth St). 9380.5996

30 Olsen Carr This art gallery specializes in Australian artists from post–World War II to the present. John Olsen—the co-director of this space with Michael Carr—is the son of Tim Olsen, one of Australia's most famous contemporary painters. It's no surprise that this gallery shows Olsen senior's work, along with a cache of other big Australian names. Exhibitions change every six to eight weeks. ♦ Tu-Sa 11AM-6PM; closed in January. 76 Paddington St (at Elizabeth St). 9360.9854

31 Grand National ★★$$ A charming old Paddington pub underwent a much-needed revamp and became a hip restaurant that's constantly buzzing with a hungry crowd. Depending on how busy things are, service can vary from smooth to nonexistent, but there's a lot to entertain while you wait— namely the action in the open kitchen and among your fellow diners. The food is a stylish take on humble pub classics. Order the chef's signature dish of pan-fried salmon with kaffir lime sauce and mashed potatoes. ♦ Modern Australian ♦ M-Tu dinner; W-Su lunch and dinner. Reservations recommended. 161 Underwood St (at Elizabeth St). 9363.4557

32 Rif Raf Clothing Company Racks of inexpensive eveningwear and nightclub garb for women are the attraction here. ♦ Daily. 414 Oxford St (between George and Elizabeth Sts). 9331.2292

San Francisco is Sydney's sister city. This makes sense considering Sydney's rolling hills and giant cliff faces that rise out of the harbor.

Lights! Action! Fox Studios Australia

Watch out Hollywood—Sydney has just entered the star-studded arena of filmdom in a big way. **Fox Studios Australia** (Driver Ave and Lang Rd, Moore Park, 9383.4000; fax 9383.4006; www.foxstudios.com.au), the site of the former headquarters of the Royal Agricultural Society (RAS), is now cultivating a whole new industry Down Under.

cinemas, and a range of retail and restaurant outlets. In its new incarnation, the heritage-listed, late–19th-century show ring boasts open-air cinema, live music, comedy shows, and circus performances.

Sydney's answer to a behind-the-scenes look into moviemaking is the studio's backlot, which will allow visitors insight into such techniques as set design, costumes, animation, and the sound factory. Some old movie sets are on display to show the "smoke and mirrors" method; there are also regularly scheduled live performances to demonstrate special effects and stunts. If your timing is right, you may also be able to spy on a film or TV show in the making on **Stages 5** and **6.**

Built in 1881, many Australians still remember this giant walled-off lot—complete with show ring, enormous pavilions, and landscaped walkways—as the site of the Royal Easter Show. The present complex, which is also a bevy of old Sydney architecture, beautifully kept grounds, and city history, is divided into three areas: the **Professional Studio, Bent Street,** and the **Fox Studios Backlot.**

The studio takes up half the 60-acre site, where films like *Babe: Pig in the City* and the two final episodes of the *Star Wars* epic were produced. Facilities here include six high-tech stages, live entertainment venues, and streets and gardens for outdoor shoots. Most of these streets have been named in honor of such famous Aussie actors as the old swashbuckler Errol Flynn and Chips Rafferty.

The entertainment and retail area revolves around **Bent Street,** which is accessible to the public year-round with no admission fee. Located here are 16

Also at **Fox Studios Australia** are the **Royal Hall of Industries** and the **Hordern Pavilion,** both of which were undergoing major renovations at press time. Many Sydneysiders can remember strolling through a trade show at the **Royal Hall,** or attending a music gig, dance party, or ball at the **Hordern.** This tradition will live on in exhibitions and concerts that will be presented here.

It looks as though Australia's sound stages will make their voices heard in the global entertainment marketplace.

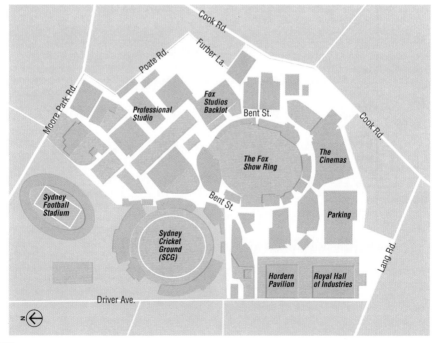

32 Calibre This menswear label from Melbourne claims to be for the smartest, chicest, and most fashionable of men. Could very well be true, since it is very popular with the 25–35-year-old set who like to be seen having the right coffee at the right cafe wearing Calibre clothes. ♦ M-Sa; Su noon-5PM. 416 Oxford St (between George and Elizabeth Sts). 9380.5993

33 Made In Japan The serenity and simplicity of Japanese design have impressed many Australians, and many of them come here to shop. Traditional lacquered bowls, boxes, origami paper, sushi plates, antique furniture, and chopsticks are just some of the exquisite treasures to be bought. ♦ Daily. 437 Oxford St (between Centennial Sq and Elizabeth St). 9360.6979

33 Bibelot This is the place for those who love stylish homewares—and don't mind paying for them. Some Australian goods are available, but most of the stock is of Italian or American design. ♦ M-W, F-Su; Th 10AM-8PM. 445 Oxford St (between Centennial Sq and Elizabeth St). 9360.6902

34 Robby Ingham Stores With the look of a modern shopping emporium, this groovy space stocks a multitude of fashion labels. Paul Smith, CP & Company, accessories from Mulberry, Comme des Garcons, and local fashion designer Jodie Boffa are just a few on offer. ♦ M-W, F-Su; Th 10AM-8PM. 422-28 Oxford St (at George St). 9332.2124

Woollahra

35 The Ritz Hotel Like good friends should, this local pub's got a few spare rooms if you need to sleep over after downing a few too many beers. ♦ Daily 11AM-11PM. 2A Oxford St (at Jersey Rd). 9360.9286

36 Claude's ★★★★$$$ Fine dining is alive and well in Woollahra here at this restaurant, which is still going strong after more than 20 years. The current owner, Tim Pak Poy, is a serious young chef who is devoted to creating faultless flavor combinations made with the best produce. The dining room is serene and intimate, more like a solemn temple than a busy restaurant, with 18th-century fabric on the walls, and the staff are world-class. The French-inspired menu changes daily; look for Australian caviar as an appetizer and any style of veal for a main course. Only a fixed-price, three-course menu is offered, and you'll need to bring along a bottle of your favorite wine—there's no bar. Book well in advance. ♦ French ♦ Tu-Sa dinner. Reservations required. 10 Oxford St (between Queen St and Jersey Rd). 9331.2325

37 Akira Isogawa The creations of this Sydney-based Japanese designer are dramatic, breathtakingly beautiful, yet simple.

Sheer fabrics from Japan and Australia are snipped and sewn into divine dresses, elegant sarongs, blouses, and skirts, all designed to complement one another. ♦ M-Sa; Su noon-5:30PM. 12A Queen St (between Moncur and Oxford Sts). 9361.5221

37 Hughenden Boutique Hotel $$ This 35-room Victorian mansion has been authentically restored, and the modern comforts don't detract from its 19th-century charm. The typically Victorian dark wood and heavy furniture are lightened by pale walls and draperies. Rooms have private baths, telephones, and TVs. Small conference facilities are available for business travelers. Dinner and Sunday high teas are served in the Victorian lounge, and a full breakfast is included in the room rate. The hotel's restaurant, **Quaife's,** also serves dinner daily. ♦ 14 Queen St (between Moncur and Oxford Sts). 9363.4333; fax 9362.0398

38 Appley Hoare Antiques Queen Street is renowned for its serious antiques shops, and this one is the queen of them all. The French Provincial theme is accented by a lovely *Sud de France* courtyard in the middle of the store. Anything from antique soup ladles to cutting boards and china is lovingly displayed on sturdy country tables and cabinets. ♦ M-Sa. 55 Queen St (at Victoria Ave). 9362.3045

39 Orson and Blake Collectibles Schedule a stop at this delightful treasure trove of tasteful homewares. Fabrics from Indonesia appear as cushion covers, soaps from France sit on stainless-steel dishes, and selected furniture makes up part of the displays. Prices are surprisingly modest for such a stylish import boutique. ♦ M-Sa; Su noon-4PM. 83-85 Queen St (between Moncur St and Victoria Ave). 9326.1155

40 Café Zigolini's ★$$ The Eastern Suburbs ladies love this restful cafe with classical music wafting through. The front room is dominated by a wooden bar with shelves displaying colorful pickled fruits and gorgeous cakes. The back room is like a small private dining room, and there are tables in a paved courtyard. The coffee is excellent and the desserts justifiably famous. ♦ Cafe ♦ M-Sa 7:30AM-midnight; Su. 107 Queen St (between Ocean and Moncur Sts). 9326.2337

40 Nostimo ★★$ Arthur Hatzis and his father opened this popular Greek-inspired cafe just a few years ago. Hatzis's wife, Marianne, designed the interior space, with bright lighting, a blue floor, and whimsical touches like stainless-steel shark's teeth jutting out of the counter. Traditional dishes, such as moussaka, are matched by lighter options of various soups and salads. The desserts, made by Arthur's mother and aunts, are marvelous. ♦ Cafe ♦ Daily. 113 Queen St (abetween Ocean and Moncur Sts). 9362.4277

41 Woollahra Hotel An old pub built in the 1930s in Art Deco style has been converted into a stylish local bar with blond wood and a large open space. Standing room is plentiful, except on Thursday and Friday night when all of the Eastern Suburbs seems to be drinking here. ♦ 116 Queen St (at Moncur St). 9363.2782

Within the Woollahra Hotel:

Bistro Moncur ★★★$$$ It's said the stylish bistro food offered here is so good that some locals have given up cooking entirely. Favorites include Chef Damien Pignolet's marinated salmon, grilled prime sirloin, and the giant-size bowl of quickly cooked French fries. The wine list is good and the service is very capable. The open dining room has wood paneling and a black-and-white abstract mural that runs the length of the wall. The only down side is that you can't make a reservation. ♦ French ♦ M-F lunch and dinner; Sa dinner; Su breakfast, lunch, and dinner. 9363.2782

42 Caffè Agostinis ★★$$ Chic and simple, this restaurant is a favorite with the Eastern Suburbs social set for a casual brunch of ricotta hot cakes and strong coffee, a leisurely lunch in the courtyard, or a quick bowl of pasta with BYO wine in the evening. Owner Margie Agostini uses only the best ingredients to create flavorful dishes like a melt-in-the-mouth risotto, corn fritters, delicate bruschetta, and the very best orange cake in town. ♦ Modern Australian/Italian ♦ M-F breakfast, lunch, and dinner; Sa brunch, lunch, and dinner; Su brunch and lunch. 118 Queen St (at Moncur St). 9328.6140

43 Jones the Grocer Delis don't get fancier than this one that stocks everything from

fresh-baked breads and homemade chocolates to tubs of olives and prepared foods. The packaged goods are so pretty that it seems a shame to open and eat them. Classical music fills the air—leading many to suspect that they've been hypnotized into buying more than they should have. ♦ M-Sa. 68 Moncur St (at Jersey Rd). 9362.1222

44 Woollahra Antiques Centre Dozens of individual dealers offer their wares from stalls in this center. Display cases filled with jewelry, colorful regiments of proud toy soldiers, model ships, and artifacts from Europe, Asia, Africa, and the Americas beckon casual shoppers and serious collectors. There's also a bookstore and a coffee shop. ♦ Daily. 160 Oxford St (between Wallis and Moncur Sts). 9327.8840

45 Centennial Hotel ★★★$$ On the fringe of Woollahra stood a tired old pub, which has been tastefully converted into an airy modern restaurant and bar. Local architect **Alex Tzannes** designed a dramatic dining room with a central wooden bar and warm white walls, which are broken here and there by golden wooden shutters and huge windows. The diverse menu offers tasty fare that ranges from char-grilled octopus salad and a surprisingly light Caesar salad to more traditional items such as roasted duck and wood-fired pizzas. ♦ Modern Australian ♦ Daily lunch and dinner. Reservations recommended. 88 Oxford St (at Victoria Ave). 9362.3838

Centennial Park/Moore Park

46 Centennial Park Opened on 26 January 1888, this 544-acre park was a Centennial gift from Britain dedicated to "the enjoyment of the people of New South Wales forever." The largest patch of green in Sydney, this remains very much a people's park, providing a much-needed recreation area for the densely

Sydney Football Stadium

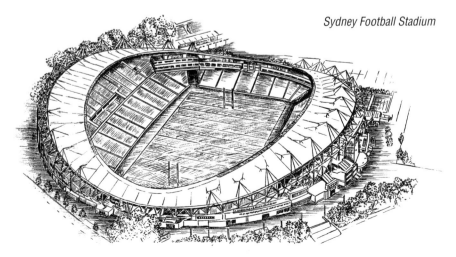

Sydney Cricket Ground

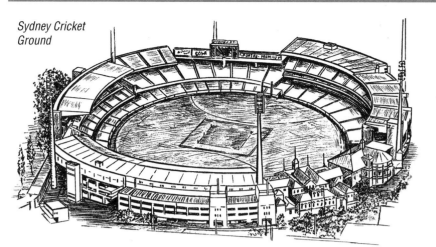

populated Eastern Suburbs. The park is ideal for a long walk, a bicycle ride, or a picnic. There are more than 35 playing fields, a beautifully maintained rose garden, equestrian grounds, a grass skiing and tobogganing area, plus bicycle, jogging, and in-line skating tracks. The park's ponds, originally known as Lachlan Swamps (after the governor), were once a source of Sydney's water; today they provide sanctuary for waterbirds. The **Australian National Parks and Wildlife Service** (9339.6699) offers a number of ranger-guided tours. ♦ Oxford St (between York Rd and Centennial Sq). 9331.5056

Within Centennial Park:

Centennial Park Cafe ★★$$ How about a bright, open cafe situated right in the middle of the park? Take a seat indoors or on the veranda to watch the cyclists, in-line skaters, and horses circling the park. The view and atmosphere almost justify the relatively expensive prices. Basic sandwiches, delicious salads, beer-batter fish and chips, and large desserts are standard offerings; a children's menu is available as well. Service can be slow. Just to the right of the entrance is a terrific little take-out cafe with a few chairs and tables. Locals sit here to take a breather after a long walk, or to avoid the production of a sit-down meal inside. ♦ Cafe ♦ Daily breakfast and lunch until 4PM. Reservations recommended. Grand and Parkes Drs. 9360.3355

47 Olympic Hotel Although it has a few guest rooms available, this hotel is most popular for its busy pub on the ground floor. Built in 1909, the structure features Federation-style architecture, accented by lovely wood moldings, stained glass, and original pub tiles. The scene is mixed, attracting everyone from sports fans in need of a refreshment break from the sports stadiums across the street to local residents in need of a schooner of beer and a chat. ♦ M-Th 10AM-11PM; F-Sa 10AM-midnight; Su 10AM-8PM. 308 Moore Park Rd (at Regent St). 9361.6315

48 Sydney Football Stadium From May through September this 42,000-capacity stadium (see illustration on page 122) hosts major rugby and soccer matches. In the winter the local Aussie Rules (a hybrid of Gaelic football) team, the **Sydney Swans**, takes over the field. This is becoming an increasingly popular event for Sydneysiders who once viewed Aussie Rules as an amusing pastime of their southern cousins in Victoria. The rest of the year it is a venue for big rock concerts. Completed in the early 1990s, the complex also features the **Stadium Fitness Center** with a 25-meter (82-foot) outdoor heated swimming pool, several tennis courts, a circuit training room, and various other sweat-inducing facilities. ♦ Fitness center: Daily 5:45AM-10PM. Driver Ave (between Lang and Moore Park Rds). General information 9360.6601; Football match information 0055.63132

49 Sydney Cricket Ground (SCG) The legendary SCG (pictured above) has been the home of Australian cricket since 1886. Test matches and the more exciting one-day international matches are played in summer months. Visit the cricket museum to get a sense of just how fanatical Sydney is about this sport, or take the **Coca-Cola Sportspace** tour through the grounds. ♦ Tours M-Sa 10AM, 1PM, 3PM. Driver Ave (between Lang and Moore Park Rds). General information 9360.6601; Tours 9380.0383; Cricket match information 0055.63132

50 Moore Park Golf Club Golfers are at home in this easily accessible club. It offers an 18-hole course and a day-and-night driving range, all at very reasonable rates. ♦ Club: daily dawn to dusk. Driving range: dawn to 10PM. Cleveland St (between Anzac Parade and S Dowling St). 9663.1064

Bests

Richard Neville
Author

Tacky and obvious, perhaps, but a cab or a bus to **Bondi Beach** on a sweltering day can provide cheap swimwear, a cradling surf, and—from the balcony of **Ravesi's Hotel**—innovative Oz tucker-with-a-view. Your last chance before the sterilizing impact of "development." At the other end of town, reached by rail, is a raffish tableau of polyglot wheeler-dealing— **Cabramatta,** with its garish bridalware; impossible skyscraper cakes; bootleg software; and emporia of inscrutable in-your-face noodles, soups, curries, and stir fries. More Asian than the malls of Bangkok.

From the gloriously Grecian **Art Gallery of New South Wales**, stroll **The Royal Botanic Gardens** to the harborside, skirting the opium poppies, and head for the wonder of the age, that monument to dreamers and gift to the tourist industry—the **Opera House.** Refreshed and empowered, you can survive the herdlike drift to **The Rocks,** with its legislated nostalgia and tawdry souvenirs, to be shocked by the new at the **Museum of Contemporary Art** and refuelled by any number of jostling cafes, where Sartre and Marx never set foot.

Ariel Booksellers is open late, strategically placed, spacious and inclined to push the cult texts of the moment, so a stint of blurb imbibing makes you feel like a professor of cultural studies.

A boring two-hour train trip to **Blackheath** in the **Blue Mountains** provides access to Grand Canyon wilderness, ferny glens, and winding, artful bushtracks for weekend or hourlong treks. If accompanied by a loved one and a bottle of plonk, you're liable to propose.

Phillipa McGuinness
Senior Commissioning Editor, Cambridge University Press

North Sydney Olympic Pool in winter. Built in Art Deco style, and situated below the northern pylon of the **Harbour Bridge** and next to **Luna Park,** this has to be one of the most atmospheric full-length swimming pools in the world. (It has a big plastic bubble over it in winter that diminishes the effect, but the journey there is still a good one, especially if you go by ferry from **Circular Quay** or to **Milsons Point** on the train.)

BBQ King—Not the most salubrious decor, and decidedly brusque service, but the food is great, especially the barbecued duck.

Gleebooks, Glebe—It's not a superstore, but it's big enough to have a superb range of books and helpful, intelligent service. The store hosts literary events, forums, and launches to which all are welcome, so the shop is a major contributor to the intellectual and cultural life in the city.

The coast walk between **Coogee** and **Bondi.** Spectacular views, lots of interesting fellow walkers to check out, and good places to stop along the way (**Waverley Cemetery,** the cafes at **Bronte,** and more).

Carla Zampatti
Executive Chairman and Company Director, Carla Zampatti Group

The Wharf (dining/theater)—Unique setting, good food. Young Australian playwrights and actors.

Art Gallery of New South Wales—Large wing dedicated to Aboriginal art. Really exciting.

Drama Theatre, Sydney Opera House—Wonderful, exciting, top quality theater.

Parsley Bay—On **Sydney Harbour,** really magical, close to city.

Sydney Harbour ferry or hydrofoil—Take a trip to **Manly** for a great day out.

Anna Volska
Actress

For early risers, **Paddy's Markets** at 7AM on summer Saturdays is when mangoes, peaches, and cherries are heaped fragrant and cheap.

When I'm feeling edgy I walk down **Oxford Street** from Queen Street in **Woollahra** as far as it takes to raise the spirits. All of it is interesting from **Centennial Park** at the beginning right down to **Taylor Square,** the gay precinct, and farther into the city. One of the juiciest bits is the bottleneck of cinemas, the bookshops, the jewelry shops full of wearable and affordable stuff, and cafes everywhere.

Ugly traffic-snarled **Cleveland Street** near Bourke Street is where you get a great range of Indian cakes and farther down towards the city great Indian, Japanese, Turkish, and Lebanese food.

Every visitor needs to be taken to the **Sydney Fish Markets** at **Pyrmont,** and for a picnic in one of the national parks.

Richard Walsh
Publisher, ACP Publishing Pty Limited

In late spring park a car above **Balmoral Beach,** preferably on a bright Saturday morning, and watch the small boats chasing each other in the dazzling sunlight across to **Manly** and listen to the birds cavorting noisily in the flowering jacarandas. This is one of the most gloriously inspiring sights in the world.

In high summer attend one of the Festival of Sydney's free entertainments, preferably "Opera in the Park" one cool evening among more than 100,000 enthusiasts, and experience first-hand the surprisingly wide appreciation of Sydneysiders for middlebrow culture.

In autumn, preferably before daylight saving has finished, take a meal at the **Wharf Theatre** in **Walsh Bay** as a prelude to your choice of show. The food is typically light, inexpensive, good-quality brasserie fare; the setting is utterly bewitching, perfect to get you in the right mood for what, unless you are terribly unlucky, is likely to be a thoroughly absorbing evening of theater.

Kate Grenville
Author

Dunking croissants into latte at **Bather's Pavilion** right on the beach at **Balmoral,** looking out through the **Heads** at a thousand miles of Pacific Ocean.

Browsing in **Gleebooks, Glebe**—books that make you think, sold by people who love them. A great range of quality Australian books here.

Beach hopping all day on the **Palm Beach** peninsula. Great surf beach one side, quiet bush-ringed bays and beaches on the other. Take the quaint putt-putt ferry and a picnic, and forget crowded **Bondi.**

Jill Dupleix
Food Editor, *Sydney Morning Herald* and *Elle Australia*/Author, *New Food*

Eating fish and chips on the beach at **Bondi.**

Watching the fireworks over the harbor in Sydney from a **Manly** ferry. When? There are *always* fireworks over the harbor in Sydney!

Going for a slow jog through my favorite jogging path in the world. Starting at the **Art Gallery of New South Wales,** around **Mrs. Macquarie's Chair,** through the **Royal Botanic Gardens,** to the **Opera House** and back.

Eating anything with caviar at **Tetsuya's** restaurant in **Rozelle.** Its modest appearance belies the exquisite pairing of flavors and immaculate timing in the tiny kitchen, and the extraordinary depth of the wine list.

Drinking Australian sparkling wine with a dozen freshly opened Pacific oysters at **Catalina, Rose Bay** in the late afternoon. It's a minimalist chic restaurant inside, with the blue spread of Rose Bay, wheeling pelicans, and landing-and-taking-off seaplanes outside.

Getting up early (5AM) and going to the **Sydney Fish Markets** to see the fish auction, or sleeping in and going later to buy fresh live mud crabs, Queensland prawns, Tasmanian lobster, local salmon, and ready-made sushi for lunch.

Having breakfast at **bills** in **Darlinghurst** (ricotta hot cakes with honeycomb butter and Grinders caffe latte) then cruising up **Oxford Street, Paddington,** going into every single shop.

Heading out to **Cabramatta** (a suburb southwest of the city) for a Vietnamese food feast that costs less than a bottle of wine.

Shopping for books late at night at **Ariel** in Oxford Street, **Paddington,** open to midnight every night.

Catching the latest exhibition at the **Museum of Contemporary Art (MCA)** in **The Rocks,** followed by roast lamb and a spectacular dessert at **Bel Mondo,** a glamorous modern Italian restaurant above **Argyle Department Store** in The Rocks.

Reading Saturday's edition of the *Sydney Morning Herald* while knocking back a great coffee sitting on a tiny stool on the pavement outside Sydney's grooviest coffee house, **Parmalat,** which is itself no bigger than a wedge of cake.

Eating my favorite noodle dishes: minced pork with noodles at the modest **Taipei** cafe in **Chinatown** for $5; and minced pork sauce with noodles at the glam **Wockpool Noodle Bar** in **Kings Cross** for $15 with a glass of wonderful Victorian Pinot Noir.

Going for a steak dinner at the plush, comfortable, neoconservative restaurant **Armstrong's** in **North Sydney,** where the sommelier will instinctively know what you are in the mood to drink.

Drinking a cold beer on a hot night in the middle of the opera. You can wander out onto the **Opera House** balcony and drink in the view of stars, harbor, and bridge during intermission.

Putting together a picnic basket of fabulous food (Mohr's smoked salmon, Maggie Beer's pheasant pâté) from the **David Jones** food hall, then walking across to **Hyde Park**—or even better, on to **The Royal Botanic Gardens**—for a picnic.

Collette Dinnigan
Director/Designer, Collette Dinnigan

Breakfast at **bills, Darlinghurst.**

Lunch at **Pier, Rose Bay**—excellent food, great view, and not too touristy.

Lunch at **Bather's Pavilion, Balmoral Beach**—great atmosphere, even good on a winter's day.

A trip to the **Sydney Fish Markets**—order a dozen oysters and a glass of Western Australian white wine and watch the fishing boats go by.

Dinner at **Bistro Moncur** in **Woollahra**—excellent food and good atmosphere.

Drive up to **Palm Beach** and walk to the lighthouse.

Shopping on **William Street, Paddington** where all the smaller designer-operated stores are located.

Cross the harbor by ferry to **Manly,** stopping in at **Taronga Zoo** on the way back.

Walking along the coast between **Bondi** and **Tamarama**—takes about an hour but the ocean views are spectacular.

First Saturday of each month take a trip to **Surry Hills Market**—good bargains from bric-a-brac to clothes.

Visit the **Brett Whitely Studio** in Surry Hills.

Eastern Suburbs/ City Beaches

After passing through the tunnel at the end of William Street at Kings Cross, motorists emerge onto **New South Head Road**, which leads directly to the Eastern Suburbs—Australia's answer to Bel Air and Beverly Hills. After the elegant, quiet enclaves of **Rushcutters Bay** and **Darling Point** comes **Double Bay**. This suburb is home to some of Sydney's poshest boutiques and most conspicuous consumers.

As New South Head Road snakes its way around the harborfront, it runs through **Rose Bay** and up to **Vaucluse**, a harbor peninsula where a giant Gothic-inspired convent sits on the side of the hill, offering some of the best views in the city. These two suburbs, along with **Bellevue Hill** and **Point Piper,** are where Sydney's ultrawealthy dwell in huge, rambling homes. Many of the houses themselves verge on the ostentatious, but they're not the point—it's the view of the harbor and the city that really makes these properties magnificent and puts them in a class by themselves. The area is not completely dominated by residential developments, but features such green oases as **Nielsen Park** and its beachfront. This park, run by the **National Parks and Wildlife Service,** is the place to begin the popular **Hermitage Foreshore Walk** back toward Rose Bay.

New South Head Road ends at the more modest, villagelike suburb of **Watsons Bay** and the giant cliff face of **The Gap** (also known as "South Head") at the mouth of the harbor. Visitors and locals converge on Watsons Bay daily to feast on seafood lunches at **Doyle's** or the **Watsons Bay Hotel** and to wander around this harborside hamlet. Just a few minutes' walk from this busy spot is The Gap, an area whose long history

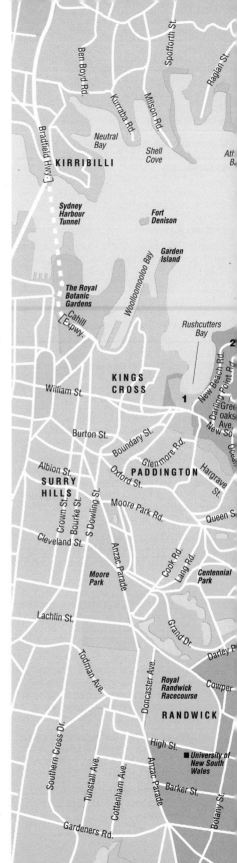

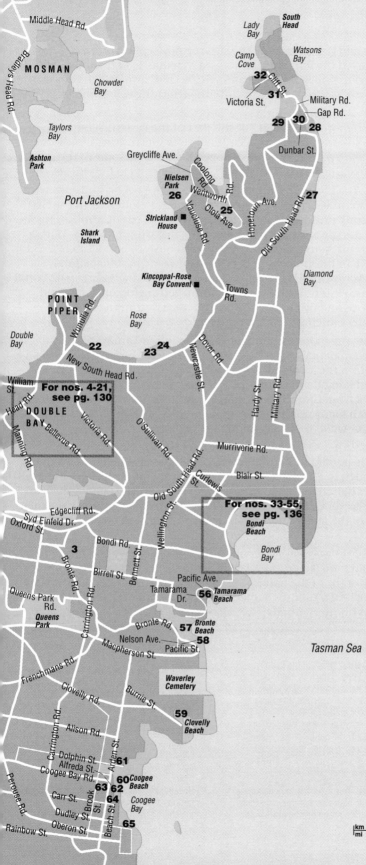

Middle Head Rd.

Bradleys Head Rd.

MOSMAN

Chowder
Bay

Taylors
Bay

Ashton
Park

Lady
Bay

**South
Head**

Camp
Cove

Watsons
Bay

32 Cliff St.

Victoria St. **31**

Military Rd.

Gap Rd.

29 **30** **28**

Dunbar St.

Greycliffe Ave.

Coolong Rd.

**Nielsen
Park**

26 Wentworth
Ave.

Vaucluse Rd.

Olola Ave.

25

Hopetown Ave.

Old South Head Rd.

27

Strickland
House

Port Jackson

Shark
Island

Diamond
Bay

Kincoppal-Rose
Bay Convent ■

Towns
Rd.

**POINT
PIPER**

Wunulla Rd.

Rose
Bay

Double
Bay

22

New South Head Rd.

23 **24**

Dover Rd.

Newcastle St.

Hardy St.

Military Rd.

William
St.

Head Rd.

**For nos. 4-21,
see pg. 130**

**DOUBLE
BAY**

Manning Rd.

Bellevue Rd.

Victoria Rd.

O'Sullivan Rd.

Old South Head Rd.

Murriverie Rd.

Curlewis St.

Blair St.

**For nos. 33-55,
see pg. 136**

*Bondi
Beach*

*Bondi
Bay*

Edgecliff Rd.

Syd Einfeld Dr.

Oxford St.

3

Bronte Rd.

Bondi Rd.

Bennett St.

Wellington St.

Birrell St.

Pacific Ave.

Tamarama
Dr.

56 *Tamarama
Beach*

Queens Park
Rd.

Carrington Rd.

**Queens
Park**

Bronte Rd.

57 *Bronte
Beach*

Nelson Ave.

58

Macpherson St.

Pacific St.

Tasman Sea

Frenchmans Rd.

Clovelly Rd.

Burnie St.

**Waverley
Cemetery**

59

*Clovelly
Beach*

Alison Rd.

Carrington Rd.

Arden St.

61

Dolphin St.

Alfreda St.

Coogee Bay Rd.

60 *Coogee
Beach*

Perouse Rd.

63

Brook St.

62

64

Carr St.

Beach St.

Dudley St.

*Coogee
Bay*

Rainbow St.

Oberon St.

65

N

mingles beauty and tragedy. Along the sheer windswept cliffs of The Gap, many have enjoyed the long walk up toward **Macquarie Lighthouse**, while others have used the steep precipice as a suicide spot, from which they can jump hundreds of feet to their deaths into the churning waves and jagged rocks below.

Less affluent and more egalitarian but still part of the Eastern Suburbs are Sydney's beach suburbs, where high culture meets surf culture. **Bondi** (pronounced *Bond*-eye), **Bronte**, and **Coogee Beaches** are some of the most accessible and exciting beaches in Sydney, all well prepared for visitors.

To local purists, the ultimate sand-and-sun experience begins and ends with world-famous Bondi Beach, only about 8 kilometers (5 miles) from the city. Here residents sunbathe on the long, golden stretch of beach, stroll along the esplanade, and mingle among backpackers and busloads of tourists. With all its cafes, restaurants, souvenir stores, hotels, and hostels, Bondi caters well to those who thrive in the atmosphere of this great gold-and-blue natural phenomenon. Many of Sydney's artists and iconoclasts have also made Bondi their home, which has prevented the area from getting too precious. And despite the crowds and litter here, the beach remains stunning and the crystal-clear water enticing on a hot Sydney day.

Farther south are the more residential beaches, such as **Tamarama** (nicknamed "Glamarama" due to the crowd it attracts), Bronte, and **Clovelly.** After pressure from the local residents, the city spared these beaches hotel development, making them wonderful alternatives to the crush of Bondi. The coastal walk from Clovelly to Bondi is also a terrific way to explore the diversity of beach landscape and culture, as joggers, surfers, families, and the odd in-line skater wend their ways along the pedestrian track.

A little farther south is Coogee Beach. This long stretch of sand (unjustly referred to as the poor man's Bondi) is only 9 kilometers (5.5 miles) from the city—close enough to visit for a morning stroll or for lunch. Coogee has been thoughtfully revitalized, has a couple of large hotels and restarants, and has become a popular venue for live music. **Wylie's Baths**, at the southern end of Coogee, is one of the larger, more well-kept public saltwater baths (pools) in Sydney.

The Eastern Suburbs may have a reputation for being showy and brash, but the beach life out here is a great social leveler. A posh element exists in Double Bay and some of the harborside suburbs, but just moments away are the neighboring beach suburbs, where all are welcome—a characteristic that in many ways is quintessentially Australian.

Eastern Suburbs

1 Rushcutters Bay Home of the **Sydney Yacht Club** and one of the less used stretches of harborfront parkland, Rushcutters Bay is where the world-famous Sydney-to-Hobart Yacht Race starts on Boxing Day (26 December) every year. The park itself is not very safe at night. The outdoor cafe next to the playing fields is open on the weekend and serves coffee and light meals. ♦ New Beach Rd (north of New South Head Rd)

2 Darling Point This suburb on a peninsula is renowned for its high-rise apartments, which have views of the city and nearby headlands, and its grand old houses, which some of Sydney's wealthiest families built in the 19th century. Some homes are visible from the street or harbor, including **Swift,** a Gothic-inspired sandstone mansion that once belonged to the old Sydney family of the same name, and **Carthona,** at the end of Darling Point Road. One of the major attractions of Darling Point is **McKell Park,** which has a jetty for ferries, and is a popular spot for wedding photos and weekend picnics. Back along Darling Point Road at **Greenoaks Avenue** sits **St. Mark's Church,** famous as the site of celebrity nuptials and as the church used in the 1994 film *Muriel's*

Wedding. Crowds gather outside the church every Saturday to witness some of Sydney's most extravagant weddings.

3 Bondi Junction Once called Tea Gardens, this suburb changed its quaint name to Bondi Junction (or, familiarly, "The Junction") in 1881, when it became a hub for the old tram system that was introduced to the area. Today it's still a hub but mainly for buses, and serves as the last train station on the Eastern Suburbs line. This is also a major suburban shopping center, with **David Jones** and **Grace Brothers** department stores and several malls tenanted with supermarket chains and small boutiques.

Double Bay

Sydneysiders have nicknamed the area "Double Pay" for good reason—the only thing cheap in Double Bay is window shopping and the view of the harbor. Ladies still lunch in this exclusive suburb from noon to late afternoon, and BMWs and Mercedes rule the roads and parking garages of **Cross, Knox,** and **Bay Streets.**

4 Double Bay Old Books If your idea of heaven is to forage for first editions of books, old postcards, musty magazines, and newspapers, then this well-stocked shop will put you on cloud nine. Proprietor Ray Swanwick is usually on hand to answer questions and make sure the authentic antique dust doesn't get brushed off too many of the publications. ♦ M-Sa; Su noon-5PM. 1D Manning Rd (between Pine Hill Ave and New South Head Rd). 9363.4936

5 Swiss Deli After you see the shelves of canned goods and kosher delicacies behind the counter, you may be forgiven for thinking you've entered a Jewish deli in New York. Proprietor David Grossman has stocked this place with a remarkable range of basic ingredients and epicurean foods. Grab a gourmet sandwich here on your way to a picnic at the nearby harborfront. ♦ M-F. 330 New South Head Rd (between Knox and Bay Sts). 9363.0629

SHERIDAN
AUSTRALIA

5 Sheridan Australia produces some of the best linen and cotton products in the world, and the mission of this more-than-25-year-old company is to make the most extravagant possible use of these materials. The two floors hold linens, cotton sheets, and towels in every size, color, and pattern imaginable. The simple, minimalist merchandising and packaging makes shopping here a breeze. ♦ M-Sa. 334-36 New South Head Rd (between Knox and Bay Sts). 9327.8355

5 Spice Market ★★$ The spicy-sweet aroma beckons you from the street at this bright and airy Thai restaurant, which also features a take-out menu. The seating is functional and the service is efficient and fast. This is a popular place for those in need of a quick, well-prepared lunch or pre-movie meal. ♦ Thai ♦ M-F lunch and dinner; Sa-Su dinner. 340 New South Head Rd (between Knox and Bay Sts). 9328.7499

Double Bay

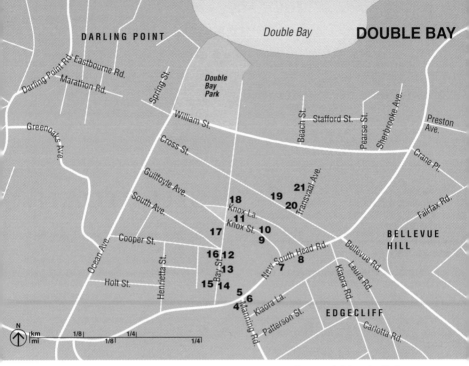

Double Bay

DARLING POINT

Double Bay Park

BELLEVUE HILL

EDGECLIFF

CHILDREN'S BOOKSHOP
LESLEY McKAY'S

5 Lesley McKay's Children's literature has a presence here in this glamorous area of Sydney. This children's bookstore holds hundreds of titles for everyone from infants to adolescents to adults who want to relive their childhoods. The toys for sale are all related to characters in the books. ◆ M-Sa. 344 New South Head Rd (between Knox and Bay Sts). 9363.0374

6 Village Double Bay Twin Cinemas The only cinema in the neighborhood shows both blockbusters and independent feature films, seven days a week. ◆ Daily. 377 New South Head Rd (at Manning Rd). 9327.1003

7 Georges ★$$ The old glass walls and glitzy decor were replaced a while ago by blond wood furniture and simpler fixtures, but this is the same restaurant that's been part of Double Bay's cafe society for decades. The new look and new menu attract the old crowd, who comfortably join the younger monied set for lavish salads, liberally garnished daily specials, and homemade desserts. Come for the scene, not the food. ◆ Modern Australian ◆ M-Sa morning tea, lunch, and dinner. 417-19 New South Head Rd (between Kiaora and Manning Rds). 9327.3672

8 The Golden Sheaf Hotel The local business crowd—and those barely of drinking

age—have made this pub a Sydney institution. The leafy outdoor beer garden at the back of the pub is popular on Saturday and Sunday afternoon for drinks and a feed. Basic pub meals—steaks, pasta, and salads—are available for lunch and dinner. ◆ Daily. 429 New South Head Rd (between Kiaora and Manning Rds). 9327.5877

9 Sir Stamford Hotel $$$ The 70 rooms of this hotel are large and lavishly decorated in dark colors and silk fabric. One of the establishment's best amenities is its 24-hour access to the pool. Although relatively small, it is well equipped for business travelers and includes two meeting rooms with views across to the surrounding parkland of Double Bay. The hotel offers room service, but has no restaurant on the premises. ◆ 22 Knox St (between New South Head Rd and Bay St). 9363.0100; fax 9327.3110

10 Dee Bee's ★★$ The reasonable prices may account for the staying power of this cafe in Sydney's most upscale neighborhood. The fare is international—everything from Mexican to Hungarian. The blackboard menu changes daily, and the desserts are all homemade. There is both outdoor and indoor seating, and service is outstanding. It is fully licensed, making it a good place to stop for a drink after some heavy-duty shopping. ◆ Cafe ◆ M-F 8AM-2AM. 27 Knox St (between New South Head Rd and Bay St). 9327.6696

11 Savoy Double Bay Hotel $$ The 35 guest rooms in this hotel are plainly decorated, but the location makes up for that. The rooms are quiet, and the rates are fair, considering that it's right in the middle of some of Australia's best shopping and dining. The hotel has no restaurant. ♦ 41-45 Knox St (between New South Head Rd and Bay St). 9326.1411; fax 9327.8464

12 Saba Specializing in the Melbourne label favored by many of Sydney's young people, this store is laden with women's knits, ready-to-wear suits, and eveningwear. Colors are seasonal and styles are always on the cutting edge. ♦ M-Sa. 39 Bay St (between New South Head Rd and Knox St). 9362.0281

12 Courtyard Cafe ★★$ For something a little more casual and less fussy than those on Knox Street, try this cafe on adjacent Bay Street. The purple-and-gray checkered rug on the floor adds to its casual ambience. There is indoor and umbrella-shaded outdoor seating. The homemade cakes are some of the best in Sydney. The staff is efficient and friendly. ♦ Cafe ♦ Daily. 37 Bay St (between New South Head Rd and Knox St). 9326.1602

13 Area ★★$$ The front terrace under the awning of this chic restaurant is clearly a prime spot for people watching. Inside, there is endless table-hopping and air-kissing. Much of the food comes from the central wood-fired oven and the rotisserie brought in from Texas. From the latter come whole legs of Illabo lamb, carved into generous slices and served with salad greens and roasted potatoes. The wood-fired oven also turns out whole baked fish, small pizzas, and delicious platters of roasted seafood. You can also order food from the bar area at dinnertime. ♦ Modern Australian ♦ M-Sa lunch and dinner. 29 Bay St (between New South Head Rd and Knox St). 9363.3656

13 Mondo Filled with modern, well-designed international—and a smattering of Australian—housewares and kitchenware, this store is very popular with those in search of that ultra-elegant but very useful gift. The staff is helpful but doesn't pressure shoppers. ♦ M-Sa. 27 Bay St (between New South Head Rd and Knox St). 9362.4964

13 Jane Lambert Hats No day at the races or similar outdoor occasion would be complete without a hat from Jane Lambert, according to local jetsetters and racing aficionados. From simple straw to lavish velvet, Lambert hats top off the outfits of some of Sydney's most discerning society women. ♦ M-Sa. 23-25 Bay St (between New South Head Rd and Knox St). 9327.8642

14 Remo Since 1988, this mail-order company has been producing its own T-shirts with groovy logos and selling all those items the upwardly mobile simply can't live without. This is the only Remo store in Sydney and stocks most of the catalog items. Pick up one of their signature Sydney mugs or T-shirts as a souvenir to take home. ♦ Daily. 19 Bay St (between New South Head Rd and Knox St). 9327.2144

15 La Deuxieme Fois This high-fashion outlet typifies the environmental ethos of our times: reduce, reuse, and recycle. Eastern Suburbs women who no longer require items from last season's wardrobe discreetly drop them off at this store, whose French name means "the second time." As if by magic, they reappear on racks—sometimes repackaged—at true bargain prices. Stock levels are very unpredictable, as the good stuff goes fast. If you're lucky, you could find anything from an Armani suit to a Gaultier bustier. ♦ M-Sa. 4-10 Bay St (at Cooper St). 9363.5775

carla zampatti

16 Carla Zampatti This Australian designer of women's prêt-à-porter sells clothes that are demure, sleek, and considered very elegant—perfect for the corporate woman or those in search of yet another little black dress. ♦ M-Sa. 24 Bay St (at Cooper St). 9326.2248

17 Bayside Natural Health Centre In the middle of all Double Bay's glitz and glamour is this tranquil health-care and food store. From skin care and iridology to holistic counseling and stress management, there is something here for every New Age warrior. ♦ Daily. 30-36 Bay St (between Cooper St and Guilfoyle Ave). 9327.8002

18 Carla Florist From the simplest red roses to the most elaborate native flower arrangement, this florist has one of the city's most diverse selections. If you drop in, the store's owner, Janine Joseph, is happy to introduce you to some of the lesser-known native flora. Otherwise, you can still expect personalized attention over the phone. ♦ M-Sa. Knox La and Bay St. 9326.2111

Topless sunbathing and swimming are permitted on all of the city's beaches.

19 The Ritz-Carlton Double Bay $$$$ Built in the late 1980s, on Double Bay's main shopping street, this luxury hotel's guests have included everyone from George Bush to Madonna. In keeping with the atmosphere of the area, the building's exterior resembles a Beverly Hills hotel. The 140 guest rooms are decorated in an elegant, classic international style. The property features an Italian-inspired courtyard and a rooftop pool with harbor views. The lounge on the second level is a perfect place for a quiet cocktail or meeting. The restaurant is elegant, the 24-hour room service prompt. The decor of the several meeting rooms is part Hollywood, part English club.♦ 33 Cross St (between Transvaal Ave and Bay St). 9362.4455, 800/241.3333; fax 9362.4744

Within The Ritz-Carlton:

Evelyn Miles Tucked inside the arcade adjoining the hotel, this is arguably Sydney's most prestigious shoe store. All the very best footwear from around the world is gathered in these plush surroundings. The store even has its own Walter Steiger concession for those in the know. Brands stocked here range from Gucci and Patrick Cox to Manolo Blahnik. ♦ M-Sa. 9327.5732

Homegrown Maria Webster and a team of other young mothers design and make the trendy children's clothes sold here. For children who need to be completely decked out, the shop also sells jewelry, accessories, and toys. ♦ M-Sa. 9328.7699

THE TEDDY BEAR SHOP
"For every bear that ever there was"

20 The Teddy Bear Shop This store's slogan is "For every bear that ever there was." With rows of toy kangaroos, koalas, and carefully dressed tartan-clad teddy bears, it seems that they have kept their promise. ♦ M-Sa. 19-27 Cross St (at Transvaal Ave). 9363.5172

BELINDA

21 Belinda Definitely a store for the stylish shoppers in the area, this up-to-the-minute boutique stocks imported clothing and features one of the best selections of elegant scarves in Sydney. English labels are a specialty, but worthy local brands include Jodie Boffa and Cloth, known for its unique fabric designs. Many residents consider this *the* Double Bay boutique. ♦ M-Sa. 8 Transvaal Ave (just north of Cross St). 9328.6288

Rose Bay

Beyond exclusive homes, what draws people to Rose Bay are the picturesque views of the harbor, either from a seaplane or from one of the restaurants listed below.

22 Pier ★★★$$$ This long, narrow restaurant (so designed because it actually sits on a pier) juts out over the shoreline where New South Head Road meets Rose Bay. This is one of the better places for Modern Australian–style seafood. It is also one of Sydney's most consistent restaurants: Dishes are always well thought out and beautifully presented, the wine list is excellent, and the staff is most attentive. For these reasons and more, this establishment has been drawing crowds since it opened in 1990.

The dining room is relatively understated, with views of Rose Bay, Vaucluse, and out into the harbor. The menu glides between seductively simple—scallops with garlic mashed potatoes—to the deliciously elaborate—*conchigliette* (small, shell-shaped pasta) with Moreton Bay bug meat (a light and sweet crustacean native to Australia), garlic, tomato, and Ligurian olives. Desserts are not to be missed, if you have room. ♦ Seafood/Modern Australian ♦ Daily lunch and dinner. Reservations recommended. 594 New South Head Rd (just east of Wunulla Rd). 9327.6561

23 Sydney Harbour Seaplanes Imagine taking a taxi to a Sydney Harbour jetty, jumping into a six-seater Beaver seaplane, taking off over the sparkling water, and marveling at the breathtaking view. After flying for a half-hour, try a big lunch at one of the restaurants hidden in the harbor coves. If that sounds good, this is the mode of sight-seeing for you. ♦ Daily. Reservations required. Rose Bay Jetty, Lyne Park, New South Head Rd (between Vickery Ave and Wunulla Rd). 9388.1978

24 Catalina ★★★$$$ The crowd here sometimes equals the food—a mélange of Sydney's finest—all on show and loving it. A great white tribute to minimalism, the interior was designed to showcase, not compete with, the view. With wraparound windows onto the bay and Sydney Harbour, through which you can see yachts bobbing on the water and seaplanes landing just in front of the restaurant, it's a great spot for a long, languid weekend lunch.

The menu is strong on seafood, and nearly always as dependable as the view. Try the salmon risotto and the wild barramundi. In the afternoon, Sydney's wealthy yachting crowd has been known to drop in here for a dozen Sydney rock oysters and a bottle of crisp white wine. ♦ Modern Australian ♦ Daily noon-midnight. Reservations recommended. Lyne Park, New South Head Rd and Vickery Ave. 9371.0555

Vaucluse

Vaucluse has the feel of an elite, closed community with style and wealth. It is by no means a gated community, although there are plenty of high fences and security in place to protect some of Sydney's most glamorous homes. There is much evidence of the old truism that having lots of money does not necessarily mean having lots of taste, but regardless of some awkward architecture, the view is reliable. This suburb has arguably the best views that money can buy of Sydney and the harbor.

25 Vaucluse House William Charles Wentworth was one of Australia's most famous early explorers, part of the triumvirate (the other two were Henry Lawson and Gregory Blaxland) responsible for crossing the Blue Mountains, part of the Great Dividing Range, into the western region of New South Wales. Beyond his achievements as an explorer, Wentworth was a lifelong proponent of representative government who also spearheaded the formation of the nation's first university and enjoyed numerous political victories. He was instrumental in drafting the

constitution that gave New South Wales self-government in 1855. His other great legacy is this house (pictured below), one of the city's only surviving 19th-century harborside estates. Built in 1803, the property features a main house, kitchen wing, stables, and outbuildings and is surrounded by 11 hectares (27 acres) of formal gardens and grounds. Wentworth, his wife, Sarah, and their 10 children lived in the house from 1827 to 1853 and again in 1861-62. The Gothic-style mansion, with its picturesque turrets and castellations, includes both lavish entertaining rooms and functional "downstairs" areas.

The estate paints a picture of the social aspirations and lifestyles of the Wentworths and their live-in servants, both convict and free. The interior includes original Wentworth family pieces, as well as representative furniture and objects from the early to mid-19th century. The extensive gardens and grounds, including a pleasure garden, parkland, bushland, and beachfront, have been restored to their 19th-century character. ♦ Admission. Tu-Su. Wentworth Rd and Olola Ave. 9388.7922

Within the Vaucluse House:

Vaucluse House Tea Rooms ★★$
This charming spot offers simple but stylish cuisine to accompany the harborside location. A variety of meat, fish, and fowl dishes are offered, as are a number of teas. ♦ Cafe ♦ Tu-Su. 9388.8188

26 Nielsen Park/Hermitage Foreshore Scenic Walk For one of Sydney's best harborfront picnic spots—complete with soft grass and shade trees—this park tops the list. And if you're looking for some pre- or post-

Vaucluse House

picnic exercise, consider taking a swim or embarking on the **Hermitage Foreshore Scenic Walk.** The Hermitage Foreshore is a narrow strip of land that extends from the park to Rose Bay. Adjacent to the residential area of Vaucluse, the walk offers an excellent opportunity to soak up the panoramic views of Sydney's magnificent harbor, with the city skyline as a backdrop. Historic mansions, such as **Strickland House,** are scattered along the route, which is set under the canopy of the Port Jackson fig trees. Linger on the sandstone rock outcroppings for their harbor views and check out the quiet fishing spots and sunny beaches where you can cool off with a swim. The route is slightly less than two kilometers (about a mile), one-way, approximately a one-hour walk at an easy pace. The degree of difficulty is between easy and medium, with a few steep sections. Start the walk from either **Nielsen Park,** Vaucluse, or near the Kincoppal-Rose Bay Convent. To get here, take bus *No. 325* from Circular Quay to Nielsen Park, or *No. 324* to Rose Bay. ♦ Transit 13.1500; National Parks and Wildlife Service 9247.5033

Within Nielsen Park:

Nielsen Park Kiosk ★★★$$$ For a delectable, leisurely lunch by the sea, stop at this charming restaurant at **Nielsen Park.** The building in which it is housed looks onto pretty Shark Beach (don't worry, there's a swimming net in place). There's a canteen with a few tables to one side of the building for the park visitors and beachgoers and a fine restaurant for lunch. The menu changes every three months, but always features classic Italian dishes carefully matched with modern flavors. Service is hospitable, but be sure not to eat here on a day when the place is booked for a weekend wedding; you may be rushed to finish your meal. A few children's meals are available. ♦ Italian ♦ Tu-Su lunch. Reservations essential on Saturday and Sunday. Greycliffe Ave (north of Vaucluse Rd). 9337.1574

Despite what you may have heard from surfers, you don't have to worry too much about shark attacks in Sydney's waters. The creatures rarely enter Sydney Harbour because the water is too polluted for their tastes, and the eastern beaches are protected by shark nets. The attacks that do happen result in an average of less than one fatality a year *countrywide.*

27 Macquarie Lighthouse This lighthouse was designed by **James Barnet** and completed in 1883. It's modeled on the original lighthouse built on this site in 1818, which was designed by the colonial architect **Francis Greenway.** Before this lighthouse existed, a team was in place atop the cliff to light a fire so that passing ships would find the mouth of the harbor. ♦ Old South Head Rd (north of New South Head Rd)

Watsons Bay

With its quaint jetty, beachside pubs and restaurants, and clusters of small waterfront homes, this tiny harborside suburb feels more like a secluded seaside village. The area was named for Robert Watson, who was harbormaster of the Sydney port in 1811 and later the first superintendent of the **Macquarie Lighthouse. Robertson Park,** with its grassy hills and children's playground, greets you as soon as you're off the ferry and is a popular picnic spot. Parking can be impossible around Watsons Bay on weekends, so a ferry, water taxi, or bus are the best bets.

28 The Gap The southern side of the harbor headland known as The Gap is one of the most beautiful coastal cliff formations in the world. Unfortunately, the area also has tragic associations for Sydneysiders; many people have taken their lives by leaping into the wave-lashed rocks below. A Cliff Rescue Unit was established in 1942 to handle hazardous rescues and to collect bodies. This is also the place where the ill-fated ship *Dunbar* was wrecked on the rocks in 1857. Only one crew member survived, and the ship's anchor is now set into the cliff directly across from the shipwreck site. The tragic history notwith-standing, it is easy to spend hours here along the walk—gazing out to the Pacific Ocean, watching tankers and cruise boats enter the harbor, or looking behind you to the west to see the giant city looming in the distance. ♦ Gap Rd (southeast of Military Rd)

29 Doyle's ★$$$ What you see is what you get at this longtime family favorite, a Sydney seafood institution. This restaurant used to be the place where Australian expats went, straight from the airport, for a bottle of Chardonnay, a plate of fish-and-chips, and a chance to renew their acquaintance with Sydney Harbour. Nowadays, there are many other (and better) options for a harborside lunch, but this place doesn't seem to be suffering from the competition. The cooking is nothing innovative, but the seafood is generally top quality. The wide variety of fish available is either grilled or fried in a light and crispy beer batter and served with thick fries. It's a great spot to take the kids; service is speedy and there's a good children's menu. Besides, the beach is there to play on if boredom sets in. This place is certainly worth a visit for the idyllic view, if nothing else. ♦ Seafood ♦ Daily lunch and dinner. Reservations recommended. 11 Marine Parade (west of Robertson St). 9337.2007

30 Picnic ★$$ This "picnic" is free of seagulls and other wildlife and is a welcome option in an area filled with seafood restaurants and pubs. You still get the view, thanks to the huge windows, which let in a grand vista and lots of light. Optional outdoor seating is well protected from the elements. There are daily specials, plus popular items like goat-cheese salad and bread-and-butter pudding, which could be considered a meal in itself. ♦ Cafe ♦ Daily 10AM-9:30PM. 3 Military Rd (between Dunbar St and Gap Rd). 9337.5221

31 Watsons Bay Hotel ★$$ There are only a few guest rooms at this waterfront pub, but most patrons are here for a beer and a seafood meal on the outdoor terrace anyway. The seafood platter is the best bet. Grab a table, order your drinks, and settle into the views of the busy jetty and the cityscape in the distance. The bar indoors is typical of old Sydney—tile walls, TV sets, beer on tap, and lots of noise. ♦ Cafe ♦ M-Tu 10AM-10PM; W-Sa 10AM-midnight; Su 10AM-8:30PM. 1 Military Rd (just west of Cliff St). 9337.4299

32 Camp Cove Avoid swimming at Watsons Bay, with its shallow, murky water and water traffic, and head straight to this beach area near South Head. This beach is at the end of **Sydney Harbour National Park**, and the area is well maintained. The water is clean, with plenty of room to swim. Take a walk out to South Head and **Hornby Lighthouse** and you'll pass Lady Bay, the nudist beach. Those so inclined may descend the steep staircase to this secluded stretch of sand and bare all. The waters of Camp Cove are not patrolled, so do not take a dip here unless you are a strong swimmer. ♦ Cliff and Victoria Sts

City Beaches

33 Bondi Beach The word "Bondi" means "the sound of waves breaking over rocks" in one of the many Aboriginal languages. Local and international visitors flock here throughout the year to enjoy the scene, ride the waves, and relax on the golden sands of this famous city beach (pictured below). In the summer months, especially on the weekend, the beach is covered with blankets, umbrellas, and a crowd of people who have come to watch the topless bathers. Others stroll along the promenade and head straight to one of the cafes along Campbell Parade. The northeastern side of the beach is often less crowded and more popular with the locals, and the southwestern end has the public baths and the rock pools and attracts backpackers and other visitors.

Bondi Beach

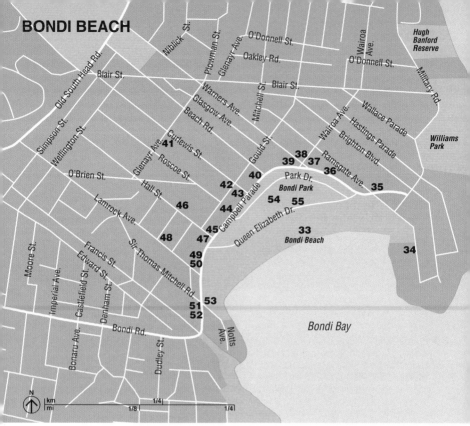

BONDI BEACH

34 Speedo's Cafe ★★$ Unlike most Bondi cafes, this one attracts fewer tourists and is very popular with North Bondi residents. Very casual is the style here: Summer weekends see the place full of families in bathing suits, covered with salt and sand as they eat breakfast after their morning dip. The pancakes are especially delicious, but the burgers, salads, and pasta dishes are quite good. There is also a take-out menu for those who want to eat on the beach. ♦ Cafe ♦ Daily. 126 Ramsgate Ave (southeast of Campbell Parade). 9365.3622

35 Sean's Panaroma ★★$$$ This eccentric little cafe at the northeastern end of Bondi Beach is not that glamorous or even that comfortable (seats are recycled school chairs), but after a lunchtime bowl of linguine with lemon, chili, and arugula, followed by a homemade sorbet, the comfort factor won't be an issue. Quality ingredients and simple, honest flavors are the draws here. At night there is a prix-fixe menu that changes daily and is always well planned. ♦ Modern Australian ♦ M-Th dinner; F lunch; Sa breakfast, lunch, and dinner; Su breakfast and lunch. 270 Campbell Parade (between Brighton Blvd and Ramsgate Ave). 9365.4924

36 Onzain ★★$$ When a restaurant has a gorgeous view to distract you, the food—even though it may be noteworthy—often plays second fiddle. Here, it doesn't. This restaurant's uncomplicated bistro food, with lots of lamb, beef, chicken, and fish, is loved by many for its big flavors that make you want to order another of whatever you've just eaten. The complimentary onion-and-garlic dip with a basket of crusty bread is an irresistible staple. Arrive at sunset so you can take a good long look at the view through the tall glass windows before you order. ♦ French ♦ M-Th dinner; F-Su lunch and dinner. Reservations recommended. Bondi Diggers' Club, 232 Campbell Parade (between Ramsgate and Warners Aves), Second floor. 9365.0763

36 Diggers' Cafe ★★★$ Delicious Turkish bread is part of most dishes at this cafe on the ground floor of the **Bondi Diggers' Club.** Since many of the patrons come straight from the health spa, the menu has lots of healthful, nutritious items—homemade muffins and organic everything. But it wouldn't be a cafe without its selection of Italian biscuits from Leichhardt (Sydney's Italian neighborhood). The view of the beach is terrific. ♦ Cafe ♦ Daily. Bondi Diggers' Club, 232 Campbell Parade (between Ramsgate and Warners Aves), Ground floor. 9365.6747

Australia's capital city is Canberra, about 300 kilometers (186 miles) southwest of Sydney.

37 Raw Bar ★★$$ It's sushi by the sea—Japanese cuisine at its most versatile, in a modern, lively atmosphere with a full view of Bondi Beach. Menu highlights include a selection of raw and cooked dishes, plus a good-value bento box. The sushi bar is often busy, and the sushi-making technique is not always perfect, but the ingredients are always extremely fresh. This place is popular with a young, largely local crowd, especially on a warm summer's night, when you can pull up a table on the pavement and watch the sun go down. ♦ Japanese ♦ Daily lunch and dinner. Warners and Wairoa Aves. 9365.7200

38 Jackie's Espresso Bar ★★$ One of Sydney's most popular cafes, this space is large and airy with a cooling, fresh, sea breeze. Take your eyes off the view of the beach long enough to order one of the well-prepared Sydney cafe standards, such as chicken schnitzel, focaccia, and Caesar salad. Service is erratic, especially on weekends, when the traffic is heavy. ♦ Cafe ♦ Daily breakfast, lunch, and dinner. 132A Warners Ave (at Wairoa Ave). 9300.9812

39 Bondi Markets For second-hand everything, including clothes, jewelry, and furniture, these small markets provide a nice break from the beach on Sunday. Lots of backpackers come here to buy the kitschy souvenirs and cheap T-shirts. ♦ Su. Bondi Beach Public School, Campbell Parade and Wairoa Ave. 9315.8988

40 Swiss-Grand Hotel $$$ With its ornamental columns and frills, this 203-room hotel looks as though it belongs in St-Tropez rather than in the more down-to-earth Bondi Beach. However, once you get past the garish exterior, the inside of this all-suite property is surprisingly simple and spacious. The hotel offers views straight out to the Pacific Ocean and provides a decent alternative to city accommodations. Meeting, conference, and dining facilities are available. ♦ Campbell Parade and Beach Rd. 9365.5666; fax 930.3545

41 City Beach Motor Inn $$ This small 26-room motel with an odd-looking green exterior is basic but comfortable. There's a swimming pool, but with the beach only a few minutes' walk away, it is hardly worth it. The rooms are very simply furnished and are equipped with refrigerators. There are in-house laundry facilities and parking for visitors. Breakfast service to the room is available, but there's no restaurant. ♦ 99 Curlewis St (at Glenayr Ave). 9365.3100; fax 9365.0231

42 Earth Food Store Mountains of organic fruit and vegetables are sold here to locals and visitors who prefer pesticide-free produce. The take-out salads are also excellent. ♦ M-Sa. 81 Gould St (at Curlewis St). 9365.5098

43 Hotel Bondi $ This 200-room hotel seems to be more popular for its four bars, beer garden, and bistro than its accommodations. Rooms are very basic and the furnishings are minimal, but every room has a refrigerator and tea- and coffee-making facilities. The hotel is a very good value, if you can cope with the noise downstairs when the music is cranked up on the weekend. ♦ 178 Campbell Parade (between Hall and Curlewis Sts). 9130.3271; fax 9130.7974

44 Fishy Affair ★$$ Lively and airy, this restaurant serves up big plates of seafood—fast—to the hordes who come here on the weekend, when the joint is jumping. It's very popular with young people, due to its moderate prices. ♦ Seafood ♦ Daily lunch and dinner. 152-62 Campbell Parade (between Hall and Curlewis Sts). 9300.0494

44 Bondi Beachside Inn $ Located right at the beach, this hotel with 70 apartments shares premises with a steak house and a seafood restaurant. You may not need either one, because 50 of the apartments come with fully equipped kitchens. The lobby is small and unpretentious, but the units are of fair size and decorated in appropriate ocean shades of blue and emerald green. Closet space is a bit cramped (with off-the-floor wardrobes), but lighting arrangements are excellent, and some of the rooms have grand ocean vistas. All rooms come with thermostatic temperature control and private balconies. ♦ 152 Campbell Parade (between Hall and Curlewis Sts). 9130.5311

The North Shore/Eastern Suburbs us-and-them mentality predates European settlement: Aborigines on each shore of the harbor called the other area *warung* ("the other side").

Breathtaking Beach Cliff Walk

The cliffs of Sydney's eastern beaches are just the place for those looking for an invigorating walk with stunning beach views and plenty of salt air—it's the quintessential Sydney experience. An additional highlight to this pleasant stroll is the opportunity to take a dip in the ocean at any point along the way.

The 10-kilometer (6-mile) walk extends along a clearly marked pathway from **Coogee Beach** to **Bondi Beach,** via **Clovelly, Bronte,** and **Tamarama Beaches.** A popular part is the leg from Bronte to Bondi, an easy, three-kilometer (two-mile) path, with spectacular, unobstructed views of the ocean along the whole route. Don't miss the Aboriginal rock carving depicting a large fish—possibly a shark—on a large, flat rock not far from the **Tamarama Surf Club** (overlooking the beach where the local surfies hang out). An eclectic range of beachside homes, some of which have been transformed from humble cottages into multimillion-dollar mansions, is also part of the scenery.

To get there by bus, catch either a *Bondi, Bronte,* or *Coogee* bus from the city or the *Bondi & Bay Explorer* bus. For those with cars it's best to start from Coogee or Bronte, as parking is very difficult in Bondi.

Coogee Beach

45 Bondi Surf Seafoods This take-out fish-and-chip shop does not serve your average greasy, heart-clogging fare. The staff will gladly grill a fillet of John Dory or a juicy salmon steak to order. Fresh oysters are also on offer and relatively inexpensive. ◆ Daily 10AM-8PM. 128 Campbell Parade (between Hall and Curlewis Sts). 9130.4554

46 Avivim ★$$ The cuisine at this kosher restaurant is more Middle Eastern than Eastern European. No matzo ball soup here—just delicious mixed plates that include hummus, *baba ganooj* (eggplant and lemon spread), tabbouleh, falafel, and generous servings of grilled meat dishes. However, the place will win no awards for decor. ◆ Middle Eastern ◆ M-Th, Su lunch and dinner. 49 Hall St (between Gould and O'Brien Sts). 9930.8302

47 Ravesi's on Bondi Beach $$ Smart but laid back, this busy boutique hotel fits right into the area's lifestyle. The 16 spacious rooms have a tropical look, furnished in simple cane and wood. All guest rooms have basic amenities, and some of the five suites have private balconies overlooking the sand and surf. If you are a light sleeper, be prepared to buy some earplugs when staying here on the weekend—Campbell Parade below attracts throngs of pubgoers. ◆ Campbell Parade and Hall St. 9365.4422; fax 9365.1481

Within Ravesi's on Bondi Beach:

Ravesi's Restaurant ★★$$ The tables on the balcony with sweeping views of the beach are what make this restaurant so special. A dozen oysters and a bottle of Champagne always fit the bill here. Brunch is one of the most popular meals, as stylish patrons in sarongs and beachwear have a bite before they hit the sand. For brunch, try the flapjacks or black sticky rice served with banana porridge and coconut cream. ◆ Modern Australian ◆ Daily breakfast, lunch, and dinner. Reservations recommended. 9365.4422

48 Thelellen Lodge $ The 14 plainly decorated rooms here are quiet and comfortable. Although pared down to the basics, all rooms have electric fans, sinks, radios, and refrigerators. Light breakfast is served in your room. A common kitchen is also a nice touch for the budget-conscious traveler. ♦ 11A Consett Ave (between Lamrock Ave and Hall St). 9130.1521

49 The Idle Tank It's a treat to have this tranquil bookstore in the middle of the crowds and cafes along Campbell Parade. Books, compact discs, and Internet service are all neatly managed in this one small space. The savvy staff is very helpful. There's a good selection of Australian literature. ♦ Daily. 84 Campbell Parade (between Lamrock Ave and Hall St). 9365.5266

50 Bondi Surf Company So you're in Australia and you can't go home without learning how to hang ten on an eight-foot swell. This store offers surfing lessons, surfboard rentals, and sells the surf gear so you can at least look the part even if you can't quite manage the waves. ♦ Daily. 72-76 Campbell Parade (between Lamrock Ave and Hall St). 9365.0870

50 Lamrock Cafe ★★$
With one of the best locations in Bondi, boasting a full view of the beach from the streetfront, this cafe is a major part of the scene here. The glass doors fold back to let in a salty sea breeze. For those who have had a late night and slept in, breakfasts and huge burgers are available any time of day. Service is casual and friendly. ♦ Cafe ♦ M-F 7AM-midnight. 72 Campbell Parade (between Lamrock Ave and Hall St). 9130.6313

50 Hugo's ★★$$ Casual but cool, this bar and restaurant on the main strip has a great view of pedestrian traffic and surf from the pavement tables. Inside, seating is snug and always filled—if you don't come for the light and delicious food, come to hang with the local hip crowd. The lunches are terrific, featuring huge grilled salads and pasta dishes. ♦ Modern Australian ♦ Daily lunch and dinner; Sa-Su breakfast and lunch. Reservations recommended. 70 Campbell Parade (at Lamrock Ave). 9300.0900

51 The Sports Bard ★★$$ As a very hip hangout, this is not some clubby gathering place for athletes but more of a casual restaurant for locals. Whether you drop in for a lazy weekend brunch or a late-night snack, the open kitchen delivers good, crowd-pleasing fare. If the walls lined with sporting paraphernalia don't inspire you to get out onto the beach and do battle with the surf, nothing will. The menu changes monthly. ♦ Modern Australian ♦ M-F dinner; Sa-Su breakfast, lunch, and dinner. 32 Campbell Parade (between Francis St and Sir Thomas Mitchell Rd). 9130.4582

52 Kelp The name of this hairdressing salon may sound a bit green and slimy, but who cares when the interior is so sleek and the patrons so stylish? "Zen and the art of hair care and maintenance" defines the look and attitude at this salon. ♦ Daily. 18 Campbell Parade (between Francis St and Sir Thomas Mitchell Rd). 9300.0808

53 Bondi Icebergs Club The "Bergs" is Australia's oldest swimming club, based at the southwestern end of Bondi Beach. Started in 1929, the club fulfills a mission to swim in the sea year-round—although they are most famous for their midwinter swims—and nurture the athletic talents of young swimmers. The club runs its own saltwater pool at the end of the beach. Admission is very reasonable. In the pool, swimmers need only worry about hypothermia, not the dangerous riptides and currents around this beach. ♦ Daily. 1 Notts Ave (at Campbell Parade). 9130.3120

54 Bondi Pavilion Built in 1928 in the middle of the beach, this public pavilion is and is considered Bondi's main landmark and locus of culture. Originally built as changing rooms and showers for swimmers, it was converted to a community center in 1978. It is now the venue for musical and theatrical performances (it has a 230-seat theater) and art exhibitions. The ballroom here is also a popular location for surf-lovers' weddings. A licensed cafe, ice cream bar, and souvenir shop are also within the building. ♦ Bondi Park, Queen Elizabeth Dr (off Campbell Parade). Schedule of events 9365.1253

Surfing was introduced to Sydney's beaches by Duke Kahanamoka of Hawaii in 1915 when he brought his long wooden board to the city for a body surfing carnival. Today the board hangs in the Freshwater Surf Club.

Bondi Beach used to be called Nelson Bay in honor of the British naval hero. It was changed to the Aboriginal name in the early 20th century.

Sydney's Architectural Style and Famous Architects

The Styles

Sydney's many impressive landmark buildings span a variety of architectural styles—from Colonial to Contemporary Expressionism—yet an Australian approach is also prominent in rows of terrace homes, bungalows, and even brand-new brick houses. In these dwellings, Australian architects have borrowed design elements from Europe and North America, ingeniously adapting them to suit Sydney's climate and using local building materials.

The following are some of the most popular architectural styles found in Sydney:

Colonial The architecture of the late 1700s to the mid-1800s was notable for its solid, stately structures with few exterior details and modest windows. Several fine examples of Colonial architecture include **Cadman's Cottage, St. James Church, Hyde Park Barracks,** and **Elizabeth Bay House.**

Victorian The late 1800s saw the advent of such grand Victorian public buildings as the **Queen Victoria Building, Town Hall,** and **Sydney Hospital** at a time when the empire was rich and made use of sandstone, stained glass, and wrought iron. This was also the period when Colonial-style two- and three-story terrace homes, featuring wrought-iron lacework on the balconies and tall ceilings, were built. **Paddington, Newtown,** and **Glebe** are the places to find them.

Federation In the early 1900s when Australia's federal government was established was a time of economic stability. Homes built then were commonly made of brick with red-tile roofs. They often had wood details and stained-glass windows, many of which depicted such native animals as kangaroos and emus. Examples of the "federation home" (as it is called today) may be found mainly in the **Inner West** suburbs of **Annandale, Burwood,** and **Strathfield.**

Post–World War II Australia's population explosion after the war caused a flurry of construction and expansion of Sydney's city limits. High-rises were not yet on the horizon (a law prohibited buildings to be taller than 150 feet). Unfortunately the architectural aesthetics from this period are unmemorable, but the style is prevalent in the bungalow-type homes in the outlying suburbs and in some modest concrete and glass International-style buildings in the **Central Business District (CBD).**

Modernism The CBD began developing vertically in the 1960s when the country went through a mining

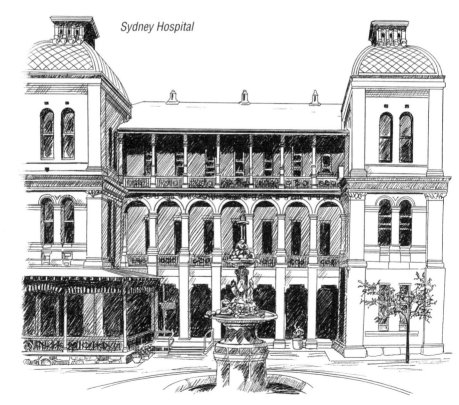

Sydney Hospital

Hyde Park Barracks

boom that resulted in a strong economy. The city's first skyscrapers were built at **Australia Square** and around **Martin Place.** Urban sprawl reached the southern and western suburbs during this period, with redbrick homes, swimming pools, and huge shopping malls edging ever outward from the city's harbor.

Postmodernism The late 1970s and early 1980s was the time when many new skyscrapers were built and the architecture reflected International Post-Modernist trends. Exterior supports were erected on office buildings and glass was liberally used to reflect the surrounding structures and the harbor. Many new homes in the **Eastern Suburbs** and **North Shore** also followed this trend.

Contemporary Expressionism/Eco Architecture
Since the late 1980s Australian architecture has developed its own style. Local architects are more likely to be commissioned than professionals from other countries and there's a new respect for domestic materials and the environment. In the city, this distinctive style—featuring the use of sandstone, granite, and wood—is found in such developments as the **Park Hyatt** at **The Rocks,** the **Governor Phillip Tower,** and the adjacent **Museum of Sydney.** Much of the Expressionist architecture of late reflects elements of nature and uses such materials as canvas, corrugated iron, and sandstone. The **Darling Harbour** development has examples of both Contemporary Expressionism and Eco Architecture.

Architects
The following architects are among those who have left their mark on Sydney:

Francis Greenway (1777-1837) A convict whose adaptable skill and methods made him the new colony's official architect, **Greenway** designed over 40 buildings in the Sydney area. Some of the better-known include **Hyde Park Barracks,** the **Conservatorium of Music,** and the **Macquarie Lighthouse** in **Vaucluse,** all of which helped him obtain Governor Macquarie's pardon.

Edmund Thomas Blacket (1817-83) One of the great civic architects of his time, **Blacket** designed many of Sydney's churches and public buildings. He is most famous for the Gothic-Revival style of the **University of Sydney**'s **Great Hall,** built in 1857.

Walter Burley Griffin (1876-1937) This North American architect's proposal plan won first prize in a world competition in 1913 to design Australia's new capital city, Canberra. In 1924, **Griffin**'s fame spread to the Sydney area when he designed the city's northern suburb of **Castlecrag.**

Jorn Utzon (1918-) Winner of the international competition to design the **Sydney Opera House,** this Danish architect started construction on this monumental public project in 1959. It wasn't completed until 1973. (Three Australian architects—**David Littlemore, Peter Hall,** and **Lionel Todd**—took over in 1966 after **Utzon** resigned in protest over how the project was being disrupted by political squabbles.)

Harry Seidler (1923-) One of Australia's more celebrated contemporary architects, **Seidler**'s company designed some of Sydney's 1960s and 1970s landmarks, including **Australia Square Tower** on **George Street** and the **MLC Centre** on Martin Place.

55 Bondi Surf Bathers' Life Saving Club

This lifesaving club was set up in 1906 to protect the growing number of swimmers and surfers at what was then already becoming Sydney's most popular beach. This club became a model for others around the nation. The lifesavers made the history books in 1938, when their services were put to the test: More than 200 people were washed out to sea after a freak wave flooded the beach. Club members managed to save 180 lives and another 15 people managed to save themselves (only five people perished). The club hosts the annual Bondi Surf Carnival, which attracts thousands of spectators.
♦ Bondi Park, Queen Elizabeth Dr (off Campbell Parade). 9365.0693

56 Tamarama Beach

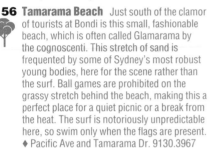

Just south of the clamor of tourists at Bondi is this small, fashionable beach, which is often called Glamarama by the cognoscenti. This stretch of sand is frequented by some of Sydney's most robust young bodies, here for the scene rather than the surf. Ball games are prohibited on the grassy stretch behind the beach, making this a perfect place for a quiet picnic or a break from the heat. The surf is notoriously unpredictable here, so swim only when the flags are present.
♦ Pacific Ave and Tamarama Dr. 9130.3967

57 Bronte Beach

The cliffs around Bronte, one of Sydney's most residential beaches, are crammed with everything from bungalow-style homes to apartment blocks. The beach itself is bordered by a rolling lawn that meets the sand. This green area is a popular place for picnics, football, and cricket games. Visitors also come to patronize the row of cafes along the southern side of the beach. A cute mini-train offers toddlers short rides around an enclosed grassy area. The old changing rooms with showers are open, as is the famous surf pool, which is busy all day every day of the year. The saltwater baths here are also a popular alternative to the rough surf for parents teaching their children to swim.
♦ Bronte Rd and Nelson Ave. Information 9389.6500

58 Bronte Cafe ★$

Everything is made on the premises at this popular beach cafe. Breakfast is the main attraction during the week, with big healthful bowls of muesli to fuel you up for the day, or fennel sausages with grilled polenta, which will jump-start your taste buds. The coffee comes in every style imaginable, and the desserts are terrific. The view of the beach isn't too shabby either. ♦ Cafe ♦ Daily. 467 Bronte Rd (east of Nelson Ave). 9387.4011

Until 1903 it was against the law in Sydney to swim in public between 6AM and 8PM.

58 Bogey-Hole Cafe ★★$

The name of this cafe makes it sound as if it should be on a golf course, but "bogey" is really an Aboriginal word, meaning swimming hole. (Bronte Beach's own bogey hole is a tidal rock pool built in the 1920s at the southern end of the beach.) This cafe serves quick breakfasts, hearty lunches, and afternoon coffee and cake. Try the smoked salmon, sour cream, and roasted capers on a bagel for breakfast, or order a Turkish-bread sandwich and eat it down on the beach. Proprietors Debra and Richard Gray have put a lot of thought into serving good, quick meals. ♦ Cafe ♦ Daily. 473 Bronte Rd (east of Nelson Ave). 9389.8829

58 Sejuiced ★$

If you can juice it, then this cafe probably serves it. Stop here after a morning swim for a wholesome breakfast of banana porridge or try one of the delicious melts for lunch. Naturally, the juice concoctions are a real treat, too. ♦ Cafe ♦ Daily. 487 Bronte Rd (east of Nelson Ave). 9389.9538

59 Clovelly Beach

Wedged between the cliffs of Waverley Cemetery and Coogee Beach is this well-protected beach. The shape of the headland makes this more of a bay than a beach, and the waters here are some of the calmest in Sydney. This creates an ideal place for children to swim, snorkel, and play in relative safety. There is also a ramp for wheelchair access into the water. ♦ Donnellan Circuit (just north of Clovelly Rd). Information 9665.1441

60 Coogee Beach

This beach got its name from the Aboriginal word "coogee," which many claim means the smell of rotten seaweed. The beach is actually very clean and smells perfectly fine. It was not until the 1840s that the land around Coogee became a small town, and later in the 1880s the area became a popular holiday spot for Sydneysiders. In the 1920s, Coogee had become so popular that a 600-foot amusement pier was built over the bay, complete with a steel shark net for safer swimming. The pier doesn't exist today, but the aquarium that was originally built in 1887 was rebuilt and opened again in 1987 at the northern end of the beach. In 1993, the redevelopment of Coogee Beach Plaza was completed, providing the area with paved promenades, terraces, and a park. ♦ Arden and Dolphin Sts. Information 9665.5138

61 Regal Pearl ★★$$ If fish-and-chips on the beach is not your style, then perhaps a Chinese meal, or dim sum (known in Australia as *yum cha*), will do the trick. The sweet pork-filled buns are as good as any in Sydney's Chinatown. This place is very popular on the weekend for inexpensive feasts. ♦ Chinese ♦ Daily lunch and dinner. 169 Dolphin St (just east of Arden St). 9665.3308

62 Pro Dive Coogee Active Coogee Beach, with its heavy surf, may not look like the ideal place to learn to scuba dive, but there are plenty of sheltered areas where an experienced instructor can teach the basics. At this store you can sign up for any number of classes and rent the gear if you didn't happen to pack it. ♦ M-Sa. 27 Alfreda St (between Arden and Brook Sts). 9665.6333

63 Coogee Bay Hotel $ This old beachside hotel is renowned for its pub and music, not its accommodations. The conference and meeting rooms, three bars, nightclub, brasserie, beer garden, and entertainment center outnumber the handful of guest rooms. However, it's a great place for an afternoon beer. ♦ 253 Coogee Bay Rd (at Arden St). 9665.0000; fax 9664.2103

63 Holiday Inn Coogee Beach $$$ Very popular as a local conference and meeting venue, this hotel is located directly opposite Coogee Beach. The 207 guest rooms and suites are simple, spacious, and clean. Most rooms have ocean views, and there is 24-hour room service. Other features include a large health club, tennis court, complimentary parking, and a swimming pool in case you are not prepared for the surf across the street. Ask about the weekend packages for couples. ♦ 242 Arden St (between Carr St and Coogee Bay Rd). 9315.7600, 800/465.4329; fax 9315.9100

64 Barzura ★★$$ Located on the south side of Coogee, this cafe and restaurant is packed every day of the week with beach lovers who have come for the Mediterranean food and the terrific southern panoramic view of the beach. There are daily specials, but the seafood dishes are the best bets. Come for a simple breakfast, or try the charcoal-grilled octopus salad for lunch. There are plenty of choices and the staff is very friendly. ♦ Modern Australian ♦ Daily breakfast, lunch, and dinner. Reservations recommended on the weekend. 62 Carr St (between Beach and Arden Sts). 9665.5546

65 Wylie's Baths There are three different public baths at Coogee, including one exclusively for women, but **Wylie's** has to be the most enticing. These baths were built in 1907 by H.A. Wylie, a famous Australian long-distance and underwater swimmer. In 1993, the local council began restoring the baths, following the original design. It's so authentic-looking that if everyone who swam here today still wore neck-to-knee swimsuits, you'd think you were back in the 1920s. There are long wooden platforms, clean changing rooms, and a giant wooden staircase built into the cliff face leading down to the baths. During the summer months, the baths offer free swimming lessons for children on Saturday morning. ♦ Admission. Neptune St and Wolseley Rd. 9665.2838

Bests

Margaret Woods
Teacher/Archivist, Rosebank College

The **Wharf Theatre**—Lunch overlooking the harbor before a matinee performance by the **Sydney Theatre Company.**

The Italian bar in **David Jones Market Street Food Hall**—Sydney's best minestrone.

The Royal Botanic Gardens—cycads—real live prehistoric plants.

Vaucluse House—Devonshire tea in 19th-century colonial mansion.

Norton Street, Leichhardt—a cappuccino crawl from cafe to cafe.

A morning walk, bike, jog around the main drive in **Centennial Park.**

Celtic mosaics in the crypt of **St. Mary's Cathedral**—see them every Sunday after listening to the choir at 10:30AM Mass.

Lunch with the city suits at **Brasserie Cassis** in **Chifley Tower.**

Nineteenth-century **Library of Australian Treasures—Mitchell Library.**

Robert Rosenblum
Professor of Fine Arts, New York University

Queen Victoria Building—the grandest grandmother of our shopping malls.

Peacock blue lizards from the Fiji Islands in the zoo.

Bondi Beach—top of the charts from sandlovers.

The subway—an endangered Edwardian species still alive and well in Sydney.

Oysters, oysters, oysters—white wine, white wine, white wine.

Australian symbolist and impressionist painting at the **Art Gallery of New South Wales.**

The Inner West

LILYFIELD

Blackmore Park

Whites Creek Valley Park

Darley Rd.

Lilyfield Rd.

City-West Link Rd.

Norton St.

Derbyshire Rd.

Balmain Rd.

Piper St.

William St.

James St.

Pioneers Memorial Park

Moore St.

Smith St.

Annandale St.

Booth St.

Allen St.

49

LEICHHARDT

Short St.

Catherine St.

Flood St.

Elswick St.

Marion St.

Leichhardt St.

Styles St.

Collins St.

Reserve St.

Day St.

Cary St.

Renwick St.

Balmain Rd.

Ferris St.

Albion St.

Johnston St.

Trafalgar St.

50

Elswick St.

Jarrett St.

Parramatta Rd. (Great Western Hwy.)

to Sydney Olympic Park

Parramatta Rd. (Great Western Hwy.)

Macaulay St.

Petersham Park

Railway St.

Westbourne St.

Albany Rd.

Percival Rd.

Salisbury Rd.

STANMORE

Brighton St.

Douglas St.

Crystal St.

Trafalgar St.

Trafalgar St.

ENMORE

Gordon St.

New Canterbury Rd.

PETERSHAM

Cavendish St.

Stanmore Rd.

Liberty St.

Newington College

Wardell Rd.

Livingstone Rd.

Newington Rd.

Frazer St.

Addison Rd.

Shaw St.

England Ave.

Wemyss St.

Enmore Rd.

Marrickville Park

MARRICKVILLE

N

km   1/4   1/2
mi 1/8   1/4

Rozelle
Bay

31

Pendrill St.

30

Glebe Point Rd.

Forsyth St.

Blackwattle
Bay

Sydney
Fish Markets

32

For nos. 34-48,
see pg. 156

ULTIMO

Wentworth
Park

Wattle St.

Bicentennial
Park

The Crescent

Toxteth Rd.

Bridge Rd.

Ferry Rd.
Taylor St.

Cardigan St.
Wentworth Park Rd.

33
Lyndhurst St.

Dargham St.

William Henry St.

ANNANDALE

Nelson St.

Minogue Cres.

Wigram Rd.

Hereford St.

29

28
GLEBE

Mitchell St.

Bay St.

Bridge Rd.

St. Johns Rd.

Derwent St.

27 Glebe Point Rd.
26
25
24
23
22
21

Cowper St.

Francis St.

Derby Pl.

Catherine St.

20

Ross St.

Arundel St.

Pyrmont Bridge Rd.

Parramatta Rd. (Great Western Hwy.)

Holme
Building

Great
Hall

Lake
Northam

Victoria
Park

City Rd.

Camperdown
Park

Missenden Rd.

Church St.

Student
Centre

Cleveland Pl.

CAMPERDOWN

19

Wentworth
Building

Salisbury Rd.

Australia St.

Carillon Ave.

City Rd.

Abercrombie St.

O'Connell St.

Campbell St.

Egan St.

2
3
4

1

Georgina St.

Queen St.

Watkin St.

6
5
7

NEWTOWN

Lennox St.

Mary St.

10
8
King St.
9

Brown St.

Wilson St.

ERSKINEVILLE

Bedford St.

Eliza St.

12
11

Erskineville Rd.

Albert St.

Gladstone St.

13

Whitehorse St.

Railway Parade

Henderson Rd.

Enmore Rd. **17**

18

14

Reiby St.

Simmons St.

Holt St.

16 **15**

Station St.

Swanson St.

Copeland St.

King St.

Concord St.

Ashmore St.

Mitchell Rd.

Camden St.

Alice St.

The Inner West

West of the Central Business District (CBD)—either as you head down George Street or through Darling Harbour—is an area referred to as The Inner West. Although The Inner West extends as far west as **Strathfield** and **Homebush Bay** (20 kilometers—12 miles—west of the city), some of the area's more accessible and exciting suburbs are **Newtown, Glebe,** and **Balmain** (and Balmain's neighbor, **Rozelle**), all approximately 4 kilometers (2.5 miles) from the city. What makes these suburbs so special is the village atmosphere they have retained from the late 19th century—there has been little new development and, for the most part, the old homes and shop fronts have been faithfully renovated and preserved.

Newtown is one of Sydney's best examples of a busy village community. Its location on the edge of the **University of Sydney** campus prevents the suburb from getting too gentrified, and the student population keeps the cafes, bookstores, and secondhand clothing stores along **King Street** in business. Meanwhile, the "DINKS" (double income, no kids) have moved in and fixed up many of the old row houses, thus encouraging the establishment of stylish cafes, restaurants, and shops.

The area was originally the site of a 1794 land grant to the free settler Nicholas Devine, who named his property **Burren Farm.** The name Newtown didn't emerge until the 1830s, when John and Eliza Webster opened a store at the end of Missenden Road called the **New Town Store.** A tiny community grew around the business and its surrounding farmland, particularly after the construction of the university in 1850. By the 1920s, King Street—the main thoroughfare—had become one of the busiest strips in the area, with major retail and manufacturing activity and a regular tram line (now defunct) running to the city.

King Street is as busy as ever, with pubs, cafes, and inexpensive restaurants that appeal to Sydney's aspiring poets, artists, designers, and the area's perennial students. Over the last several years, Newtown has also become a center for Sydney's gay and lesbian community: its pubs, such as the **Newtown Hotel,** feature drag nights and other gay-friendly entertainment. Farther down King Street, past its train station, is **Enmore,** where the scene becomes a little rougher around the edges and less appealing to those who don't know where they are going.

The **University of Sydney** acts as an unofficial dividing wedge between the villages of Newtown and Glebe. Both suburbs are home to a lot of students, but Glebe prides itself (even if the residents are sometimes loath to admit it) on being slightly more refined. Its main thoroughfare, **Glebe Point Road,** starting at **Parramatta Road** and running down to **Rozelle Bay,** is lined with a curious mix of inexpensive cafes, fine restaurants, bars, secondhand bookstores, and blocks of original row houses. There is still the odd junk shop, bohemian cafe, and the old **Valhalla** cinema, but among these and in between some of the more working-class Victorian residences sit some old 19th-century mansions—reminders that this area was once even more prestigious than it is today.

Glebe's gentrified edge may also be attributed to its history and close proximity to the harbor at **Blackwattle Bay.** Richard Johnson, the First Fleet chaplain, was granted 400 acres of land by Governor Arthur Phillip in 1789. He and his wife, Mary, occupied this land, which came to be known as **Glebe Estate.** ("Glebe" means land assigned to clergy.) By the end of the 19th century, Glebe had become a simple working-class suburb, with some grand homes built at the end of Glebe Point Road near the water and on the hill (such as **Lyndhurst**), while workers' cottages were clustered near Parramatta Road.

Across **Johnstons Bay**, over the ultramodern **Glebe Island Bridge**, is the suburb of Balmain. This harborside suburb and its neighbor, Rozelle, have become two of Sydney's most sought-after addresses. This is remarkable to many Sydneysiders, considering that Balmain was the epitome of an urban working-class community less than 30 years ago. Throughout the 19th century, Balmain was an industrial area, with shipyards, dry docks, and a coal mine, which provided some of Sydney's fuel. The concentration of sailors and dock workers made this one of the most economically deprived sections of Sydney, and also one of the toughest, a phenomenon that lasted well into the mid-20th century. Remnants of this past can be seen in some of the original wooden and stone cottages, the narrow Victorian row houses, and public buildings such as the **Watch House** on **Darling Street.**

Like Glebe, today's Balmain offers a curious mix of old and new, affluent and working class. Since the 1970s, those in search of a terrace house near the city ("Ten minutes on the ferry!") have converged on the suburb, buying up anything for sale and renovating it in its original style. What were once old wooden workers' cottages are now, in many cases, meticulously restored and painted family homes. Some of Balmain's pre-gentrification residents are still there, giving the place a bit of a reality check, but things are changing fast: Properties are hard to come by and, since the early 1990s, the Balmain fire has been fueled by a number of elegant restaurants, such as **Bistro Deux** and **Tetsuya's**, that attract hordes of Sydneysiders from all corners of the city.

Darling Street is really what gives Balmain its wonderful village atmosphere. On the weekend, it swarms with families and individuals who have come to brunch at their favorite cafe or stroll around the **Balmain Markets**, open each Saturday and Sunday on the grounds of **St. Andrew's Congregational Church.** The markets attract a diverse crowd of shoppers, who browse among stalls that sell antiques, old jewelry, various arts and crafts, aromatic essential oils, and herbal remedies.

Many Sydneysiders will rightly claim that trips to The Inner West should also include other neighborhoods such as **Leichhardt** and **Annandale.** These suburbs also mix Victorian working-class architecture with new money, making them wonderful places to explore on foot. But for the time being, Newtown, Glebe, and Balmain are the more developed main attractions.

Newtown

Thai Land RESTAURANT

1 Thai Land ★$$ For a traditional Thai dining experience, turn right as you enter and sit at the low tables with cushions. To the left is a Western table-and-chairs arrangement. However you choose to be seated, the extensive menu remains the same, featuring the standard Thai curries and soups. The green-curry chicken is a house specialty worth sharing. Daily specials appear on a blackboard. Service is friendly and fast, although a touch sloppy. ♦ Thai ♦ Daily dinner. 74-78 King St (between Queen and Georgina Sts). 9516.1127

2 Fresh on King ★$ Seafood dishes are the specialty at this simple, inexpensive cafe. The ingredients are very basic and very fresh (as the name suggests) and the preparation is consistent and reliable. The menu ranges from fish-and-chips to grilled local catches, such as snapper and John Dory. ♦ Seafood ♦ Daily lunch and dinner. 89 King St (between Little Queen St and Missenden Rd). 9550.5866

3 Fish Tank ★★$$ This breezy modern restaurant has a lovely courtyard in the back and offers well-presented seafood dishes with a minimum of fuss. Order such old standards as beer-batter fish and crispy chips, or specials like mussels in saffron broth and tuna steak with artichoke salad. A blackboard menu offers catch-of-the-day specials. The wine list is simple, and many varieties are offered by the glass. ♦ Seafood ♦ M-Th dinner; F-Su lunch and dinner. 119 King St (between Little Queen St and Missenden Rd). 9557.5627

The Sydney area has been inhabited for at least 50,000 years.

Shaiza's
Curry House

3 Shaiza's Curry House & Indian Seafood Restaurant ★$$ The portions of tandoori cooking here are larger than life—sort of like this restaurant's lavish Indian decor of dark wood and brass. Dishes are reasonably priced, with a wide selection of Indian classics—from chicken *vindaloo* (with a very spicy sauce) to prawns *biryani* (cooked with a cumin, coriander, and chili sauce). Vegetarians are also well taken care of, and the chef is prepared to alter the spices for those less inclined to have their taste buds go into shock. ♦ Indian ♦ Daily dinner. 121 King St (between Little Queen St and Missenden Rd). 9516.2165

4 Has Beans Cafe and Worlds-Up-Art ★$ This cozy yet quirky cafe and art gallery with an outdoor terrace is popular with students and local bohemians in need of basic food and coffee. The ground floor houses the cafe, which serves an eclectic mix of Italian and Mexican food in the midst of walls lined with contemporary art. This is also a popular venue for poetry readings on the first Sunday of every month. ♦ Cafe ♦ M, W-Su breakfast, lunch, and dinner. 153A King St (between Missenden Rd and Stephen St). 9519.9317

5 Newtown Hotel As a former corner pub for working-class Newtown, this place still has an old-Sydney-pub feel, but the crowd is mainly gay men. Midweek drag shows start at 11PM at the ground floor, while the cocktail bar on the second floor is less flashy. ♦ Daily 11AM-midnight. 174 King St (at Watkin St). 9557.1329

CAФE
XORE

6 Cafe X Core ★★$$ The loud, colorful decor at this popular Mediterranean restaurant/cafe makes it a rather festive environment. The Greek-inspired menu, with its hefty portions, has changed little since the place opened in 1994 and still offers diners old Greek standards (featuring lots of seafood), plus some familiar Middle Eastern dishes, all using very fresh

ingredients. Weekends are busiest here, although it's a great spot for a midweek lunch. The staff always seems to be smiling, courteous, and fast. ♦ Cafe/Greek ♦ Daily breakfast, lunch, and dinner. 191 King St (between O'Connell and Egan Sts). 9516.4970

7 The Bookshop Those in need of a good novel or a hard-to-find art book know that this store, which specializes in gay and lesbian fiction and nonfiction, is the perfect place to browse. The staff is more than willing to help you find what you're looking for—and even what you didn't know you were looking for. The shop also features readings and book signings by local authors. ♦ Daily 10AM-9PM. 186 King St (between Watkin and Brown Sts). 9557.4244

8 Noo Noo's This pleasant shop sells unusual, eclectic gifts and knickknacks from around the world, including such items as thumb pianos and other crafts from Afghanistan and Zimbabwe. ♦ M-Sa. 238 King St (at Whateley St). 9516.4368

The Cornstalk Bookshop

9 The Cornstalk Bookshop This rambling, crowded, secondhand bookstore, which also has a branch in Glebe, attracts students and browsers in search of classic paperbacks or rare first editions. ♦ Daily 10AM-11PM. 262 King St (between Whateley St and Erskineville Rd). 9550.3566. Also at: 112 Glebe Point Rd (between Mitchell St and St. Johns Rd). 9660.4889

10 Dendy Cinema The students and film buffs of The Inner West don't have to travel to the city to see the latest art-house films from Australia and abroad, now that this theater (of Martin Place fame) has opened a branch here. ♦ Daily. 261 King St (between Church and Mary Sts). 9550.5699. Also at: 19 Martin Pl (between Castlereagh and Pitt Sts). 9233.8166

11 Thai Pothong ★★$$ Quick service with a smile is the order of the day at this popular Thai restaurant, whose patrons include a mixture of down-to-earth students, professors, and some locals. There's a wide selection of traditional Thai dishes, with such noteworthy items as Thai fish cakes and stuffed chicken wings as appetizers. ♦ Thai ♦ M-F lunch and dinner; Sa-Su dinner. 298 King St (between Erskineville Rd and Wilson St). 9550.6277

12 Eastern Flair This decorative arts and crafts store has a large selection of cards, rugs, and gifts, including original carvings from Borneo and pieces from Nigeria and the Ivory Coast. ♦ M-Sa. 319-21 King St (between Mary and Eliza Sts). 9565.1499

So What Exactly Is "Modern Australian Cuisine"?

Only in recent years has Australia's culinary world laid claim to having its own cuisine. "Modern Australian" defines a style of fusion cooking that combines the finest Australian products with food preparation techniques from the Mediterranean and Asia. Restaurants offering this cuisine usually indicate on their menus that local products—Sydney Rock Oysters, Illabo lamb, or South Australian olive oil, for example—are used in preparing dishes, and wine lists generally feature labels from Australian vineyards. The blending of cultures is apparent in such delights as kangaroo fillet served on a bed of steamed bok choy next to potato dumplings, and grilled blue-eyed cod with a rich salsa verde and Tasmanian potato fries.

Prior to the massive post–World War II immigration that brought Mediterranean and Asian cooking to Australia, most of what Australians ate was derived from blander English standards. (Curried egg or lamb with mint sauce were about as exotic as the dishes got.) Sydneysiders considered the French restaurant as the ultimate gastronomic experience.

The culinary scene started to change in the 1950s and 1960s with the opening of Italian, Greek, and Lebanese restaurants and delis, although most of these establishments imported prepared meats, cheeses, herbs, and spices from Europe and the Middle East. Asian immigrants made their mark on the food scene in the 1970s, offering new tastes from China, Malaysia, Vietnam, and Thailand. These cuisines took hold and became as popular as Mediterranean fare.

In the early 1980s chefs at major hotels and restaurants started introducing Australian bush foods (some—like wattle seed, witchetty grubs, and bush berries—that had been used by Aborigines for thousands of years) and products in their preparation of European dishes, while others borrowed Mediterranean and Asian techniques and flavors for their cooking. This phenomenon has caught on throughout the city and today's dining experience is a far cry from the steak-and-kidney pies of yesteryear. Some of the pioneers of Modern Australian cuisine, as well as some establishments where you can indulge your tastebuds, are described below.

Neil Perry is the talent behind some of Sydney's greatest gastronomic institutions, including **Rockpool** (see page 28), **Wockpool** (see page 81), and **MCA Cafe** (see page 28). He was one of the earliest people to popularize the use of Australian products.

Gay Bilson and her ex-husband Tony introduced Sydneysiders to native Australian products prepared European style at the now-closed **Berowra Waters Inn** on **Hawkesbury River.** Gay and Tony continue to offer their progressive cuisine at **& (Ampersand)** (see page 82).

Belgian-born Serge Dansereau has been executive chef at the **Regent Sydney** hotel and promoting Modern Australian cuisine at its **Kable's** (see page 25) for over a decade. He uses more French-style preparation techniques in his cooking than many other Modern Australian chefs.

Christine Manfield is renowned for her use of Asian and Mediterranean flavors and techniques at **Paramount** (see page 107). The restaurant sells its own cookbook (written by Manfield) for those who want to introduce Modern Australian fare into their kitchens.

Stefano Manfredi blends traditional Italian fare with Australian products at **Bel Mondo** (see page 32) in **The Argyle Department Store.**

At **Bather's Pavilion** at **Balmoral Beach** (see page 167), Victoria Alexander offers seafood prepared with Asian and Mediterranean spices.

David Thompson of **Darley Street Thai** (see page 102) and **Sailor's Thai** (see page 33) delivers traditional Thai cuisine using the best Australian meat, seafood, and vegetables. The atmosphere of his restaurants is also a study in successfully fusing vivid bright colors from Thailand with contemporary Australian design using local woods and metal.

KEELY EDWARDS

13 Three Five Seven King ★★$$ In an area renowned for its abundance of Thai restaurants is this casual terra-cotta–filled bistro serving Italian food with Modern Australian flair. Service is professional but relaxed. The simple menu—including such dishes as seared tuna steak on a bed of shaved fennel and homemade sausages and mushrooms with heavenly polenta—is reasonably priced, and there is an interesting wine list, featuring selections from small wineries, that offers many items by the glass. Don't leave without picking up a bottle of the house chickpea-and-garlic dressing. ◆ Modern Australian ◆ M-Sa dinner. Reservations recommended. 357 King St (at Enmore Rd). 9519.7930

14 Sandringham Hotel Fondly referred to by area residents as "The Sando," this old, yet-to-be-gentrified pub offers music by local artists of every description seven nights a week. Each night, the place attracts a different crowd: for example, on Monday night, there are poetry readings; Tuesday is reserved for acoustic music; and Wednesday features a motley crew of new bands. ◆ Daily 8PM-midnight. 387 King St (between Holt and Goddard Sts). 9557.1254

15 Lime Cafe ★★$ White walls, concrete floors, and basic modern furnishings make this cafe an odd find along King Street, where the restaurants are usually a little cozier and funkier. The simple blackboard menu reflects the seasonal vegetables and fruits, and all the biscuits (cookies) and tarts are made on the premises. The hazelnut shortbread is divine, and the fresh mint tea is a brisk alternative to caffeine. ◆ Cafe ◆ Tu-Su breakfast and lunch. 420 King St (at Whitehorse St). 9517.2337

16 The Red Arrow ★$ At the end of King Street is this old shop that has been converted into an eccentric cafe. Don't be surprised if you're served by someone with a lot of facial piercing. The big window lets you see all the wild and wonderful Newtown types parading up and down the main street. The homemade tangy ginger beer is a real treat, and the "Big Knock-Up" breakfast will satisfy the heartiest

appetite. ◆ Cafe ◆ M-W, Su breakfast and lunch; Th-Sa breakfast, lunch, and dinner. 417 King St (between Camden and Holt Sts). 9557.5728

17 Bastante Regular ★$ The piped-in jazz music keeps customers' feet tapping at this tiny (18-seat) cafe. The decor features stainless-steel seats, floral displays, and old benches from a doctor's waiting room. The menu is your basic cafe fare. Try the delicious sandwiches, with such tasty fillings as grilled vegetables, served on crusty baguettes. The meat loaf and mango chutney sandwich is superb. ◆ Cafe ◆ Daily. 50 Enmore Rd (at Station St). 9557.8691

ENMORE THEATRE

18 Enmore Theatre Most Sydneysiders know Enmore for its inexpensive housing and for this famous old theater. Originally built in 1908, it had an Art Deco face-lift in the 1930s and became a movie house. Today it hosts rock-and-roll acts from Australia and abroad—everything from Patti Smith to Public Enemy—and some stage productions. ◆ Call for hours. ◆ 130 Enmore Rd (between Reiby and Simmons Sts). 9550.3666

Within the Enmore Theatre:

Box Office Cafe ★$ Buy tickets or see a performance, then stop in here for a snack or light meal. The dimly lit, redwood interior evokes the feeling of the 1930s. The menu is standard cafe food: bacon and eggs, cereal, or croissants for breakfast; nachos, pastas, burgers, and schnitzels for lunch and dinner. Sample the huge range of teas and coffees, especially the aromatic sage tea. ◆ Cafe ◆ Daily breakfast, lunch, and dinner. 9550.3666

19 University of Sydney The main quadrangle of this university campus is reminiscent of Oxford or Cambridge—the Sydney university buildings (illustrated on page 151) bear more than a passing resemblance to those English models. Founded in 1850, the University of Sydney is Australia's oldest college and this, its main campus, in an area called **Camperdown**, is located only three kilometers (two miles) from the city center, where the suburbs of Newtown and Glebe meet. The university's **Great Hall**—situated at the northwest corner of the main quad—is one of the two grandest surviving 19th-century halls in Australia (the other is the **Centennial Hall** in the **Sydney Town Hall**). The work of the architect **Edmund Thomas Blacket,** it is the venue for the university's graduation ceremony each year. Today the university has almost 30,000

Sydney University

students and nearly 5,000 staff. Apart from this main campus, there are 10 others, housing schools of music, visual arts, dentistry, law, agriculture, and veterinary science. University bookshops and stores (stocking university sweaters, mementos, and the like) are located at the **Holme** and **Wentworth** buildings (open Monday through Friday). You can obtain a map of the from the **Student Centre** during business hours. ◆ To get to the university, catch a *Newtown No. 422, 423,* or *426* or *Glebe* bus from the city to the corner of Parramatta and Glebe Point Rds

Glebe

20 UniLodge $ Housed in the old Grace Brothers building with an enormous lit globe on the roof, this new property is the place to stay for those looking for a basic, well-maintained room without any of the frills found in the higher-priced hotels. The 590 rooms are simply furnished, with kitchenettes, bathrooms, double beds, desks, dining tables, and TVs. There's a cafe, in-house parking, a laundry, and a business and conference center. An indoor lap pool, spa, sauna, and rooftop training track will keep the fitness-minded content. Its location just opposite the **University of Sydney** and on the fringe of Glebe makes this place popular with traveling students and academics. ◆ Broadway and Bay St. 9338.5000; fax 9338.5111

21 Essential Energies This store specializes in aromatherapy, holistic treatments, and many other alternative schools of healing. The staff is happy to explain the medicinal properties attributed to various substances and to recommend their favorite brands. ◆ M-Sa. 16 Glebe Point Rd (between Parramatta Rd and Derby Pl). 9552.3538

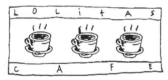

22 Lolita's ★$ An old Glebe institution, this cafe consistently serves good simple meals and coffee to the Sydney university crowd. Besides the regular menu, a daily specials board lists soup, pasta, and rice dishes. Big, hearty breakfasts are the draw here on the weekend. ◆ Cafe ◆ M-F breakfast, lunch, and dinner; Sa-Su breakfast and lunch. 29 Glebe Point Rd (between Parramatta Rd and Francis St). 9692.0493

22 Phoenix Rising Booksellers Incense fills the air in this New Age bookstore, which specializes in books on natural therapies and self-help. The shop will mail books to customers and fill special orders. ◆ M-Sa. 31A Glebe Point Rd (between Parramatta Rd and Francis St). 9566.2157

Parliament House of New South Wales on Macquarie Street was inaugurated in 1829. It is the oldest continuously used parliamentary building in the world.

Restaurants/Clubs: Red   **Hotels:** Blue
Shops/ Outdoors: Green   **Sights/Culture:** Black

The Olympic Torch Comes to Sydney

From 15 September to 1 October 2000, Sydney will host the **Games of the XXVII Olympiad.** The main venue for the events is the **Sydney Olympic Park** at **Homebush Bay,** 15 kilometers (9 miles) west of Sydney, although some will take place in other areas of **Greater Sydney** and beyond. With the exception of preliminary football events that will be played in Adelaide, Brisbane, Canberra, and Melbourne, spectators will easily be able to see more than one event a day. Sydney's gone all out to host this important celebration of world harmony, including the building of several new hotels and sports arenas which will be used in future international sporting events.

Events

The 28 sports on the 16-day program include two new Olympic events—tae kwon do and triathlon—as well as an addition to gymnastics—trampolining. Some events held outside the **Olympic Park** include boxing, judo, weightlifting, wrestling, and volleyball at **Darling Harbour;** equestrian events at **Horsley Park;** shooting at **Holsworthy;** and canoeing, kayaking, and rowing at **Penrith Lakes.** Several free activities include a 42-kilometer (26-mile) marathon through the city, sailing and cycling events, and a triathlon. The **Sydney Harbour Regatta,** a sailing race in which more than 35 countries will participate, will also take place during the games.

Transportation to the Games

An extensive train, bus, and hydrofoil system between the city center and **Olympic Park** will facilitate travel to events at all sites within the Greater Sydney area. In addition to the frequent public transportation service, there will be park-and-ride stations in designated areas for those wishing to drive.

How to Get Tickets

At press time, tickets were expected to go on sale by mail order in mid-1999, with 75 percent of them reserved for Australians. Non-Australians should contact the Olympic Organizing Committee in their home countries (in the US, the **USOC,** 1750 E Boulder St, Colorado Springs, CO, 80909-5764, 719/632.5551) or visit the web site of the **Sydney Organising Committee for the Olympic Games** (**SOCOG**) (www.sydney.olympic.org) for details on how to obtain tickets.

Olympic Arts Festivals

To celebrate the idea of the games bringing more understanding, harmony, and cultural exchange to the world, **SOCOG** is sponsoring a four-year program of cultural festivals leading up to 2000. The first, the Festival of Dreaming in 1997, honored the world's indigenous cultures with an emphasis on Australian Aborigines. The second, A Sea Change, explored diversity in Australian cultures and landscape (1998). At press time, two remained: Reaching The World, an international event that will carry Australian culture to the five continents represented in the Olympic rings (1999); and Harbour of Life, a focus on Sydney and Australia, with an emphasis on what defines Australian cultural life (2000). Each runs from the middle of September through the first week of October, with the exception of the last, which is from 1 August to 24 October.

Visit **SOCOG**'s web site (see above) for the most current information on sites, events, tickets, and festivals.

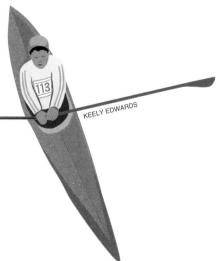

KEELY EDWARDS

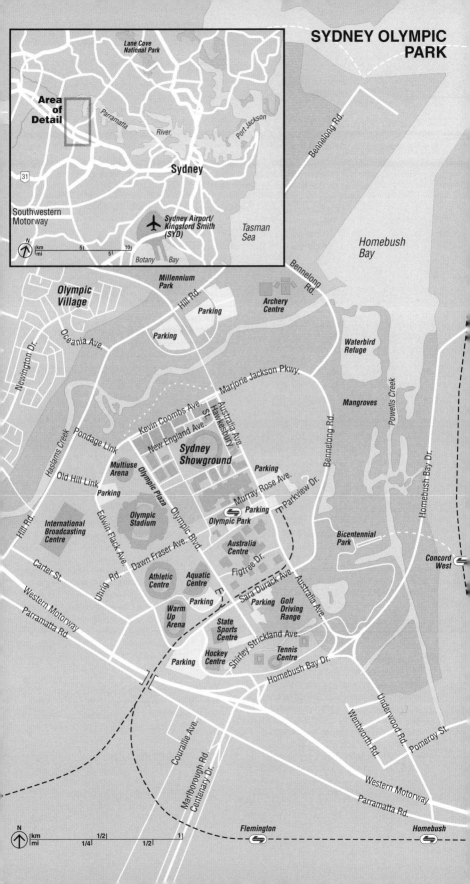

Cafe

22 Well-Connected Café ★★$ Grab your caffeine and get ready to ride the information superhighway. This two-level cafe has 12 computer terminals so you can enjoy Internet access along with your coffee and cake. The place attracts the hippest travelers in cyberspace and offers basic cafe food. ♦ Cafe ♦ Daily 10AM-10PM. 35 Glebe Point Rd (between Parramatta Rd and Francis St). 9566.2655

22 Badde Manors $ People come to this neighborhood institution, favored by **University of Sydney** students and local bohemians, for the scene. The food is nothing special—just basic and inexpensive focaccia, small salads, and cakes. The sometimes surly staff is known for helping the cafe remain true to its name. ♦ Cafe ♦ Daily breakfast, lunch, and dinner. 37 Glebe Point Rd (at Francis St). 9660.3797

23 Siena ★★$$$ This restaurant stands out like a proverbial sore thumb (albeit a pleasant one) amid the casual students' cafes on lower Glebe Point Road: The decor is delicate and light, the tablecloths are crisp and white, and the service is very proper indeed. For the most part, the patrons at this restaurant look as though they just popped in from the posh Eastern Suburbs. Though the management claims the kitchen "specializes in Tuscan-inspired Australian cuisine," touches of the Middle East and Asia appear on the menu in dishes that feature ginger, lime, and Chinese greens. The daily risotto always seems light and delicious. ♦ Modern Australian ♦ Tu-F lunch and dinner; Sa dinner. 43 Glebe Point Rd (between Francis and Cowper Sts). 9552.1541

23 Gleebooks Proprietors David Gaunt and Roger Mackell have two well-organized and well-run bookstores on Glebe Point Road. This one, the first, is home to 35,000 new titles and a very impressive program of literary events and readings, while down the road, the second store stocks used books, including modern and antiquarian first editions and children's books. The second store is popular with students in search of a cheaper textbook or novel—or those wanting to sell used volumes for extra cash. ♦ M-Sa 8AM-9PM; Su 9AM-9PM. 49 Glebe Point Rd (between Francis and Cowper Sts). 9660.2333. Also at: 191 Glebe Point Rd (at St. Johns Rd). 9660.5144

24 Kafenio ★★$ Hearty helpings of focaccia and quiche, huge portions of soup, and desserts with such names as Louisiana Fat Boy Double Chocolate Fudge Brownie—phew!—are the draws for a mix of students, locals, and businesspeople. As the name suggests, the coffee is terrific and there are several house blends of tea on the menu. Sit at a stool by the window or at one of the dark wooden tables farther inside. ♦ Cafe ♦ M-Sa breakfast and lunch; Su brunch and lunch. No credit cards accepted. 72 Glebe Point Rd (between Derby Pl and Mitchell St). 9552.3610

25 Kill City This well-organized and rather spartan bookstore is dedicated to crime fiction and nonfiction—not pest control. You could spend hours skimming though the thrillers and discovering some bizarre accounts of human misdeeds. The knowledgeable staff includes several crime-fiction fanatics. ♦ M-Sa. 85 Glebe Point Rd (between Cowper and Mitchell Sts). 9692.9060

26 Nature's Energy Staffed by herbalists and a "flower essence consultant," this aromatic store sells essential oils, burners, and anything else that hasn't been processed and smells good. ♦ M-Sa. 115 Glebe Point Rd (at Mitchell St). 9660.8342

27 Darling Mills Restaurant and Farm ★★ $$$ This restaurant's claim to fame is that it has its own farm (on the Darling Mills Creek in New South Wales's Hills district) that provides fresh produce for the kitchen. This is evident in the terrific salads and in the flavors of the fresh herbs that dominate the main courses. The seafood on the menu comes from all over the country. Native Australian specialties include Tasmanian salmon, King Island kangaroo, and the mud crab. The decor of this two-floor restaurant, which has a sandstone facade and interiors dating back to the 1850s, is very rustic in the midst of an ultra-urbane neighborhood. ♦ Modern Australian ♦ Tu-F lunch and dinner; M, Sa-Su dinner. Reservations recommended. 134 Glebe Point Rd (between Mitchell St and St. Johns Rd). 9660.5666

28 The Valhalla A Glebe institution attracts the local student population and those Sydneysiders in search of films the big theaters wouldn't dream of showing. For years it has been screening old classics, alternative flicks, and the odd new release. The Sunday double feature is very popular. If you haven't consumed too much junk food during the flick, stop in at their cafe afterward for some sticky date pudding and a round of strong caffe latte. Ask about the five-ticket discount. ◆ 166 Glebe Point Rd (at Hereford St). 9660.8050

29 Haven Inn $$$ The 55 spacious rooms here are built around a plant-filled inner courtyard featuring a simple swimming pool. The atmosphere is very casual, but the rooms have all the modern conveniences, including VCRs; there's also a huge in-house video library. The furnishings are rustic, done in simple pastel colors and dark woods. Amenities include a country-style restaurant and cocktail bar, 24-hour room service, secretarial services, and meeting rooms with audio-visual equipment. The management offers courtesy bus service to Darling Harbour and the city. ◆ 196 Glebe Point Rd (at Wigram Rd). 9660.6655; fax 9660.6279

30 Trickett's Bed and Breakfast $$ The details on the ornate ceiling in this stately but charming seven-room bed-and-breakfast have been carefully preserved from the days when this Victorian building was the Glebe children's court. Each room is decorated differently, with period furniture and big, sturdy queen-size beds; all have private baths. Enjoy complimentary continental breakfast in the conservatory, and make the most of the tiled, shaded verandas and balconies. It's hard to believe that you're only 10 minutes from the city. ◆ No credit cards accepted. 270 Glebe Point Rd (at Pendrill St). 9552.1141; fax 9692.9462

31 Blackwattle Canteen ★★$ Hidden at the end of Glebe Point Road in a warehouse that houses artist's studios, this loft-style cafe has old chairs and tables, a wooden floor, and a corrugated iron ceiling. Order a coffee, sit back, and take in the beautiful views of Rozelle Bay. Local artists and students favor this spot for breakfast, staggering in early for eggs, toast, and grilled tomatoes to start their day. The service is casual and friendly. ◆ Cafe ◆ Daily breakfast and lunch. 465 Glebe Point Rd (at Federal Rd). 9552.1792

32 The Boathouse on Blackwattle Bay ★★★$$$ With its casual waterside dining room, seafood menu, stylish patrons, and relaxed yet efficient service, this restaurant provides a typical Sydney dining experience. The owners of the successful **Bayswater Brasserie** (see page 102) opened this spot close enough to the city to be convenient, yet just far enough removed from the hustle and bustle so that diners can relax. The restaurant, a gleaming modern structure that is actually anchored in the bay, has views of the waters surrounding the majestic cables of the Glebe Island Bridge. The view of the **Sydney Fish Markets** reassures you that the seafood hasn't had to travel far. Oysters and crustaceans are the stars of the menu here. Try the steamed Moreton Bay scallops, local yabbies (crayfish), or the Asian-inspired dish known as drunken prawns. ◆ Seafood ◆ Tu-Su lunch and dinner. Reservations recommended. Ferry Rd (northeast of Taylor St). 9518.9011

33 Lyndhurst Between 1833 and 1836 this Regency-style mansion was built for the inspector of colonial hospitals, Dr. James Bowman, with **John Verge** as the architect. Bowman told him to spare no expense—and he didn't, thus creating one of the stateliest homes in Sydney at the time. Through the mid-1800s, it was a religious college, then the surrounding property was subdivided in the late 1870s. Nearly one hundred years later, in 1972, the Department of Main Roads purchased the house with plans to demolish it for a new expressway. But when a new state government came to power in 1976, officials scrapped the plans to build the expressway and the remains of the mansion were salvaged. In the 1980s, it was restored and is now occupied by the Historic Houses Trust of New South Wales. ◆ M-F. 61 Darghan St (between Lyndhurst and Cardigan Sts). 9692.8366

Balmain

34 The Watch House By the mid-1800s, Balmain already had more than 1,300 residents, who petitioned the government in 1851 to provide them with a police station and jail to manage the area's growing crime. In 1852, the Legislative Council committed money to the project and commissioned architect **Edmund Thomas Blacket** to find a site and come up with a design for the new building. In 1855, the one-story sandstone Georgian-style lockup (or "watch house," another term for police station), with its striking facade, was completed and ready to handle the local criminals. Another floor was added to the building in the 1880s, and the facility continued operating until the early 1920s, when the jail was moved to a new building. For almost 50 years, the building was a private home; in 1970, it was saved from demolition by the Balmain Association, which made it their headquarters. ◆ 179 Darling St (at St. John St)

The mascots of the Sydney 2000 Olympic Games are Syd, a platypus; Millie, an echidna; and Olly, a kookaburra.

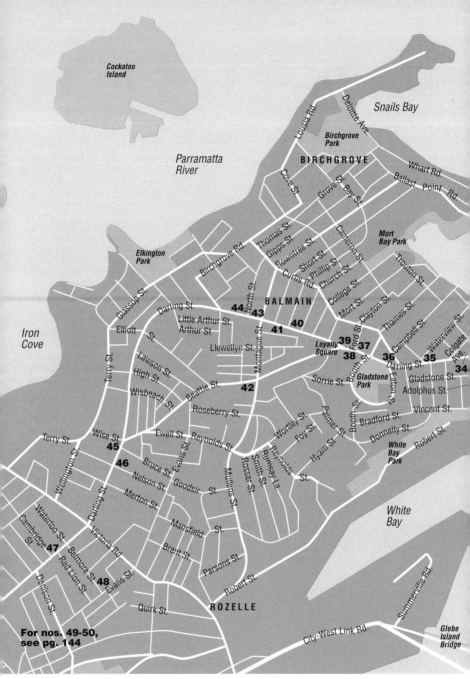

35 L'Avventura ★$$ A New York–born Italian runs this restaurant, which offers old favorites like eggplant parmigiana as well as such seafood and contemporary dishes as porcini mushroom risotto. The service can be erratic, but the good-quality comfort food and the setting—in a beautiful old sandstone building—make up for that. ◆ Italian ◆ Daily dinner. 1 Queens Pl (at Darling St). 9818.5361

36 Balmain Stars at Gigi's ★★$$ A pizzeria that names its pizzas after the signs of the zodiac? Yep, it's hard to believe, but seeing is believing, and everything—decor and toppings—is so tasteful that it wouldn't matter what they called the pizzas. Old favorites are offered next to more gourmet-inspired ingredients like pesto, chèvre, and roasted eggplant. It's a perfect place for families: parents can go gourmet while the kids chomp on their pepperoni and sausage. ◆ Pizza ◆ Daily lunch and dinner. 229 Darling

Restaurants/Clubs: Red	**Hotels:** Blue
Shops/ Outdoors: Green	**Sights/Culture:** Black

156

Goat Island

Mort Bay

Darling Harbour

Johnstons Bay

PYRMONT

Casino

37 The Monkey Bar ★★$$ Local urban professionals love this renovated pub with an outdoor courtyard. The street-level bar looks like a club and is furnished with new leather couches, wooden chairs, steel counters and tables, and pale walls. The kitchen has yet to prove itself, but daily specials and a selection of meat and seafood dishes are always offered. ◆ Modern Australian ◆ Daily brunch, lunch, and dinner. 255 Darling St (at Ford St). 9810.1749

38 Peninsula Bistro ★★$$ The large colorful faces painted on the walls light up this bistro and create a busy, jolly atmosphere. The food is equally snazzy, featuring all the French bistro classics cooked with popular Australian seafood and meats. Try the delicious confit of duck or the creamiest crème brûlée. The cheese plate is also wonderful. ◆ French ◆ M-Sa dinner; Su lunch and dinner. 264 Darling St (between Booth St and Loyalty Sq). 9810.3955

38 Holy Sheet! From bedspreads to rubber duckies, this store specializes in affordable contemporary bed linens and other home furnishings. With its very helpful staff, this is a good place to find a gift. ◆ M-Sa. 270 Darling St (between Booth St and Loyalty Sq). 9810.3091. Also at: 320 Oxford St (between William and Underwood Sts), Paddington. 9360.3111

39 Pentimento Bookshop New books, photography, graphics and prints, and art supplies make this store a mix of the visual and the literary. There's a wide selection of Australian writers and children's literature. The sofas where you can sit and read at your leisure are a nice touch. ◆ M-Sa. 275 Darling St (at Loyalty Sq). 9810.0707

St (between Curtis Rd and McDonald St). 9818.2170

37 Café Berlin ★$ Coffee and pastries in the German tradition, like Sacher torte and linzertorte, star here. Also come here if you're in the mood for some heartier Teutonic fare. The German-style salads, which are anything but light and are usually made with potatoes, are worth trying. ◆ German ◆ Daily lunch and dinner. 249 Darling St (between McDonald and Ford Sts). 9810.2336

Nova Peris-Kneebone, the first Aboriginal athlete to win an Olympic gold medal, will be the first person to carry the Sydney 2000 Olympic Torch when it reaches Australia for the Torch Relay event.

Omnivore

40 Omnivore ★$$ The name of this restaurant invites the right patrons—those who eat anything. Try the famous breakfast of scrambled eggs with home-smoked salmon or one of the huge antipasto plates for lunch or dinner. The dining room is sleek, with its wooden floors, ocher accents, and flowers, while the rooms upstairs have views of the Harbour Bridge. ◆ Modern Australian ◆ Daily breakfast, lunch, and dinner. 333 Darling St (between Church and Phillip Sts). 9810.1393

41 Jiyu No Omise ★★$$ With more than a decade in the business, this Japanese restaurant has built up a crowd of loyal patrons. The sushi plates feature such popular Australian fish as ocean trout, bream, and tiger prawns. The simple decor and friendly service make dining here seemingly effortless—until you read the long menu. Ask the staff to help you choose. ◆ Japanese ◆ Daily dinner. 342 Darling St (between Loyalty Sq and Montague St). 9818.3886

42 Exchange Hotel/Safari Bar/Beattie Street Bar Here's a popular old Balmain corner pub that now attracts hordes of urban professionals who like to spend Sunday drinking with their mates. Upstairs is the colonial-themed **Safari Bar,** complete with animal skins and weapons, while downstairs is the **Beattie Street Bar,** with its TVs and sports-bar ambience. ◆ M-Sa noon-midnight; Su noon-10PM. 94 Beattie St (at Mullens St). 9810.1171

The five most popular attractions in Sydney are: retail stores, the Sydney Opera House, Darling Harbour, The Rocks, and Sydney Harbour cruises.

43 Logue's Eating House ★★$$ Once famous only for her fabulous take-out food and catering business a few doors down, Simone Logue has taken the hint from her customers and opened up a casual restaurant. Good advice, it seems, as the place is always filled with hungry diners seated at old wooden tables enjoying flavorsome home cooking: comforting bowls of soup, risotto, and such rich puddings as banana with butterscotch sauce. This is true Australian food served with a wonderfully fresh, casual approach. Ask to sit outdoors on a warm evening. ◆ Modern Australian ◆ Daily breakfast, lunch, and dinner. 359 Darling St (at Rowntree St). 9810.3415

44 The Manor House Edmund Thomas Blacket, the colonial architect, designed and built this sandstone residence for his family in 1870, a year after his wife, Sarah, had died. The two-story house is a mixture of Victorian and Georgian in style, with wrought-iron lacework and wooden shutters. **Blacket** only lived here for five years, after which the house was occupied in turn by a number of schools and other tenants. In 1976, it was sold and converted to a stylish restaurant, which now operates only as a catering hall and reception room for special occasions. The structure is protected by the National Trust of Australia. The building is not open to the public, unless, of course, you're invited to a function here. ◆ 393 Darling St (between North St and Birchgrove Rd)

Rozelle

45 Bistro Deux ★★$$$ Inner West fans of **Bistro Moncur** in Woollahra now have a favorite spot of their own—a restaurant owned by the same proprietors and supervised by the same head chef. Situated within the **Sackville Hotel,** this is a stylish bistro with all the characteristics of its older sibling: wonderful flavors, faultless cooking, and a very capable, friendly staff. Patrons return for the sirloin steak and homemade sausages. The simple modern interior is dominated by a giant mural by artist Michael Fitzjames. It's more relaxed than **Bistro Moncur,** but that's a standard difference between Rozelle and Woollahra. ◆ French ◆ Tu-Su lunch and dinner. 599 Darling St (at Wise St). 9555.7555

46 About Life Offering a very healthful alternative to traditional supermarkets, this deli/supermarket/cafe, with a modern, glass-and-chrome interior, stocks its own and other brands of packaged and prepared foods for the health-conscious. Anyone who wants to enjoy preservative-free food that also tickles the taste buds will enjoy shopping here. From the assortment of dairy substitutes down to the pet food, all basics are covered. The fresh sushi is a special draw. ♦ M-F 7AM-8PM; Sa-Su. 600 Darling St (between Nelson and Bruce Sts). 9555.2695

47 Tetsuya's ★★★$$$ Forget harbor views and up-to-the-minute decor: the food is the star here, at one of Sydney's best-loved restaurants. Award-winning chef Tetsuya Wakuda has mastered a deliciously smooth blend of French, Japanese, and Australian influences. Take a few hours to sit back and enjoy the parade of flavors in the prix-fixe lunch or dinner menu, punctuated with a selection of wines by the glass chosen especially to complement each course. Expect to reserve up to six weeks in advance for this unforgettable Sydney dining experience. The menu changes frequently, but Tetsuya is always proud to feature native Australian ingredients. ♦ French/Japanese ♦ W-Sa lunch and dinner; Tu dinner. Reservations essential. 729 Darling St (at Cambridge St). 9555.1017

48 Rose, Shamrock and Thistle Nicknamed the "Three Weeds" hotel (an obvious play on its name), this typical Sydney pub, with its old, beer-stained bar, is something of an institution, featuring live music with an emphasis on blues and folk. ♦ M-Sa 11AM-midnight; Su noon-10PM. 193 Evans St (at Belmore St). 9810.2244

Leichhardt

49 Bar Italia ★★$ Right in the heart of Sydney's Italian neighborhood, this undistinguished cafe—complete with laminated tabletops and plastic chairs—enjoys an atmosphere created by the crowd, not the decor. All the basics appear on the menu—seafood, veal, chicken, focaccia, pasta, and salads—and offer good quality for very little money. Leave room for some of the best gelati in Sydney. ♦ Cafe/Italian ♦ Daily breakfast, lunch, and dinner. 169-71 Norton St (between Short and Allen Sts). 9560.9981

50 Cafe Barzu ★★$$ This cafe didn't win the local small business achievement award for nothing. The front window panels of the converted warehouse space slide open, making the cafe light and breezy. There are three dining areas; upstairs, downstairs, and in the courtyard. The lunch menu consists mainly of focaccia sandwiches and melts, whereas the dinner menu has gourmet pizzas with such toppings as roasted pumpkin, feta cheese, kalamata olives, and pesto. There are 12 cakes from which to choose—all heavy, all delicious. ♦ Cafe ♦ Daily brunch, lunch, and dinner. 21 Norton St (between Parramatta Rd and Marion St). 9550.0144

Bests

Angelique Mentis
Attorney, Skadden, Arps, Slate, Meagher & Flom

Taking a run or walk along the **Bondi** to **Bronte** ocean cliffs on a weekend morning, followed by a leisurely brunch at one of the trendy laid-back cafes (in summer, add a swim before brunch).

Hanging out at the **Tropicana Expresso Bar** with the Sunday papers.

Having my boyfriend pick me up in his speedboat after work on a summer's afternoon from the **Opera House,** cruising out to **Camp Cove** for a swim and then heading back to **Watsons Bay** for a few drinks in the beer garden or dinner at **Doyle's** on the beach.

Catching a seaplane to fly you over glorious Sydney and then along the coast.

Walking through **The Royal Botanic Gardens,** along **Mrs. Macquarie's Chair,** and along the foreshores to the **Opera House.**

Walking home through the city at dusk.

The **Manly** to **The Spit** walk along the harbor foreshores.

Taking a plunge at Bronte or **Tamarama** early in the summer while the water's still chilly.

Driving or walking across the **Harbour Bridge** at night and watching the city lights.

Staring out my office window across the harbor and watching the colorful spinnakers of yachts sail by in the Wednesday afternoon twilight races.

Rum, easily produced from sugar cane, was used as currency in Sydney's early days.

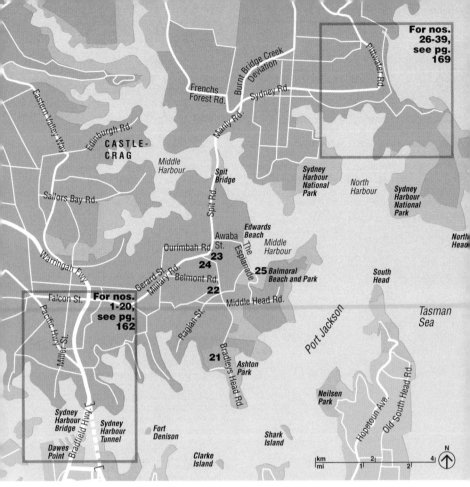

For nos. 26-39, see pg. 169

For nos. 1-20, see pg. 162

North Sydney/North Shore

Linked to the city and Eastern Suburbs by the **Sydney Harbour Bridge** and **Harbour Tunnel** is the verdant, hilly North Shore, a suburban area that also is very much a part of Sydney's cultural history. Running north up the **Pacific Highway** and east along **Military Road,** the area is divided by tiny harbor inlets, coves, beaches, national parkland, and numerous tree-lined neighborhoods. But though its varied landscape may prove confusing to the newcomer, there are a number of places here that are well worth a visit.

Across Sydney Harbour is the commercial area of Sydney known as North Sydney. This is essentially a city within a city, almost an offshoot of the Central Business District (CBD), which developed after the bridge and rail system made this side of the harbor easily accessible for commercial purposes. In the 1960s and 1970s, lured by inexpensive land costs and leases, major companies established headquarters and branch offices here, dotting the landscape with high-rise office buildings. Today the area is known for its many advertising agencies and insurance companies.

A century ago, before the streets of North Sydney started filling out and up, the North Shore was considered a remote region—although it was only little more than 3.5 kilometers (2 miles) across the harbor. But in the late 1860s, ferry service from the southern shore changed this conception, and the North Shore became a desirable place to live: a safer part of Sydney in which one could raise a family, enjoy the unspoiled bushland, and yet still be close to business. By the turn of the century, harborside suburbs such as **Mosman** and **Milsons Point** rivaled the Eastern Suburbs as prized residential areas.

The streets of North Sydney are definitely more sedate than those of the CBD. Perhaps this is because it is newer and not as developed and densely populated as other urban areas. Add to this the abundance of nearby well-tended parkland and the splendid harbor and city views at almost every turn—especially from Milsons Point, and **Kirribilli**, the Prime Minister's official Sydney residence—and you'll understand the residents' pride.

Farther east along the North Shore is the delightful, elegant suburb of Mosman. As the harbor ferry glides into **Mosman Bay**, passengers see a wooded inlet with old homes perched in the surrounding hills. A hundred years ago, this was a small whaling town run by Archibald Mosman. Today the town's original whaling hut has been turned into a Cub Scout hall, and rowing and sailing are the only sports engaged in on these waters.

On Athol Bay is **Taronga Zoo,** one of the world's most beautiful and brilliantly designed animal habitats. The cages and enclosures seem to blend with their surroundings, giving visitors the impression that they are actually on safari rather than visiting a living museum. The views of the harbor from some of the sites here are unrivaled.

Down the hill, north of Mosman, is the major harbor inlet of **Middle Harbour.** This area is well protected from the Pacific Ocean and has a number of smaller harbor beaches, including the most famous, **Balmoral Beach**, with its excellent restaurants, parkland, and turn-of-the-century promenades.

Within the area known as **North Harbour** is the tourist-friendly, overdeveloped beach community of **Manly,** just 14 kilmoters (9 miles) from the city. Some claim that the most beautiful thing about Manly is the trip there and back on the hulking *Manly Ferry*. The ride takes about 40 minutes (unless you opt for the speedier JetCat), and passes some of Sydney Harbour's most memorable sights, including the **Opera House, Fort Denison,** the Eastern Suburbs harbor beaches and homes, and some of the unspoiled land of **Sydney Harbour National Park.**

In 1857, English entrepreneur Henry Gilbert Smith started developing the tiny fishing village of Manly into an ocean resort town for Sydney. Soon after, his investments paid off and families came to Manly to stroll along the esplanade under the shade of the Norfolk Island pines (planted by Smith), providing a Southern Hemisphere interpretation of old Brighton Beach, England. However, decades passed before visitors could enjoy the pleasures of the clear waters, as public bathing was considered indecent and, therefore, prohibited until 1902.

Today Manly is a curious cross between the old-fashioned seaside resort it once was and the overcommercialized beachside theme park it has become. Not surprisingly, Manly is not for everyone, but provides many diversions for families. At the **Manly Ferry Wharf**, visitors are greeted by an old-fashioned fun park, **Oceanworld,** and some tour operators selling tours of the harbor, beaches, and anything else they can conjure. (The **Visitors' Centre** is right at the wharf as you leave the ferry.) To get to the beach, walk down what is called **The Corso,** which will take you right to the enormous beachfront known as **Manly Beach.** Large terraced hotels, restaurants, cafes, and surf-and-sports stores line the long esplanade of **North** and **South Steyne.** Musicians and other buskers stroll the walkways along the beach on the weekends; there is an annual food festival in June and a jazz festival in

October, both of which attract big crowds. Take your time to decide where to eat here; the best time to visit is during the week, when fewer people mean more dining options.

If this scene is all too much for you, head east to tiny **Shelly Beach**, a refreshing change from its loud and colorful older sibling. (On the way, you'll see the giant sandstone **St. Patrick's Seminary** looming large on the top of this penninsula.) Surrounded by parkland from **Sydney Harbour National Park**, the water here is usually very calm, making it perfect for children to swim safely. Visitors tend to seek out **Le Kiosk**, a famous old sandstone restaurant tucked in the bushland behind the beach serving Modern Australian cuisine.

In many ways, the North Shore and Manly are worlds apart although they are geographically linked in their location on the same side of the harbor—much as Double Bay is to Bondi Beach.

North Sydney/ Lower North Shore

1 Harbourside Apartments $$ All of the 82 executive- and family-size units of this apartment complex (all with maid service) boast spectacular views of Sydney Harbour and the city. Apartments—ranging in size from studio to two-bedroom—have comfortable, contemporary furnishings and well-equipped kitchens. The pool here is one of the main attractions: Perched at the harbor's edge, it gives swimmers the sensation of being able to just float out among the boats. ♦ 2A Henry Lawson Ave (east of Blues Point Rd). 9963.4300; fax 9922.7998

2 Fare Go Gourmet ★★$$$ Giving someone a "fair go" in Australia translates as "treating someone well." Owner Monique de Vries manages to treat everyone who dines at her restaurant very well indeed, serving up dishes with ingredients indigenous to Australia, such as barramundi (a fish found in the North Australian waters) with herb salsa, kangaroo kebabs, and even more exotic offerings such as soy-crusted brains. The decor isn't quite as modern as the food. ♦ Modern Australian ♦ Tu-Sa dinner. Reservations recommended. 69 Union St (between Chuter and Thomas Sts). 9922.2965

3 Greenwood Plaza The architectural integrity of this Victorian Gothic sandstone building—originally **St. Leonards Public School**—has been painstakingly maintained despite its conversion into a commercial and retail center. Built in 1877 in the heart of North Sydney, the building was designed by **George Allen Mansfield,** who designed several other schools around the same time. It was originally called **Greenwood** after Nimrod Greenwood, headmaster from 1884 to 1914. The building remained a school until 1969; in 1993 it was restored and reopened as the **Green-wood Hotel** (pictured at right), a "pub" housing restaurants and meeting rooms. ♦ 36 Blue St (between Walker and Miller Sts)

Within Greenwood Plaza:

Greenwood Hotel ★★$$ Beautiful old sandstone walls and highly polished wood floors juxtaposed with lots of contemporary furniture and fast service set the stage at this large, popular restaurant. The food is as comforting as the surroundings, with lots of lamb, beef, and English standards, including sausages and mash. The ubiquitous sticky toffee pudding is just one of the delicious calorie-laden dessert tempters and there's a good wine list, too. For a more leisurely dining experience, avoid the weekday lunchtime rush. ♦ Modern Australian ♦ M-F lunch and dinner; Sa dinner. Reservations recommended. 9964.9968

Plaza Grill ★★$$$ North Sydney now boasts an impressive number of first-rate restaurants, and this is one of them. Not big on decor, with simple wood tables in a warm setting, this place, owned by **Armstrong's**

Greenwood Hotel

Mark Armstrong, is a haven for meat lovers—local businesspeople and visitors alike who appreciate the serious selection of aged steaks ready for grilling. If your tastes lie elsewhere, there's also wood-fired rotisserie of spatchcock, quail, and duck. The wine list complements the fare. ♦ Steak house ♦ M lunch; Tu-F lunch and dinner. Reservations recommended. 9964.9766

4 Centra North Sydney $$$ Set in the heart of North Sydney's commercial center, this modern, 212-room hotel means business—from the secretarial services to the conference rooms. There's a pleasant plus: Most of the guest rooms are decorated in light woods and pastels and have great views of the cityscape and the Harbour Bridge. The **Blues Bar and Restaurant** serves Modern Australian fare; there's also room service. ♦ 17 Blue St (at Pacific Hwy). 9955.0499; fax 9922.3689

5 Yamakasa ★★$$ This reasonably priced, split-level Japanese restaurant in downtown North Sydney does very well thanks to its comfortable wooden furniture, friendly staff, and great seafood. The extensive menu includes everything from sushi and sashimi to tempura and teriyaki. There's also an impressive sake and wine list. ♦ Japanese ♦ M-F lunch and dinner; Sa dinner. Reservations recommended. 155 Miller St (between Pacific Hwy and Berry St). 9957.4895

6 Blueberries An unpretentious nightclub, this place attracts a fairly well-dressed crowd. There's a brasserie that serves basic fare—grilled meats and hearty salads—and a huge cocktail bar. Dance off the calories to top 40 favorites. ♦ M-W noon-2AM; Th-Sa noon-4AM. 107 Mount St (at Arthur St). 9954.4919

7 The Walker It may look old-fashioned, circa 1950s to be exact, but this cinema boasts state-of-the-art sound and visual equipment and mainly screens independent films. Discounted tickets are offered every Wednesday; movie buffs can take advantage of the discounted Walker Pass. ♦ Daily. 121 Walker St (between Mount and Berry Sts). 9959.4222

8 Bistro Pavé ★★$$ This modern bistro attracts a local business crowd with superb French cuisine served in a pleasing setting of warm cream walls, simple wood and chrome chairs, and tile floors. Chef Colin Holt is fast becoming one of Sydney's culinary stars, departing from the trend toward Modern Australian cuisine and instead serving rich, French food with contemporary twists. The menu features well-prepared standards such as duck terrine, boudin noir (blood pudding), and rillettes (potted meat or fish preserved in fat), all presented with minimalist aplomb. Still true to his heritage, however, Holt's wine list features selections from many of

Australia's finest vineyards. ♦ Modern French ♦ M-W lunch; Th lunch and dinner; F-Sa dinner. 181 Miller St (between Pacific Hwy and Berry St), Suite 1. 9956.8583

9 Armstrong's ★★$$$ A clubby brasserie in the business-dominated locale of North Sydney, its power lunchers are a noisy lot, hurried and hungry for a steak, a bowl of chips, and a glass of wine. In the evening the cuisine is the same—steaks, and various grilled seafood dishes—but the atmosphere is much more subdued, and definitely more formal. Ths place enjoys a loyal following for its excellent wine list, thoughtful service, and that memorable sticky toffee pudding. ♦ Modern Australian ♦ M-F lunch and dinner; Sa dinner. Reservations recommended. 1-7 Napier St (between Charles and Berry Sts). 9955.2066

10 McLaren $$ Boutique hotels like this are rare in Sydney—especially in a commercial hub such as North Sydney. An old Victorian mansion and a new section decorated in keeping with the period make this a popular destination. Attached to the mansion is **The Atrium Garden** cafe/bar, with cane furniture, hanging ferns, and a glass ceiling lending a tropical greenhouse air. The old mansion is protected by the National Trust, so any renovations here have been carefully carried out to make this a very special experience indeed. Although small (28 rooms), the popular hotel offers room service and hearty breakfasts. Book well in advance. ♦ 25 McLaren St (between Miller and Angelo Sts). 9954.4622; fax 9922.1868

11 Rydges North Sydney $$$ There are 167 accommodations at this hotel in the middle of North Sydney's commercial district. With 48 one- and two-bedroom suites complete with kitchen facilities—ideal for families—this hotel resembles a well-maintained modern apartment complex. There is a restaurant and cocktail bar on the premises, and basic room service is available. The executive boardroom and convention facilities have space for meetings of 10 to 250 persons. ♦ 54 McLaren St (between Walker and Miller Sts). 9922.1311; fax 9922.4339

12 The Independent Theatre Built around 1900, this Baroque-style structure was formerly a part of the North Sydney Tram shed. Now nearing its hundredth birthday, the building has been, in turns, a variety theater, a vaudeville house, a boxing arena, an experimental theater venue, and a cabaret. In its current incarnation—under the auspices of owners Seaborn, Broughton and Walford Foundation for the Performing Arts—the building serves as a venue for everything from theater to dance. ♦ 269-71 Miller St (between McLaren and Ridge Sts). 9955.6794

13 Millers Treat ★$ Seemingly unfazed by the burgeoning business community that now surrounds it, this unassuming, rustic-looking cafe has been here for years. A welcome respite for high-pressured corporate types, it's a cozy place—with old wooden chairs and tables, a slate floor, and an open fire to take the chill off winter nights. The surrounding area may be different, but the menu hasn't changed much over the years; customers still order such long-time favorites as shepherd's pie, nachos, and banana splits. Though lunchtime tends to be a bit frenetic, evenings at the cafe are more convivial, as the candles on the tables are lit and local singers provide background music. Outdoor seating is in an umbrella-shaded courtyard. ♦ Cafe ♦ M-F 10:30AM-midnight; Sa-Su 10AM-midnight. 232 Miller St (between McLaren and Ridge Sts). 9955.7427

14 Playfair House Also known as "Delamaire," this is the former home of Thomas Playfair, mayor of Sydney from 1885 to 1889. The three-story house was built in 1881 and is in the style of a Victorian terrace house (town house). The house adjoins six other smaller houses that were a part of the original Playfair property and passed on to his children. These days the terraces have been converted to commercial offices. Thomas Playfair is also honored by Playfair Street and Playfair Stairs in The Rocks on the other side of Sydney Harbour. ♦ 2-14 Ridge St (between Ridge La and West St)

15 The Duxton Hotel $$$ Opened in 1992, this relatively stylish hotel has 165 well-appointed rooms, including 36 suites, all with contemporary blond wood furniture and pastel accents. Most of the suites have splendid harbor views. Facilities include **The Rio Cielo Restaurant and Bar,** a heated outdoor swimming pool, sauna, and conference facilities. ♦ 88 Alfred St (at Cliff St). 9955.1111; fax 9955.3522

Luna Park

16 Luna Park Beside the **North Sydney Olympic Pool** sits a huge amusement park built in the 1930s that operated through the 1980s. Though the park—modeled after Luna Park in Coney Island, New York—met with financial woes and is now open only for private functions, the giant-size clown's face that marks the entrance has become something of a Sydney landmark (see illustration on page 165). More like a miniature ghost town on the edge of the harbor, it's still worth a look—if only to imagine echoes of the screams from the now-silent rollercoaster at the harbor's edge. ♦ Northcliff and Paul Sts

17 North Sydney Olympic Pool Arguably one of the best locations for a public pool in the world, this Olympic-size saltwater pool is perched at the harbor's edge right beside the Harbour Bridge. In winter the pool is heated and covered. There's also a wading pool. ♦ Admission. M-F 6AM-9PM; Sa-Su 7AM-7PM. Alfred St S and Northcliff St. 9955.2309

18 Kirribilli House This rambling Victorian Gothic harborside home is the official Sydney residence of the prime minister of Australia. Originally built for businessman Adolphus Feez in 1855, it was purchased by the commonwealth in 1920. Since 1956 this architecturally splendid home with its sweeping harbor views has been the exclusive domain of the prime minister and his family. There are no public tours of the house; the best way to appreciate its grandeur is from the harbor or from the **Opera House.** ♦ Kirribilli Ave (just east of Mirradong Pl)

19 Admiralty House Next door to **Kirribilli House** (see above), this two-story Victorian house—built in 1842 by Lieutenant Colonel John Gibbs—is currently the Sydney residence for the Queen's representative, the governor general of Australia. The New South Wales government purchased the house in 1900, and used it as the residence for the naval commander-in-chief for Her Majesty's ships until 1913. Since that time it has been loaned to the federal government to accommodate a variety of dignitaries—from royalty to diplomats. Though there is no public access to the house, it may also be viewed from the harbor. ♦ Waruda St and Mirradong Pl

20 Ensemble Theatre An acting school and a theater company popular with—and supported by—local residents occupy this performance space. Productions include local and international works. ♦ Daily. 78 McDougall St (at Willoughby St). 9929.0644

The number of motor vehicles in the city has increased by about one-third since 1996.

Mosman

21 Taronga Zoo To get up-close-and-personal with indigenous Australian animals, head for this extraordinary zoo boasting more than 400 species and 2,000 specimens from Australia and around the world. The views are as impressive as the exhibits: the sprawling, 75-acre property at the edge of Sydney Harbour affords some of the best views of Sydney from almost every vantage point. Over the last 20 years, **Taronga** has made many changes to its exhibits, embracing the international change in attitude about the care and public display of wild animals. Just about all of the caged enclosures are gone—replaced by more natural, more spacious areas that are constantly being updated and improved. The zoo is also involved with conservation programs for endangered animals, and has developed breeding programs for such diverse denizens as chimpanzees, rhinoceros, iguana, and Australian mammals. Gorillas—also part of the conservation program—are the star attractions of the new **McDonald's Gorilla Forest,** a $3.8-million update of, and a vast improvement over, the sad concrete pens of the past. This is also the first time since 1980 that gorillas have been on display here. Be sure to see the family of 10 Western Lowland gorillas led by a giant 200-kilogram (441-pound) male named Kibabu, who is something of a celebrity at the zoo. And there's more: Apart from having Sydney's only platypus exhibit, the zoo also has *Koala Encounters,* where you can have your photo taken with a koala between 10:30 and 11:30AM and 1:30 and 2:30PM daily, and an exhibit, *Australian Walkabout,* in which you can meet kangaroos, wallabies, and other indigenous Australian animals. Other popular exhibits are the *McDonald's Orangutan Rainforest* and *Cats of Asia,* which includes a white tiger and rare Sumatran tigers. The zoo offers special tours for groups and independent travelers, including breakfast tours, educational tours, and "behind the scenes" with Australian animals. Alternatively, short tours can be arranged through the **Information Centre,** located inside the main entrance. Also, try to catch one of the keeper talks, animal shows, and feedings that take place throughout the day. Among the free daily presentations is the seal theater show

(1 and 2:30PM) and the up-close-and-personal petting sessions (2PM). There are six eateries located throughout the property. Souvenirs are also available, at the top (main) entrance and in the middle of the zoo, opposite the flamingos. The zoo is a 12-minute ferry ride across Sydney Harbour, from Circular Quay Wharf 2. It is also easily accessible by bus or car and there is ample parking. ♦ Admission. Daily. Bradleys Head and Beach Rds. 9969.2777

22 White Everything sold in this oasis of minimalism is either white, glass, or stainless steel. Selected housewares from tableware to bed linen are dramatically displayed in the crispy clean surrounds. It almost resembles a museum. ♦ M-Sa; Su noon-4PM. 785 Military Rd (between Raglan St and Avenue Rd). 9968 4559

23 I Piatti ★★$$ North Shore ladies lunch here along with anyone else who appreciates good, well-prepared food and an oh-so-elegant setting. You might be seated inside, but the inventive design of this cafe—lots of natural light and excellent acoustics—will give you the feeling that you are dining alfresco. Delicious, oversize omelettes are on the menu all day, with sides of black bread and all the condiments you could ever dream of. Dinner includes big Caesar salads and grilled octopus on a bed of mixed greens. The coffee is terrific (but strong) and all the desserts are made here. ♦ Cafe ♦ Daily. 710 Military Rd (between Mandolong and Spit Rds). 9968.3054

24 Accoutrement For serious home chefs or anyone in search of fine kitchenware, this is where Sydney's gastronomes come to buy their knives and hard-to-get accessories for their Alessi-clad kitchens. ♦ M-Sa; Su 11AM-4PM. 611 Military Rd (between Gouldsbury and Vista Sts). 9969.1031

25 Balmoral Beach and Park A terrific place for family picnics, games, and cycling, this well-manicured parkland—including the park, the beach promenade, and its classically styled rotunda—was developed in the 1930s through a public works program. The Art Deco style of the **Bather's Pavilion** lends an old seaside resort feel to the area. As pretty as it is today, Balmoral also has an interesting history behind some of its structures. In 1924

a group of Theosophists (a religious movement that developed in the late 19th century) built the **Star Amphitheater,** at the northern end of Balmoral (also known as "Edwards Beach"). This group believed that the Second Coming of Jesus Christ would take place at Balmoral at this spot. The group—which held regular prayer meetings here until the 1940s—disbanded, leaving the theater vacant. Today it is used as a venue for outdoor theater performances and concerts. ♦ The Esplanade

On Balmoral Beach:

Watermark ★★$$$ This restaurant shares the same exclusive beachside strip as **Bather's Pavilion**—just a little farther down at the opposite end of Balmoral Beach. A great view of the water is balanced with a fairly simple interior. When the weather is right, take a table outside under the shade of a beautiful old Moreton Bay fig tree. Given a bottle of wine, a delicate scallop salad, and a Sydney sunset, you'll have to be forcibly removed from your spot. This place is packed for weekend brunch. ♦ Modern Australian ♦ Daily breakfast, lunch, and dinner. 2A The Esplanade (at Botanic Rd). 9968.3433

Bather's Pavilion ★★★$$$ Balmoral Beach has an old English seaside town feel to it—the waves here are gentle, and there is a long, paved promenade to stroll along and a parkland for picnics and games. But though the restaurant (or "Bather's," as the locals call it) seems to fit comfortably into its old English setting, it is very much an Australian experience. It offers everything Australians love about dining out—it's on the water, the dining room is casual, the famous Sydney seafood takes center stage on the menu, and the service is attentive without being too fussy. The weekends are extra busy here, with patrons dining on such **Bather's** classics as seared sea scallops with cumin-spiced relish, salmon with saffron rice, or barramundi with coconut curry sauce. Old-fashioned desserts such as trifle and puddings are worth shedding diet worries for. There is an outdoor area overlooking the beach for drinks and coffee only. This is a Sydney institution for good reason. ♦ Modern Australian ♦ M-F lunch and dinner; Sa-Su breakfast, lunch, and dinner. Reservations required. 4 The Esplanade (at Awaba St). 9968.1133

The Australian flag has three parts. In the top left corner is the Union Jack, which symbolizes its colonization by Britain. At the bottom left is the Star of Federation—its seven points represent the country's six states and one territory. The Southern Cross constellation fills the right half.

Sydney by Night— Nightclubs, Jazz Joints, and Pubs

With hot dance spots, smooth jazz clubs, and local pubs offering comedy, poetry readings, and theater, Sydney has something for every night owl. **Macleay Street** in **Kings Cross**, and **Oxford Street** in **Darlinghurst** are the two centers of late-night Sydney, although the pubs in **Inner West** and around **The Rocks** are also hubs of live entertainment and serious drinking. Dress codes are usually lax at most pubs and jazz joints, but only those wearing the latest duds will be allowed into the ultrahip nightclubs. The following are some of the city's more popular late-night haunts.

Clubs

Blackmarket Just off the beaten track in Inner West, this club is a happening (although very bizarre) spot where deejays crank out the latest tunes. "The Hellfire Club" on Friday night features leather and bondage and is definitely not for those who are easily shocked. Come during the day on Saturday and Sunday and you won't even know that it's not midnight. ♦ F 10PM-5AM; Sa-Su 6AM-6PM. 111 Regent St (between Meagher and Queen Sts), Chippendale. 9283.5555

The Cauldron This long-running, popular club with both live and canned music caters to a well-heeled, well-dressed crowd, and unlike some other nightspots, suits are de rigueur (no jeans are allowed). Although the club also serves food, eat beforehand at one of the restaurants on Victoria Street. ♦ Tu-Sa 6PM-3AM. 207 Darlinghurst Rd (at Farrell Ave), Darlinghurst. 9331.1523

Comedy Store A changing line-up of local, interstate, and international talent (Robin Williams has performed here) are on stage at Sydney's leading stand-up comedy venue. Don't miss the famous open-mike evening on Tuesday, especially for those with enough nerve to get up and take a stab at stardom. ♦ Daily 6PM-midnight. 450 Parramatta Rd (at Crystal St), Petersham. 9564.3900

D.C.M. Although it's primarily a gay men's club, this noisy place welcomes anyone who comes with the right attitude and a powerful urge to bump and grind on the dance floor. A very young, hip, and extroverted crowd comes here for the hardcore music. ♦ M-F, Su 8PM-3AM; Sa 8PM-10:30AM. 33 Oxford St (between Pelican and Brisbane Sts), Darlinghurst. 9267.7380

The Harold Park Hotel Innovative theater, stand-up comedy, and author readings are the draws at this old pub. Monday night is stand-up comedy night, while Tuesday features "Writers in the Park," when authors read their own work. Wednesday through Sunday is comedy theater, and Thursday through Saturday has a theater restaurant show. ♦ Daily 6PM-midnight. 115 Wigram Rd (at Ross St), Glebe. 9552.1791

Kinselas This three-story spot has stunning Art Deco detailing throughout, especially in the lovely ground-floor bar, where live entertainment is frequently featured. The small bar on the middle floor is often reserved for special events and "members." The dance floor is on the top level where the music varies according to the DJ who's spinning that night. ♦ M-Sa 8PM-3AM; Su 8PM-midnight. 383 Bourke St (between Campbell St and Taylor Sq), Darlinghurst. 9331.3100

Riva Located in the **Sheraton on the Park** hotel, this nightclub has two bars and a room with sofas for those looking to relax. Live pop, rock, and cabaret bands often play here, but for the most part this joint is rather sophisticated and sedate. Don't dress too casually. ♦ Daily 8PM-1AM. 130 Castlereagh St (between Park and Market Sts), Central Business District. 9286.6666

Round Midnight This suave spot with intimate lounge areas features funk, blues, and soul music from many regular visiting and local acts. ♦ Tu-Th, Su 8PM-3AM; F-Sa 8PM-5AM. 2 Roslyn St (at Darlinghurst Rd), Kings Cross. 9356.4045

Jazz

The Basement The local and international performers at this popular place are the main reason to come here, but its restaurant also serves good hearty comfort food. ♦ M-F noon-midnight; Sa-Su 7PM-midnight. 29 Reiby Pl (between Macquarie Pl and Pitt St), Circular Quay. 9251.2797

Orient Hotel Jazz music and heavy drinking are two reasons to drop in at this place. It's lots of fun for those who like to stay up late and party hearty. ♦ M-Th 9PM-midnight; F-Sa 7PM-2:30AM; Su 3:30-11:30PM. 89 George St (at Argyle St), The Rocks. 9251.1255

Soup Plus This place features excellent jazz and blues. The inexpensive, basic fare (soup, of course) will ensure a long stay. Live jazz is on tap six days a week; Monday is Big Band night. ♦ M-Th noon-midnight; F-Sa noon-1AM. 383 George St (between Market and King Sts), Central Business District. 9299.7728

KEELY EDWARDS

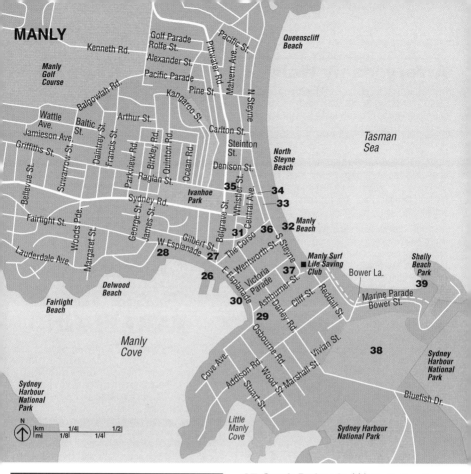

MANLY

Golf Parade
Rolfe St.
Kenneth Rd.
Alexander St.
Pacific Parade
Pacific St.
Pittwater Rd.
Malvern Ave.
N Steyne
Queenscliff Beach

Manly Golf Course
Balgowlah Rd.
Kangaroo St.
Pine St.
Carlton St.

Wattle Ave.
Baltic St.
Daintrey St.
Francis St.
Arthur St.
Parkview Rd.
Birkley Rd.
Quinton Rd.
Ocean Rd.
Kangaroo St.
Steinton St.
Denison St.
North Steyne Beach

Jamieson Ave.
Griffiths St.
Bellevue St.
Suwarrow St.
Margaret St.
Woods Pde.
Raglan St.
George St.
James St.
Sydney Rd.
Ivanhoe Park
Belgrave St.
Whistler St.
Central Ave.
35
34
33
Tasman Sea

Fairlight St.
Gilbert St.
W Esplanade
The Corso
Wentworth St.
S Steyne
31
36
32 Manly Beach

Lauderdale Ave.
28
27
E Esplanade
Victoria Parade
37
Manly Surf Life Saving Club
Shelly Beach Park
39

Delwood Beach
26
Ashburner St.
Darley Rd.
Cliff St.
Reddall St.
Bower La.
Marine Parade
Bower St.

Fairlight Beach
30
29
Osbourne Rd.
Vivian St.
38
Sydney Harbour National Park

Manly Cove
Cove Ave.
Addison Rd.
Wood St.
Marshall St.
Stuart St.

Sydney Harbour National Park
Little Manly Cove
Sydney Harbour National Park
Bluefish Dr.

N
km 1/4 1/2
mi 1/8 1/4

Manly

26 Manly Wharf In the center of Manly Cove is this wharf where the **Manly** ferry docks (see illustration on page 170). Also here is a string of shops, restaurants, cafes, and fast-food places.

On Manly Wharf:

Quayside Booking Centre From this center, book accommodations, harbor tours, and day trips; also available here is information about local attractions. ♦ Daily. 9977.5296

Armstrong's Manly ★$$ If you take the ferry from the city to Manly, you won't have far to walk to find a decent restaurant. This place is right on Manly Wharf, huddled between tacky tourist shops and hamburger joints. Despite its garish neighbors, the eatery boasts a great view onto Manly Cove. Striped umbrellas shield alfresco diners from the harsh summer sun while they tuck into the great fish and chips, kangaroo rump, and Asian-inspired salads. The same first-rate fare is served in the large dining room. ♦ Modern Australian ♦ Daily lunch and dinner. Reservations recommended. Shop 213. 9976 3835

27 Grande Esplanade $$$ The first two floors of this building house very modern studio, one- and two-bedroom full-service apartments— right on Manly Cove. Each of the 54 rooms and 6 suites has a kitchen and washer/dryer. Decor is beach-house at its best, casual and bright. There is a gym and complimentary parking for guests. There's a two-week minimum stay in the suites. ♦ W Esplanade and Belgrave St. 9976.4600; fax 9976.4699

28 Manly Art Gallery and Museum Established in 1930, this institution is run by the local council to provide locals and visitors a glimpse into Manly's history and culture. Permanent exhibitions include a retrospective of Australian beach fashions, photography, and other visual arts related to Manly's beach life. There are also a number of changing exhibits. A bookshop stocks souvenirs, postcards, and posters. ♦ Admission; children and Manly residents free. Tu-Su. W Esplanade and Commonwealth Parade. 9949.1776

A Very Manly Walk

One of the most scenic harborside walking tracks in Sydney, the **Manly Scenic Walkway** goes from the beach community of **Manly** to the **Spit Bridge.** Along the almost–10-kilometer (6-mile) walk is natural bushland that has changed little in 200 years, mainly because of its preferred status as a national park. Highlights include modern harborside suburbs, weathered Aboriginal sites, native coastal heath, and pockets of subtropical rain forest in the **Sydney Harbour National Park.** The panoramic views of the entrance to Sydney Harbour alone are worth the trek.

It's a three-to-four-hour stroll at a leisurely pace, with a mixture of easy and hard walking, including a steep section in the national park. Start the walk at either the Spit Bridge or at **Manly Wharf.** There's plenty of parking at both ends. Or take a ferry or *JetCat* (hydrofoil) from **Circular Quay,** or bus from Circular Quay or **Wynyard Station** to Manly Wharf (call 13.1500 for schedules). For more information on the park, contact the **National Parks and Wildlife Service** (9977.6522).

KEELY EDWARDS

OCEANWORLD

28 Oceanworld This large aquarium is the first thing you'll see as the ferry pulls into Manly Cove. Considered a poor relation to the grand **Sydney Aquarium** at Darling Harbour, it's still a place where you can watch sharks being fed and check out popular fur seals. The moving walkway runs through a huge tank filled with marine life. ♦ Admission. Daily. W Esplanade and Commonwealth Parade. 9949.2644

29 Periwinkle Guesthouse $ Built in 1895, this family-run guesthouse has wrought-iron terraces overlooking a central courtyard. There are 18 spacious, high-ceilinged rooms, a cozy guest lounge with an open fireplace— a perfect place to wind down or warm up—a sun room with a color TV, a guest kitchen, and a laundromat. Bathrooms are shared. ♦ 18-19 E Esplanade (at Ashburner St). 9977.4668; fax 9977.6308

Sydney Harbour PARAFLYING

30 Sydney Harbour Paraflying Some people like to view stunning Sydney Harbour from the deck of a ferry or even aboard a sea plane, while those with an adventurous bent prefer to see the sights while suspended in the air by ropes and a Para-Sail. If you fall into the last category, then this company can turn your dream into a reality. They operate a cable/winch Para-Sailing boat, meaning you both take off and land on the boat—allowing you to keep relatively dry and, by the way, avoid those pesky sharks. Tickets may also be purchased from the **Quayside Booking Centre.** Advance reservations recommended. ♦ Daily. 21/38 E Esplanade (at Victoria Parade). 9977.6781

Manly Wharf

Manly Beach

31 Jipang ★★$ This small Japanese noodle house along Manly's Corso is an ideal hunger-pleaser on the way to or from a stroll along the beach. A simple restaurant with indoor and outdoor seating, it offers an inexpensive range of noodle dishes, including ramen with seafood and rice with chicken teriyaki. ♦ Japanese ♦ Tu-Su lunch and dinner. 37-39 The Corso (between N Steyne and Whistler St). 9977.4436

32 Manly Beach It takes about 40 minutes by ferry, and about 45 minutes by car to get to this ocean beach from the CBD. Captain Arthur Phillip named the area Manly due to the "confidence and manly behavior" of the local Aborigines he saw there. The beachfront is now lined with tall Norfolk Island pines that were planted years ago when the area was developed as a posh vacation destination for Sydneysiders. This was one of the first beaches to allow public bathing (in 1902). As Manly's popularity grew (along with the growth of Sydney), it became an extension of Sydney's Northern Suburbs, and many locals made Manly their full-time home. Along The Corso, which leads from Manly Cove in Sydney Harbour to Manly Beach on the ocean, there is a lingering sense that this remains a tourist-friendly, seaside town. But though the hotels and restaurants along the beachfront make it an interesting destination for visitors, the scene here can seem a bit contrived at times. The **Manly Surf Life Saving Club**, located at the southern end of the beach, patrols the beaches here. Call for 9977.2742 for information on beach conditions. ♦ S Steyne

33 Brazil ★★$$ A small, light-hearted spot on the surf at Manly, the prime seating here is upstairs, where the view of the water is dazzling. Food is confidently Asian and Mediterranean, casual menu by day (large salads and pasta dishes) and more serious fare at night (Chinese glazed chicken with Asian greens and noodles). Save room for one of the rich, sumptuous Italian-inspired desserts. The place can get pretty busy on weekends, especially for breakfast and late morning brunch. ♦ Modern Australian ♦ Daily breakfast, lunch, and dinner. 46 N Steyne (between The Corso and Raglan St). 9977.3825

33 Manly Blades This stores claims to have the largest selection of in-line skates in Sydney. Rent your Rollerblades here and head for the esplanade; if you feel a bit wobbly, get the staff to give you a few pointers. All protective gear is included in the rental. Skateboards are also for hire. Rates are very reasonable, with overnight, three-day, and group rental options. ♦ Daily 10AM-sunset. 49 N Steyne (between The Corso and Raglan St), Shop 2. 9976.3833

The UK and Ireland still represent the largest immigrant population in Sydney. Southern Europe runs a close second, while Southeast Asia is the third-largest group.

In the early days of Sydney, foreign ships anchored off the North Shore until their captains made their intentions clear, hence the name "Neutral Bay."

North Sydney's Independent Theatre is rumored to be haunted. There have been sightings of an old woman in the dress circle, a white figure on stage, and a man in the dressing rooms.

34 Manly Pacific Parkroyal $$$ A modern hotel overlooking Manly Beach, its 169 rooms are basic—pastel colors, with glass, Formica, and marble accents—but the ocean views more than compensate. There are two restaurants, two bars, a gymnasium, sauna, swimming pool, and spa. Secretarial services and seven meeting rooms that can accommodate 800 people give this hotel a corporate air. ♦ 55 N Steyne (between Raglan and Denison Sts). 9977.7666; fax 9977.7822

35 Manly Backpackers Beachside $ For backpackers or those prepared to share rooms, these very basic accommodations are ultracheap. There also are some twin rooms. Shared kitchen facilities are available. ♦ 28 Raglan St (at Pittwater Rd). 9977.3411; fax 9977.4379

36 Cafe Tunis ★$$ The Tunisian owners of this sleek, long, brightly colored restaurant have successfully introduced some aromatic flavors from the North African kitchen to Manly. Breakfast is a real treat, especially when eggs are accompanied by merguez sausage; dinner has spicy seafood dishes with couscous and tagines of chicken and lamb. Wine may be ordered by the glass. Service is friendly and relaxed. ♦ North African ♦ Daily breakfast, lunch, and dinner. Reservations recommended. 30 S Steyne (between Wentworth St and The Corso). 9976.2805

37 Radisson Kestrel Hotel $$$ With 83 rooms (32 are suites) at the south end of Manly Beach, this is a relatively small and charming property for this international chain. All of the brightly colored guest rooms have elegant, modern furnishings and look out over the ocean. The most lavish accommodation is the enormous **Ocean View Spa Suite** with panoramic views of Manly Beach and a large sitting room. The **Sorrel Restaurant**, serving breakfast, lunch, and dinner, has an impressive outdoor deck for alfresco dining. 8-13 S Steyne (between Ashburner St and Victoria Parade). 9977.8866, 800/333.3333; fax 9977.8209

38 St. Patrick's Seminary You can't miss this mammoth Neo-Gothic sandstone Catholic seminary perched on the hilltop as you look southeast from Manly Beach. The Catholics are renowned for securing some of the most prized land and best views wherever they set up. This is surely the case with this seminary (pictured below), which overlooks Manly Beach and borders **Sydney Harbour National Park.** The grand structure was built in 1885 to the chagrin of the predominantly Protestant government of the time. The seminary and its grounds are currently leased out to a hotel management school. ♦ Darley Rd (between Bluefish Dr and Vivian St)

39 Shelly Beach One of Sydney's most protected ocean beaches, it also is considered by many as a haven from the commercial buzz of Manly Beach. The tiny beach is surrounded by woodland and is an ideal spot to take the family for a dip in the ocean. From the water you can enjoy beautiful views of the national park and **St. Patrick's Seminary** on the hill. Parking, changing rooms, and picnic facilities are available. Although the water is relatively tranquil here, the area is not patrolled by surf life savers. ♦ Marine Parade (east of Bower La)

On Shelly Beach:

St. Patrick's Seminary

Le Kiosk ★★★$$$ Just around the corner from the bustle of Manly is this sandstone restaurant sitting on the hillside looking back toward Manly. The restaurant retains much of the style it had as a 1920s tea room, with high ceilings and carved wood moldings, although the kitchen is another matter. Contrary to the name of this breezy, outdoorsy sounding place, wonderful Asian-inspired cuisine with an emphasis on seafood is served here. Try the chili crab with glass noodles or the large seafood platter. The wine list is strictly Australian. ♦ Modern Australian ♦ Daily lunch and dinner. Reservations recommended. 1 Marine Parade. 9977.4122

Sydney as the Star

In the early 20th century Australia was considered a pioneer in filmmaking, producing some of the world's first silent movies. Even today Australian films continue to make an impact on the world. Many of these have been shot in Sydney, where the landscape, culture, and people are central to the movie's plot line. The following selection is undeniably Sydney:

The Adventures of Priscilla, Queen of the Dessert (1994) Stephan Elliot wrote and directed this outrageous film—starring Terrence Stamp, Hugo Weaving, and Guy Pearce—about three drag queens who take a bus journey to the desert in search of meaning in their lives. Although it takes place mainly in the outback, the beginning and end are set in Sydney pubs.

Bliss (1985) Based on the Peter Carey novel of the same name, Ray Lawrence's film deals with an advertising man's extraordinary search for identity. It is set in Sydney and the bush.

Careful He Might Hear You (1983) Wendy Hughes, Robin Nevin, and John Hargreaves star in Jill Robb's story of a 1920s custody battle between a wealthy Sydney woman and her sister.

Children of the Revolution (1996) Peter Duncan wrote and directed this offbeat political satire starring Judy Davis and Sam Neill that's set in post–World War II Sydney. It's a tale of a woman who raises her boy, who may be the son of Stalin (played by F. Murray Abraham). As he gets older, he develops an affinity for fascist-style rule of Australia. It's good for lots of laughs with some insight into political masterminding.

Don's Party (1976) A David Williamson play with the same title was the basis for this dramatic film starring the late John Hargreaves about a wacky election-night party in Sydney that leads to frayed friendships and marriages.

For the Term of His Natural Life (1927) This story of a convict's harrowing experience when he was transported to Sydney was taken from Marcus Clarke's 1874 novel. Norman Dawn directed this epic tale.

The Last Days of Chez Nous (1992) Gillian Armstrong directed this film set in **The Inner West** suburb of **Glebe** about a woman who is dealing with her French lover's feelings of alienation and her sister's betrayal. It stars Lisa Harrow and Bruno Ganz.

The Last Wave (1977) One of Peter Weir's earlier haunting films stars Richard Chamberlain as a white lawyer who gets caught up in Aboriginal culture and mysticism while investigating a murder. Weir cleverly contrasts the statutes and mores of modern Sydney with the tribal laws of the Aborigine in the outback.

Muriel's Wedding (1994) P.J. Hogan wrote and directed this comic tragedy (much of it set in Sydney) about a young woman in search of her place in the world. It stars Toni Collette, Rachel Griffiths, and Bill Hunter.

Oscar and Lucinda (1997) A transplanted English clergyman (Ralph Fiennes) and an ambitious young woman (Cate Blanchett) from the Australian countryside are drawn together by their passion for gambling in this tale set in mid–19th-century Sydney and the outback. Gillian Armstrong directed.

Puberty Blues (1981) This story of teen life in a fictional southern beach Sydney suburb was directed by Bruce Beresford of *Driving Miss Daisy* fame.

Strictly Ballroom (1992) Set in the battlefield of ballroom dancing competitions in suburban Sydney, this hilarious cult classic stars Paul Mercurio and Tara Morice.

The Sum of Us (1994) Russell Crowe and Jack Thompson are featured in the adaptation of David Stevens's sometimes comic play about a father's idiosyncratic way of accepting his gay son's lifestyle.

They're A Weird Mob (1966) Michael Powell directed this classic comic film about the "New Australians" in Sydney.

Walkabout (1971) Jenny Agutter, Lucien John, and David Gulpilil star in this visually stunning film about a brother and sister who become stranded in the wilderness. They are saved by a young aborigine on his coming-of-age "walkabout," who shows them how to survive in the desert. Directed by Nicolas Roeg, this movie is also known for its haunting musical score and social commentary about the contrast between life in the city (Sydney) and in the outback.

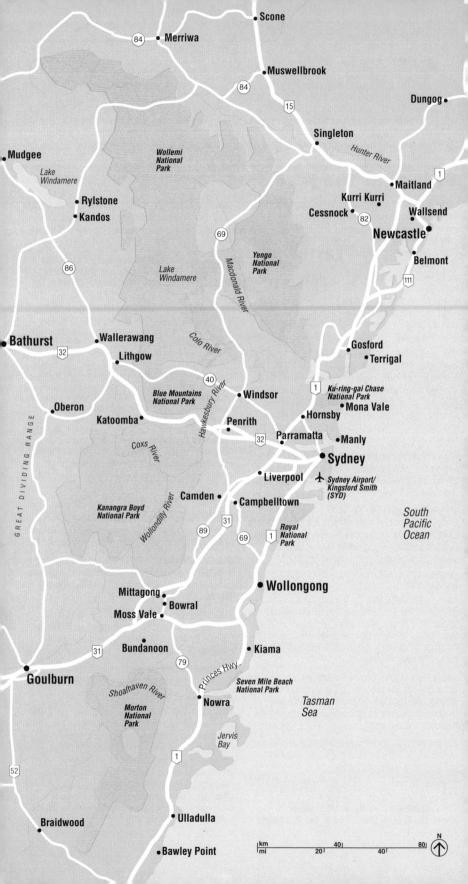

Beyond Sydney

Although Sydney's metropolitan area spreads out for about 50 kilometers (31 miles) in each direction from the harbor, within two hours of the Central Business District (CBD) are some remarkable natural wonders to experience on a day trip or a one- or two-night jaunt.

The outskirts of **Greater Sydney** contain national parks, walking trails, and beaches—all close enough to visit in a single day. Most are accessible by bus and rail (call the **State Transit Authority** at 13.1500 for schedules), or even by taxi, since they are considered part of the Sydney metropolitan area.

The **Northern Suburbs** remained relatively undeveloped until the middle of the 19th century, when a ferry system and roads were in place. Then the land around the harbor inlets and coves became ripe for growth. Still, although now more heavily populated, this area manages to remain leafy and green and has varied charms: from superb hiking and quiet bird watching at **Lane Cove National Park** and **Ku-ring-gai Chase National Park** to the siren song of the seaside in the beach towns around **Pittwater** and **Mona Vale.**

While the Northern Suburbs are renowned for bush walks and nature trails, Sydney's **Western Suburbs,** particularly around **Parramatta,** are known for historic sites and colonial homes. This area was developed early: By the late 1700s, the colony started spreading west as it grew along the banks of the **Parramatta River.**

The terrain in Southern Sydney is flat and sandy. **Botany Bay National Park,** just east of **SydneyAirport/Kingsford Smith,** was the site of Captain Cook's landing in 1770 and the site of Captain Arthur Phillip's landing in 1788. Seventeen kilometers (11 miles) farther down the coast the **Royal National Park,** only the second national park in the world (Yosemite in the US was the first), offers beautiful beaches and dense low woodland. Both parks are accessible by public transportation.

Farther afield, overnight-excursion territory begins. Most of these areas are best visited by car, but **Countrylink** (13.2232) and the **State Transit Authority** (13.1500) offer tours and provide regular, scheduled transportation as well.

The **Central Coast** features a string of beach towns frequented by Sydneysiders and visitors alike. **Gosford** and **Terrigal** are the most well-known, although stopping at one of the smaller hamlets has the advantage of smaller crowds. Also in the area is **Old Sydney Town**, a re-creation of the days of the original colony.

About 120 kilometers (74 miles) northwest of Sydney is **Hunter Valley**, one of Australia's most famous wine districts. Its landscape has been compared to California's Sonoma Valley and its climate is similar to France's Burgundy and Bordeaux regions. A day trip from Sydney will allow you to explore one or two vineyards, but there are more than 50 wineries in this valley, so a longer trip might be in order, especially for wine connoisseurs. A longer trip also allows more time to enjoy the area's luxury resorts and award-winning restaurants.

On a clear day in Sydney, look out from **Centrepoint Tower** and you'll see the outline of a dark mountain range running along the western horizon. This is a segment of the Great Dividing Range called the **Blue Mountains,** less than a two-hour drive from the city. Many of the 26 towns that make up this region have been built alongside magnificent cliffs that drop into deep undulating valleys, cascading waterfalls, and some of the most unspoiled dense bushland in Australia. The resorts and restaurants here make the most of the fresh air and gorgeous views.

The **Southern Highlands** are only a 90-minute drive southwest of Sydney. With dense green forests, small farms, large old sandstone and wooden homes with well-tended gardens, and an unhurried pace, this area is Sydney's answer to an English country village. Some of the old estates built on the land surrounding the towns of **Mittagong, Bowral,** and **Moss Vale** have been converted into guest houses, spas, and country-style restaurants, while the towns themselves are lined with antiques and craft shops and cafes.

Head south along the old **Princes Highway** for about 100 kilometers (62 miles) and you enter some of Australia's less populated, most unspoiled beach territory known as the **South Coast** or the **Illawarra District.** Visit the small coastal town of **Kiama, Seven Mile Beach National Park,** and **Jervis Bay.** The green rolling hills running down to brilliant white beaches and churning blue sea provide a wonderfully scenic drive.

City code 2 unless otherwise indicated.

Greater Sydney

Not far from the thriving northern suburb of **Chatswood,** and only 10 kilometers (6 miles) from the city center is **Lane Cove National Park** (9412.1811). The park is accessible by public transportation—take the **North and Western** *Bus No. 551* or *550* to **Fullers Bridge** (for schedules, call 9816.2622). There are three entrances to the park: **Lane Cove Road** from the west; and two at **Fullers Bridge,** off **Delhi Road** and **Lady Game Drive.** Starting at a bushy ridgetop at Lady Game Drive, a walking track climbs down and meanders along the banks of the **Lane Cove River.** The river draws droves of Sydneysiders, who enjoy leisurely paddlewheel cruises or rent rowboats or canoes (9419.3159). The relatively easy walking path leads through sandstone overhangs and caves, offering opportunities to see the amazing local birds, including lorikeets, herons, white egrets, and kookaburras. The track ends at **De Burghs Bridge** where you can cross the river and return along the opposite bank. An entire round-trip trek covers about 10 kilometers (6 miles) and takes a good 4 hours to complete.

About 10 kilometers (6 miles) beyond Chatswood is the suburb of **Wahroonga**—accessible from the city by train or taxi, site of the **Rose Seidler House** (71 Clissold Road, off Burns Rd, 9989 8020). This modernist architectural masterpiece (pictured below), built between 1948 and 1950, was the first commission for architect **Harry Seidler,** who reached the height of his fame in the 1960s and 1970s. The Viennese-born **Seidler** came to Australia imbued with the philosophy of modernism, having studied in America with **Walter Gropius** and other Bauhaus proponents, **Joseph Albers** and **Marcel Breuer. Seidler** built this house for his parents, Rose and Max, who lived here until 1967. Innovative when it was built in 1952, the **Rose Seidler House** has remained influential, still stimulating much

Rose Seidler House

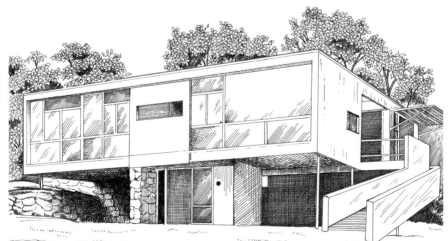

KEELY EDWARDS

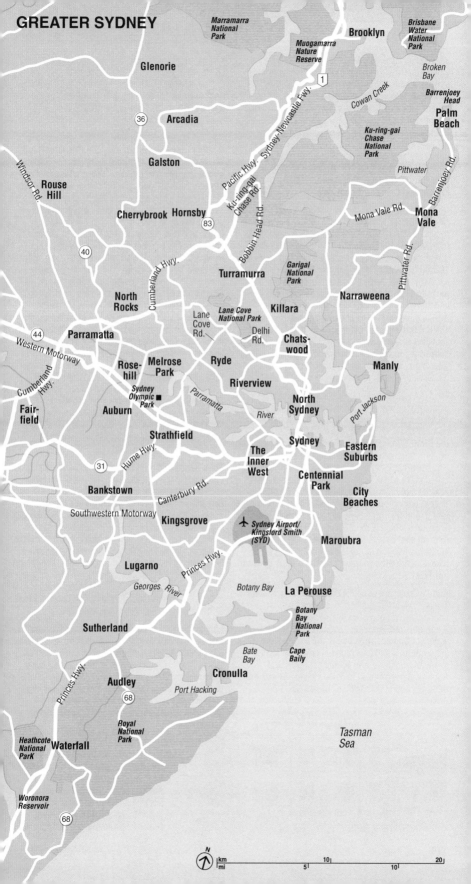

GREATER SYDNEY

Marramarra National Park

Brooklyn

Brisbane Water National Park

Glenorie

Muogamarra Nature Reserve

Broken Bay

1

Arcadia

Cowan Creek

Barrenjoey Head

36

Palm Beach

Galston

Ku-ring-gai Chase National Park

Windsor Rd.

Rouse Hill

Cherrybrook

Hornsby

Pittwater

Mona Vale Rd.

Mona Vale

40

Ku-ring-gai Chase Rd.

83

Cumberland Hwy.

North Rocks

Turramurra

Garigal National Park

Killara

Narraweena

Pittwater Rd.

44

Parramatta

Lane Cove Rd.

Lane Cove National Park

Delhi Rd.

Chats-wood

Western Motorway

Rose-hill

Melrose Park

Ryde

Manly

Cumberland Hwy.

Auburn

Sydney Olympic Park

Riverview

Parramatta

River

North Sydney

Port Jackson

Fair-field

Strathfield

Sydney

Eastern Suburbs

31

Hume Hwy.

The Inner West

Centennial Park

City Beaches

Bankstown

Canterbury Rd.

Southwestern Motorway

Kingsgrove

✈ Sydney Airport/ Kingsford Smith (SYD)

Maroubra

Lugarno

Princes Hwy.

Georges River

Botany Bay

La Perouse

Botany Bay National Park

Sutherland

Bate Bay

Cape Baily

Princes Hwy.

Audley

Cronulla

68

Port Hacking

Tasman Sea

Heathcote National Park

Waterfall

Royal National Park

Woronora Reservoir

68

N

km
mi

5

10

10

20

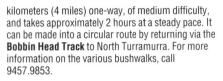

intellectual discourse. The house, which is nestled into natural bushland, has been carefully restored to its authentic 1950s state, incorporating the Modernist features of open planning, minimal color scheme, modern appliances, and revolutionary labor-saving devices. The original furniture by Saarinen, Hardoy, and Eames is one of the most important postwar design collections in Australia. The house is open only on Sunday; there is an admission fee. From its generous expanse of glass walls and sun-filled deck, this house has panoramic views of nearby **Ku-ring-gai Chase National Park.**

Only 25 kilometers (15.5 miles) from the city, **Ku-ring-gai Chase National Park** is easily accessible by public transportation. Take **Shorelink** *Bus No. 567* from **Wahroonga Station** to the end of Grosvenor Street; or **Shorelink** *Bus No. 577* from **Turramurra Station** to **Bobbin Head.** For timetable information, call 9457.8888. Australia's second-oldest national park, **Ku-ring-gai Chase** was established in 1894, and it offers a chance to experience a bit of the Aussie bush without having to travel far from the city. The **Kalkari Visitors' Centre** (Ku-ring-gai Chase Rd, east of Sydney-Newcastle Fwy, 9457.9322), open daily, is a good source of information both about the Aborigines who originally inhabited the area and the native wildlife still found in the park.

Throughout the park, sheer cliffs dramatically drop into the water, and hundreds of Aboriginal rock-art sites dot the area. The park features a number of excellent bush-walking trails, of which the **Gibberagong Track** is one of the best. It begins on the ridgetop, with a spectacular display of wildflowers; zigzags down to the **Gibberagong** water holes where eastern water dragons (native lizards) sun on the rocks; then follows **Cockle Creek,** linking up with a boardwalk over a mangrove forest; and finally ends up at scenic **Bobbin Head.** This walk, which is mostly downhill with some difficult sections, is 6.5 kilometers long (4 miles) and takes about 3 hours to complete. For a full-day hike, link the **Gibberagong** with the **Mount Ku-ring-gai Track.**

Another excellent option is the **Sphinx-Warrimoo Track.** Rain forest, gullies, and rugged sandstone country all help to make this walk a real adventure. A half-day trek, it provides scenic views along the waters of **Cowan Creek.** Along the banks of the creek are numerous middens (accumulations of shells, charcoal from fires, and animal bones) where Aboriginal people used to gather to dine on oysters, mussels, and other shellfish. The walk is 6.5

kilometers (4 miles) one-way, of medium difficulty, and takes approximately 2 hours at a steady pace. It can be made into a circular route by returning via the **Bobbin Head Track** to North Turramurra. For more information on the various bushwalks, call 9457.9853.

Heading north from **Ku-ring-gai** along **Mona Vale Road** or from Sydney proper along **Pittwater Road,** you reach Sydney's **Northern Beaches.** On public transportation, take *Bus No. 190* from **Wynyard Station;** call 13.1500 for information. Since the turn of the century these beach towns have developed as weekend-cottage communities. At **Mona Vale,** connect with the main beach artery, **Barrenjoey Road,** and take your pick of sandy spots. The most popular ocean beaches along this peninsula are **Newport, Bilgola, Avalon, Whale,** and **Palm.** Whale and Palm Beaches, in particular, are ultrawealthy communities and the location for some spectacular beach homes built right into the cliffs overlooking the surf. They have quite a reputation for their Hollywood- and Hamptons-style parties throughout the summer months, and the beachwear seen on these shores is the epitome of "beach chic". These two suburbs, not incidentally, also have some of the area's best restaurants. Try **Jonah's** (69 Bynya Rd, between Surf and Norma Rds, Whale Beach, 9974.5599) for great service and French-inspired Mediterranean cuisine.A little farther down the road is the aptly named **Beach Road Restaurant** (1 Beach Rd, at Barrenjoey Rd, Palm Beach, 9974.1159), which serves fine Modern Australian fare to an adoring local and city crowd.

Palm Beach Wharf (at the end of this peninsula on the Pittwater side) is a good spot to sit and watch ferries and sail boats ply the harbor inlet. North of Palm Beach the peninsula ends at **Barrenjoey Head.** A steep climb up the hill leads to the old sandstone **Barrenjoey Lighthouse,** which provides excellent views of the headland, the mouth of the **Hawkesbury River,** and the Pittwater region. For information on the lighthouse and local walking tours (the fourth Sunday of every month) call 9457.9853. For general information on the region, its beaches, accommodations, and restaurants, visit or call the **Pittwater Visitors' Information Centre** (1 Park St, at Barrenjoey Rd, Mona Vale, 9979.8717).

Heading west from Sydney, either along **Parramatta Road** or the **Western Motorway,** leads to the densely populated **Western Suburbs.** Despite the crush of modern humanity, a number of historic sites have been preserved, making for interesting full- or half-day visits. Most are accessible by rail and bus; staff members at most sites are happy to answer telephone requests for directions and information on guided tours.

Parramatta (Aboriginal for "where eels lie down to sleep"), 23 kilometers (14 miles) away from the city by road, is also accessible by train and by hydrofoil (13.1500) from **Circular Quay**). The town is the site of Australia's oldest surviving public building, **Old Government House** (Parramatta Park, Macquarie

Old Government House

Rouse Hill House

KEELY EDWARDS

and Pitt Sts, 9635.8149), which was erected in 1799. The building's two-story central section is brick, plastered over to give the appearance of solid stone. Between 1812 and 1818 two wings were added and in 1816 a Doric-columned porch, attributed to convict/architect **Francis Greenway,** was added. The austere furniture makes up one of Sydney's few remaining collections of home furnishings from the turn of the 18th century. The house (pictured on page 178) is managed by the Historic Houses Trust and can be visited only by guided tour. It is open Tuesday through Sunday and has an admission fee.

Also in Parramatta is **Experiment Farm** (9 Ruse St, east of Harris St, 9635.5655). In 1789, ex-convict James Ruse and his wife Elizabeth were given a 1.5-acre parcel of land here to cultivate. Governor Arthur Phillip named the property "Experiment Farm" two years later when he granted Ruse an additional 30 acres as a reward for cultivating the colony's first successful wheat crop. The farmhouse that exists today was built by the next owner, John Harris, in the 1830s. This small house, with its well-preserved Australian red cedar woodwork and English period furniture, is well worth the admission fee; it is open Tuesday through Thursday and Sunday.

Another important colonial site can be found in nearby **Rosehill.** Built in the 1790s, **Elizabeth Farm**

(Alice St, between Arthur and Alfred Sts, 9635.9488) contains some of the oldest surviving European buildings in Australia; it also holds an important place in the national consciousness. It has been said the country's economy "rides on the sheep's back"—wool production and export. The farm (pictured at lower left) was the home of John and Elizabeth MacArthur, who conducted some of the earliest experiments in Merino wool production. Now part of the Historic Houses Trust, the farm reflects the colony's first 50 years of architectural ambitions and provides a glimpse into early colonial Australia. From a typical English cottage (part of the original roof still survives), it evolved into the distinctive form of the Australian bungalow with deep, shady verandas. The interior rooms are sparsely furnished with reproductions of furniture, portraits, and objects belonging to the MacArthurs; draperies, floor coverings, and plants typical of an early 19th-century home have also been added. The house is surrounded by an 1830s-style garden that contains bunya pines, olive trees, and early plantings from the Macarthurs' time. The site is open Tuesday through Sunday, with an admission fee.

There are only a few early colonial homes that have remained unaltered over the years. Fewer still have remained within one family. **Rouse Hill House** (980 Windsor Rd, at Guntawong Rd, Rouse Hill) was built between 1813 and 1818 for Richard and Elizabeth Rouse and was occupied by seven succeeding generations of Rouses for 180 years. The original property included a house, 1,200 acres of farmland, outbuildings, and gardens. The surrounding rural community was small but thriving, with a church and school. In 1978 the property was purchased by the New South Wales government, and in 1986 it was transferred to the New South Wales Historic Houses

Trust for conservation and care. Touring the home is like entering a sepia snapshot of early Sydney life. The house is open once a month to visitors for guided tours; call 9692.8366 for more information. Today only 30 acres remain and many of the outbuildings are mere ruins. But the home itself retains its original character: a four-square Georgian house with 11 rooms in the main structure and two mid–19th-century service wings. Built of sandstone, the house has had several paint jobs. On the interior, the ground floor chimney pieces and front door were changed in the mid-19th century, but the original first-floor fireplace area survives.

For a completely different experience, take **CityBus** *No. 394* or *398* from Circular Quay and head for Southern Sydney. Sand dunes and heathlands dominate **Botany Bay National Park,** which covers the north and south headland of historic **Botany Bay.** From clifftop paths, wildflowers frame spectacular views of rugged coastline. This is a bird-watcher's paradise: terns, kestrels, cormorants, and white-breasted sea eagles are regular visitors to **Tabbigai Gap.** Near **Cape Baily Lighthouse** are the remnants of World War II bunkers. The **Cape Baily Coast Walk** (at the end of Solander Drive) is one of the easier walking routes; the 5-kilometer (3 miles) round-trip hike takes about 2 hours. For a more extended ramble, hook up with the 5-kilometer (3 miles) **Muru Track** (opposite the Discovery Centre). For public transportation to the Muru Track, catch **Kurnell Coaches** *Bus No. 987* from **Cronulla Railway Station.** For timetable information, call 9524.8977. For information about the walk, call 9668.9111.

La Perouse Museum (Anzac Parade, La Perouse, 9311.3379) in the northern part of the park is managed by the National Parks and Wildlife Service. It's a memorial to the French explorer who arrived in the area only six days after Captain Arthur Phillip and the First Fleet in January 1788. This was La Perouse's last expedition before he and his ship vanished somewhere in the South Pacific. Guided tours in English and French are offered; bookings are essential.

Just 29 kilometers (18 miles) from the city proper, majestic coastal cliffs and small white sandy beaches dominate the landscape. **Royal National Park** (Princes Hwy, Waterfall, general information, 9542.0648, information on walks, 9524.0666) was established by the New South Wales government in 1879 and was the world's second national park. With more than 150 kilometers (93 miles) of walking tracks, the park is a hikers' paradise, excellent for a long day trip or an overnight camping trip. There are eight campsites, some with bathrooms and wheelchair accessibility.

Although it is home to some of Australia's most famous vineyards, the Hunter Valley produces only three percent of Australia's wines.

For public transportation from Sydney, take a train on the *Illawarra Line* to **Waterfall Station.** By car, drive south along the **Princes Highway** to the town of **Waterfall.** Park at the southern end of **Lady Carrington Drive,** which cuts through the park, and follow the signs to the **Forest Island Path,** which traverses 4.5 kilometers (3 miles) along the lower slopes of **Forest Island** and under dense canopies of the lush rain forest. From this path, which is of easy-to-medium difficulty and takes about two hours to complete, quiet and lucky observers might see lyrebirds, bowerbirds, and even wallabies. Stop in **Audley** for pamphlets and maps and to visit the park's gift shop.

The Central Coast

Hundreds of beach towns dot the coastline of New South Wales. Just 80 kilometers (50 miles) north of Sydney and only one hour away by road or rail, the Central Coast is known for its good surf and terrific golden sandy beaches. It's also noted for block upon block of beachside hotels and row upon row of suburban housing. Still, if you don't mind the development, it's an easy one- or two-day jaunt when the salt air beckons.

By car, it's about a one-hour drive from Sydney to **Gosford,** the largest town on the Central Coast, via the **Sydney-Newcastle Freeway** north, but a car isn't necessary. One major reason for this area's popularity is that it is extremely easy to get to, and to get around via public transportation. **CityRail** (13.1500) has direct service to Gosford; **Peninsula Bus Lines** (4341.1433) and **The Entrance Red Bus Service** (4332.8655) connect Gosford and the surrounding beach communities.

Developed in the 1830s and named for a British earl, today Gosford is a modern, shopping-mall–filled city. However, some historic attractions remain; for example, the old sandstone **Court House** (Georgina and Main Sts, no phone), which was built in 1868 and is the oldest public building on the Central Coast. About 9 kilometers (6 miles) west of the city is **Old Sydney Town** (4340.1104). Short on authenticity but long on entertainment value, this tourist attraction romantically re-creates the early days of the colony, offering crafts demonstrations and plenty of street theater. It's open Wednesday through Sunday.

Despite its name, **Brisbane Waters National Park** (4324.4911) is more oriented toward the land than the sea. Its rugged sandstone topography is laced through with walking trails that are part of the **Great North Walk** trail system. One of the park's most popular attractions is the **Bulgandry Aboriginal Engraving Site,** a good example of this indigenous art form.

About 12 kilometers (7 miles) east of Gosford, **Terrigal** is the more upscale of the Central Coast's beach communities. The **Central Coast Tourism Office** (Terrigal Dr, 800/80.6258) is a good place to gather information about local happenings. Accommodations are plentiful and are seldom completely booked up, except for school holidays. This is a terrific beach for families with children. The waves are usually gentle—at least by Australian standards. At **Terrigal Haven** on the southern end of the beach, the surf is so gentle that young children and timid swimmers may splash around in relative safety. Contact the **Terrigal Surf Life Savers Club** (4384.3554) for beach conditions.

For accommodations, it's hard to overlook the 196-room **Holiday Inn Crowne Plaza Terrigal** (Pine Tree La, 4384.9111; fax 4384.5798), a gigantic resortlike hotel with three restaurants, two bars, and a nightclub, where every guest room provides a view of the beach. The hotel's **Aromas On Sea** (4384.3501) dishes up relatively inexpensive big American-style breakfasts; burgers and fresh salads at lunch; and Modern Australian fare, particularly lamb and local seafood, for dinner. Another of the hotel's restaurants, **Le Mer** (4384.9111) offers a more formal dining experience and specializes in a delicious array of game meats. For a fancy night out, dine at **Jardines** (150 Terrigal Dr, 4384.1621), famous for its classic chateaubriand and mouth-watering, calorie-laden desserts.

A few kilometers south of Terrigal is the quieter **Avoca Beach.** The beach itself is well tended and tidy, studded with natural rock pools. Although **North Avoca Beach** is said to have the best surf in the area, its lack of retail concessions means smaller crowds—and more beach towel room. Call the **Avoca Surf Life Saving Club** (4382.1514) for beach and surf conditions. Accommodations are not as plentiful here as in Terrigal, but there is the **Bellbird Resort** (360 Avoca Dr, Avoca Beach, 4382.2322; fax 382.3806), which boasts a good restaurant called **Feathers** (serving simple Australian cuisine), a cocktail bar, tennis courts, and a pool for those who are not ready to brave the blue surf just a stone's throw across the road. In addition to 36 standard guest rooms, the resort has 7 private villas with balconies.

The Entrance, about 15 kilometers (9 miles) north of Terrigal, is the Central Coast's second-largest beachside town. Situated on **Tuggerah Lake,** it is more of a suburban community than a seaside resort. It does have a spectacular and popular surfing beach and inland waterways—the contiguous Tuggerah Lake, **Budgewoi Lake,** and **Lake Munmorah**—that are popular boating and fishing destinations.

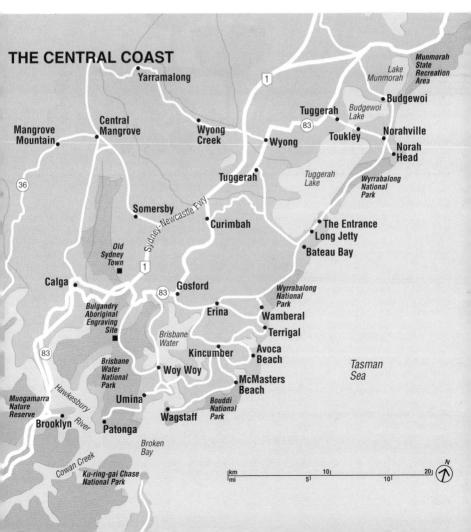

THE CENTRAL COAST

Wine Country Tours

When a driving tour of the wine country is not an option, consider a guided excursion through the region. Several tour companies offer day trips from Sydney to **Hunter Valley.** The excursions generally are scheduled on Tuesday, Thursday, Saturday, and Sunday. Costs and departure times are subject to change, so be sure to call for up-to-date information. All require advance bookings.

AAT Kings (9252.2788) offers one-day "Hunter Valley Winetaster" bus tours, which include visits to four wineries, including **Petersons, Hunter Cellars,** and the renowned **Wyndham Estate,** where day-trippers are treated to a traditional Australian lunch of beef, damper (Australian -bush bread), and salad. There's also a stop in the historic town of **Wollombi,** where you can stretch your legs, do a bit of souvenir shopping, and learn a little about the history of the region. Tours depart from **Circular Quay West,** with additional pickups at major hotels, every Tuesday, Thursday, and Sunday.

Australian Pacific Tours (131.304) offers a similar one-day bus trip to four Hunter Valley wineries. The stops include **Petersons, McGuigan's,** and **McWilliams' Mount Pleasant** estate, with lunch at **Wyndham Estate.** This operator also offers a two-day excursion to Hunter Valley, with tasting visits to four wineries, a special tour of the **McWilliams** winery to see the wine-making process, and an overnight stay at the charming **Peppers Guesthouse** (see page 184). Breakfast is included, as is loads of

knowledgeable commentary from the cheery drivers. Tours depart from Circular Quay West with additional pickups at major hotels, every Tuesday, Thursday, and Sunday.

Countrylink (13.2322), the smartly run state rail system, also offers excursions to Hunter Valley. The adventure begins with a scenic train ride up the North Coast along the winding **Hawkesbury River** to Newcastle, with a connection to **Cessnock** where a bus awaits to convey day-trippers to the various wineries for tours and tastings. Scheduled stops include **Peterson's** and **Wyndham Estate.** The starting point of the journey is Sydney's **Central Railway Station;** check schedules and make reservations at the **Countrylink Travel Center** in the station.

KEELY EDWARDS

Hunter Valley

A 2-hour drive of 120 kilometers (74 miles) north leads to Hunter Valley. Although it is close enough for a simple day trip, the "Hunter" (as it is commonly called) is better appreciated over two or three days of serious relaxing, wine tasting, and exploring. Most of the grape-growing activity takes place in and around the historic towns of **Wollombi, Cessnock, Pokolbin,** and **Branxton.** Although Hunter is a year-round tourist destination, two annual events are particularly popular: the Hunter Vintage Walkabout in the harvest season of February and March, and the Hunter Wine and Food Festival in September. The **Hunter Valley Wine Society** (4998.7397) in Cessnock is a good source of information about these festivals and about the region in general.

Early in the 19th century, before the rich alluvial soil was planted with grapes, the coal-mining industry attracted settlers to towns like Cessnock and **Maitland.** In the early 1830s a free settler by the name of James Busby wrote *A Treatise on the Culture of the Wine* and *The Art of Making Wine,* works so impressive that the governor granted him 2,000 acres in the Hunter in the hope that wine would compete

with hard rum, a spirit that was thought to be ruining the colony. Busby took off to Europe, returning with 700 vine clippings from France and Spain. Half of the clippings went to **The Royal Botanic Gardens** in Sydney (some specimens remain today) while the other half went to his property near the town of Pokolbin (a few miles northwest of Cessnock).

It took about a hundred years before Busby's vine stocks, which are said to be the foundation of the more than 50 vineyards that operate in the Hunter today, began producing prize-winning white Burgundies and Clarets. It was not until the 1950s and 1960s that Australians, and a new population of European immigrants following World War II, began noticing these local wines.

Hunter Valley is best explored by car, particularly if you have a designated driver. A car (or bicycle for the more adventurous) allows the freedom to discover the "boutique" vineyards that are too small to distribute their wines nationally and abroad.

An ideal starting point for such a tour is Cessnock, the gateway to the Lower Hunter, at the base of the

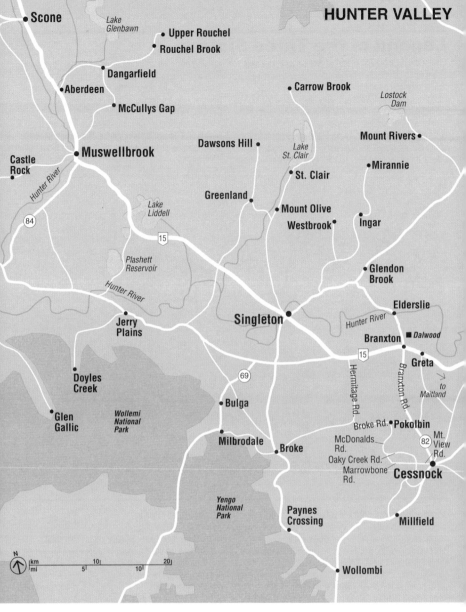

Scone

Lake
Glenbawn

Upper Rouchel

Rouchel Brook

Dangarfield

Aberdeen

McCullys Gap

Carrow Brook

Lostock
Dam

Muswellbrook

Dawsons Hill

Lake
St. Clair

Mount Rivers

Mirannie

Castle
Rock

Hunter River

St. Clair

Greenland

Lake
Liddell

Mount Olive

Westbrook

Ingar

84

15

Plashett
Reservoir

Hunter River

Glendon
Brook

Elderslie

Jerry
Plains

Singleton

Hunter River

Branxton

Dalwood

Doyles
Creek

69

Greta

Hermitage Rd.

Branxton Rd.

to
Maitland

Glen
Gallic

Wollemi
National
Park

Bulga

Broke Rd.

Pokolbin

Milbrodale

Broke

McDonalds
Rd.

Oaky Creek Rd.

Marrowbone
Rd.

82

Mt.
View
Rd.

Cessnock

Yengo
National
Park

Paynes
Crossing

Millfield

N

km
mi

10

5

20

10

Wollombi

Brokenback Range. This town, named after Cessnock Castle in Scotland, was a coal-mining center well into the 1930s. The **Cessnock Visitors' Information Centre** (Turner Park, Aberdare Rd, 4990.4477; fax 4991.4518) provides touring maps and advice about accommodations, vineyards, and attractions. Another good source of information, especially for advance bookings of accommodations and tours, is **Hunter Central Reservations** 4929.9434, 800/654.558).

From Cessnock, head west about 10 kilometers (6 miles) along **Mount View Road** and **Marrowbone Road** to Pokolbin, a little town in the Upper Hunter Valley that is surrounded by some of Australia's most famous vineyards. On the way to Pokolbin is **Petersons Vineyard** (Mount View Rd, 4990.1704),

one of the Hunter's best boutique wineries. Although **Petersons** only began producing wine in 1981, it has won more than a hundred national and international medals. This vineyard doesn't distribute its wines, so the only way to buy is to visit and stock up. **Hungerford Hill** (McDonalds Rd, 4998.7666), **Tyrells** (Broke Rd, 4998.7509), **Rothbury Estate** (Broke Rd, 4998.7672), **Lindemans** (McDonalds Rd, 4998.7501), and **McWilliams Mt. Pleasant** (Marrowbone Rd, 4998.7505) are all in the vicinity of Pokolbin. These vineyards offer well-organized tours and exhibitions; all are open daily; most have their own cafes and restaurants; some offer accommodations as well.

Legend of the Three Sisters

The three rock formations that rise up next to **Echo Point** are a part of local Aboriginal legend. It is said that a shaman by the name of Tyawan left his daughters Meehni, Wimlah, and Gunnedoo high on a cliff to protect them from the Bunyip (a mythical evil creature). Meehni was frightened by a centipede and threw a stone at it. This woke the Bunyip from its sleep below, and it lurched at the sisters, trying to attack them. Seeing this attack, Tyawan pointed his magic bone to turn his girls into stone so the Bunyip would not be able to harm them. Unfortunately, Tyawan became trapped by a rock and changed himself into a lyrebird as protection against the Bunyip. In the scuffle, Tyawan lost his magic bone and could not change his daughters back into humans. They sit here today as **The Three Sisters,** waiting to be changed back, but still safe from the Bunyip.

KEELY EDWARDS

In and around Pokolbin are nearly 30 restaurants, most of which adjoin the vineyards' rustic inns and resort accommodations. The **Convent at Peppertree** (Halls Rd, Pokolbin, 4998.7764; fax 4998.7323) has been transformed from a Catholic convent into a luxury hotel. One of the most popular attractions at this rambling resort, part of the **Peppertree Wines** estate (4998.7539), is **Robert's Restaurant** (4998.7330), a rustic-looking restaurant that is entered though an 1876 cottage. The food here is anything but old-fashioned—the kitchen turns out thoroughly Modern Australian cuisine prepared with fresh local products. The wine list is outstanding, featuring the vineyard's own wines and many other local labels.

The Convent

Peppers Guest House (Ekerts Rd, Pokolbin, 4998.7596; fax 4998.7739) is another fine old mansion that has been revamped into an upscale resort. Set amid vineyards and beautiful native gardens,

and providing great service and food, **Peppers** showcases the bounty of the Hunter Valley region. Its amenities include a lovely pool and a prime location right next to **Cypress Lakes Golf Course.** Contrary to its French name, **Chez Pok At Peppers** (4998.7596) serves delicious Modern Australian cuisine in an elegant candlelit dining room and on the veranda.

Casuarina Country Inn and Cottages (Hermitage Rd, Pokolbin, 4998.7888; fax 4998.7692), only a moment's drive from the golf course is another popular destination. Many of the rooms are decorated with a particular theme—from an over-the-top French bordello to rustic cabins. Most rooms overlook the valley and the **Brokenback Range. Casuarina Restaurant** serves hearty, well-prepared Australian country-style cuisine. **Kirkton Park Country House** (Oaky Creek Rd, Pokolbin, 4998.7680; fax 4998.7775) looks like a rambling country estate complete with tennis courts and swimming pool. The rooms have mountain views and are decorated with Australian and English antiques. The house restaurant, **Leith's,** dishes up good country food that makes the most of locally grown products.

For something less expensive, but still close to many of the wineries, try **Grapeview Villas** (Thompsons Rd, Pokolbin, 4998.7630; fax 4998.7644). These eight fully equipped villas can accommodate from two to six people.

The terrain around Pokolbin is relatively flat, so if you are up for a bit of exercise between wine tastings and lunch, rent a bicycle at **Grapemobile Bicycle Hire** (82 Greta St, Pokolbin, 4991.2339). This establishment also organizes cycling and walking tours, for a day or a weekend, year-round.

In Branxton, approximately 20 kilometers (12 miles) north of Cessnock, is **Balloon Aloft** (Branxton Rd, 4938.1955), which runs hot-air balloon tours high above the perfect vine rows and the hills of **Brecken**

Ridge. Try to take off in the early morning before the sun heats up the earth and vineyards or go later in the day when the setting sun makes the hills golden and smooth.

Branxton is a country town, curiously dotted with Greek Revival buildings, its legacy from its days as a rich regional center for farming and cattle ranching. On its outskirts the National Trust of Australia maintains **Dalwood** (Dalwood Rd, Dalwood, 4938.3444), a stately home built in 1838 for the Wyndhams, the family that introduced Hereford cattle to Australia.

Adjoining **Dalwood** is the **Wyndham Estate Winery** (049/38.3444). The continent's oldest winery, it has been a household name for generations of Australians.

About 100 kilometers (62 miles) northwest of Branxton, on the fringe of wine country, is the town of **Scone.** Here **Belltrees Homestead** (Gundy Rd, 6545.1668; fax 6546.1122) is still run by the White family, who built the property in the late 1880s. The exterior features white Victorian lattice work and the large guests rooms are decorated in an elegant Australian country style. Room rates include breakfast and dinner, and tours of the property and the original homestead (built 1830s) are led by members of the White family.

Belltrees Homestead

KEELY EDWARDS

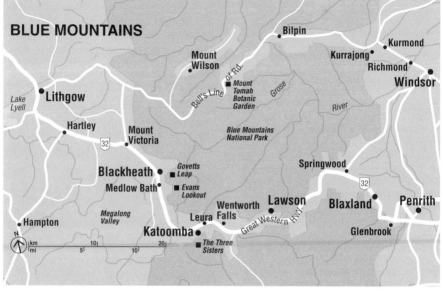

BLUE MOUNTAINS

Bilpin

Kurmond

Mount
Wilson

Kurrajong

Richmond

Windsor

Lake
Lyell

Lithgow

Bell's Line of Rd.

■ Mount
Tomah
Botanic
Garden

Grose

River

Hartley

32

Mount
Victoria

Blue Mountains
National Park

Springwood

Blackheath ●

■ Govetts
Leap

Medlow Bath ●

■ Evans
Lookout

Wentworth
Falls

Lawson

Blaxland ●

Penrith

Hampton

Megalong
Valley

Leura ●

32

Katoomba ●

■ The Three
Sisters

Glenbrook

km
mi

10

5

10

20

Blue Mountains

Named for the blue haze that the eucalyptus forests create in the atmosphere, the Blue Mountains begin only an hour's drive due west of Sydney on the **F4 Freeway.** Rising to a height of more than 1,300 meters (4,265 feet), the mountains have richly forested canyons and gorges that are a wonderful example of the diversity of geography around Sydney. This landscape, along with the crisp mountain air, the vast sandstone valleys lined with waterfalls, and little mountain towns of timber and stone, has drawn visitors since the late 1800s. Some have been so seduced by the region that they relocated permanently. Others are happy to come for the day or night, eat a big lunch at one of the great

restaurants, browse around an antiques shop, and take a stroll around one of the many lookouts.

The main road through the Blue Mountains is the **Great Western Highway** (now part of the F4 Freeway), which climbs along a ridge through a succession of 26 mountain towns from **Glenbrook,** near the foot of the mountains, through to places like **Wentworth Falls, Leura, Katoomba, Medlow Bath, Blackheath,** and **Mount Victoria,** ending on the other side of the mountains in the old mining town of **Lithgow.** These towns are so accessible today that it is difficult to imagine that this mountain range prevented the early colony from expanding westward until an 1813 expedition, led by explorers Blaxland, Wentworth, and Lawson, found a way across. Many have followed their route since, and there is now a tremendous range of

Yester Grange

KEELY EDWARDS

resorts, hotels, guest houses, restaurants, and tour companies.

Wentworth Falls

A car is the best way to travel if you plan to ramble off the beaten path, but it is not the only option. A number of tour companies offer packages to the Blue Mountains; go to **Quayside Bookings** at Circular Quay or ask at any city hotel. **State Rail** (13.1500) offers regular train service from Sydney with stops at nearly every mountain town, most of which are small enough to walk around. In Katoomba there are bus and cab companies that offer transportation to the lookouts. Cycling is another option for the fit and energetic; rent bikes at **Katoomba Mountain Bike Hire** (38 Waratah St, 4782.6600).

There are two main visitor centers for information about the Blue Mountains: the **Tourist Information Centre** (4739.6266) on the highway at Glenbrook on the left just as you start climbing the mountain, and **Echo Point** (4782.0756) in Katoomba at the very top of the mountains. Both centers, which are open daily, provide maps of bush-walking trails and details on museums, galleries, gardens, and guest houses. Another good source of information is the **Heritage Centre** (Govetts Leap Rd, Blackheath, 4787.8877), which is run by the National Parks and Wildlife Service. In addition to its own lectures and exhibitions, the center provides maps and information related to **Blue Mountains National Park.** It's particularly useful if you wish to hike or mountain bike.

Wentworth Falls was the first major town built along the mountain ridge. Named for both the explorer William Charles Wentworth and for the area's magnificent double waterfall (illustrated above), this town overlooks the green expanse known as **Jamison Valley.** Be sure to include a visit to **Yester Grange** (Yester Rd, 4757.1110), a restored Victorian country home (pictured on page 186) built in 1888. The property, with tea rooms, a restaurant, and a craft shop, is open daily. If you don't eat here, try **The Whistle Stop Cafe** (8 Station St, 4757.3161) for some hearty home-style Australian cooking.

Another town also overlooking the Jamison is Leura, known for its luxury resorts and fine restaurants and a popular locale for small conferences. The village has been classified by the National Trust, which means that many of the cafes and boutiques are housed in protected turn-of-the-century buildings.

Three of the best restaurants in the mountains are here: **Cafe Bon Ton** (192 The Mall, 4782.4377) and **Silk's Brasserie** (128 The Mall, 4784.2534), both serving Modern Australian cuisine. The aptly named **Fork N View Restaurant** (Cliff Dr, 4782.1164) serves simple seasonal Australian cuisine in a dining room with spectacular views of the valley below.

One of Leura's most popular attractions is **Everglades Gardens** (37 Everglades Ave, 4784.1938), open Wednesday through Sunday, which is run by the National Trust. Designed by Danish landscape architect Paul Sorensen in the early 1930s, the gardens consist of six acres of beautifully kept gardens, grottos, and a natural amphitheater surrounded by fragrant pine trees.

The hub of mountain activity and tourism is Katoomba, whose name supposedly means "shiny, falling water" in one of the Aboriginal languages. **Katoomba Street,** the main thoroughfare, runs from the railway station right down to Echo Point. Along this stretch, the grand old **Carrington Hotel** (10-16 Katoomba St, 4782.1111) stands as a reminder of the area's heyday in the 1930s. At press time, the place was undergoing renovation that was scheduled to be completed by 2000.

At Echo Point, the **Three Sisters** (see page 184) rock formation sits out on a sheer rocky promontory. Once here, it is easy to see why this is the most visited lookout in Australia; as the cliff face and mountain gorges drop hundreds of meters into the

Blue Mountains

KEELY EDWARDS

Jamison Valley below. You could spend hours here studying the cloud formations and breathing in the crisp mountain air or, alternatively, take the **Giant Stairway** walking path into the valley, which takes some time (two to three hours) and energy to complete, but is well worth the effort. West of Echo Point on an adjacent cliff face is **Katoomba Falls** and the **Scenic Railway** and **Scenic Skyway** (Cliff Dr, 4782.2699). The cable-car trip is definitely more scenic than the railway, which drops at virtually a 90° angle into the valley below. (The railway's original purpose was to transport coal miners in the valley.) Both attractions are open daily.

From budget motels to luxury resorts, accommodations line every street of Katoomba. One of the most beautiful hotels is **Lilianfels** (Lilianfels Ave, Katoomba, 4780.1200; fax 4780.1300), near Echo Point. With its health club, gym, tennis courts, and pool, the hotel seems much like a luxury mountain spa. Every room has a view of the valley, and the adjacent **Darley's Restaurant** (4780.1200), housed in an old mountain estate, serves some of the best Modern Australian cuisine in the country.

A few kilometers farther west is the tiny town of Medlow Bath. Other than views and walking trails, one of the main attractions here is the old **Hydro Majestic Hotel** (Great Western Hwy, 4788.1002; fax 4788.1063). The hotel has had various face-lifts and tends to attract busloads of tourists who come to have a quick lunch overlooking the **Megalong Valley.** It's worth a visit to see the restored 1920s architecture, complete with long timber-lined corridors and tall arched ceilings.

Blackheath is one of the most idyllic examples of an Australian mountain town and is a welcome contrast to the often tourist-busy Katoomba. It's friendly, has a couple of local pubs, some special guest houses, and lots of natural attractions close by. In the 1820s Governor Macquarie named the town after its "black,

wild appearance"; today it is considerably more sophisticated. The **Heritage Centre** (see above) on **Govetts Leap Road** will provide maps and suggestions for walks. Make sure you don't miss **Evans Lookout** (Evans Lookout Rd), **Govetts Leap,** and **Anvil Rock** (Govetts Leap Rd), all overlooking the untouched, dense eucalyptus forests of **Grose Valley.** These are some of the most breathtaking views in the Blue Mountains, still untouched by commercial development.

For any overnight stay in Blackheath, try **Glenella Guesthouse** (56 Govetts Leap Rd, 4787.8352) for its elegant lodgings and even more impressive food. Book well in advance for dinner (served Thursday through Sunday only), as the Modern Australian cuisine turned out by the kitchen here has been attracting crowds of gourmands for decades. For a slightly more rugged experience, the delightful **Jemby-Rinjah Lodge** (336 Evans Lookout Rd, 4787.7622; fax 4787.6230) offers environmentally sensitive cabins and lodges near **Evans Lookout** and is perfect for the more active, bush-loving visitor.

Another lookout point favored by the locals is on the Megalong Valley side of Blackheath. It's too far to walk, but if you have a car, turn off the Great Western Highway across the railway tracks at **Blackheath Station** and head out along **Shipley Road** to **Shipley Plateau.** Another local favorite is a trip down into the lush rain forest valley along **Megalong Road** with a stop at **Megalong Valley Tearooms** (Megalong Rd, 4787.1233) for tea or a light lunch.

One of the last major towns of the Great Western Highway stretch of the Blue Mountains is historic Mount Victoria. The **Hotel Imperial** (Great Western Hwy and Darling Cswy, 4787.1233; fax 4787.1461) occupies the corner across from the old sandstone tollgate house. This rambling hotel provides modest, comfortable lodgings, and features a large dining room and pub. Near the town's railway station are a number of fine antiques shops and bookstores and the **Mount Victoria Museum of Australiana** (Station St, 4787.1210). The museum, which is only open Saturday and Sunday from 2 to 5PM, displays Australian memorabilia from the 19th and early 20th centuries.

ROYAL BOTANIC GARDENS

An alternative route back to Sydney is via the little two-lane **Bell's Line of Road.** The trip will be considerably longer, but it's highly recommended for anyone with time to spare. Roll down the car windows to hear the bell birds chirping in the trees; you might even be lucky enough to spot a native lyrebird. Stop off at the delightful village of **Mount Wilson,** famous for its gardens and the big wood-and-stone homes that were built as mountain retreats during the 1920s and 1930s. East of the Mount Wilson turnoff, **Mount Tomah Botanic Garden** (Bell's Line of Rd, Mount Tomah, 4567.2154) boasts a spectacular setting and many native species of temperate plants. It serves as the cool-climate garden of **The Royal Botanic Gardens** and is open daily; admission is nominal. One of the finer accommodations in Mount Wilson is the **Blueberry Lodge,** famous for its gardens and the big wood-and-stone (Chimney Cottage Waterfall Rd, 4756.2022; fax 4756.2022). Although it looks rather like a North American ski chalet in architectural style, the setting is tranquil and the rooms are very comfortable.

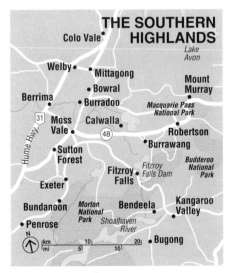

The Southern Highlands

Situated about 130 kilometers (81 miles) southwest of Sydney along the **Hume Highway,** the Southern Highlands are synonymous with cozy English-style comfort. About 700 meters (2,300 feet) above sea level, the Highlands are part of the **Great Dividing Range,** which runs down most of the east coast of Australia. The rich soil, high rainfall, and cooler climate attracted the landed gentry who settled here in the mid-1800s, building grand English-manor–style houses and gardens. The Highlands became known as the "Sanitarium of the South" because the air was thought to purify the lungs after too much exposure to the "nasty, subtropical atmosphere" of Sydney. In 1865 the area received its best endorsement when the New South Wales government leased **Throsby Park Homestead** in **Moss Vale** as a summer home for the governor. Sydneysiders have been flocking here for short breaks, weekend retreats, or retirement ever since. The main towns of **Mittagong, Bowral,** and Moss Vale have many excellent restaurants, pubs, cafes, and inns that charm the short-term visitor as well. And in addition to offering relief from the sometimes oppressive summer heat, the Southern Highlands can be delightful during the chilly winter months of July and August. Many hotels offer mid-year "Christmas" packages that include holiday decorations, lunches, and other extras.

Although driving is the best way to explore the Highland towns, it's possible to take the train from Sydney's **Central Station** to the Mittagong, Bowral, or Moss Vale stations and then explore by foot or taxi. A trip to the Highlands often begins in Mittagong. And the first stop should be the **Southern Highlands Visitors' Information Centre** (Winifred West Park, Old Hume Hwy, 4871.2888), which is open daily and will help visitors book accommodations, choose restaurants and cafes, and decide how to explore the area. There are also maps and information on the local golf courses and clubs.

The name "Mittagong" comes from the Aboriginal word meaning "little mountain," yet others claim it means "plenty of native dogs." Whatever its definition, the town used to be one of the more industrial settlements in the region when Australia's first iron works were built here in 1848. By the 1880s dairy farms and fruit plantations had become the leading enterprises. Many of the sandstone cottages still seen were built in this period.

For some parkland near the town, visit the reserve of **Lake Alexander** (Queen St). It's hard to believe that this gorgeous expanse is actually an artificial lake, created at the turn of the century to supply trains with water. The banks now make idyllic picnic grounds and walking trails. Another popular outdoor space in Mittagong is **Kennerton Green** (Bong Bong Rd, 4871.1110). This exotic private garden was designed by Marilyn Abbott, a weekend resident who left her pride and joy to the town in her will.

The **Sturt Craft Centre** (Waverley Parade and Range Rd, 4871.1279) is a popular stop for those interested in local crafts. The center features pottery, weaving, and textile workshops, as well an exhibition gallery and a gift shop. It was established in 1941 by Winifred West, a former headmistress from nearby Frensham Girls School.

Other than a few cafes, milk bars (delis), and pubs, Mittagong offers some pleasant culinary surprises such as **Thonburi** (60 Bowral Rd, 4872.1511). This Thai restaurant gets a lot of patronage in the town's highly Anglo-Saxon environment. Expect beautifully prepared traditional Thai dishes made with local products and at inexpensive prices.

On the drive out of Mittagong on the way to Bowral, **Mount Gibraltar** rises on the left. Once at its peak, you will find yourself rewarded with wonderful picnic spots and lookouts offering panoramic views of the towns below and some of the national park in the distance.

Bowral is the most developed town and probably the best one to visit for a taste of the Highlands if time is limited. Meaning "high" in Aboriginal, Bowral was once a part of the estate of the explorer and surveyor-general John Oxley. The railway finally made it here in 1867, bringing with it soon after hordes of Sydneysiders looking for respite from the harsh city summers. More farmers moved in, rambling country homes were built, and residents re-created English country gardens.

Gardens remain one of the major attractions of Bowral. The Bowral Tulip Festival in late September is the Highlands' largest drawing card. Participating gardens exhibit their mass plantings of tulips over two weekends. The streets are decked out with tulip symbols everywhere and the pretty gardens are ablaze with the red and yellow tulip cups. Sydneysiders are so crazy about this flowering festival that hotels are booked up months in advance, and the local restaurants and cafes are packed to the rafters.

The **Bowral Schoolhouse and Museum** (Boolwey and Bendooley Sts, 4861.1086) is a good stop for a little history lesson on the area. It is open daily in summer and during the annual spring Tulip Festival. Another museum is the **Bradman Museum** (Jude St, 4862.1247), dedicated to the life and career of Bowral's most famous resident and Australia's most famous cricket player, Sir Donald Bradman. Open daily, the museum has general cricket memorabilia and most of Bradman's cricket gear.

A portion of the Zig Zag railway line, the first to cross the Blue Mountains, is now a walking trail in Glenbrook.

Bong Bong Street is the main drag, lined with trendy cafes, country-style pubs, antiques

shops, and craft stores. For food, try **The Catch** (250 Bong Bong St, 4862.2677) and **Janek's** (Corbett Plaza, 4861.4414), both serving excellent Modern Australian cuisine. Bowral has the best accommodation options in the Southern Highlands, thanks to the many old estates that have been converted into fine resorts or bed-and-breakfasts. **Milton Park** (Horderns Rd, 4861.1522; fax 4861.4716) is one of the best. Only 5 kilometers (3 miles) from Bowral, this was the former residence of the famous Hordern family from Sydney. The 700-acre grounds of the residence are approached along an avenue of silver-barked gums and feature a garden of both native and English plantings. Guests can enjoy tennis, croquet, horseback riding, and an 18-hole golf course. The 40 rooms are large and furnished with some antiques. The resort's restaurant serves superior Modern Australian cuisine at reasonable prices.

Across from **Milton Park** is **Bong Bong Racecourse** (4862.2155), the venue for the annual Bong Bong Picnic Races each November. This event attracts a smart set of Sydneysiders and locals who come dressed in their best country clothing to cheer for local thoroughbreds while sipping Champagne and dining on picnic lunches.

Other accommodations in the area include **Briars Country Lodge** (Moss Vale Rd, 4868.3566; fax 4868.3223), just off the main road on the way out of town heading toward Moss Vale. The 30 rooms here are spacious and decorated with simple country furniture. Right next door is the famous **Briars Inn** restaurant, built in 1845, whose cozy dining room has served as the setting for many a romantic dinner and wedding luncheon.

Parts of Moss Vale appear to be right out of the late 19th century. The town was established in 1834 from a land grant given to Dr. Charles Throsby. Thirty years later Throsby subdivided the land and Moss Vale became the administrative center for the district. **Throsby Park Homestead** (4887.7270) is an old Georgian home that the family leased to the New South Wales government in 1865 for the governor's summer residence. The grand, well-preserved homestead is now run by the **National Parks and Wildlife Service,** which schedules tours the last Sunday of each month.

Visit **Cecil Hoskins Nature Reserve,** just two kilometers (one mile) north of Moss Vale on the banks of the **Wingecarribee River,** if the urge for a picnic lunch strikes. It's quiet and peaceful; colorful native birds abound, and the hiking and swimming are excellent.

Berrima Courthouse

KEELY EDWARDS

For accommodations, try the historic **Hotel Moss Vale** (Argyle St, 4868.1007), which was built in 1850 and features cozy fireplaces. The **Dorme House** (Moss Vale Golf Club, 4868.1014; fax 4868.1258) also offers comfortable, inexpensive accommodations for those who like the Highlands golfing scene.

About 10 minutes drive northwest of Moss Vale is the town of **Berrima.** Major Mitchell surveyed this site in 1829 and declared that it would be a perfect area for regional manufacturing. This led to the construction of an impressive Georgian-style sandstone courthouse in 1838 (pictured above); there's an enormous jail, which still operates today. Unfortunately Mitchell's vision was thwarted when the railway bypassed the town (in favor of Moss Vale) in 1860. Berrima appears to have recovered from its economic woes and is now a busy historic arts and crafts village. The town is small enough to park your car and just wander.

Visit **Berrima Courthouse** (Camden Valley Way, 4877.1505) for a lesson on mid-19th–century colonial legal methods. Just across the street is **Berrima Gaol**, a Georgian sandstone jail that was completed in 1839 and has gone from being a maximum security prison to a minimum security facility where the inmates make crafts for the local stores on Camden Valley Way.

Harper's Mansion (Camden Valley Way, 4861.2402) is a historic home that has been carefully renovated and converted into the local headquarters for the National Trust. Open Saturday through Monday, the mansion contains fine examples of 19th-century woodwork and furniture. After a visit, have a drink at the **Surveyor-General Inn** (Camden Valley Way, 4877.1226),

Australia's oldest continuously licensed hotel (pub). The pub still has its original walls and remains

popular for its well-presented bistro meals.

Book lovers will want to make time to browse in **Berkelow's Book Barn** (Hume Hwy, 4877.1370). This musty, cozy bookstore is something of an institution in these parts. The well-versed staff will help you wade through the colossal inventory of second-hand titles—from inexpensive paperbacks to rare leather-bound first editions.

The little Highland town of **Bundanoon** capitalizes on its Scottish heritage every April with a Brigadoon Festival. The attractions include bagpipe bands, caber-tossing competitions, and the "fine art" of haggis hurling. Just beyond the town, **Fitzroy Falls** and **Gambells Rest** provide access to **Morton National Park** (4887.7270), and its walking trails, creeks, and waterfalls. The park covers 380,380 acres and features deep river gorges that have cut into the sandstone basin. It is not unusual for walkers to see gray kangaroos, wallabies, lizards, and flocks of native birds.

Approximately three square feet of land in La Perouse near Botany Bay is technically French soil. A monument on this spot is dedicated to Comte La Perouse, who sailed into Sydney Harbour only three days after Captain Arthur Phillip's British First Fleet.

Illawarra and the South Coast

The main road heading south from Sydney, **Princes Highway,** winds through the southern suburbs, eventually leading to parklands and some of the most picturesque coastal towns and unspoiled beaches in all of New South Wales. Compared to the Central Coast north of Sydney, which is a somewhat overdeveloped tourism site, the South Coast feels relatively unpopulated. For this reason, the accommodations and the restaurants here aren't as fancy, and there are few tours of the region. So if you are prepared to rent a car and play it by ear, you'll not be disappointed.

Princes Highway runs along the **Royal National Park** (see "Greater Sydney," above) down into a valley where the large industrial town of **Wollongong** sits on the edge of the South Pacific Ocean. Although this town has its share of gorgeous beaches, the true beauty of the South Coast isn't revealed until you head farther south.

If driving, stop at **Kiama,** about 120 kilometers (74 miles) from the city. Kiama is an Aboriginal word meaning "sound of the sea" and probably refers to the town's famous ocean blowhole. The beach here is lined with Norfolk Island pines and is very popular with surfers. Visit the **Kiama Visitors' Centre** (Blowhole Point, 4232.3322) to get a listing of some the historical and natural attractions here, farther inland and south. For example, about 10 kilometers (6 miles) west of Kiama is the historic town of **Jamberoo,** which offers an abundance of arts and crafts galleries. Near Jamberoo are **Minnamurra Falls** and **Minnamurra Rainforest** (4236.0469) where 1.2 kilometers (0.75 miles) of elevated boardwalk allows

you to roam through 988 acres of rain forest where cabbage tree palms, staghorn ferns, and the native Illawarra fig tree dominate the landscape.

A few minutes drive south of Kiama leads to the townships of **Gerringong** and **Gerroa,** which abut **Seven Mile Beach National Park,** known for its sand dunes and banksia heaths. Get a glimpse of this remarkable stretch of beach from the **Charles Kingsford Smith Memorial and Lookout** (Fern St and Headland Dr, Gerringong), the site that commemorates the aviator's historic 1933 journey from Seven Mile Beach to New Zealand. Local accommodations mostly consist of budget hotels and holiday trailer parks; one noteworthy exception is **Beachview Resort** (Fern St, Gerringong, 4234.1359; fax 4234.1495) with its swimming pool, tennis courts, and access to **Werri Beach.**

About 20 kilometers (12 miles) southwest of Gerringong is the delightful town of **Berry.** It's sometimes referred to as "The Town of Trees," a name given to the area because 19th-century settlers planted rows of oaks, elms, and beech trees. The surrounding area, situated at the foot of the Illawara coastal escarpment, is predominantly dairy farmland. It was originally called **Broughton's Creek,** but was renamed in 1880 in honor of Alexander Berry, one of the first settlers. It has since become a weekend retreat for Sydneysiders who appreciate the town's boutique hotels, antiques and craft shops, pubs, restaurants, and cafes. The **Berry Museum** (Queen St, 4464.1280), which is open Saturday and Sunday and on public holidays, is a good place to start a tour of the region. Built as a bank in 1886, this museum has a permanent exhibition on Berry's past as a farming area and bustling rural town.

Bunyip Inn

KEELY EDWARDS

The Bunyip Inn

The reasonably priced, colonial-style sandstone and brick **Bunyip Inn Guest House** (122 Queen St, 4464.2064; fax 4464.2324), see illustration on page 192, provides a rustic retreat in the middle of town. Another good option is **Woodbyne Guest House** (4 O'Keefe La, Jaspers Brush, 4448.6200; fax 4448.6211), a few kilometers south of town, which has four large, well-decorated rooms, a spacious art gallery where guests dine each night, classically inspired gardens, and a wading pool. **Silo's Restaurant** (Princes Hwy, Jaspers Brush, 4448.6160), which uses fruits, vegetables, and herbs grown on its own little farm, is staffed by a cheerful crew who serve up a simple, well-presented Australian meal.

About 180 kilometers (112 miles) south of Sydney, just past the busy town of **Nowra**, is **Jervis Bay.** In 1992 Jervis Bay was classified as a marine reserve, and it features a series of small golden swimming beaches bounded by green national parkland. The crystal waters are home to a group of bottle-nosed dolphins and other sea life. **Bowen Island,** at the entrance to the bay, has a colony of penguins; from September through November humpback whales often visit as they migrate south to cooler waters. **Dolphin Watch Cruises** (74 Owen St, Huskisson, 4441.6311) offers wildlife-watching tours of the bay. Scuba diving, with strict guidelines to ensure protection of the reserve, is also permitted. The **Jervis Bay National Park Visitors' Centre** (Jervis Bay Rd, Jervis Bay, 4443.0977) is the best source of information about the many motels and bed-and-breakfasts in the surrounding area.

The town of **Huskisson** has a history of boat building and fishing. It's the most populated town and the gateway to the area. A ferry built in Huskisson, the *Lady Denman,* saw many years of service in Sydney and was returned here to be converted to the **Lady Denman Heritage Complex** (Dent St, 4441.5675). It's open Tuesday through Sunday, and includes a museum, boardwalk, and bush-walking track. Places in the area such as **Hyams Beach,** with its tiny general store, bottle shop, and gas station, and **Cave Beach** are delightful finds and great for a long, lazy swim in the gentle surf of the bay. **Jervis Bay Botanic Gardens** (Cave Beach Rd, 4443.0977) is an annex of the Australian National Botanic Gardens in Canberra, and is open daily from April through October. This cool, lush area is a perfect sanctuary for a couple of hours, and is especially nice on a very hot day.

About 230 kilometers (143 miles) south of Sydney is the scenic fishing village of **Ulladulla,** which is liberally sprinkled with motels and pubs.

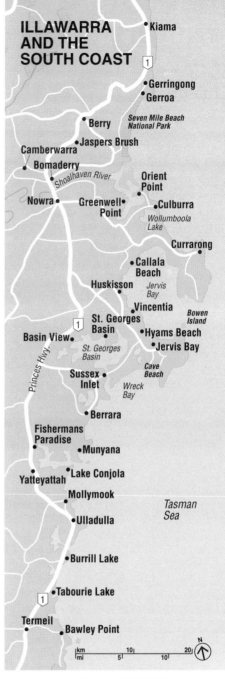

ILLAWARRA AND THE SOUTH COAST

Kiama
Gerringong
Gerroa
Berry   Seven Mile Beach National Park
Jaspers Brush
Camberwarra
Bomaderry
Shoalhaven River
Orient Point
Nowra   Greenwell Point   Culburra
Wollumboola Lake
Currarong
Callala Beach
Huskisson   Jervis Bay
Vincentia   Bowen Island
St. Georges Basin   Hyams Beach
Basin View   Jervis Bay
St. Georges Basin
Cave Beach
Sussex Inlet   Wreck Bay
Princes Hwy
Berrara
Fishermans Paradise
Munyana
Yatteyattah   Lake Conjola
Mollymook
Tasman Sea
Ulladulla
Burrill Lake
Tabourie Lake
Termeil
Bawley Point
km   10   20
mi   5   10
N

Cookaburra's (10 Wason St, 4454.1443) sophisticated kitchen dishes up everything from kangaroo loin to local crab tails. About another 20 minutes south along Princes Highway is the very popular **Barry's Country Guest House** (Old Princes Hwy, Termeil, 4457.1188) where—if you book far enough in advance—the jolly staff will feed you some of the best Modern Australian cuisine south of Sydney and keep you in cozy comfort for the night. Also try **Bawley Point Guest House** (17 Johnston St, Bawley Point, 4457.1011), not only for its comfy, elegant lodgings in a 1930s house, but for its terrific Modern Australian fare.

History

40,000-50,000 years ago After being in almost total isolation for 40,000 years, Australia is inhabited by Aboriginal people who are believed to have come from Southeast Asia. Sydney's coastal Aboriginal population are known as the Eora.

1770 Captain James Cook and the crew of the *Endeavour* arrive at **Botany Bay** on 29 April. Cook claims the continent for Britain. It is named **Terra Australis,** the nomenclature used in Britain at that time.

1779 Following the end of transportation of convicts to the American colonies in 1776, suggestions are made in England that New South Wales (NSW) become a penal colony to alleviate the mother country's overflowing jails.

1788 The British First Fleet of 11 ships, under the command of Captain Arthur Phillip, sails into Botany Bay on 26 January with 1,044 people, including 736 convicts, on board. (A few days later, two French vessels, commanded by La Perouse, arrive.) Phillip decides Botany Bay is too swampy and sails north to what is now **Sydney Harbour** (named after Lord Sydney, the British Home Department's Secretary of State). The official colony of NSW is proclaimed, comprising 2,100,000 square miles—half of Australia. Arthur Phillip is appointed the first governor.

1789 Bennelong, a local Aborigine, is held against his will and forced to act as intermediary between the British and the indigenous population. The site of the **Sydney Opera House** is later named **Bennelong Point** after him.

1793 The first free settlers land in Sydney. Population of Sydney is now 3,120. Two-thirds of the colony are convicts.

1803 First issue of Australia's first newspaper, *Sydney Gazette,* is published.

1804 An uprising of 400 Irish convicts takes place at **Castle Hill,** northwest of Sydney. Australia's second major settlement and penal colony is founded in Hobart, Tasmania by Lieutenant David Collins.

1806 Captain William Bligh (of *Mutiny on the Bounty* infamy) becomes governor.

1808 Governor Bligh is overthrown in the "Rum Rebellion," a mutiny by army officers.

Sydney's population rises to 9,100.

1813 The previously impenetrable **Blue Mountains** are finally explored by Wentworth, Lawson, and Blaxland, opening up rich farmlands in the west.

1816 Governor Lachlan Macquarie is new head of the colony. He and his wife, Elizabeth, set out to improve the "degenerating" morals of the colonists.

The colony's convict architect, **Francis Greenway,** designs the **Macquarie Lighthouse** at the mouth of Sydney Harbour.

1817 Australia is adopted as the continent's new name.

1836 Charles Darwin, naturalist and author, visits Sydney on the *HMS Beagle.*

1838 **David Jones** department store opens, featuring women's and men's fashions imported from London.

1851 Edward Hargreaves discovers gold near Bathurst, west of the Blue Mountains.

Sydney's population almost doubles in the next 10 years.

1856 Transportation of convicts to NSW ceases.

1888 Sydney celebrates its centenary with the opening of **Centennial Park.**

1900 Bubonic plague breaks out in **The Rocks.**

1901 The six colonies of Australia—NSW, Victoria, South Australia, Western Australia, Queensland, and Tasmania—are formed into a federation on 1 January in **Centennial Park.** The self-governing Commonwealth of Australia is proclaimed.

1908 Canberra, halfway between Sydney and Melbourne, is chosen as the nation's capital.

1914 Australia enters World War I on the side of Britain; 60,000 Australians are killed in action.

1932 Construction on the **Sydney Harbour Bridge,** which joins the city center to the **North Shore,** is completed. The opening ceremony is interrupted when Royalist Francis de Groot slashes the ribbon in the name of the King of England.

Sydney's population reaches 1 million.

1934 Australia's national airline, **Qantas,** begins regular flights from Sydney to London.

1939-45 Australian troops fight overseas during World War II. Over 33,500 are killed.

1942	Three Japanese midget submarines creep into Sydney Harbour and torpedo a ferry. All are sunk.
1947	Postwar immigration brings large influx of Europeans.
1965	Australia sends troops to Vietnam. The total number sent by the end of Australia's involvement reaches 50,000.
1966	Australia adopts the dollar as decimal currency.
	Lyndon Johnson is the first US president to visit Australia. His visit sparks many demonstrations and riots over the Vietnam War.
1973	Queen Elizabeth II opens the **Sydney Opera House.**
1979	The Aboriginal Land Trust regains possession of 144 properties.

1988	On 26 January Australia celebrates 200 years of European settlement.
1992	The **Harbour Tunnel** is opened, relieving severe traffic congestion on the Sydney Harbour Bridge.
1993	Sydney wins the race against Beijing to host the 2000 Olympic Games.
1994	The city suffers some of the worst bush fires in its history.
1995	NSW Governor Gordon Deane is removed from his residence by the Labor government, paving the way for the move to make Australia a republic by 2001.
1998	On Boxing Day (26 December), the Sydney to Hobart Yacht Race ends in tragedy when six people perish at sea because of heavy storms. It's the largest sea rescue operation in Australia's history.

New South Wales Government House

Index

Index

Index

Restaurants

Only restaurants with star ratings are listed below. All restaurants are listed alphabetically in the main (preceding) index. Always call in advance to ensure a restaurant has not closed, changed its hours, or booked its tables for a private party. The restaurant price ratings are based on the average cost of an entrée for one person, excluding tax and tip.

★★★★ An Extraordinary Experience
   ★★★ Excellent
      ★★ Very Good
         ★ Good

$$$$ Big Bucks ($30 and up)
   $$$ Expensive ($20-30
      $$ Reasonable ($10-$20)
         $ The Price Is Right
            (less than $10)

Hotels

The hotels listed below are grouped according to their price ratings; they are also listed in the main index. The hotel price ratings reflect the base price of a standard room for two people for one night during the peak season.

$$$$ Big Bucks ($275 and up)
$$$ Expensive ($200-$275)
$$ Reasonable ($125-$200)
$ The Price Is Right
  (less than $125)

$$$$

$$$

Index

Features

Bests

Maps

CITYRAIL SYSTEM

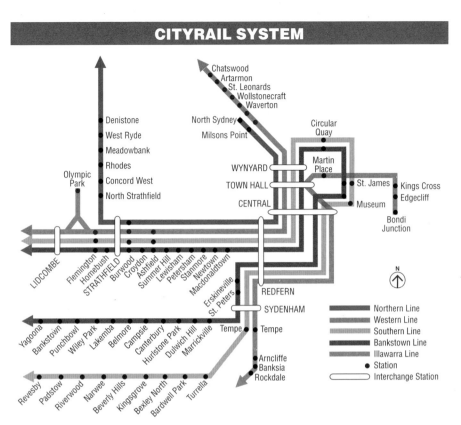

Chatswood
Artarmon
St. Leonards
Wollstonecraft
Waverton

North Sydney
Milsons Point

Denistone
West Ryde
Meadowbank
Rhodes
Concord West
North Strathfield

Olympic Park

Circular Quay

WYNYARD
TOWN HALL
CENTRAL

Martin Place
St. James
Museum

Kings Cross
Edgecliff

Bondi Junction

LIDCOMBE
Flemington
Homebush
STRATHFIELD
Burwood
Croydon
Ashfield
Summer Hill
Lewisham
Petersham
Stanmore
Newtown
Macdonaldtown
Erskineville
St. Peters

REDFERN
SYDENHAM

Tempe · Tempe

Arncliffe
Banksia
Rockdale

N

Yagoona
Bankstown
Punchbowl
Wiley Park
Lakemba
Belmore
Campsie
Canterbury
Hurlstone Park
Dulwich Hill
Marrickville

Revesby
Padstow
Riverwood
Narwee
Beverly Hills
Kingsgrove
Bexley North
Bardwell Park
Turrella

Legend:
- Northern Line
- Western Line
- Southern Line
- Bankstown Line
- Illawarra Line
- · Station
- Interchange Station

SYDNEY FERRIES

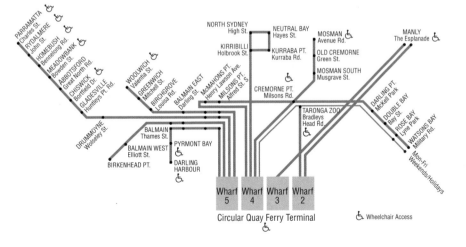

PARRAMATTA Charles St.
RYDALMERE John St.
HOMEBUSH Bennelong Rd.
MEADOWBANK Bowden St.
ABBOTSFORD Great North Rd.
CHISWICK Bortfield Dr.
GLADESVILLE Huntleys Pt. Rd.
DRUMMOYNE Wolseley St.

WOOLWICH Valentia St.
GREENWICH Mitchell St.
BIRCHGROVE Louisa Rd.
BALMAIN EAST Darling St.

BALMAIN Thames St.
BALMAIN WEST Elliott St.
BIRKENHEAD PT.

PYRMONT BAY
DARLING HARBOUR

NORTH SYDNEY High St.
KIRRIBILLI Holbrook St.
McMAHONS PT. Henry Lawson Ave.
MILSONS PT. Alfred St. S.
CREMORNE PT. Milsons Rd.

NEUTRAL BAY Hayes St.
KURRABA PT. Kurraba Rd.

MOSMAN Avenue Rd.
OLD CREMORNE Green St.
MOSMAN SOUTH Musgrave St.

TARONGA ZOO Bradleys Head Rd.

MANLY The Esplanade

DARLING PT. McKell Park
DOUBLE BAY Bay St.
ROSE BAY Lyne Park
WATSONS BAY Military Rd.
Mon-Fri
Weekends-Holidays

Wharf 5
Wharf 4
Wharf 3
Wharf 2

Circular Quay Ferry Terminal

♿ Wheelchair Access

SYDNEY EXPLORER

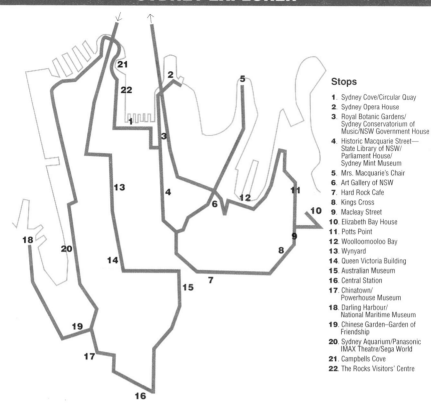

Stops

1. Sydney Cove/Circular Quay
2. Sydney Opera House
3. Royal Botanic Gardens/ Sydney Conservatorium of Music/NSW Government House
4. Historic Macquarie Street— State Library of NSW/ Parliament House/ Sydney Mint Museum
5. Mrs. Macquarie's Chair
6. Art Gallery of NSW
7. Hard Rock Cafe
8. Kings Cross
9. Macleay Street
10. Elizabeth Bay House
11. Potts Point
12. Woolloomooloo Bay
13. Wynyard
14. Queen Victoria Building
15. Australian Museum
16. Central Station
17. Chinatown/ Powerhouse Museum
18. Darling Harbour/ National Maritime Museum
19. Chinese Garden–Garden of Friendship
20. Sydney Aquarium/Panasonic IMAX Theatre/Sega World
21. Campbells Cove
22. The Rocks Visitors' Centre

BONDI & BAY EXPLORER

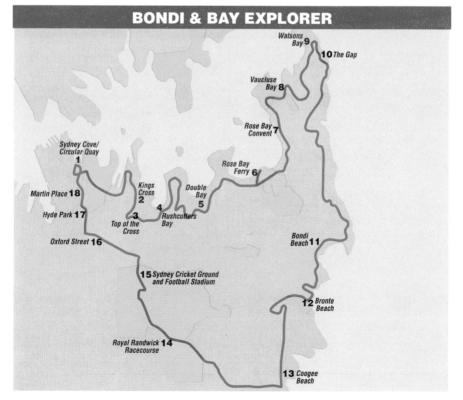

ACCESS® Guides

Orde**r** by phone, toll-free: 1-800-331-3761   Travel: Promo # R00111

Name _____   Phone _____

Address _____

City _____   State _____   Zip _____

Pleas**e** send me the following ACCESS® Guides:

- [ ] **ATLANTA** ACCESS® $18.50
  0-06-277156-6
- [ ] **BOSTON** ACCESS® $19.00
  0-06-277197-3
- [ ] **CAPE COD, MARTHA'S VINEYARD, & NANTUCKET** ACCESS® $19.00
  0-06-277220-1
- [ ] **CARIBBEAN** ACCESS® $20.00
  0-06-277252-X
- [ ] **CHICAGO** ACCESS® $19.00
  0-06-277196-5
- [ ] **CRUISE** ACCESS® $20.00
  0-06-277190-6
- [ ] **FLORENCE & VENICE** ACCESS® $19.00
  0-06-277222-8
- [ ] **GAY USA** ACCESS® $19.95
  0-06-277212-0
- [ ] **HAWAII** ACCESS® $19.00
  0-06-277223-6
- [ ] **LAS VEGAS** ACCESS® $19.00
  0-06-277224-4
- [ ] **LONDON** ACCESS® $19.00
  0-06-277225-2
- [ ] **LOS ANGELES** ACCESS® $19.00
  0-06-277259-7
- [ ] **MEXICO** ACCESS® $19.00
  0-06-277251-1
- [ ] **MIAMI & SOUTH FLORIDA** ACCESS® $19.00
  0-06-277226-0
- [ ] **MINNEAPOLIS/ST. PAUL** ACCESS® $19.00
  0-06-277234-1
- [ ] **MONTREAL & QUEBEC CITY** ACCESS® $19.00
  0-06-277160-4
- [ ] **NEW ORLEANS** ACCESS® $19.00
  0-06-277227-9
- [ ] **NEW YORK CITY** ACCESS® $19.00
  0-06-277235-X

- [ ] **NEW YORK RESTAURANTS** ACCESS® $13.00 0-06-277218-X
- [ ] **ORLANDO & CENTRAL FLORIDA** ACCESS® $19.00 0-06-277228-7
- [ ] **PARIS** ACCESS® $19.00
  0-06-277229-5
- [ ] **PHILADELPHIA** ACCESS® $19.00
  0-06-277230-9
- [ ] **ROME** ACCESS® $19.00
  0-06-277195-7
- [ ] **SAN DIEGO** ACCESS® $19.00
  0-06-277185-X
- [ ] **SAN FRANCISCO** ACCESS® $19.00
  0-06-277169-8
- [ ] **SAN FRANCISCO RESTAURANTS** ACCESS® $13.00 0-06-277219-8
- [ ] **SANTA FE/TAOS/ALBUQUERQUE** ACCESS® $19.00 0-06-277194-9
- [ ] **SEATTLE** ACCESS® $19.00
  0-06-277198-1
- [ ] **SKI COUNTRY** ACCESS® Eastern United States $18.50 0-06-277189-2
- [ ] **SKI COUNTRY** ACCESS® Western United States $19.00 0-06-277174-4
- [ ] **WASHINGTON DC** ACCESS® $19.00
  0-06-277232-5
- [ ] **WINE COUNTRY** ACCESS® France $19.00 0-06-277193-0
- [ ] **WINE COUNTRY** ACCESS® California $19.00 0-06-277258-9

Prices subject to change without notice.

Total for ACCESS® Guides:	$
Please add applicable sales tax:	
Add $4.00 for first book S&H, $1.00 per additional book:	
Total payment:	$

- [ ] Check or Money Order enclosed. Offer valid in the United States only. Please make payable to HarperCollins*Publishers*.
- [ ] Charge my credit card [ ] American Express [ ] Visa [ ] MasterCard

Card no. _____   Exp. date _____

Signature _____

Send orders to: HarperCollins*Publishers*
P.O. Box 588
Dunmore, PA 18512-0588

ACCESS®
Makes the World Your Neighborhood

Access Destinations

- Atlanta
- Boston
- Cape Cod, Martha's Vineyard, & Nantucket
- Caribbean
- Chicago
- Cruise
- Florence & Venice
- Gay USA
- Hawaii
- Las Vegas
- London
- Los Angeles
- Mexico
- Miami & South Florida
- Minneapolis/St. Paul
- Montreal & Quebec City
- New Orleans
- New York City
- New York Restaurants
- Orlando & Central Florida
- Paris
- Philadelphia
- Rome
- San Diego
- San Francisco
- San Francisco Restaurants
- Santa Fe/Taos/Albuquerque
- Seattle
- Ski Country Eastern US
- Ski Country Western US
- Washington DC
- Wine Country France
- Wine Country California

Pack lightly and carry the best travel guides going: ACCESS. Arranged by neighborhood and featuring color-coded entries keyed to easy-to-read maps, ACCESS guides are designed to help you explore a neighborhood or an entire city in depth. You'll never get lost with an ACCESS guide in hand, but you may well be lost without one. So whether you are visiting Las Vegas or London, you'll need a sturdy pair of walking shoes and plenty of ACCESS.

HarperResource
A Division of HarperCollins*Publishers*
http://www.harpercollins.com